THE BEATLES PHENOMENON

THE BEATLES PHENOMENON

A Celebration in Words, Pictures and Music

OMNIBUS PRESS
Part of The Music Sales Group

London | New York | Paris | Sydney | Copenhagen | Berlin | Madrid | Tokyo

Published by
Omnibus Press
in association with
Wise Publications
14-15 Berners Street,
London W1T 3LJ, UK.

Exclusive Distributors:
Music Sales Limited
Distribution Centre,
Newmarket Road,
Bury St Edmunds,
Suffolk IP33 3YB, UK.
Music Sales Pty Limited
20 Resolution Drive, Caringbah,
NSW 2229, Australia.
Australian Booktrade:
Macmillan Distribution Services
56 Parkwest Drive, Derrimut,
Vic 3030, Australia.

Order No. NO91190
ISBN 978-1-84772-253-9
This book © 2008 Omnibus Press,
a division of Music Sales Limited.

Arranging and engraving
supplied by Camden Music.
Compiled by Chris Charlesworth.
Text by Barry Miles.
Music and text edited by
Ann Barkway, Tom Farncombe,
David Harrison and Andy Neill.
Book design by Stephen Coates
and Henrietta Molinaro.
Photo research by Sarah Bacon.
Cover photograph courtesy
Fiona Adams/Redferns.

Your Guarantee of Quality:
As publishers, we strive to produce
every book to the highest commercial
standards. This book has been carefully
designed to minimise awkward page
turns and to make playing from it a
real pleasure.
Particular care has been given to
specifying paper made from pulps
which have not been elemental
chlorine bleached. This pulp is from
farmed sustainable forests and was
produced with special regard for the
environment.
Throughout, the printing and
binding have been planned to ensure
a sturdy, attractive publication which
should give years of enjoyment.
If your copy fails to meet our high
standards, please inform us and we will
gladly replace it.

www.omnibuspress.com
www.musicsales.com

Printed in China

Contents

A Note from the Music Editors

This collection of 100 of the greatest songs by the greatest band ever has been freshly transcribed, arranged and engraved. For the guitarist, we have aimed to produce guitar shapes that reflect as accurately as possible the original main rhythm guitar part, or else – where there is no substantial guitar part in the original – we've provided shapes that in our opinion give the most satisfying route through a song. Often, where chords in the original music are indistinct or inconsistent, or where opinions are famously divided on the correct voicing or name (e.g. the opening chord of 'A Hard Day's Night') we've simply settled on the one that provokes least disagreement.

Where a capo is required for the guitar part, the chord shape name is given above diagram, with the chord name at sounding pitch below.

As for lyrics, from the 'for' in verse 2 of 'Ticket To Ride' (which is never fully audible but appears on the original lyric sheet) to the mildly risqué 'tit-tit-tit' in the chorus of 'Girl' (to which John Lennon owns up in a 1970 interview with *Rolling Stone*), and the spelling of 'sneid' in 'I Am The Walrus', we've been as scrupulous as possible.

In those cases where no definitive version of the chords or lyric exists, we are grateful to the many musicians and aficionados who have pitched in with enlightening suggestions.

David Harrison
Tom Farncombe

The Last Great Band in Black and White
By Barry Miles

The Beatles were "a Sixties group", encompassing the entire decade, literally beginning in 1960, when they went to Hamburg, and ending in 1970, when Paul sued to end their partnership. Other groups, like The Shadows, lived through it, but they hailed from the previous era and managed to hang on indefinitely. The Beatles both reflected the enormous changes in society through the Sixties and were themselves catalysts for that change. They came together during the era of 'How Much Is That Doggie In The Window?' and 'The Deadwood Stage', and went professional at the time of The Avons' 'Three Little Girls Sitting In The Back Seat' and Ricky Valence's 'Tell Laura I Love Her'. By the time they broke up, Jimi Hendrix, Brian Jones's Rolling Stones and Syd Barrett's Pink Floyd had been and gone. The Beatles were both precursors and survivors.

They started it all, entering the music business when the BBC had a monopoly on radio, and the industry giants EMI and Decca dominated the record charts. Before the Beatles, an American would have been hard pressed to name one British singer or group; after The Beatles, British acts occupied a large percentage of the American charts. They paved the way for The Rolling Stones, The Who, The Kinks, The Yardbirds, The Animals, Herman's Hermits and scores of other groups that constituted "The British Invasion".

Pop music, as it was known in the days before "rock", was seen as part of show business: to their bosses at EMI, there was little difference between The Beatles and Alma Cogan. They were on the cusp between music hall and MTV, playing variety shows along with hoofers, jugglers and comedians, though there is no recorded instance of them following a performing dog act. It is unlikely that Oasis would consider sharing top billing on a TV show with a glove puppet, but The Beatles did. Pop groups were regarded as variety acts, and in these pages The Beatles can be seen playing *Sunday Night At The London Palladium*, and Mike and Bernie Winters' *Big Night Out*, alongside Arthur Askey, Bruce Forsyth, Morecambe and Wise and the like, where they were expected to take part in skits as well as play their latest single. (In fact, as pop music has become more of a packaged commodity, new bands did much the same thing in the Nineties, but in the heady days of "rock" it was a point of principle for Led Zeppelin *never* to appear on television, regardless of the show.)

Live performance was more important to The Beatles than to many present day acts because that was how they made their money, at least in the early years. Their royalties from EMI were so derisory that the greatest benefit of having a record in the charts came from the ability to charge more for live performances. No-one expected to make serious money from record sales, but with records in the charts you could play a lucrative summer season in a seaside resort and a sold-out Christmas panto. The Beatles did all of this after their initial success. Of course, all that would change. Indeed, they sold so many records that even on a farthing per record each they were able to get rich, and when it came time to renew their contract with EMI they got their own back by driving an incredibly hard bargain.

Their workload was astonishing: more than 800 hours on stage in Hamburg, 292 performances at The Cavern alone. On top of that, Brian Epstein experimented with bookings, trying out new markets, booking The Beatles into a public school here, a débutante dance there, three weeks at the Paris Olympia, Carnegie Hall. Brian was determined to present them as a class act. Looking through the chronology it is fascinating to see who else was on the bill, particularly in the early days. At The Cavern, with its origins as a jazz club, they were often as not sharing the bill with one or two traditional jazz bands. Trad jazz enjoyed a period of popularity just as The Beatles were getting going. It was a peculiar business, bearing little relationship to its supposed origins in Twenties' New Orleans. All its original practitioners were either dead or in their seventies and eighties. Acker Bilk headlined in a bowler hat and striped waistcoat and The Temperance Seven were cool and languid in a smooth flapper style that owed little to a New Orleans street band. This was what The Beatles were up against. Not great competition admittedly, but their energy and belief in themselves and their music saw them through, blowing their rivals off the stage one by one, first in Hamburg, then Liverpool, then London and finally the world.

Why The Beatles and not, say, Rory Storm and The Hurricanes who already featured Ringo Starr? The answer lies in their extraordinary ability as composers. It was fortuitous that Lennon and McCartney should meet because not only were they rock'n'roll fanatics, but they were also both already writing songs. The chemistry between them worked perfectly and together they composed an extraordinary body of work. The Beatles recorded 184 original songs without which they would almost certainly not have enjoyed such world-wide success. It was remarkable that they wrote songs at all, coming from their background, but what made The Beatles unstoppable was the momentum they created in their work, striving to make each album and single different, relying not on a tried and tested blues format or a series of traditional pop hooks, but experimenting with harmonies and rhythms, changing tempos and even tagging on whole new melodies. Songs poured out of them, so many that they didn't need to use singles on albums to fill the space. In the modern era, up to three years or more often elapse between album releases by top recording acts, but The Beatles – *the* top act in the world – managed to release 12 original albums, including one double, in the eight years between 1963 and 1970, not to mention around 30 non-album tracks, including many of their biggest and best loved hit singles. Astonishingly, the third member of the group, George Harrison, also flowered as a songwriter. To his chagrin, Frank Sinatra always introduced 'Something' as "a Lennon and McCartney composition" and Harrison didn't get his full due until after the group split up. Even Ringo wrote the odd song, such as 'Octopus's Garden', but his best songs came later: 'It Don't Come Easy', 'Back Off Boogaloo'.

The Beatles heralded the singer-songwriter, hastening the collapse of the Brill Building and its commercial song writing teams. Before the Beatles it was rare to sing your own material: Elvis never wrote a song. After the Beatles it was seen as a sign of weakness if you didn't sing your own stuff. As old time rocker Jerry Lee Lewis said, referring to the demise of Bobby Vee, Bobby Darin, Bobbie Vinton and all the other Bobbies as The Beatles wiped the board clean: "Thank God for The Beatles, they cut' em down like wheat before the sickle".

They turned touring upside down too. Before the Beatles there were no stadium concerts: after they filled Shea Stadium to its 56,000 capacity – the biggest rock' n'roll audience ever assembled at that time – the American stadium tour became the norm for a world-class act. The Beatles toured America with two roadies and a driver, playing hockey arenas and baseball stadiums, using whatever existing PA there was and with no foldback speakers on stage. Modern groups tour with an entourage of 150 crew and have more volume in their stage monitors than The Beatles had for a whole stadium, but once again it was The Beatles that led the way.

As if all this wasn't enough, during the Beatlemania years of non-stop touring and recording they also somehow found the time to make two full-length feature films, scores of live radio and TV appearances and give more media interviews in a day than today's superstars are inclined to give in a year. Somehow, amidst all this, they also coped with being the most famous and sought after people on the planet. In some cities, notably in Australia, half the population would turn out to welcome them, crowding into the streets, waiting for them to make personal appearances on balconies just like the Royal Family.

No other group developed so much. It would have been easy to retire, or at least settle back into comfortable celebrity after Beatlemania, but instead the Four Moptops transformed themselves into the Princes of Psychedelia and began a whole new life and a whole new series of experiments, dragging pop music forever out of Denmark Street and Tin Pan Alley and into the realm of art. *Revolver* had been a landmark album, filled with beautifully crafted songs and yet using experimental studio techniques that had other groups consulting with their studio managers. It was hard to see how they could better it. Everyone was waiting to see what The Beatles did next.

Sgt Pepper was the world's first "concept" album, the first to print the lyrics on the sleeve (another blow to Denmark Street), and musically, it blew everyone's minds. It had the huge iconic chord on 'A Day In The Life' and it even had an iconic sleeve that was much parodied and copied over the years. It was their "masterpiece" in the traditional Renaissance sense of a piece of work to prove you knew your craft.

Drugs certainly helped this transformation and, because LSD and marijuana were illegal, The Beatles found themselves assigned yet another pioneering role as spokesmen for the newly emerging drug culture: they signed (and paid for) the "pot ad" in *The Times*, they recorded psychedelic music that was banned by the BBC and were interviewed about LSD by serious newspapers. Naturally they were also busted. Having abandoned their identity as the Fab Four, the nation's favourite boys, they were fair game for the drugs squad,

though it now seems likely that in the case of both John and George the drugs were planted in their homes by the police themselves.

The strain of it all took its toll. They were tired to their bones, stressed and taking too many drugs. John, perhaps, felt it most keenly. Once again they both mirrored and led the direction of Sixties' popular culture when they became involved in meditation and the Maharishi Mahesh Yogi. The Maharishi might have been a passing interest had Brian Epstein not died when The Beatles were on one of his meditation courses. His words helped them deal with their grief and the next year they set off to India, in John and George's case with no clear idea of when, if ever, they might come back.

In the event, they did not become yogis, but their period of enforced sobriety allowed scores of songs to come flowing from them, many of which appeared on the double 'White Album' and *Abbey Road*. Ultimately it all came to an end: first Ringo, then George left the group and both returned. Then John left but the news was witheld. When Paul got fed up with waiting around instead of getting on with a solo career, he revealed that The Beatles were no more in a press release that accompanied his first solo album. The press misunderstood the story and thought that he was the one who had left. They soon found out the truth, and in looking for someone to blame, picked on Yoko Ono. Yoko certainly played a role in the break-up by sticking close to John in the studio, inhibiting the close-knit working relationship they had previously enjoyed, something that the other Beatles' wives and girlfriends did not do – and something that John would have objected to strenuously if anyone else had done it. But the group had run its course. They had grown apart. It was a marriage approaching divorce, and, as with many divorces, it was acrimonious, doubly so because it attracted the media spotlight. With so much money at stake there were powerful conflicting forces at work, one of which was their last "manager" Allen Klein, who later went to jail for financial skulduggery.

The Beatles have become icons: just as the Eiffel Tower is for Paris, Big Ben for London, the Empire State Building for New York, a clip of Hitler ranting locates us at the beginning of the World War II. For the Sixties we have Harold Wilson puffing his pipe, Christine Keeler sitting astride her famous chair, and there, jigging their guitars on some forgotten stage, their fringes covering their foreheads, screaming girls drowning out their words: The Beatles – the last great band in black and white.

Miles

1933-59

1933
18 February
→ Yoko Ono born in Tokyo, Japan.

1934
19 September
→ Brian Epstein born in Liverpool.

1940
23 June
→ Stuart Sutcliffe born in Edinburgh, Scotland.

7 July
→ Richard Starkey born at 9 Madryn Street, Liverpool 8, in the Dingle.

9 October
→ John Winston Lennon born at Oxford Street Maternity Hospital, Liverpool, to Alfred Lennon and Julia Lennon, née Stanley. John lived at 9 Newcastle Road, Liverpool 15, with his mother, his Aunt Mimi and his grandparents. His father was away at sea.

1941
24 September
Linda Louise Eastman was born in Scarsdale, New York.

24 November
→ Pete Best born in Madras, India.

1942
18 June
→ James Paul McCartney born at Walton Hospital, Liverpool, to James McCartney, cotton salesman, and Mary Patricia McCartney, née Mohin, midwife. Jim's job at Napiers aircraft factory was classifed as war work, so they were able to get a small house in Wallasey, at 92 Broadway, across the Mersey.

1943
25 February
→ George Harrison born at 11:42 pm to Louise Harrison, née French, a Liverpool shopgirl, and Harold Hargreaves Harrison, a bus conductor

**Above: Paul McCartney, aged 6 and behind him, his younger brother Michael.
Opposite: John Lennon in Dovedale Primary School uniform.**

since 1937 and for ten years before that a ship's steward on the Liverpool White Star Line. George was their fourth and last child, and grew up in a little two-up-two-down house at 12 Arnold Grove, Wavertree, Liverpool 15.

January
→ The McCartney family move to a bungalow in Roach Avenue, Knowsley Estate, Liverpool.

1945
12 November
→ John went to his first school: Mosspits County Primary School on Mosspits Lane.

1946
→ John expelled from Mosspits County Primary School for misbehaviour. He was five and a half. John was enrolled in Dovedale Road Primary School.
→ Aided by the money that Mary McCartney was now earning as a midwife, the McCartney family moved to a ground-floor flat in Sir Thomas White Gardens, Liverpool city centre, and not long afterwards to a new council house at 72 Western Avenue, Speke.

1947
September
→ Paul started at Stockton Wood Road Primary School, Speke. Within a year, he transferred to the Joseph Williams Primary School in Belle Vale, a bus ride away from his home.

1948
September
→ George went to Dovedale Road Primary School. John was still there but two years ahead, so they never met.

1949
→ George's family moved to a new two-up-two-down council house at 25 Upton Green, Speke.

1952
→ Paul's family moved to 12 Ardwick Road, Speke.

September
→ John started at Quarry Bank High School, having left - in July. Within a few weeks, he had attracted a reputation as a troublemaker, having been discovered in possession of an obscene drawing.

1953
Spring
→ In his final months at Joseph Williams Primary School, Paul was awarded a prize at a ceremony in Picton Hall, Liverpool, for an essay he had written about the Queen's coronation. McCartney later returned to Picton Hall in 1984 to receive his Freedom of the City of Liverpool honour.

September
→ Paul entered the Liverpool Institute school.

1954
September
→ George started at the Liverpool Institute. Paul was already there, in the year above.

1955

→ Paul's family moved to 20 Forthlin Road, Allerton, Liverpool 18. The property has since been bought by the National Trust, which has opened it to the public restored to the way it looked in 1955.

September

→ John was now in the C stream at school because his marks were so poor. By the final term, he was 20th in the class: the bottom of the bottom class.

1956

18 June

→ For his 14th birthday, Paul's father bought him a trumpet. After taking a few lessons on the instrument, Paul swapped it at Rushworth & Drapers store in Liverpool for a Zenith acoustic guitar, priced £15.

31 October

→ Paul's mother dies of breast cancer, aged 47. Within a few weeks of his mother's death, Paul had written his first song, 'I Lost My Little Girl'.

1957

→ George's mother buys him a guitar from a boy at school who was selling it for £3. It soon becomes obvious that he needs something better and his mother saves up until she can buy him a £30 model with a cut-away neck.
→ John's Aunt Mimi lends him the money to buy a £17 Gallotone Champion guitar by mail-order, complete with a sticker promising that the instrument was 'Guaranteed not to split'. Included in the deal is a book, *Play The Guitar*.

March

→ Inspired by Lonnie Donegan and Elvis Presley, John and his school friend Pete Shotton start a skiffle group which they called The Blackjacks. Pete played washboard. The traditional skiffle-group line-up was completed shortly afterwards by the addition of Bill Smith on tea-chest bass. John handled almost all of the lead vocals, with the other members adding the choruses. They played

skiffle standards like 'Rock Island Line', 'Maggie Mae', 'Freight Train' and 'Don't You Rock Me Daddy-O'.

May
→ With a line-up change, the Blackjacks changed their name to The Quarry Men, since they were all from Quarry Bank High School. The line-up now was John on vocals and guitar; Eric Griffiths on guitar; Colin Hanton on drums; Len Garry on tea-chest bass; Pete Shotton on washboard; and Rod Davis on banjo.

24 May
→ The Quarry Men played their ???????first gig:

John: "Our first a appearance was in Rose Street, it was their Empire Day celebrations. They all had this party out in the street. We played from the back of a lorry. We didn't get paid or anything."

9 June
→ The Quarry Men entered the ABC TV *TV Star Search* talent contest held at the Empire Theatre, Liverpool. They didn't pass the audition.

22 June
→ The Quarry Men played at an outdoor street party at Roseberry Street, Liverpool, to celebrate the 750th anniversary of King John granting a charter to Liverpool making it a free borough.

Summer
→ George and his brother Pete, together with Pete's school friend Arthur Kelly and Alan Williams (not to be confused with the future manager of The Beatles), played a gig at the British Legion Club in Speke as The Rebels. Since no other band scheduled to play had turned up, they were forced to play all through the evening. The next morning on the bus to school, George told Paul about the gig. After that, Paul began to join George in the Harrisons' front room, where they played their way through his chord books.

6 July
→ John and Paul met for the first time, at the Woolton Parish Church Garden Féte, held at St. Peter's Church. The Quarry Men Skiffle Group performed four times that day, twice during the afternoon in the Lower Church field and twice that evening at the church hall, where John's group was supporting The George Edwards Band. After their 5.45 performance, McCartney was introduced to Lennon by their mutual friend, Ivan Vaughan.
→ Two songs from the Quarry Men's evening performance survived on a reel-to-reel tape 'Puttin' On The Style' and 'Baby Let's Play House'. They were sold at auction in London in 1994 to EMI Records for £78,500. Only 30 seconds of 'Puttin' On The Style' has been released. Other songs The Quarry Men are known to have performed that day include 'Worried Man Blues', 'Come Go With Me', 'Railroad Bill', 'Maggie Mae' and 'Cumberland Gap'.

29 July
→ Paul and his brother Michael went to Scout camp at Hathersage in Derbyshire. A few days earlier, John's friend Pete Shotton had passed

Left: A 13-year-old George Harrison practices guitar.
Opposite: The Quarry Men on stage at the Walton Village Féte, 6 July 1957 – the day that John met Paul for the first time.

on the invitation for Paul to join The Quarry Men, an offer that he eagerly accepted.

7 August
→ The Quarry Men play the Cavern, after the Cavern Club owner Alan Sytner heard them perform at Childwall Golf Club. They began with 'Come Go With Me' but John blasted straight into 'Hound Dog' followed by 'Blue Suede Shoes', prompting Sytner to send a note on-stage reading 'Cut out the bloody rock!'

18 October
→ Conservative Club, New Clubmoor Hall, Liverpool. Paul's first gig with The Quarry Men.
Paul: "That night was a disaster because I got sticky fingers and blew the solo in 'Guitar Boogie Shuffle', which is one of the easiest things in the

Paul: "At Woolton village féte I met him. I was a fat schoolboy and, as he leaned an arm on my shoulder, I realised that he was drunk. We were 12 then but, in spite of his sideboards, we went on to become teenage pals."

John: "The day I met Paul I was singing 'Be-Bop-A-Lula' for the first time on stage. There's a picture of me with a checked shirt on, holding a little acoustic guitar – and I am singing 'Be-Bop-A-Lula'."

world to play. That alone made me resolve never to become a lead guitarist."

Autumn
➔ Paul and John began to practise their guitars and by January they were writing songs together.

John: "When Paul and I started writing stuff, we did it in the key of A because we thought that was the key Buddy Holly did all his songs in."

7 November
➔ Wilson Hall, Garston. A notorious teddy boy hangout. The Quarry Men played there four times on Charlie Mac's Thursday 'Rhythm Nights'.

16 November
➔ Stanley Abattoir Social Club, Liverpool.

23 November
➔ New Clubmoor Hall, Conservative Club, Liverpool. The line-up of The Quarry Men now consisted of John, Paul, Eric Griffiths, Colin Hanton and Len Garry.

7 December
➔ Wilson Hall, Garston, Liverpool. Around this time George saw The Quarry Men play for the first time.

George: "I remember being very impressed with John's big thick sideboards and trendy teddy boy clothes. He was a terribly sarcastic bugger right from day one, but I never dared back down from him. ...I was never intimidated by him. Whenever he had a go at me I just gave him a little bit of his own right back."

1958

10 January
➔ New Clubmoor Hall, Garston, Liverpool.

24 January
➔ The Cavern (evening), with the Merseysippi Jazz Band. They were billed as 'The Quarry Men Skiffle Group'. This was Paul's Cavern début. The first of 292 shows there.

6 February
➔ Wilson Hall, Garston, Liverpool. After the gig (or, according to some sources, the gig at the Morgue in March), John accompanied Paul and George part of the way home.

Paul: "George slipped quietly into one of the seats on this almost empty bus we were on, took out his guitar and went right into 'Raunchy'. Some days later I asked John,

➔ The Quarry Men line-up now consisted of: John, Paul, George, Len Garry, Eric Griffiths and sometimes John 'Duff' Lowe on piano.

Paul: "We had a bloke called Duff as pianist for some time, but his dad wouldn't let him stay out late. He'd be playing away one minute, and the next he would have disappeared, gone home in the middle of a number."

Griffiths left The Quarry Men soon after George was recruited.
➔ Despite joining The Quarry Men, George also continued to perform occasionally with his own band, The Rebels.

13 March
➔ The Morgue Skiffle Cellar, Broadgreen, Liverpool. The first of several appearances at this illegal club held in the cellar of a Victorian mansion. The police closed it down a month later.

15 July
➔ John's mother, Julia, was killed in a road accident as she left her sister Mimi's house. She was run down by a policeman who was driving illegally alone on 'L'-plates, speeding because he was late for work.

'Well, what do you think about George?' He gave it a second or two and then he replied, 'Yeah, man, he'd be great.' And that was that. George was in and we were on our way."

Paul: "The only way I could help John was to empathise, as I'd had the same thing happen to me. There wasn't anything I could say that would magically patch him up. That kind of hurt goes far too deep for words."

➔ Julia's death affected John very deeply. His work at art college – poor at the best of times – suffered badly and he virtually lost interest in the group. The Quarry Men played very few gigs during 1958.

19 July
➔ John's mother Julia was buried after a funeral service at Allerton Cemetery, Liverpool.
➔ That year (in either late spring or early autumn; none of the participants can clearly remember the date) John Lennon arranged for a recording of The Quarry Men to be made at a small studio in the back room of a house at 38 Kensington, Liverpool 7, where Percy Phillips would record two sides of music for 17 shillings and sixpence. Phillips advertised himself as a 'Professional Tape & Disc Recording Service', and continued to operate from the same address until the late 1960s.
➔ Only one copy of the single was cut and the tape itself was destroyed 24 hours later, once the record had been paid for. The A-side featured John singing Buddy Holly's *That'll Be The Day*, while on the B-side was a love song credited to Paul and George (the only known example of

them writing as a team) entitled 'In Spite Of All The Danger', loosely built around the tune of Elvis Presley's 'Trying To Get To You'. The line-up on the recording was John, Paul, George, Colin Hanton and John 'Duff' Lowe. On the day of the session, The Quarry Men could only muster 15 shillings between them, so Phillips held on to the disc until one of the group returned the next day with the correct money.

John 'Duff' Lowe: "It was just a shellac demo disc. The more you played it, the worse the quality became. It was just done for a giggle. It was passed around. Anyone who had a friend could borrow it for a couple of days. No-one ever asked me to lend it, so it must have come to me after everyone else had had a go. People forgot about it, and it was at the bottom of a linen drawer in my house."

Paul bought the disc from John Lowe in 1981 for an unspecified sum in excess of £5,000. During the 1980s he pressed up a limited quantity of reproductions of the single, which he gave to friends. Edited versions of both songs eventually appeared on *Beatles Anthology 1*.

Autumn
➔ John and fellow Liverpool Art College student Cynthia Powell

began a relationship, after dancing together at a lunchtime party. Cynthia declined John's initial request for a date, but the couple still spent that night together at his Gambier Terrace flat.

20 December
→ The group played at the wedding reception of George's brother Harry to Irene McCann, in Speke.

Late in the year
→ The Quarry Men failed an audition for ABC Television in Manchester. Drummer Colin Hanton left the group after an argument with Paul following a gig at Finch Lane Bus Depot. The lack of a regular drummer severely hampered The Quarry Men's progress over the next year.

1959

1 January
→ Wilson Hall, Garston, Liverpool. Speke Bus Depot Social Club.

24 January
→ Woolton Village Club, Woolton, Liverpool.

Summer
→ Because The Quarry Men were doing very few gigs, George began playing with other groups, particularly The Les Stewart Quartet.

29 August
→ Casbah Coffee Club, West Derby, Liverpool. The Les Stewart Quartet (featuring George on guitar) was booked for the opening night of Mona Best's new club, held in the basement of her house, but that afternoon Les Stewart had a terrific row with his bass player, Ken Brown, resigned from the group and stalked off. Ken Brown asked George if he knew anyone who could help out and John and Paul were called in. The Quarry Men played the gig and every Saturday night for the next seven weeks. The Quarry Men line-up for these gigs had been reduced to John, Paul, George and Ken Brown. No drummer, but as they always told promoters,

"The rhythm's in the guitars".

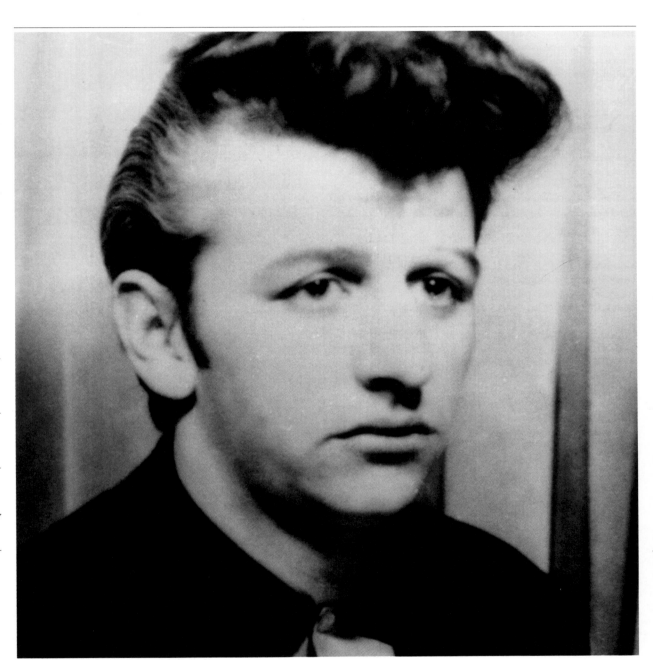

10 October
→ Casbah Coffee Club, West Derby, Liverpool. Ken Brown left the group over an argument about wages. Paul objected when Mona Best paid Brown his 15 shillings even though he had not played that evening because of a heavy cold. The future Beatles closed ranks and walked away.

Mid October
→ The group changed their name to Johnny & The Moondogs for another audition for Carroll Levis's *TV Star Search* at the Empire Theatre. This time they qualified for the final round. They appeared twice during the week and qualified for the next round.

15 November
→ Hippodrome Theatre, Ardwick, Manchester. The final round of *TV Star Search*. Johnny & The Moondogs lost out because they had nowhere to stay and couldn't be there for the voting.

17 November
→ The Second Biennial John Moores Exhibition was held in Liverpool at the Walker Gallery. John's friend from art school, Stuart Sutcliffe, submitted a large canvas entitled 'Summer Painting'. The painting was accepted for the show, and John Moores himself bought it for £65 when the show ended in January.

1960

17 January
→ John persuaded Stuart Sutcliffe that what he really wanted to do with his John Moores money was buy a bass guitar and join Johnny & The Moondogs. He bought a Hofner President, more for its looks than for its sound, since he was unable to play it.

23 April
→ John and Paul hitchhiked down to Caversham in Berkshire, to stay with Paul's older cousin, Bett Robbins, who, together with her husband Mike, ran a pub called The Fox and Hounds. Prior to this they had been redcoats at Butlin's, and Mike had a small amount of showbusiness experience – appearing on the radio and being interviewed by local newspapers – which their visitors were delighted to hear about. John and Paul worked behind the bar and on Saturday night performed in the tap room as The Nerk Twins (they were advertised on the door of the saloon bar as such). They sat on high barstools with their acoustic guitars and opened with an old Butlin's favourite, 'The World Is Waiting For The Sunrise', before moving on to their usual repertoire.

24 April
→ The Fox and Hounds, Caversham. The Nerk Twins performed in the tap room again this lunchtime before hitchhiking back to Liverpool.

May
→ Allan Williams was asked by John to be the band's manager. Williams owned the Jacaranda Coffee Bar on Slater Street, a regular meeting place for Liverpool groups such as Rory Storm & The Hurricanes and Derry Wilkie & The Seniors. The Jac featured live shows in the tiny basement which Williams had converted in to a tiny dance floor. His friends, The Royal Caribbean Steel Band, were the residents. Williams was not too impressed by The Moondogs but agreed to manage them.
→ The Moondogs were unhappy with their name. One night at Stuart's Gambier Street flat, John and Stuart came up with a new name for the group, taken from Marlon Brando's film *The Wild One*:

Lee Marvin to Marlon Brando: "You know I've missed you. Ever since the club split up I've missed you. Did you miss him?" Motorcycle gang: "Yeah."

Lee Marvin: "We all missed you,' points to the girls in the gang. 'The beetles missed yuh, all the beetles missed yuh. C'mon Johnny, let's you and I..."

Stuart suggested The Beetles because it was like Buddy Holly's Crickets. John then modified the name by changing an 'e' to an 'a' to make a pun on beat. Allan Williams didn't like it and suggested Long John and The Silver Beatles. Other names considered at that time were The Silver Beats, Silver Beetles and Beatals.

5 May
→ Allan Williams found the group a drummer called Tommy Moore and

Allan Williams: "I thought The Beatles were a right load of layabouts. It was true that they were different: they had strong personalities, somehow compelling, and they were oddly impressive in a way hard to define. There seems to be something about my personality that attracts the losers and fringe people of the world, and The Beatles just seemed to be part of the crowd."

Opposite: George, Stuart Sutcliffe and John pictured in Hamburg. Photographer Astrid Kirchherr took this and other classic images of the early Beatles. Below: Royston Ellis

allowed them to practise at the Jacaranda in return for doing odd jobs.

10 May
→ Wyvern Social Club.
Looking for musicians who would play for low wages, London promoter Larry Parnes came to Liverpool to audition groups to back Billy Fury (who was himself from Liverpool) on a tour of northern England and Scotland. Fury himself attended the auditions, as did every hopeful group in Liverpool. John dropped the "Long John" and they attended Parnes's audition as The Silver Beatles. Drummer Johnny "Hutch" Hutchinson of Cass and The Cassanovas stood in at the audition as Tommy Moore arrived late. Larry Parnes considered that the group, except for Tommy, had some potential – despite Stuart Sutcliffe's blatant deficiences as a bassist and a few days later he contacted Williams with a job offer.

14 May
→ Lathom Hall, Liverpool, as The Silver Beats.

Royston Ellis

The London 'Beat' poet, 19-year-old Royston Ellis (right), author of *Jiving To Gyp: A Sequence of Poems* (Scorpion Press, London, 1959), was booked to read his poems at the University of Liverpool. He met The Beatles and convinced them to back him for a reading at the Jacaranda. At this time reading poetry to a jazz backing had been popularised in the US by Jack Kerouac, Kenneth Patchen and Lawrence Ferlinghetti, and in Britain by Christopher Logue. After the reading Ellis visited Gambier Terrace, where John and Stuart were then living, and showed them how to unscrew a Vick's inhaler to get the Benzedrine out. Years later it was Ellis who inspired John by introducing him to Polythene Pam.

18 May

→ The group were offered a job by Larry Parnes as backing group for the little-known Liverpool pop singer Johnny Gentle on a nine-day tour of Scotland. They decided to adopt pseudonyms for the occasion; Paul changed his to Paul Ramon, George became Carl Harrison (after Carl Perkins) and Stu changed Sutcliffe to deStael (after the then-fashionable painter). They chose as their name The Silver Beetles. Tommy and George arranged time off work, John and Stuart skipped college and Paul persuaded his father that the trip would enable him to study for his A-levels. The tour itinerary was May 20: Town Hall, Alloa, Clackmannanshire; May 21; Northern Meeting Ballroom, Inverness and May 23: Dalrymple Hall, Aberdeen. On the way to this venue, Johnny Gentle crashed the car. Tommy Moore was concussed and lost several teeth. He was taken to hospital but the manager of Dalrymple Hall was outraged that the group had no drummer and stormed into the hospital and dragged Tommy from his bed to take his place on stage.

25 May

→ The Johnny Gentle tour continued at St Thomas' Hall, Deith, Banffshire; May 26: Town Hall, Forres, Morayshire; May 27: Regal Ballroom, Nairn, Nairnshire ending at Rescue Hall, Peterhead, Aberdeenshire and arriving back in Liverpool on May 29.

30 May

→ Jacaranda Coffee Bar, Liverpool. Allan Williams engaged The Silver Beetles to play Monday night "fill-in" performances (when not otherwise engaged) on the evenings that the house band, The Royal Caribbean Steel Band, took the night off. Their fee was Coca-Cola and beans on toast.

2 June

→ The Institute, Neston, Wirral, as The Beatles.
An event promoted by Les Dodd's Paramount Enterprises arranged by Williams while the group had been away in Scotland. This was the first of their Thursday night sessions at this notoriously rough venue. During

one Silver Beetles set at The Institute, a 16-year-old boy was nearly kicked to death.
→ *The Heswall And Neston News And Advertiser* documented the group's appearance:
There was no mention of 'Silver Beetles' in this account, suggesting that the group were operating under both names at this time.

4 June

→ Grosvenor Ballroom, Liscard.

6 June

→ Grosvenor Ballroom, Liscard, a special Whitsun bank holiday, Jive and Rock session.

9 June

→ The Institute, Neston, Wirral.

11 June

→ The Grosvenor Ballroom, Liscard. Another rowdy Saturday night. The group had no drummer since Tommy Moore had resigned, having had enough of John's malicious wit, and of the pressure from his girlfriend to "get a proper job". John asked if anyone in the audience could play drums and "Ronnie", the drunk, grinning leader of a local gang of teddy boys, settled himself behind Moore's kit (still on hire-purchase). Though Ronnie had obviously never played drums before,

no one dared take them off him. In the interval John managed to phone Allan Williams who drove over to the Grosvenor and saved them.

13 June

→ The Jacaranda as The Silver Beetles. This was Tommy Moore's last gig with the group before he went back to being a fork-lift truck-driver at the Garston bottle works.

16 June

→ The Institute, Neston, Wirral.

18 June

→ Grosvenor Ballroom, Liscard.

23 June

→ The Institute, Neston, Wirral.

25 June

→ Grosvenor Ballroom, Liscard.

30 June

→ The Institute, Neston, Wirral.

July

→ With no drummer The Silver Beatles (as they were now called) were reduced to playing at Williams' strip club.
In early July Allan Williams and his friend 'Lord Woodbine' opened an illegal strip club in Upper Parliament Street called the 'New Cabaret Artists Club'. He offered the group 10 shillings (50p) each every night to provide the music for a stripper called Janice.

Paul: "John, George and Stu and I used to play at a strip club in Upper Parliament Street, backing Janice the Stripper. At the time we wore little lilac jackets... or purple jackets or something. Well, we played behind Janice and naturally we looked at her... the audience looked at her, everybody looked at her, just sort of normal. At the end of the act she would turn round and... well, we were all young lads, we'd never seen anything like it before, and all

> "A Liverpool rhythm group, The Beatles, made their debut at Neston Institute on Thursday night."

blushed... four blushing, red faced lads. Janice brought sheets of music for us to play all her arrangements. She gave us a bit of Beethoven and the Spanish Fire Dance. So in the end we said, 'We can't read music, sorry, we can play the Harry Lime Cha-Cha which we've arranged ourselves, and instead of Beethoven you can have 'Moonglow' or 'September Song' – take your pick... and instead of the 'Sabre Dance' we'll give you 'Ramrod'. So that's what she got. She seemed quite satisfied, anyway. The strip club wasn't an important chapter in our lives, but it was an interesting one."

→ According to Williams they played two sets each night for a week, with Paul on drums. The *Sunday People* of newspaper featured photographs John and Stuart Sutcliffe's flat in an expose entitled 'The Beatnik Horror, for though they don't know it they are on the road to hell'. This dubious 'publicity', John's first appearance in the national press, was arranged by Allan Williams.

2 July
→ The Grosvenor Ballroom, Liscard. Johnny Gentle, visiting his home in Liverpool on a weekend off, stopped by the Jacaranda to look up his old backing group. Williams told him where The Silver Beatles were playing and Gentle and his father went over to the Grosvenor, where Gentle leaped up and joined the group on stage for a few numbers.

7 July
→ The Institute, Wirral.

9 July
→ First of a four-week residency at the Grosvenor Ballroom, Liscard.
→ Without bothering to inform Allan Williams, The Royal Caribbean Steel

Band, his resident group at the Jacaranda, accepted an engagement at a club in Hamburg in late June and simply failed to turn up one night. They happily wrote to Williams telling him there was a good market for British bands in Hamburg and urging him to visit.
→ Williams, always looking for a new angle, visited the city with his friend Lord Woodbine and met Bruno Koschmider, owner of the Kaiserkeller. Since American rock'n'roll bands would have been too expensive to bring over, Koschmider was delighted to find that cheap rock groups were available in Britain, and at the end of July, Williams sent one of his groups, Derry & The Seniors, to Hamburg to play at the Kaiserkeller.

2 August
→ Bruno Koschmider wrote to Allan Williams asking if he could supply another group, and Williams offered the engagement to The Silver Beatles, provided they could find a drummer.
→ Around this time, Paul wrote to a friend that since Norman Chapman's departure from the group, he had been acting as their drummer. He also noted that The Beatles had been promised a second tour of Scotland as a reward for completing their first trip successfully.

6 August
→ With their usual Saturday night engagement at the Grosvenor cancelled, the group went over to Mona Best's Casbah Coffee Club where they found The Blackjacks performing, with Mona's son, Pete, playing a brand new drum kit. The Blackjacks were about to split up, so The Beatles shrewdly asked Pete if he wanted to come to Hamburg with them and arranged for Pete to audition for them the following Saturday.

12 August
→ Pete Best was auditioned by John, Paul and George to be their permanent drummer and go with them to Hamburg. Since he was their only hope of getting a drummer and therefore getting the gig, he passed the audition. It was just before the Hamburg tour that the group changed their name to The Beatles.

Above: Pete Best at the Casbah Coffee Club. Opposite: The Silver Beatles audition for Larry Parnes, Liverpool, 10 May, with Johnny Hutchinson on drums.

Pete Best: "A few years ago I used to sit in with various groups at The Casbah, Heyman's Green, and also had a trio called The Blackjacks. The Beatles used to play at the club and I got to know them there. They were auditioning for a drummer at the Wyvern Club, Seel Street (now the Blue Angel) and asked me to come along. They desperately needed a drummer at the time as they had to go to Germany within a few days' time. They asked me to join the group and two days later I was in Hamburg with them..."

16 August
→ The Beatles, accompanied by Allan Williams, his wife, her brother and Lord Woodbine, left Liverpool for Hamburg in Williams' old Austin van. They stopped off in London for a

Previous page: The five-man Beatles line-up pose at Heiligengeistfield Square, Hamburg. L-R: Pete Best, George, John, Paul, Stuart Sutcliffe.

further passenger, Herr Steiner, an Austrian then working at the Heaven & Hell coffee bar on Old Compton Street, who was to act as Koschmider's interpreter. They took the ferry from Harwich to the Hook of Holland.

17 August

→ The Beatles and company arrived in Hamburg in the early evening. The contract signed between Allan Williams' Jacaranda Enterprises and Bruno Koschmider was to provide a five-piece band called The Beatles who were to be paid DM30 per day of work.

→ They began work right away at the Indra, at 58 Grosse Freiheit.

→ They were to play seven days a week from 8 until 9; from 10 until 11; 11 until 12 and from 1 until 2. On Saturdays they began work at 7, playing until 8. Then from 9 until 10; 10 until 11; 12 until 1 and 1 until 3am. On Sundays they began even earlier: 5 until 6, 6:30 until 7:30, 8 until 9, 9:30 until 10:30, 11 until 12 and 12:30 until 1:30.

Paul: "You revved your engines up so much that when you let them go, you just coasted. Like at Hamburg we often played an eight-hour day! Playing like that, you get to have a lot of tunes, if nothing else. So what we used to do, even on our eight-hour stint, was to try not to repeat any numbers. That was our own little ambition to stop us going round the bend. That gave us millions of songs, though some we could only just get away with – 'Dum-da-dum-da-dum-da-dum!' for half-an-hour! We'd shout out a title the Germans wouldn't understand to keep ourselves amused, like 'Knickers', but eventually we built up quite a programme."

George: "Sure we come from

George: "When you think about it sensibly, our sound really stems from Germany. That's where we learned to work for hours and hours on end, and keep on working at full peak even though we reckoned our legs and arms were about ready to drop off."

Liverpool. There are hundreds of groups there, many on an R & B kick. But you won't hear us shouting about a Liverpool Sound, or Merseybeat, simply because it's been dreamed up as an easy way to describe what's going on with our music. 'Hamburg Stamp and Yell' music might be more accurate. It was all that work on various club stages in Germany that built up our beat."

→ Only John and Paul did vocals before the first Hamburg trip, but the eight-hour sessions meant that George had to share the work, and by the time they returned to Liverpool they had three vocalists.

Paul: "Hamburg was a good exercise really in commercialism – a couple of students would stick their heads round the door, and we'd suddenly go into a piece of music that we thought might attract them. If we got people in, they might pay us better. That club was called the Indra – which is German for India. We were nicking left, right and

centre off other bands there; we'd see something that we'd like, and after they left Hamburg, we'd put it in our set. Well you've got to, haven't you? We used to like going up and watching Tony Sheridan, 'cos he was a little bit of the generation above us; he used to play some blues, real moody stuff."

→ The Beatles got on well with Tony Sheridan and his group, The Jets. Paul and Iain Hines, the keyboard player with The Jets, used to double date two Hamburg barmaids: Paul's was called Liane.

Iain: "Every evening, when we'd finished working, Liane used to pick us up in her tiny Volkswagon and take us to her flat for coffee and a record session. Paul and I used to play Elvis and Everly records while Liane prepared a supper of Deutsch Beefsteak (hamburgers) and coffee."

It was already 4am when she picked them up from the club.

→ When The Beatles arrived at the Indra they were completely broke. Rosa, the cleaning lady, gave them

a few marks so they could go across the street to Harold's café for a meal of potato fritters, cornflakes and chicken soup. Rosa washed their shirts and socks, gave them chocolate bars, and for a time, Paul lived in her small bungalow down on the docks.

Rosa: "I remember when young Paul used to practise guitar on the roof of my little place. We used to get crowds of burly old Hamburg dockers hanging around, just listening. They shouted out things in German, but Paul didn't understand them. It's odd. They were a very hard audience who didn't really know what Paul was playing, but somehow they took to him."

→ The Beatles' accommodation was two shared rooms behind the screen of the Bambi-Filmkunsttheater where they had to use the cinema bathrooms to wash. There were no cooking facilities and the group used to frequent the British Sailors' Society, where the manager, Mr Hawk, would feed them cornflakes and pints of milk.

1 – 30 September

→ Indra Club, Grosse Freiheit, Hamburg.

Paul: "The first time we went to Hamburg we stayed four and a half months. It's a sort of blown up Blackpool, but with strip clubs instead of waxworks; thousands of strip clubs, bars and pick-up joints, not very picturesque. The first time it was pretty rough but we all had a gear time. The pay wasn't too fab, the digs weren't much good, and we had to play for quite a long time."

Liverpool musician Howie Casey: "At the beginning, they

still played a lot of The Shadows' numbers, but gradually turned to R&B. When they came over, they had very, very pointed shoes in grey crocodile. They had mauve jackets, black shirts and pants, and also brown jackets with half-belting at the back. The length of their hair caused a great stir – it was thick at the back, almost coming over their collars."

→ During their time at the Indra, Stuart Sutcliffe briefly left The Beatles to play with Howie Casey's group, The Seniors.

"The Beatles did their nuts because Stu was playing with us", Casey recalled.

1 – 3 October
→ Indra, Grosse Freiheit, Hamburg.

4 October
→ Police pressure caused by noise complaints – mostly from the old woman who lived above the club – caused Bruno Koschmider to stop using the Indra as a music club and bring back the strippers. So after 48 nights on stage, The Beatles moved to the much larger Kaiserkeller, at 36 Grosse Freiheit. Here they alternated with Rory Storm & The Hurricanes who had arrived in Hamburg three days before, after playing a summer season at Butlin's. The drummer with The Hurricanes was Ringo Starr.

10 October
→ Allan Williams returned to Hamburg on a visit. The Beatles had a problem with the stage at the Kaiserkeller, which was much larger than they were used to and made them appear like frozen waxworks. Koschmider complained to Williams who yelled
"Make a show, boys!"
and encouraged them to move around. Koschmider, who spoke no English, took up the chant:
"Mach schau!"

In future, every time they slowed down or looked tired, Koschmider would exhort them to "Mach schau!"
→ Their act was transformed: first John and then the others began to throw microphones and instruments about the stage. They smoked, drank and sometimes even fought on stage. John once performed wearing only his underwear and a toilet seat around his neck. They painted swastikas on old Afrikka Corps caps, and goose-stepped around the stage giving illegal Seig Heil salutes and yelling at the audience,
The audience loved it. Insulting the customers not only went down well but also began to attract large crowds. Half the time the band were drunk or – with the exception of Pete – on Benzedrine; there was no other way they could get through the two final sets. The gangsters in the audience would send up crates of beer and hand them preludin; it was sensible not to refuse gifts from these people.

→ The Beatles and Rory Storm had a competition to see which group could demolish the club's unstable and potentially dangerous stage. Rory Storm won the bet during an enthusiastic version of 'Blue Suede Shoes'. The outraged Koschmider fined him DM65 to pay for the damage.

15 October
→ Walter Eymond, the singer and bass player with The Hurricanes, made an amateur recording of 'Summertime' at the small Akustik studio by the railway station, at Kirchenallee 57, Hamburg – a place where messages to family and friends could be recorded on 78rpm discs. Eymond's stage name was Lou Walters but everyone knew him as Wally. Backing him were Ringo, also in The Hurricanes, and

"Clap your hands, you fuckin' Nazis."

Left: The Beatles on stage at the Top Ten Club in Hamburg.

John, Paul and George from The Beatles. Stuart was there as an observer as he couldn't play well enough for recording, so for the first time on record, John, Paul, George and Ringo played together. Wally and Ringo also made recordings of 'Fever' and 'September Song', possibly during the same session. Nine copies of the 'Summertime' 78 were cut, but only one copy has surfaced.

16 October

→ The Beatles' contract was extended until December 31. They were making good money for Koschmider.

→ The audience was composed mostly of gangsters, people in the sex industry, rockers and visiting sailors. Then one day, an art student happened by, attracted by the sound of Rory Storm & The Hurricanes. Klaus Voormann was an "exi" – an existentialist – the sworn enemies of the rockers, and felt a certain trepidation at venturing into their territory, but having seen The Beatles do their set he was so excited that he returned the next day, and the one after, this time bringing with him his girlfriend, the photographer Astrid Kirchherr. Astrid and Stuart Sutcliffe soon became a couple (their engagement was announced in November), encouraging Astrid to take some of the best-known photographs of the group from that time.

→ Though Stuart was regarded by many as the most attractive member of the group, he had still not learned how to play his bass guitar, preferring to pose with it and look moody. This caused a tremendous friction in the group with Paul complaining to John, and both John and Paul complaining to Stuart. John was torn between friendship and his desire for the group to make it. He knew that Paul was right and The Beatles could never be any good musically as long as Stuart remained in the group. But at the same time he loyally defended his friend to the hilt, threatening to leave himself if Stuart was forced out.

Paul: "The problem with Stu was that he couldn't play bass guitar. We had to turn him away in photographs because he'd be doing F-sharp and we'd be holding G. Stu and I had a fight once on stage in Hamburg but we were virtually holding each other up. We couldn't move, couldn't do it. The thing that concerned me was the music, and that we get on musically, and we didn't. Same with Pete Best."

30 October

→ The Beatles made a verbal agreement with Peter Eckhorn to play the Top Ten Club in April provided that he sort out their immigration problems.

1–3 November

→ Kaiserkeller, Grosse Freiheit, Hamburg.

1 November

→ Bruno Koschmider terminated The Beatles' contract. His notice to quit read:

"I the undersigned hereby give notice to Mr. George Harrison and to Beatles' Band to leave on November 30th, 1960. The notice is given to the aboveby order of the Public Authorities who have discovered that Mr. George Harrison is only 17 (seventeen) years of age."

→ Besides discovering that George was under age, Koschmider was more likely moved to dismiss The Beatles because he had discovered that they were planning to transfer to the Top Ten Club, run by his rival, Peter Eckhorn.

21 November

→ George was deported from Germany for being too young to work in nightclubs.

22 November

→ Despite the loss of their lead

Paul: "There was an article on the group in a German magazine. I didn't understand the article, but there was a large photograph of us in the middle page. In the same article there was a photograph of a South African negro pushing the jungle down. I still don't quite know what he has to do with us, but I suppose it has some significance."

guitarist The Beatles were expected to continue playing at the Kaiserkeller normally. The work sheet for this date gives the exact times they were expected on stage: 7:30 pm until 9; 9:30 until 11; 11:30 until 1; 1:30 until 2:30 am: five and half hours of playing time, seven days a week.

29 November

Paul: "One night we played at the Top Ten Club and all the customers from the Kaiserkeller came along. Since the Top Ten was a much better club, we decided to accept the manager's offer and play there. Naturally the manager of the Kaiserkeller didn't like it."

→ During a change of digs from the Bambi-Filmkunsttheater to quarters provided by Peter Eckhorn, Pete and Paul accidentally set their old room on fire: there was no light and so as they were packing, they set fire to a condom in order to see. Though no damage was done except for one singed mark on the wall, Koschmider had them arrested and deported for arson.

Peter Eckhorn: "They were working at the Kaiserkeller in Hamburg at the time, but they didn't like it there and so they came to see me and ask if there was any work to be had at the Top Ten. To show what they could do they played a couple of numbers for me. I liked them. I said OK, I'd give them a job. But before I could hire them, the owners of the Kaiserkeller made a complaint about the boys to the police, saying they'd tried to set fire to the club! It wasn't true, of course, but the complaint had the desired effect: The Beatles were deported. It took seven months to get them back again. They stayed three months and were very popular, not so much for

Opposite: Being only 17, George was deported from Hamburg on 21 November after being found underage to perform in the Reeperbahn's nightclubs.

their music [which wasn't so different from the other groups], but for their personalities. Nobody in particular shone out – they were all well liked."

December 1
→ Paul and Pete arrived back in England after being deported from Germany.

10 December
→ John, who had decided to stay on in Germany with Stuart rather than returning home with Paul and Pete, finally set off for England by train. Stuart stayed on in Hamburg with Astrid, conveniently solving the problem of how to remove him from the group.

15 December
→ John finally contacted Paul, George and Pete, having arrived home broke and depressed four days earlier. This was his first contact with his band-mates since their deportation, leading them to fear that he was no longer interested in playing with The Beatles.

16 December
→ George wrote to Stuart Sutcliffe in Hamburg:

"Come home sooner… It's no good with Paul playing bass, we've decided, that is if he had some kind of bass and amp to play on!"

17 December
→ Casbah Coffee Club, West Derby, Liverpool with ex-Blackjack Chas Newby, on bass.

24 December
→ Grosvenor Ballroom, Liscard.

27 December
→ Litherland Town Hall, where they were advertised as "Direct from Hamburg".
→ This "Welcome Home" engagement had been booked for them by Bob Wooler with Brian Kelly for a fee of £6. The Beatles played their normal Hamburg set, which had an electrifying effect on the young audience. Immediately after the show Brian Kelly booked them for another 36 dances – at £6 to £8 a gig – before any other promoter could get to them.

31 December
→ Casbah Coffee Club, West Derby, Liverpool. Chas Newby's final engagement with the group before returning to college.

John: "In Liverpool, people didn't even know we were from Liverpool. They thought we were from Hamburg. They said, 'Christ, they speak good English!' Which we did of course, being English. But that's when we first stood there being cheered for the first time."

1961

January

→ John tried to get George to play bass but this met with a solid refusal and so Paul, who had been playing both rhythm guitar and piano, was deputed to take the job. He put together a bass out of a Solid 7 model and three piano strings. It was not very satisfactory, but it still sounded better than Stuart had done.

→ Beatlemania was beginning. Girls began screaming and rushing the stage, mostly for Pete Best who on one occasion was nearly pulled into the audience.

5 January

→ Litherland Town Hall.

6 January

→ St John's Hall, Bootle.

Below: The leather-clad Beatles in front of their van outside the Cavern Club, Mathew Street, Liverpool.
Opposite: George, Stuart and John (with Paul at the piano), on stage at the Top Ten Club, Hamburg.

7 January

→ Aintree Institute, Liverpool and Lathom Hall, Seaforth, Liverpool. Two gigs in one evening.

13 January

→ Aintree Institute, Liverpool.

14 January

→ Aintree Institute, Liverpool.

15 January

→ Casbah Coffee Club, West Derby, Liverpool.

18 January

→ Aintree Institute, Liverpool.

19 January

→ Alexandra Hall, Crosby, Liverpool.

20 January

→ Lathom Hall, Seaforth.

21 January

→ Lathom Hall, Seaforth and Aintree Institute, Liverpool.

25 January

→ Hambleton Hall, Huyton, Liverpool.

26 January

→ Litherland Town Hall.

27 January

→ Aintree Institute, Liverpool.

28 January

→ Lathom Hall, Seaforth and Aintree Institute, Liverpool.

29 January

→ Casbah Coffee Club, West Derby, Liverpool.

The Cavern: 9 February

This was the first time the group played The Cavern under the name of The Beatles. The club would become forever associated with the group. George arrived in blue jeans, which were banned from the club, but fortunately he was able to convince the bouncer, Paddy Delaney, that he was part of the act.

30 January

→ Lathom Hall, Seaforth.

1 February

→ Hambleton Hall, Huyton, Liverpool.

2 February

→ Litherland Town Hall.

3 February

→ St. John's Hall, Bootle.

4 February

→ Lathom Hall, Seaford.

5 February

→ Blair Hall, Walton, Liverpool.

6 February

→ Lathom Hall, Seaforth.

7 February

→ Merseyside Civil Services Club, Liverpool.

8 February

→ Aintree Institute, Liverpool and Hambleton Hall, Huyton, Liverpool.

9 February

→ The Cavern, Liverpool (an unadvertised lunchtime session).

10 February

→ Aintree Institute, Liverpool and Lathom Hall, Seaforth.

11 February

→ Lathom Hall, Seaforth and Cassanova Club, Sampson & Barlow's New Ballroom, Liverpool.

12 February

→ Casbah Coffee Club, West Derby, Liverpool.

14 February

→ Cassanova Club, Sampson & Barlow's New Ballroom, Liverpool and Litherland Town Hall.

→ The second booking of the night was a St Valentine's Day Special. Paul sang Elvis's 'Wooden Heart' wearing a red satin heart bearing the names of the group pinned to his jacket. The heart was raffled but when the winner climbed up on stage to receive her prize and a kiss from Paul, the stage was

1961

inundated with squealing girls and the group had to be rescued by bouncers.

15 February
→ Aintree Institute, Liverpool and Hambleton Hall, Huyton, Liverpool.

16 February
→ Cassanova Club, Sampson & Barlow's New Ballroom, Liverpool and Litherland Town Hall.

17 February
→ St John's Hall, Tuebrook, Liverpool.
→ This gig was promoted by Pete Best's mother, Mona, who negotiated a number of The Beatles' bookings at this stage in their career.

18 February
→ Aintree Institute, Liverpool.

19 February
→ Casbah Coffee Club, West Derby, Liverpool.

21 February
→ The Cavern (lunchtime), Cassanova Club, Sampson & Barlow's New Ballroom, Liverpool and Litherland Town Hall. Three bookings in one day was not uncommon for The Beatles during 1961.

22 February
→ Aintree Institute, Liverpool and Hambleton Hall, Huyton, Liverpool.

Playing in Hamburg: 1 April

The Beatles began a three-month, 13-week season at the Top Ten Club, at Reeperbahn 136; a venue of about the same size as the Kaiserkeller, with a couple of dozen small tables surrounding a square dance floor by the stage. Their residency at the Top Ten Club lasted from April 1 until July 1, playing seven-hour sessions on week nights and eight hours at weekends with a 15-minute break every hour. They alternated first with The Jaybirds and later with Rory Storm & The Hurricanes. Beatles historian Mark Lewisohn has calculated that they spent 503 hours on stage over 92 nights.

In Hamburg they were reunited with Stuart Sutcliffe, who had returned there two weeks before and sometimes sat in with them. Stuart's decision not to remain in the band was now final. It was during this Hamburg visit that Astrid dressed Stuart in black leather, an outfit which the rest of the group then had copied by a tailor on the Reeperbahn. She also brushed Stu's hair forward, to look like her 'exi' friends. The other Beatles did not go for this – yet.

24 February
→ Grosvenor Ballroom, Liscard.

25 February
→ Aintree Institute, Liverpool and Latham Hall, Seaforth.

26 February
→ Casbah Coffee Club, West Derby, Liverpool.

28 February
→ The Cavern (lunchtime), Cassanova Club, Sampson & Barlow's New Ballroom, Liverpool and Litherland Town Hall.
→ In late February, Stuart Sutcliffe returned to Liverpool to see his parents but stayed only for a couple of weeks – though that proved long enough to cause dissension within the Beatles' ranks, when John insisted that despite his musical shortcomings, Stu should resume his former role as the group's bass player.

1 March
→ Aintree Institute, Liverpool.

2 March
→ Litherland Town Hall.

3 March
→ St John's Hall, Bootle.

4 March
→ Aintree Institute, Liverpool.

5 March
→ Casbah Coffee Club, West Derby, Liverpool.

6 March
→ The Cavern (lunchtime) and The Liverpool Jazz Society (the previously named and later to be renamed Old Iron Door Club).

7 March
→ Cassanova Club, Sampson & Barlow's New Ballroom, Liverpool.

8 March
→ The Cavern (lunchtime), Aintree Institute, Liverpool and Hambleton Hall, Huyton, Liverpool.

10 March
→ The Cavern (lunchtime), Grosvenor Ballroom, Liscard and St. John's Hall, Tuebrook, Liverpool.

11 March
→ Aintree Institute, Liverpool and Liverpool Jazz Society (Old Iron Door Club).

12 March
→ Casbah Coffee Club, West Derby, Liverpool and Cassanova Club, Sampson & Barlow's New Ballroom, Liverpool.

13 March
→ The Cavern (lunchtime) and Liverpool Jazz Society (Old Iron Door Club).

14 March
→ The Cavern (lunchtime).

15 March
→ The Cavern (lunchtime), Liverpool Jazz Society (afternoon).
→ Stuart Sutcliffe returned to Hamburg to his girlfriend, Astrid Kirchherr, and the State College of Art where he was studying painting.

16 March
→ The Cavern (lunchtime).

17 March
→ Mossway Hall, Croxteth and Liverpool Jazz Society (Old Iron Door Club).

19 March
→ Casbah Coffee Club, West Derby, Liverpool.

20 March
→ The Cavern (lunchtime) and Hambleton Hall, Huyton, Liverpool.

21 March
→ The Cavern (evening) with The Remo Four, Dale Roberts & The Jaywalkers and The Swinging Bluegenes, on a Bluegenes guest night. This was The Beatles' first evening gig at the Cavern.

22 March
→ The Cavern (lunchtime).

24 March
→ The Cavern (lunchtime).

Above: Stuart and John, Hamburg. While Sutcliffe's musical abilities were limited, John defended his friend's position in The Beatles until Stuart left to pursue his art career.

26 March
→ Casbah Coffee Club, West Derby, Liverpool.

27 March
→ The Beatles returned to Hamburg by train to play at the Top Ten. They received DM35 per man per day and accommodation: the fourth-floor attic above the club.

1-30 April
→ Top Ten Club, Reeperbahn, Hamburg.

20 April
→ Allan Williams in Liverpool had discovered that The Beatles did not intend to pay him his managerial commission on their earnings at the Top Ten Club, and that they considered he was no longer their manager. He wrote them a stormy letter, accusing them of forgetting who had helped them in the past, and describing them as 'swollen-headed'.

Allan Williams: "I am very distressed to hear you are contemplating not paying my commission out of your pay, as we agreed in our contract for your engagement at the Top Ten Club.

May I remind you, seeing you are all appearing to get more than a little swollen-headed, that you would not ever have smelled Hamburg if I had not made the contracts.

So you see, lads, I'm very annoyed you should welsh out of your agreed contract. If you decide not to pay I promise that I shall have you out of Germany inside two weeks through

1961

several legal ways and don't
you think I'm bluffing.

I don't want to fall out with
you but I can't abide anybody
who does not honour their word
or bond, and I could have sworn
you were all decent lads, that is
why I pushed you when nobody
wanted to hear you."

Williams no longer acted as
The Beatles' manager after this
point, and was unsuccessful in
pursuing his financial claim
against the group.

Late May/early June
→ Having watched the group
perform at the Top Ten Club in early
May, German orchestra leader,
composer and record label executive
Bert Kaempfert signed The Beatles
(John, Paul, George and Pete) to a
recording contract which ran from
July 1st 1961 to June 30th 1962.
Kaempfert let them tape some of
their own material, but his primary
interest was for them to be a backing
group for the London rock'n'roll
singer, Tony Sheridan, whom he had
also recently signed.

1 – 30 June
→ Top Ten Club, Reeperbahn, Hamburg.

22/23 June
→ Friedrich-Ebert-Halle, Hamburg-
Harburg.
→ The Beatles, with Paul on bass,
backed Tony Sheridan on three days
of recording for Bert Kaempfert. The
equipment consisted of nothing more
than a portable tape recorder set up on
the stage of an orchestral hall with the
curtains drawn.
→ At the orchestral hall, they
recorded four tracks backing Sheridan:
'My Bonnie (Lies Over The Ocean)',
'When The Saints Go Marching In',
'Why (Can't You Love Me Again)' and
'Nobody's Child'. They also did one of
their own, 'Cry For A Shadow', an
instrumental credited to John Lennon
and George Harrison.
→ The single 'My Bonnie'/'The Saints'
was released in Germany as Polydor 24

Opposite: George
sits among The Beatles'
instruments, the Top Ten
Club, Hamburg.
Above: A surly-looking
John pictured in
Hamburg.

673 in October. The Beatles were
renamed 'The Beat Brothers' for this
release because their name sounded
too much like 'Peedles', a German slang
term for male genitalia.

24 June
→ Studio Rahlstedt, Rahlau 128,
Tonndorf, Hamburg.
→ A further track with Tony Sheridan
was recorded: Jimmy Reed's '(If You
Love Me Baby) Take Out Some
Insurance On Me', plus the pre-war
standard, 'Ain't She Sweet', recorded by
The Beatles without Sheridan and with
John on lead vocal.

2 July
→ The Beatles set off for Liverpool
from Hamburg, arriving the next day.

6 July
→ Bill Harry, a local writer, published
the first issue of his fortnightly beat
music paper named *Mersey Beat*
which included a humorous article
written by John, entitled 'Being a
Short Diversion on the Dubious
Origins of The Beatles translated from
the John Lennon'.

13 July
→ St John's Hall, Tuebrook, Liverpool.

14 July
→ The Cavern (lunchtime and evening),
the latter a 'Welcome Home Night'.

15 July
→ Holyoake Hall, Wavertree,
Liverpool.

1961

28 July
→ Aintree Institute, Liverpool.

29 July
→ Blair Hall, Walton, Liverpool.

30 July
→ Blair Hall, Walton, Liverpool.

31 July
→ The Cavern (lunchtime) and Litherland Town Hall.

2 August
→ The Cavern (lunchtime and evening).

4 August
→ The Cavern (lunchtime) and Aintree Institute, Liverpool.

5 August
→ The Cavern (evening).
→ An all-night session with The Cimmerons, The Panama Jazz Band, The Mike Cotten Jazz Band, The Kenny Ball Jazzmen and The Remo Four.

6 August
→ Casbah Coffee Club, West Derby, Liverpool. The Beatles first gig here in three months

7 August
→ Town Hall, Litherland.

8 August
→ The Cavern (lunchtime).

9 August
→ The Cavern (evening).

10 August
→ The Cavern (lunchtime) and St. John's Hall, Tuebrook, Liverpool.

11 August
→ The Cavern (evening).

12 August
→ Aintree Institute, Liverpool.

13 August
→ Casbah Coffee Club, West Derby, Liverpool.

14 August
→ The Cavern (lunchtime).

16 July
→ Blair Hall, Walton, Liverpool.

17 July
→ The Cavern (lunchtime) and Litherland Town Hall.

19 July
→ The Cavern (lunchtime and evening).

20 July
→ St John's Hall, Tuebrook.
→ The second issue of *Mersey Beat* featured a picture of The Beatles on the cover with a report on their recording session with Tony Sheridan, under the grammatically dubious heading: 'Beatle's Sign Recording Contract!'
→ Noting the immediate popularity of *Mersey Beat's* first issue, Brian Epstein ordered 12 dozen copies of the new edition for his record shop, NEMS.

21 July
→ The Cavern (lunchtime) and Aintree Institute, Liverpool.

22 July
→ Holyoake Hall, Wavertree, Liverpool.

23 July
→ Blair Hall, Walton, Liverpool.

24 July
→ Litherland Town Hall.

25 July
→ The Cavern (lunchtime and evening).

26 July
→ The Cavern (evening).

27 July
→ The Cavern (lunchtime) and St John's Hall, Tuebrook.

Above: L-R: Stuart, George and John back Tony Sheridan at the Top Ten Club, Hamburg.

16 August
→ The Cavern (evening).

17 August
→ St John's Hall, Tuebrook, Liverpool.

18 August
→ The Cavern (lunchtime) and Aintree Institute, Liverpool.

19 August
→ Aintree Institute, Liverpool.

20 August
→ Hambleton Hall, Huyton, Liverpool.

21 August
→ The Cavern (lunchtime).

23 August
→ The Cavern (lunchtime and evening).

24 August
→ St John's Hall, Tuebrook, Liverpool.

25 August
→ The Cavern (lunchtime) and a 'Riverboat Shuffle' on the M.V. *Royal Iris*, River Mersey, with Acker Bilk and His Paramount Jazz Band.

26 August
→ Aintree Institute, Liverpool.

27 August
→ Casbah Coffee Club, West Derby, Liverpool.

28 August
→ The Cavern (lunchtime).

29 August
→ The Cavern (lunchtime).

30 August
→ The Cavern (evening) with The Strangers.

31 August
→ St John's Hall, Tuebrook, Liverpool.
→ *Mersey Beat* reported that a 'Beatles' fan club had been started. 'The club will open officially in September...'

1 September
→ The Cavern (lunchtime).

2 September
→ Aintree Institute, Liverpool.

3 September
→ Hambleton Hall, Huyton, Liverpool.

6 September
→ The Cavern (evening).

7 September
→ The Cavern (lunchtime).

8 September
→ St John's Hall, Tuebrook, Liverpool.

9 September
→ Aintree Institute, Liverpool.

10 September
→ Casbah Coffee Club, West Derby, Liverpool.

11 September
→ The Cavern (lunchtime).

13 September
→ The Cavern (lunchtime and evening).

14 September
→ Litherland Town Hall.
→ John's satirical column 'Around and About', written under the pseudonym Beatcomber, first appeared in *Mersey Beat* magazine, alongside a selection of his fake classified ads.

15 September
The Cavern (lunchtime), Grosvenor Ballroom, Liscard and Village Hall, Knotty Ash.

16 September
→ Aintree Institute, Liverpool.

17 September
→ Hambleton Hall, Huyton, Liverpool.

19 September
→ The Cavern (afternoon).

1961

20 September
→ The Cavern (evening).

21 September
→ The Cavern (lunchtime) and Litherland Town Hall.

22 September
→ Village Hall, Knotty Ash.

23 September
→ Aintree Institute, Liverpool.

24 September
→ Casbah Coffee Club, West Derby, Liverpool.

25 September
→ The Cavern (lunchtime).

27 September
→ The Cavern (lunchtime and evening.

28 September
→ Litherland Town Hall.

29 September
→ The Cavern (lunchtime) and Village Hall, Knotty Ash.

30 September
→ Paul and John set off to hitchhike to Paris, financed by some cash from an aunt in Scotland which John had been given as an early 21st birthday present.

October
→ The single 'My Bonnie'/'The Saints' by Tony Sheridan & The Beat Brothers was released in Germany as Polydor NH 24673.
→ The EP *My Bonnie* by Tony Sheridan and The Beat Brothers was released in Germany on Polydor EPH 21485: Side A: 'My Bonnie', 'Why'; Side B: 'Cry For A Shadow', 'The Saints'.

5 October
→ The Beatles were named as Liverpool's top group in Bob Wooler's regular column in *Mersey Beat*.

9 October
→ John spent his 21st birthday in Paris with Paul. They visited Jürgen Vollmer, a friend from the Reeperbahn, who had moved there to study photography. He wore his hair brushed forward in a fashion which was popular among some French youths, and was a style he had been introduced to by Astrid Kirchherr, who cut Stuart Sutcliffe's hair that way when they were all in Hamburg. John and Paul decided they wanted their hair like Jürgen's and asked him to do it.
→ Astrid had initially copied the style from a Jean Cocteau movie, the 1959 *Le Testament d'Orphée* where Jean Marais wore his hair brushed forward to play Oedipus; the ultimate origin of the famous Beatles haircut.

15 October
→ Albany Cinema, Northway (lunchtime).

16 October
→ The Cavern (lunchtime).

17 October
→ David Lewis Club, Liverpool. Promoted by The Beatles' newly formed fan club.

18 October
→ The Cavern (lunchtime and evening).

19 October
→ Litherland Town Hall.

20 October
→ The Cavern (lunchtime) and Village Hall, Knotty Ash.

21 October
→ The Cavern (all night session) with The Panama Jazz Band, The Remo Four, Gerry & The Pacemakers, The Yorkshire Jazz Band and The Collegians Jazz Band.

22 October
→ Casbah Coffee Club, West Derby, Liverpool.

24 October
→ The Cavern (lunchtime).

25 October
→ The Cavern (evening).

26 October
→ The Cavern (lunchtime).

27 October
→ Village Hall, Knotty Ash.

Jürgen Vollmer: "I gave both of them their first Beatles haircut in my hotel room on the Left Bank."

28 October
→ Aintree Institute, Liverpool.
→ This was the legendary day on which Raymond Jones supposedly asked Brian Epstein for a copy of 'My Bonnie' by The Beatles at NEMS record store. The record was released only in Germany at that time and was by Tony Sheridan and The Beat Brothers, not The Beatles, so it took Epstein a little while to track it down.
→ Epstein's assistant, Alistair Taylor, subsequently claimed that this legendary occurrence was actually a myth, and that there was no 'Raymond Jones'.

Alistair Taylor: "The truth is that we were being asked for 'My Bonnie', but no one actually ordered it. Brian would order any record once we had a firm order for it. I thought that we were losing sales, and I wrote an order in the book under the name 'Raymond Jones', and from that moment the legend grew."

29 October
→ Hambleton Hall, Huyton, Liverpool.

30 October
→ The Cavern (lunchtime).

31 October
→ Litherland Town Hall.

1 November
→ The Cavern (lunchtime and evening).

3 November
→ The Cavern (lunchtime).

4 November
→ The Cavern (evening).

6 November
→ The British arm of Polydor Records released 'My Bonnie' by Tony Sheridan & The Beatles in the New Year.

7 November
→ The Cavern (lunchtime), Merseyside Civil Service Club and The Cavern again (evening).

8 November
→ The Cavern (evening).

9 November
→ The Cavern (lunchtime) and Litherland Town Hall.
→ Brian Epstein, accompanied by his assistant, Alistair Taylor, visited the Cavern for the first time. His presence was announced by DJ Bob Wooler over the PA:

"We have someone rather famous in the audience today."

It is a measure of how small-town Liverpool was in 1961 that a record shop owner could be regarded as a famous celebrity.
→ Despite feeling very out of place among the lunch-time 'cave-dwellers' in the primitive, sweaty atmosphere of the Cavern, Epstein began to visit the club regularly to see The Beatles, always taking time to have a few words with them.

10 November
→ Tower Ballroom, New Brighton, Wallasey, Village Hall Knotty Ash. The Beatles played two sets, the first at 8 and the second at 11:30. In between sets they drove to Knotty Ash for the other gig.

11 November
→ Aintree Institute, Liverpool.

12 November
→ Hambleton Hall, Huyton, Liverpool.

13 November
→ The Cavern (lunchtime).

14 November
→ The Cavern (lunchtime) and Merseyside Civil Service Club.

15 November
→ The Cavern (lunchtime and evening).

17 November
→ The Cavern (lunchtime) and Village Hall, Knotty Ash.

18 November
→ The Cavern (evening).

19 November
→ Casbah Coffee Club, West Derby, Liverpool.

21 November
→ The Cavern (lunchtime) and Merseyside Civil Service Club.

22 November
→ The Cavern (evening).

23 November
→ The Cavern (lunchtime).

24 November
→ Casbah Coffee Club, West Derby, Liverpool and Tower Ballroom, New Brighton, Wallasey.

26 November
→ Hambleton Hall, Huyton, Liverpool.

27 November
→ The Cavern (lunchtime).

28 November
→ Merseyside Civil Service Club.

29 November
→ The Cavern (lunchtime and evening shows).

1961

1 December
→ The Cavern (lunchtime) and Tower Ballroom, New Brighton, Wallasey. The latter was one of Sam Leach's 'Operation Big Beat' sessions, with The Beatles heading the bill of six groups.

2 December
→ The Cavern (evening).

3 December
→ Casbah Coffee Club, West Derby, Liverpool.
→ The first meeting between the group and Brian Epstein to discuss his becoming their manager was held at Epstein's office at NEMS. The Beatles were not sure and went away to think about it.

5 December
→ The Cavern (lunchtime).

6 December
→ The Cavern (evening).
→ The Beatles' second meeting with Brian Epstein. John, acting as the spokesman for the group, accepted Brian's proposal but no documents were drawn up.

8 December
→ The Cavern (lunchtime) and Tower Ballroom, New Brighton, Wallasey.

9 December
→ Palais Ballroom, Aldershot.
→ The newspaper advertisement for the gig had not been printed and The Beatles arrived at an empty hall. A quick run round the local coffee bars asking people to come to a free dance resulted in an audience of 18 people.

10 December
→ Hambleton Hall, Huyton, Liverpool.
→ The group came to an informal agreement with Brian Epstein, making him their manager providing he could get them a recording contract.

11 December
→ The Cavern (lunchtime).

13 December
→ The Cavern (lunchtime and evening).
→ Brian Epstein used his influence to persuade the A&R Manager of Decca Records, Mike Smith, to visit Liverpool to see them play The Cavern. After

John: "We were in a daydream till he came along. We'd no idea what we were doing. Seeing our marching orders on paper made it all official. Brian was trying to clean our image up. He said we'd never get past the door of a good place. He'd tell us that jeans were not particularly smart and could we possibly manage to wear proper trousers. But he didn't want us suddenly looking square. He let us have our own sense of individuality. We respected his views. We stopped chomping at cheese rolls and jam butties on stage. We paid a lot more attention to what we were doing. Did our best to be on time. And we smartened up, in the sense that we wore suits instead of any sloppy old clothes."

Above: The Beatles pose for Albert Marrion's camera on 17 December. A month later, they were voted the top group in Liverpool thanks to a *Mersey Beat* newspaper poll.

watching them play he agreed to audition them in London.

15 December
→ The Cavern (lunchtime) and Tower Ballroom, New Brighton, Wallasey.

16 December
→ The Cavern (evening).

17 December
→ Casbah Coffee Club, West Derby.

18 December
→ The Cavern (lunchtime).

19 December
→ The Cavern (lunchtime).

20 December
→ The Cavern (evening).

21 December
→ The Cavern (lunchtime).

23 December
→ The Cavern, all-night session with The Micky Ashman Ragtime Jazz Band, The Remo Four, Gerry & The Pacemakers, The Saints Jazz Band and The Searchers.

26 December
→ Tower Ballroom, New Brighton, Wallasey. A 'Boxing Night Big Beat Ball'.

27 December
→ The Cavern (evening) with Gerry & The Pacemakers and Kingsize Taylor & The Dominoes. Advertised as 'The Beatles' Xmas Party'.

29 December
→ The Cavern (evening).

30 December
→ The Cavern (evening).

1962

1 January

➔ The Beatles auditioned for Mike Smith, an A&R manager at Decca Records, at Decca's studios in Broadhurst Gardens, West Hampstead, north London. They got started at 11 am and finished about an hour later. The group recorded a mixture of oldies, some of their own compositions and a selection of recent chart hits, chosen by Brian Epstein intending to show all sides of their ability, from rock'n'roll to ballad standards: 'Like Dreamers Do' (Lennon/McCartney), 'Money (That's What I Want)', 'Till There Was You', 'The Sheik Of Araby', 'To Know Her Is To Love Her', 'Take Good Care Of My Baby', 'Memphis, Tennessee', 'Sure To Fall (In Love With You)', 'Hello Little Girl'(Lennon/McCartney), 'Three Cool Cats', 'Crying, Waiting, Hoping', 'Love Of The Loved' (Lennon/McCartney), 'September In The Rain', 'Besame Mucho' and 'Searchin'.

➔ Mike Smith cut a number of acetates for his boss Dick Rowe, the head of 'Pop' A&R at Decca, singling out the Lennon & McCartney songs 'Hello Little Girl' and 'Like Dreamers Do' as the most interesting items on the tape. But Rowe turned the group down, famously telling Brian Epstein:

"Groups of guitars are on the way out, Mr Epstein. You really should stick to selling records in Liverpool." "Electric guitars", he told him, were now "old hat".

He became known as 'The man who turned down The Beatles' but later made up for it by signing The Rolling Stones to Decca in 1963 – on George Harrison's advice.

3 January

➔ The Cavern (lunchtime and evening).

4 January

➔ A poll of 5,000 readers of *Mersey Beat* magazine to find Liverpool's most popular group showed The Beatles at number one.

5 January

➔ The Cavern (lunchtime). The single 'My Bonnie'/'The Saints'

Above: The smartly groomed Beatles after Brian Epstein cleaned up their image into matching suits. Opposite: George, John and Paul pictured in the back yard of the McCartney home at 20 Forthlin Road, Allerton, Liverpool.

by Tony Sheridan and The (now-correctly-named) Beatles was released in the UK by Polydor: an Epstein promotional plan which meant that 'Polydor Recording Artists' could be now added to posters and advertisements even though there was little chance of the record getting into the charts.

6 January

➔ The Cavern (evening).

7 January

➔ Casbah Coffee Club, West Derby, Liverpool.

9 January

➔ The Cavern (lunchtime).

10 January

➔ The Cavern (evening).

11 January

➔ The Cavern (lunchtime).

12 January

➔ The Cavern (evening). Tower Ballroom, New Brighton, Wallasey.

13 January

➔ Hambleton Hall, Huyton.

14 January

➔ Casbah Coffee Club, West Derby, Liverpool.

15 January

➔ The Cavern (lunchtime).

17 January

➔ The Cavern (lunchtime and evening).

19 January

➔ The Cavern (lunchtime) and Tower Ballroom, New Brighton, Wallasey.

20 January

➔ The Cavern (evening).

21 January

➔ Casbah Coffee Club, West Derby, Liverpool.

22 January

➔ The Cavern (lunchtime) and Kingsway Club, Southport.

1962

24 January
→ The Cavern (lunchtime and evening).
That afternoon The Beatles finally signed a management contract with Brian Epstein, witnessed by his assistant Alistair Taylor, at Brian's NEMS office. He was to receive 25 per cent of their gross earnings. The four Beatles divided what was left after their expenses had been deducted. This meant that Brian always received more money than any individual Beatle and, when their expenses became enormous, he received considerably more. The normal management percentage in those days was 10 per cent.

26 January
→ The Cavern (lunchtime and evening) and Tower Ballroom, New Brighton, Wallasey.

27 January
→ Aintree Institute, Liverpool.

28 January
→ Casbah Coffee Club, West Derby, Liverpool.

29 January
→ Kingsway Club, Southport.

30 January
→ The Cavern (lunchtime).

31 January
→ The Cavern (evening).

1 February
→ The Cavern (lunchtime) and Thistle Café, West Kirby.

2 February
→ Oasis Club, Manchester.

3 February
→ The Cavern (evening).

4 February
→ Casbah Coffee Club, West Derby, Liverpool.

5 February
→ The Cavern (lunchtime) and The Kingsway Club, Southport.
Pete Best was ill and couldn't make these two gigs. Ringo Starr stood in as

The path to George Martin: 8 February

Brian Epstein had the Decca audition tape made into 78rpm acetates at EMI's His Master's Voice record shop at 363 Oxford Street, London. Jim Foy, the disc-cutter, was impressed by their performance, and when Brian told him that John and Paul wrote some of their own material, he suggested that Brian should meet Sid Coleman, the head of EMI's record publishing company, Ardmore and Beechwood, whose offices were on the top floor.
Coleman eventually published two of John and Paul's songs, 'Love Me Do' and 'P.S. I Love You'. When Epstein mentioned his problem in finding the Beatles a record deal, Coleman suggested Brian should see George Martin, head of A&R at Parlophone Records.

The Beatles' drummer for both performances.

7 February
→ The Cavern (lunchtime and evening).

9 February
→ The Cavern (lunchtime and evening) and Technical College Hall, Birkenhead.

10 February
→ Youth Club, St. Paul's Presbyterian Church Hall, Tranmere, Birkenhead.

11 February
→ Casbah Coffee Club, West Derby, Liverpool.

12 February
→ The Beatles were auditioned by Peter Pilbeam, who produced BBC Radio programmes for teenage audiences made in the North of England. He booked them to record a session for *Teenagers' Turn* on March 7.

13 February
→ The Cavern (lunchtime).

14 February
→ The Cavern (evening).

15 February
→ The Cavern (lunchtime) and Tower Ballroom, New Brighton, Wallasey, with Terry Lightfoot and his New Orleans Jazz Band. Billed as the 'Pre-Panto Ball' as there was to be a 'Panto Ball' at the Tower the next night. Between them they drew a large audience of 3,500.

16 February
→ Technical College, Birkenhead and Tower Ballroom, New Brighton, Wallasey.

17 February
→ The Cavern (evening).

18 February
→ Casbah Coffee Club, West Derby, Liverpool.

19 February
→ The Cavern (lunchtime).

20 February
→ Floral Hall, Southport. 'A Rock 'n' Trad Spectacular'.

21 February
→ The Cavern (lunchtime and evening).

23 February
→ The Cavern (lunchtime), Tower Ballroom, New Brighton, Wallasey (sets at 9 and 10.45 pm) and Technical College, Birkenhead.
→ The group just had time between sets at the Tower to squeeze in a half-hour appearance at Birkenhead.

24 February
→ YMCA Wirral and a Cavern all-night session.

26 February
→ Kingsway Club, Southport.

27 February
→ The Cavern (lunchtime).

28 February
→ The Cavern (evening).

1 March
→ The Cavern (lunchtime).

2 March
→ St John's Hall, Bootle and Tower Ballroom, New Brighton, Wallasey. Billed as the 'Mad March Rock Ball'.

3 March
→ The Cavern (evening).

4 March
→ Casbah Coffee Club, West Derby, Liverpool.

5 March
→ The Cavern (lunchtime) and Kingsway Club, Southport.

6 March
→ The Cavern (evening) with Gerry & The Pacemakers on the Bluegenes Guest Night.

7 March
→ The group drove to the Playhouse Theatre in Manchester to record their first BBC radio broadcast for the Light Programme show *Teenagers' Turn – Here We Go*. They did three numbers, all covers of American hits, before a teenage audience: Roy Orbison's 'Dream Baby (How Long Must I Dream)', Chuck Berry's 'Memphis, Tennessee' and the Marvelettes' 'Please Mister Postman'. It was broadcast March 8.

8 March
→ Storyville Jazz Club.

9 March
→ The Cavern (lunchtime and evening).

10 March
→ St Paul's Presbyterian Church Youth Club, Church Hall, Tranmere, Birkenhead.

11 March
→ Casbah Coffee Club, West Derby, Liverpool.

12 March
→ The Cavern (lunchtime).

13 March
→ The Cavern (lunchtime).

14 March
→ The Cavern (evening).

15 March
→ The Cavern (lunchtime).

Below: Onstage at the Cavern, 7 April. Opposite: Astrid Kirchherr and Stuart Sutcliffe. Stu died tragically young on 10 April.

16 March
→ The Cavern (evening).

17 March
→ Village Hall, Knotty Ash. A 'St Patrick's Night Rock Gala'.

18 March
→ Casbah Coffee Club, West Derby, Liverpool.

19 March
→ Kingsway Club, Southport.

20 March
→ The Cavern (evening).

21 March
→ The Cavern (lunchtime).

22 March
→ The Cavern (evening).

23 March
→ The Cavern (lunchtime and evening).

24 March
→ Heswall Jazz Club, Barnston Women's Institute, Heswall, Wirral, with The Pasadena Jazzmen. For the first time, The Beatles wore suits on stage for this prestigious event.

25 March
→ Casbah Coffee Club, West Derby, Liverpool.

26 March
→ The Cavern (lunchtime).

28 March
→ The Cavern (lunchtime and evening).

29 March
→ Odd Spot Club, Liverpool.

30 March
→ The Cavern (lunchtime and evening).

31 March
→ Subscription Rooms, Stroud in Gloucestershire.

1 April
→ Casbah Coffee Club, West Derby, Liverpool.

2 April
→ The Cavern (lunchtime) and Liverpool Pavilion with 'Ireland's Pride', the Royal Show Band from Waterford. The Beatles were billed as 'Merseyside's Joy'.

4 April
→ The Cavern (lunchtime and evening).

5 April
→ The Cavern (evening).

6 April
→ The Cavern (lunchtime) and Tower Ballroom, New Brighton, Wallasey.

7 April
→ The Cavern (evening) and Casbah Coffee Club, West Derby, Liverpool.
→ The Cavern show was advertised as 'The Beatles Farewell Show' before they left for Hamburg. George was ill and couldn't play these two gigs.

10 April
→ Stuart Sutcliffe, who had remained in Hamburg, was rushed to hospital with a brain haemorrhage, but died in the ambulance. He was 22.

11 April
→ The Beatles, except George, flew to Hamburg from Ringway Airport, Manchester. They were greeted on arrival by Stuart Sutcliffe's distraught girlfriend, Astrid Kirchherr, who managed to stammer out her tragic news. To her surprise, John exhibited no outward emotion at all – though she later credited John as having 'saved' her from her grief, by insisting that she come out to see The Beatles perform every evening rather than maintaining a lonely vigil in her room.

13-30 April, 1 – 31 May
→ The Beatles played a seven-week season at the Star-Club, Grosse-Freiheit, Hamburg ending on May 31, with only one day off: April 20, when the club closed for Good Friday. For the first two weeks they were on the same bill as Gene Vincent.

9 May
→ George Martin met with Brian Epstein at Abbey Road at the suggestion of Sid Coleman. On the strength of the Decca audition tapes, Martin offered Brian a provisional recording contract before he had even seen the group play.

24 May
→ The Beatles once again acted as Tony Sheridan's backing band at the Studio Rahlstedt. They were joined for the session, which began at 6pm, by Roy Young (piano) and Ricki Barnes (saxophone). Two songs were recorded, 'Sweet Georgia Brown' and 'Swanee River'. Paul was credited in Polydor's paperwork as the arranger for 'Sweet Georgia Brown'.

25 May
→ With their obligations to Bert Kaempfert complete, Brian Epstein and Kaempfert signed an agreement cancelling The Beatles' German recording contract with immediate effect. This freed The Beatles to record for George Martin at Parlophone a few days later.

28 May
→ The Beatles opened what the Star-Club billed as their 'Rockin'-Twist Festival 62.

June
→ The album *My Bonnie* by Tony Sheridan & The Beat Brothers was released in Germany on Polydor LPHM 46612 (mono) and SLPHM 237112 (stereo). The album, the first anywhere in the world to feature The Beatles' work, included 'My Bonnie' and 'The Saints', credited on the rear cover as 'Accompanied by The Beatles'.

6 June
→ The Beatles recorded four numbers in studio three at EMI Studios, 3 Abbey Road, St. John's Wood, north London: 'Besame Mucho', 'Love Me Do', 'P.S. I Love You' and 'Ask Me Why'. The session was produced by Ron Richards. George Martin only showed up when the balance engineer, Norman Smith, liked their first Lennon and McCartney composition and sent the tape operator, Chris Neal, to fetch him. George Martin saw the potential in what he heard, and ordered the final signature to be placed on the contract. The Beatles were now EMI artists.

9 June
→ The Cavern (evening): 'The Beatles' Welcome Home Show' 900 fans managed to squeeze into the airless basement for this gig, breaking the Cavern's attendance record.

11 June
→ The group recorded another set for the BBC Light Programme's *Teenagers' Turn – Here We Go*, at the BBC's Playhouse Theatre, Manchester. They played 'Ask Me Why', 'Besame Mucho' and 'A Picture Of You'. It was broadcast on the 15th.

12 June
→ The Cavern (lunchtime and evening).

13 June
→ The Cavern (lunchtime and evening).

15 June
→ The Cavern (lunchtime and evening).

16 June
→ The Cavern (evening).

19 June
→ The Cavern (lunchtime and evening).

20 June
→ The Cavern (lunchtime and evening).

21 June
→ Tower Ballroom, New Brighton, Wallasey. Bruce Channel topped the bill with Delbert McClinton and The Barons as his backing group.

22 June
→ The Cavern (lunchtime and evening).

23 June
→ The Victory Memorial Hall, Northwich in Cheshire.
→ Brian Epstein formed NEMS Enterprises Limited to deal with The Beatles' affairs.

24 June
→ Casbah Club, West Derby, Liverpool. The Beatles's final appearance at Mona Best's club.

25 June
→ The Cavern (lunchtime) and Plaza Ballroom, St Helen's in Lancashire. 'Big Beat Bargain Night'.

27 June
→ The Cavern (lunchtime and evening).

28 June
→ Majestic Ballroom, Birkenhead, 'Merseyside's luxury ballroom'. The Beatles' first booking with the Top Rank Organisation.

29 June
→ The Cavern (lunchtime). Tower Ballroom, New Brighton, Wallasey. 'Operation Big Beat III', a five-and-a-half hour 'Cavalcade of Rock 'n' Twist'.

30 June
→ Heswall Jazz Club at the Barnston Women's Institute in Heswall.

1 July
→ The Cavern (evening) with Gene Vincent & Sounds Incorporated.

2 July
→ Plaza Ballroom, St Helen's in Lancashire.

3 July
→ The Cavern (lunchtime).

4 July
→ The Cavern (evening).

5 July
→ Majestic Ballroom, Birkenhead.

6 July
→ Riverboat Shuffle on board the M.V. *Royal Iris*, organised by The Cavern.
→ Also on the bill were Acker Bilk's Paramount Jazz Band.

7 July
→ Golf Club Dance, Hulme Hall, Port Sunlight, Birkenhead.

8 July
→ The Cavern (evening).

9 July
→ Plaza Ballroom, St Helens.

10 July
→ The Cavern (lunchtime).

11 July
→ The Cavern (evening).

12 July
→ The Cavern (lunchtime) and Majestic Ballroom, Birkenhead.

13 July
→ Tower Ballroom, New Brighton, Wallasey.

14 July
→ Regent Dansett, Rhyl, Wales.

15 July
→ The Cavern (evening).

16 July
→ The Cavern (lunchtime) and Plaza Ballroom, St Helen's.

17 July
→ McIlroy's Ballroom, Swindon.

18 July
→ The Cavern (lunchtime and evening).

19 July
→ Majestic Ballroom, Birkenhead.

20 July
→ The Cavern (lunchtime) and The Bell Hall, Warrington.

21 July
→ Tower Ballroom, New Brighton, Wallasey.

22 July
→ The Cavern (evening).

23 July
→ Kingsway Club, Southport.

24 July
→ The Cavern (lunchtime).

25 July
→ The Cavern (lunchtime and evening) and Cabaret Club, Liverpool. The latter booking was not a success.

26 July
→ Cambridge Hall, Southport, supporting Joe Brown & The Bruvvers.

27 July
→ Tower Ballroom, New Brighton, Wallasey, supporting Joe Brown & The Bruvvers.

28 July
→ The Cavern (evening) and Majestic Ballroom, Birkenhead, Cheshire.

30 July
→ The Cavern (lunchtime) and Blue Penguin Club, St John's Hall, Bootle in Lancashire.

1 August
→ The Cavern (lunchtime and evening).

3 August
→ Grafton Ballroom, Liverpool.

4 August
→ Victoria Hall, Higher Bebington in the Wirral.

5 August
→ The Cavern (evening).

7 August
→ The Cavern (lunchtime and evening).

Below: Paul and George onstage at the Tower Ballroom, 27 July. The Beatles original road manager, Neil Aspinall can be seen bottom left.

8 August
→ Co-op Ballroom, Doncaster.

9 August
→ The Cavern (lunchtime).

10 August
→ Riverboat Shuffle on the *Royal Iris*.

11 August
→ Odd Spot Club, Liverpool.

12 August
→ The Cavern (evening).

13 August
→ The Cavern (lunchtime) and Majestic Ballroom, Crewe.

15 August
→ The Cavern (lunchtime and evening).
These were Pete Best's last performances as drummer with The Beatles before he was unceremoniously fired.
→ John Lennon telephoned Ringo Starr in Skegness, where he was about to complete a summer season with

Below: Before Ringo
Starr joined The Beatles
in August, he was a
bearded drummer with
top Liverpool group,
Rory Storm and The
Hurricanes.

Rory Storm & The Hurricanes at Butlin's Holiday Camp, and confirmed that he was to become The Beatles' new drummer. Ringo and The Beatles had already had several clandestine meetings about him replacing Pete Best.

16 August

→ Riverpark Ballroom, Chester. In the morning, Brian Epstein told Pete he was no longer in The Beatles. Johnny 'Hutch' Hutchinson, drummer with The Big Three, filled the empty drum stool at Chester.

17 August

→ Majestic Ballroom, Birkenhead and Tower Ballroom, New Brighton, Wallasey with 'Hutch' Hutchinson on drums.

18 August

→ Horticulture Society Dance, Hulme Hall, Port Sunlight, Birkenhead. This was Ringo's debut as a Beatle. They managed a two-hour rehearsal together before the 10 pm gig.

19 August

→ The Cavern (evening). Ringo's Cavern début as a Beatle. Pete Best had many fans who were aggrieved at his dismissal and the group were attacked as they entered the club. George received a black eye.

20 August

→ Majestic Ballroom, Crewe.

22 August

→ The Cavern (lunchtime and evening).

23 August

→ Riverpark Ballroom, Chester. John had got his girlfriend Cynthia Powell pregnant and so he 'did the right thing'. They were married at the Mount Pleasant Register Office with Paul as best man. George, Brian Epstein, Cynthia's brother Tony and his wife Marjorie were the only guests. John's harridan Aunt Mimi boycotted the event. Afterwards Brian Epstein took them all to Reece's cafe for a set lunch of roast chicken with all the trimmings followed by fruit salad. The cafe did not sell alcohol so they toasted each other with water. Brian allowed the couple to move into a small bachelor flat he maintained near the art college. John spent his wedding night on stage.

24 August
→ The Cavern (lunchtime) and Majestic Ballroom, Birkenhead, Wirral.

25 August
→ Marine Hall Ballroom, Fleetwood, Lancashire.

26 August
→ The Cavern (evening).

28 August
→ The Cavern (evening).

29 August
→ Floral Hall Ballroom, Morecambe.

30 August
→ The Cavern (lunchtime) and Riverpark Ballroom, Chester.

31 August
→ Town Hall, Lydney, Gloucestershire.

1 September
→ Subscription Rooms, Stroud, Gloucestershire.

2 September
→ The Cavern (evening).

3 September
→ The Cavern (lunchtime) and Queen's Hall, Widnes, Cheshire.

4 September
→ Abbey Road. The Beatles flew from Liverpool Airport to London, where they checked into a small hotel in Chelsea. Neil Aspinall had already driven their equipment down and was waiting with it at the studio. They rehearsed until 5 pm, then George Martin took the group to his favourite Italian restaurant for dinner to get to know them a bit.
→ They recorded a number of takes of 'Love Me Do' and, much against their wishes, 'How Do You Do It', a song written by professional pop composer Mitch Murray, which George Martin intended as their first A-side. The group's lack of enthusiasm

Above: The Beatles with their new drummer Ringo onstage at the Cavern. Pete Best's sacking angered many loyal fans.

was evident from the lacklustre performance captured on tape.
→ Photographer Dezo Hoffmann documented the session for posterity, and traces of the black eye that George received on August 19 can be seen in his photographs.

5 September
→ The Cavern (evening).

6 September
→ The Cavern (lunchtime) and Rialto Ballroom, Liverpool.

7 September
→ Newton Dancing School, Village Hall, Irby, Heswall in the Wirral.

8 September
→ YMCA Birkenhead, and Majestic Ballroom, Birkenhead.

9 September
→ The Cavern (evening).

10 September
→ The Cavern (lunchtime) and Queen's Hall, Widnes, Cheshire.

11 September
→ Abbey Road. The group recorded 'Love Me Do', 'P.S. I Love You' and 'Please Please Me'. George Martin had

elected to use a session drummer named Andy White in place of Ringo, who was relegated to tambourine and maracas - a demotion which led him to fear that he would soon be following Pete Best out of The Beatles. The recording of 'Love Me Do' featuring Ringo on drums eventually appeared on their first single, while the White version was first released on The Beatles' debut LP, and later pressings of the single. The differences in the drumming are almost minimal.

12 September
→ The Cavern (evening).

13 September
→ The Cavern (lunchtime) and Riverpark Ballroom, Chester.

14 September
→ Tower Ballroom, New Brighton, Wallasey. 'Operation Big Beat V'.

15 September
→ The Victory Memorial Hall, Northwich, Cheshire.

16 September
→ The Cavern (evening).

17 September
→ The Cavern (lunchtime) and Queen's Hall, Widnes.

19 September
→ The Cavern (evening).

20 September
→ The Cavern (lunchtime).

21 September
→ Tower Ballroom, New Brighton, Wallasey.

22 September
→ Majestic Ballroom, Birkenhead.

23 September
→ The Cavern (evening).

25 September
→ Heswall Jazz Club, The Barnston Women's Institute, Heswall.

26 September
→ The Cavern (lunchtime and evening).

1962

28 September
→ The Cavern (lunchtime) and 'A Grand River Cruise' aboard the M.V. *Royal Iris*.

29 September
→ Oasis Club, Manchester.

30 September
→ The Cavern (evening).

1 October
→ The group signed a second management contract with Brian Epstein. It ran for five years and gave him 25 per cent of their gross earnings.

2 October
→ The Cavern (lunchtime).

3 October
→ The Cavern (evening).

4 October
→ The Cavern (lunchtime).

5 October
→ The Beatles' first single, 'Love Me Do'/'P.S. I Love You', was released in the UK as Parlophone 45R 4949. Brian Epstein is reputed to have bought 10,000 copies for his NEMS chain of record stores because he knew that was how many they would have to sell to make it into the Top 20. Sales across Liverpool were so heavy that the single immediately topped the 'official' Merseyside Top Twenty chart published in *Mersey Beat*.
→ Radio Luxembourg played the record for the first time this evening, to the thrilled disbelief of The Beatles.

6 October
→ Horticultural Society Dance, Hulme Hall, Port Sunlight, Birkenhead.

7 October
→ The Cavern (evening).

8 October
→ The Beatles recorded an interview session at EMI's headquarters in London for *The Friday Spectacular* show on Radio Luxembourg.

10 October
→ The Cavern (lunchtime and evening).

Above: The Beatles pose during a photo shoot around their native Liverpool. Opposite: The Beatles onstage during their final run at the Star Club, Hamburg.

11 October
→ Rialto Ballroom, Liverpool.

12 October
→ The Cavern (lunchtime) and Tower Ballroom, New Brighton, Wallasey with The Beatles second to Little Richard on a five and a half hour bill.

13 October
→ The Cavern (evening).

15 October
→ Majestic Ballroom, Birkenhead.

16 October
→ La Scala Ballroom, Runcorn, Cheshire.

17 October
→ The Cavern (lunchtime) and (evening). Between Cavern shows the group appeared on Granada Television's *People And Places* singing 'Some Other Guy' and 'Love Me Do', transmitted live from Manchester. This was their first television appearance to be broadcast.

19 October
→ The Cavern (lunchtime).

20 October
→ Majestic Ballroom, Hull.

21 October
→ The Cavern (evening).

22 October
→ Queen's Hall, Widnes.

25 October
→ The group recorded 'Love Me Do', 'A Taste Of Honey' and 'P.S. I Love You' for the Light Programme's *Here We Go* at the BBC studios in Manchester.

26 October
→ The Cavern (lunchtime) and Public Hall, Preston.
'Love Me Do' entered the *New Musical Express* charts at number 49.

27 October
→ Hulme Hall, Port Sunlight, Birkenhead.

28 October
→ Empire Theatre, Liverpool as support for Little Richard.

29 October
→ The Beatles made a second visit to Granada Television's Manchester studios to record for *People And Places*. They performed 'Love Me Do' and 'A Taste Of Honey'.

30 October
→ The Beatles flew to Hamburg for 14 nights at the Star Club sharing the bill with Little Richard. With her husband now likely to be absent for the rest of the year, Cynthia Lennon moved in with Aunt Mimi at Mendips, where she was quickly educated into the behaviour that her aunt-in-law expected from her.

1 – 14 November
→ Star Club, Grosse Freiheit, Hamburg, with Little Richard. The Beatles deeply resented having to fulfil this booking, at a time when it seemed as if their debut single might be about to become a sizeable hit in the UK.

17 November
→ Matrix Hall, Coventry.

18 November
→ The Cavern (evening). A 'Welcome Home' gig.

19 November
→ The Cavern (lunchtime), Smethwick Baths, Smethwick, Staffordshire and Adelphi Ballroom, West Bromwich. Three gigs in one day.

20 November
→ Floral Hall, Southport. Two sets.

21 November
→ The Cavern (lunchtime and evening).

22 November
→ The Cavern (lunchtime) and Majestic Ballroom, Birkenhead.

23 November
→ St James's Church Hall, Gloucester Terrace, London, and Tower Ballroom, New Brighton, Wallasey.

24 November
→ Royal Lido Ballroom, Prestatyn, Wales.

25 November
→ The Cavern (evening).

26 November
→ Abbey Road. The group recorded 'Tip Of My Tongue', 'Ask Me Why' and 'Please Please Me'. George Martin was pleased with the results and told the group that 'Please Please Me' would be a number one hit. The 'Tip Of My Tongue' recording didn't survive.

27 November
→ The group recorded 'Love Me Do', 'Twist And Shout' and 'P.S. I Love You' for the BBC Light Programme's *Talent Spot* at the BBC Paris Studio on Lower Regent Street, London.

28 November
→ The Cavern (evening) and The 527 Club, top floor of Lewis's Department Store, Liverpool - 'The Young Idea Dance' for the shop staff.

29 November
→ Majestic Ballroom, Birkenhead.

30 November
→ The Cavern (lunchtime) and Town Hall, Earlstown, Newton-le-Willows in Lancashire - 'The Big Beat Show'.

1 December
→ The Victory Memorial Hall, Northwich in Cheshire, and Tower Ballroom, New Brighton, Wallasey.

2 December
→ Embassy Cinema, Peterborough as support for Frank Ifield.

3 December
→ The group appeared on *Discs-a-Go-Go*, live from Bristol's TWW (Television Wales and West) studio.

4 December
→ The Beatles sang 'Love Me Do', 'P.S. I Love You' and 'Twist And Shout' live on *Tuesday Rendezvous*, a children's show presented by Gary Marshall, transmitted live from Associated-Rediffusion's Kingsway studio, London.

5 December
→ The Cavern (lunchtime and evening).

6 December
→ Club Django, Queen's Hotel, Southport.

7 December
→ The Cavern (lunchtime) and Tower Ballroom, New Brighton, Wallasey.

8 December
→ Oasis Club, Manchester.

9 December
→ The Cavern (evening). George Martin attended this performance to see if a live album could be recorded at The Cavern.

10 December
→ The Cavern (lunchtime).

11 December
→ La Scala Ballroom, Runcorn, Cheshire.

12 December
→ The Cavern (lunchtime and evening).

13 December
→ Corn Exchange, Bedford.

14 December
→ Music Hall, Shrewsbury.

15 December
→ Majestic Ballroom, Birkenhead, followed at midnight by the *Mersey Beat* Poll Winners Award Show. The Beatles were voted most popular group for the second year running and closed the show at 4 am.

16 December
→ The Cavern (evening).

17 December
→ The Beatles played live on Granada Television's *People And Places* show.

18 – 31 December
→ The Star Club, Grosse Freiheit, Hamburg. The Beatles' fifth and final residency in Germany, arranged before their chart success and growing concert revenues. As with the previous Hamburg booking they were reluctant to go, but had no option.

27 December
→ 'Love Me Do' got to number 17 in the *Record Retailer*'s Top 50 charts, its highest position.

Love Me Do

Words & Music by John Lennon
& Paul McCartney
© Copyright 1962 MPL Communications
Limited, 1 Soho Square, London W1
All Rights Reserved.
International Copyright Secured.

(Harmonica)

Love, love me do,____ you know I love you,____ I'll

al - ways be true,____ so plea - ea - ea - ease____ love me

do.____ Oo,____ love____ me do.____

Some - one to love, some - bod - y new,____ some - one to

1963

3 January
→ Two Red Shoes Ballroom, Elgin, Morayshire.
→ John flew from Liverpool to Scotland, arriving barely in time for the show.

4 January
→ Town Hall, Dingwall, Ross and Cromarty.

5 January
→ Museum Hall, Bridge of Allan, Stirlingshire. The group were billed for the night as 'The 'Love Me Do' Boys'.

6 January
→ Beach Ballroom, Aberdeen.

8 January
→ The group appeared live on Scottish TV's *Round-Up*, transmitted locally from the Theatre Royal, Glasgow,

10 January
→ Grafton Rooms, Liverpool, where they headed a bill of five acts.

11 January
→ The Cavern (lunchtime) and Plaza Ballroom, Old Hill, Staffordshire.
→ The single 'Please Please Me'/'Ask Me Why' was released in the UK as Parlophone 45-R 4983 to favourable reviews.
→ The Beatles appeared on ABC TV's *Thank Your Lucky Stars*, performing 'Please Please Me'.

12 January
→ Invicta Ballroom, Chatham, Kent.

13 January
→ Alpha TV Studios, Birmingham, where the group recorded an appearance on ABC TV's *Thank Your Lucky Stars*.

14 January
→ Wolverham Welfare Association Dance, Civic Hall, Wirral.

16 January
→ Granada TV Centre, for the *People And Places*, for which they mimed to 'Please Please Me' and 'Ask Me Why'.
→ Playhouse Theatre, Manchester to record their spot on *Here We Go*, for which they sang 'Chains', 'Please

Below: The Beatles onstage at the Cavern. Their last (and 292nd) appearance at this legendary venue, which helped to establish their reputation in Liverpool and beyond, occurred on 3 August. Opposite: George lovingly polishes his Gretsch guitar before a performance.

Please Me', 'Three Cool Cats' and 'Ask Me Why'.

17 January
→ The Cavern (lunchtime) and Majestic Ballroom, Birkenhead, where 500 disappointed fans had to be turned away.
→ 'Please Please Me' entered the charts.

18 January
→ Floral Ballroom, Morecombe, Lancashire.

19 January
→ Town Hall Ballroom, Whitchurch, Shropshire.

20 January
→ The Cavern (evening).

21 January
→ EMI House, London, to record EMI's plug show, *The Friday Spectacular,* for Radio Luxembourg'.

22 January
→ BBC Paris Studio, London, where they were interviewed live on the radio programme *Pop Inn* to promote their new single 'Please Please Me'.
→ Playhouse Theatre, London, to rehearse and record their first appearance on the BBC radio pop programme *Saturday Club*. The group recorded 'Some Other Guy', 'Love Me Do', 'Please Please Me', 'Keep Your Hands Off My Baby' and 'Beautiful Dreamer'.
→ BBC Paris Studio, London, to record a BBC Light Programme show *The Talent Spot*. They sang 'Please Please Me', 'Ask Me Why' and 'Some Other Guy' before a studio audience.

23 January
→ The Cavern (evening).

24 January
→ Assembly Hall, Mold, Wales.
→ Earlier, The Beatles signed copies of 'Please Please Me' at NEMS record

1963

shop in Liverpool and gave a short acoustic performance to assembled fans.

25 January
→ Co-operative Hall, Darwen - a local Baptist Church youth club event billed as 'The Greatest Teenage Dance'.

26 January
→ El Rio Club, Macclesfield, Cheshire, and King's Hall, Stoke-on-Trent, Staffordshire.
→ John and Paul began work on 'Misery', intended for Helen Shapiro, backstage at this gig. They completed the song en route to the following night's performance in Manchester but her management rejected it as 'too miserable'.

27 January
→ Three Coins Club, Manchester.

28 January
→ Majestic Ballroom, Newcastle upon Tyne.

30 January
→ The Cavern (evening).

31 January
→ The Cavern (lunchtime) and two shows (because of demand for tickets) at the Majestic Ballroom, Birkenhead.

1 February
→ Assembly Rooms, Tamworth, Staffordshire, and Maney Hall, Sutton Coldfield, Warwickshire.

2 February
→ Gaumont Cinema, Bradford.
→ A nationwide tour began with Helen Shapiro, where The Beatles were effectively bottom of the bill. The gig itinerary was 5 February: Gaumont Cinema, Doncaster; 6 February: Granada Cinema, Bedford; 7 February: Regal Cinema, Wakefield; 8 February: ABC Cinema, Carlisle, and 9 February: Empire Theatre, Sunderland.
→ The programme opened with The Red Price Band, followed by The Honeys, compere Dave Allen, The Beatles, and Danny Williams who closed the first half. The Red Price Band again opened the second set, followed by The Kestrels and Kenny

Lynch, and then Dave Allen introduced 16-year-old Helen Shapiro. The Beatles wore burgundy suits with velvet collars, designed by Paul, and their hair brushed forward 'French style'.
→ 'Please Please Me' entered the *Music Week* charts at number 16.

3 February
→ The Cavern (evening), an eight-hour 'Blues Marathon'

4 February
→ The Cavern (last lunchtime session).

11 February
→ Abbey Road. All 10 new tracks needed to make the *Please Please Me* album were recorded in one 10-hour session (the other four tracks were already out as sides A and B of their two singles). The tracks were chosen by George Martin from the Beatles' Cavern set in an attempt to re-create the atmosphere of the group's live performance. John was suffering from a severe head cold, and was in imminent danger of losing his voice – as a cursory listen to the rendition of 'Twist And Shout' that closed their debut album will reveal.

12 February
→ Azena Ballroom, Sheffield, and Astoria Ballroom, Oldham.

13 February
→ Majestic Ballroom, Hull.

14 February
→ Locarno Ballroom, Liverpool - a St Valentine's Day dance.

15 February
→ Ritz Ballroom, King's Heath, Birmingham.

16 February
→ Carfax Assembly Rooms, Oxford.

17 February
→ Teddington Studio Centre, Middlesex, to record an appearance on ABC TV's *Thank Your Lucky Stars*, where they sang 'Please Please Me'.

18 February
→ Queen's Hall, Widnes - two sets.

> **Paul:** "We'd been playing the songs for months and months and months before getting a record out. So we came into the studio at 10 in the morning, started it, did one number, had a cup of tea, relaxed, did the next one, a couple of overdubs... we just worked through them, like the stage act. And by about 10 o'clock that night, we'd done ten songs and we just reeled out of the studios, John clutching his throat tablets!"

19 February

→ Cavern Club (evening).

→ The queue began to form two days before the doors opened. Bob Wooler announced from the stage that The Beatles' 'Please Please Me' now occupied the number one position in the *NME* charts. It was also, supposedly, the last time that any of The Beatles saw Pete Best, though they took great pains to ensure that their paths crossed at no time during the evening. Afterwards The Beatles drove through the night to London.

20 February

→ St James St Swimming Baths, Doncaster.

→ Earlier, the group appeared live on the BBC Light Programme's *Parade Of The Pops*, presented by Denny Piercy, singing 'Love Me Do' and 'Please Please Me'. This was their first live BBC transmission.

21 February

→ Majestic Ballroom, Birkenhead.

22 February

→ Oasis Club, Manchester.

→ *New Musical Express*, the first pop paper to reach the news-stands, confirmed that 'Please Please Me' had now reached the No. 1 position in the British sales chart.

→ The music publishing company Northern Songs was set up by Dick James to control the rights to all compositions by John and Paul.

23 February

→ 'Please Please Me' reached No. 1 in the *Disc* singles chart.

→ Granada Cinema, Mansfield, Nottinghamshire started the second leg of the Helen Shapiro tour. This was followed by gigs on 24 February: Coventry Theatre, Coventry; 26 February: Gaumont Cinema, Taunton, Somerset; 27 February: Rialto Theatre, York; 28 February: Granada Cinema, Shrewsbury; 1 March: Odeon Cinema, Southport; 2 March: City Hall, Sheffield; 3 March: Gaumont Cinema, Hanley, Staffordshire.

→ By the end of the tour, The Beatles spot had been moved and they closed the first half of the show. In the coach on the way to Shrewsbury, John and

Above: Larking about on a British tour, as captured by the lens of NEMS Enterprises' employee Tony Bramwell. As the Beatles fame grew, their Liverpool-based organisation NEMS expanded, necessitating its relocation to London.

Paul wrote 'From Me To You', which became their third single, in preference to the original choice of 'Thank You Girl'.

25 February

→ Casino Ballroom, Leigh, Lancashire, for Brian Epstein's NEMS Enterprises 'Showdance'.

→ The single 'Please Please Me'/'Ask Me Why' was released in US as Vee Jay VJ 498, The Beatles' first American record under their own name, although some copies mispelt it as 'Beetles.'

2 March

→ Didsbury Studio Centre: After their second set at Sheffield, The Beatles drove to Manchester to be interviewed live with Brian Epstein by David Hamilton for ABC TV's evening talk

show, *ABC At Large*. A short clip of 'Please Please Me' was shown.

4 March

→ Plaza Ballroom, St Helens.

5 March

→ Abbey Road. The group recorded 'From Me To You', 'Thank You Girl' and 'The One After 909'. Before the session the group took part in an unused photographic session on the steps of the studio and at Manchester Square intended for the *Please Please Me* album cover.

6 March

→ Playhouse Theatre, Manchester. The Beatles recorded another session for the BBC Light Programme's *Here We Go*, singing 'Misery', 'Do You Want To Know A Secret?' and 'Please Please Me'.

7 March

→ Elizabethan Ballroom, Nottingham, with Gerry & The Pacemakers, The Big Three and Billy J. Kramer & The Dakotas. Everyone on the bill of this 'Big Beatle Show' was managed by Brian Epstein, who also promoted the event. This was the first of six 'Mersey Beat Showcase' events promoted by NEMS, where the artists accompanied by 80 paying fans were taken by coach to venues across the country.

8 March

→ Royal Hall, Harrogate.

9 March

→ Granada Cinema, East Ham, London.

→ The Beatles' second package tour, this time supporting visiting American stars Tommy Roe and Chris Montez. The group metaphorically wiped the stage with them at the early show on this first night and took over top billing for the day's second performance. Their set for the tour was 'Love Me Do', 'Misery', 'A Taste Of Honey', 'Do You Want To Know A Secret?', 'Please Please Me' and 'I Saw Her Standing There'.

→ The tour continued on 10 March: Hippodrome Theatre, Birmingham; 12 March: Granada Cinema, Bedford (George and Paul took over all the singing for the night, fronting a three-man Beatles as John was in bed with

a cold). 13 March: Rialto Theatre, York (without John); 14 March: Gaumont Cinema, Wolverhampton (without John); 15 March: Colston Hall, Bristol (with John back for both sets); 16 March: City Hall, Sheffield ; 17 March: Embassy Cinema, Peterborough; 18 March: Regal Cinema, Gloucester; 19 March: Cambridge; 20 March: ABC Cinema, Romford; 21 March: ABC Cinema, West Croydon; 22 March: Gaumont Cinema, Doncaster; 23 March: City Hall, Newcastle upon Tyne; 24 March: Empire Theatre, Liverpool; 26 March: Granada Cinema, Mansfield; 27 March: ABC Cinema, Northampton; 28 March: ABC Cinema, Exeter; 29 March: Odeon Cinema, Lewisham, London; 30 March: Guildhall, Portsmouth; 31 March: De Montfort Hall, Leicester.

11 March
→ The Beatles went to EMI House to record their last interview for *The Friday Spectacular* to be broadcast on Radio Luxembourg.
→ The Beatles also appeared on the BBC Light Programme's *Here We Go*.

13 March
→ Abbey Road. John was considered well enough to take part in an overdub session to put harmonica on to 'Thank You Girl'.

16 March
→ Broadcasting House, London. The Beatles performed live 'I Saw Her Standing There', 'Misery', 'Too Much Monkey Business', 'I'm Talking About You', 'Please Please Me' and 'The Hippy, Hippy Shake' on the BBC Light Programme's *Saturday Club*.

21 March
→ BBC Piccadilly Studios, London, recording 'Misery', 'Do You Want To Know A Secret?' and 'Please Please Me' for BBC Light Programme's *On The Scene*.

22 March
→ The album *Please Please Me* was released in the UK as Parlophone PMC 1202 (mono) and PCS 3042 (stereo). Side A: 'I Saw Her Standing There', 'Misery', 'Anna (Go To Him)', 'Chains', 'Boys', 'Ask Me Why', Please Please Me'; Side B: 'Love Me Do', 'P.S. I Love You', 'Baby It's You', 'Do You Want To Know A Secret?',

'A Taste Of Honey', 'There's A Place', 'Twist And Shout'.

25 March
→ The Beatles spent the day being photographed and filmed by Dezo Hoffmann. Among the photos which resulted from this session was the famous 'bombsite' shot which was later used on the cover of the *Twist And Shout* EP.

1 April
→ BBC Piccadilly Studios, London. The group recorded two programmes for the BBC Light Programme's *Side By Side*. For the first show, The Beatles sang 'Side By Side' with The Karl Denver Trio, followed by 'I Saw Her Standing There', 'Do You Want To Know A Secret?', 'Baby It's You', 'Please Please Me', 'From Me To You' and 'Misery'. For the second show they once more sang 'Side By Side' with The Karl Denver Trio followed by 'From Me To You', 'Long Tall Sally', 'A Taste Of Honey', 'Chains', 'Thank You Girl' and 'Boys'.

3 April
→ Playhouse Theatre, London, to record a session performing 'Please Please Me', 'Misery' and 'From Me To You' for BBC Radio's *Easy Beat*.

4 April
→ BBC Paris Studio, London, to record a third *Side By Side* broadcast. The Beatles performed 'Too Much Monkey Business', 'Love Me Do', 'Boys', 'I'll Be On My Way' and 'From Me To You'.
→ After the recording session The Beatles travelled north to play an afternoon session at Roxburgh Hall, Stowe School, where the all-male public schoolboy audience sat in neat rows and did not scream.

5 April
→ EMI House, London. During an award ceremony in which they were presented with their first silver disc for 250,000 sales of the single 'Please Please Me', the group gave a private performance for EMI executives.
→ Swimming Baths, Leyton, London.

6 April
→ Pavilion Gardens Ballroom, Buxton, Derbyshire.

Opposite and above: Recording a session for the BBC Light Programme. Between 1962 and 1965, The Beatles made 53 radio appearances for the Beeb which often featured material from the group's stage act which they never officially recorded.

7 April
→ Savoy Ballroom, Portsmouth.

8 April
→ John and Cynthia's son, John Charles Julian Lennon, was born at six am at Sefton General Hospital, Liverpool.

9 April
→ BBC Paris Studio, London, to do a live interview for the BBC Light Programme lunchtime show *Pop Inn*, during which The Beatles' forthcoming single 'From Me To You' was played.
→ Associated-Rediffusion's Wembley Studios for a live appearance on the children's programme *Tuesday Rendezvous*. They mimed 'From Me To You' and 'Please Please Me'.
→ The Ballroom, Gaumont State Cinema, Kilburn, London.

10 April
→ Majestic Ballroom, Birkenhead.
→ John finally saw Cynthia and Julian at Sefton General Hospital before the evening's show.

11 April
→ Co-operative Hall, Middleton, Lancashire.
→ The single, 'From Me To You'/'Thank

You Girl', was released in the UK as Parlophone R 5015.

12 April
→ Cavern Club, for a Good Friday, eight-hour 'R&B Marathon'.

13 April
→ Studio E, Lime Grove Studios, London, for rehearsals and the recording of BBC Television's *The 625 Show*. The Beatles performed: 'From Me To You', 'Thank You Girl' and were joined by the rest of the cast to close the show with 'Please Please Me'.

14 April
→ ABC Television's Teddington Studio Centre, Teddington. The Beatles mimed to 'From Me To You' for the following week's edition of *Thank Your Lucky Stars*.
→ That evening, The Beatles saw The Rolling Stones play at the Crawdaddy Club in the Station Hotel, Richmond. The Beatles appeared at the club identically dressed in long suede leather jackets acquired in Hamburg. It was an intentionally intimidating image, later described by Jagger as a 'four-headed monster'.

15 April
→ Riverside Dancing Club, Bridge Hotel, Tenbury Wells, Worcestershire.

16 April
→ Granada TV Centre, Manchester. The Beatles mimed to 'From Me To You' on *Scene At 6.30* which was broadcast live.

17 April
→ Majestic Ballroom, Luton.

18 April
→ Royal Albert Hall, London, with Del Shannon, The Springfields, Lance Percival, Rolf Harris, The Vernons Girls, Kenny Lynch, Shane Fenton & The Fentones, and George Melly.
→ A two-part concert - the second half of which was broadcast live by BBC radio as *Swinging Sound '63*. In the first half, The Beatles played 'Please Please Me' and 'Misery' and in the second 'Twist And Shout' and 'From Me To You'. The show closed with a fade-out with the entire cast performing Kurt Weill's 'Mack The Knife'.
→ It was at this concert that Paul met

Above and opposite: 1963 held a hectic schedule for The Beatles with recording sessions, TV and radio appearances, interviews and photo sessions slotted between almost nightly concert appearances. All this hard work paid off and by the end of the year, they were the biggest group in Great Britain.

Jane Asher, his girlfriend for much of the Sixties.

19 April
→ King's Hall, Stoke-on-Trent. The second of Brian Epstein's 'Mersey Beat Showcase' events.

20 April
→ Ballroom, Mersey View Pleasure Grounds, Frodsham, Cheshire.

21 April
→ Empire Pool, Wembley, for the *NME*'s '1962-63 Annual Poll-Winners' All Star Concert', starring Cliff Richard and The Shadows.
→ As the poll had been conducted in 1962, The Beatles hadn't actually won anything, but they were included because of their two recent number one singles. They played 'Please Please Me', 'From Me To You', 'Twist And Shout' and 'Long Tall Sally' to an audience of 10,000 people, and were regarded by media observers as having stolen the show from the headliners.
→ Pigalle Club, Piccadilly, London. \The Beatles travelled into London's West End after the *NME* concert for a performance at this more select venue.

23 April
→ Floral Hall, Southport.

24 April
→ Majestic Ballroom, Finsbury Park, London.
→ Another of Brian Epstein's 'Mersey Beat Showcase' promotions.

25 April
→ Ballroom, Fairfield Hall, Croydon.
→ A 'Mersey Beat Showcase'.

26 April
→ Music Hall, Shrewsbury.

27 April
→ The (Victory) Memorial Hall, Northwich, Cheshire.

28 April
→ George, Paul and Ringo flew to Santa Cruz, Tenerife for a 12-day holiday.
→ At Brian's expense, John and Brian Epstein flew to Torremolinos, Spain, for a vacation together, leaving Cynthia and her new born baby in Liverpool. The decision alarms and hurts Cynthia, while the news that Lennon and his overtly gay manager had holidayed together prompts much amusement and gossip among the Merseybeat community.

11 May
→ Imperial Ballroom, Nelson. A record 2,000 attendance.

12 May
→ Alpha TV Studios, Birmingham, for another recorded *Thank Your Lucky Stars* appearance. The Beatles mimed 'From Me To You' and 'I Saw Her Standing There'.

14 May
→ Rink Ballroom, Sunderland.

15 May
→ Royal Theatre, Chester.

16 May
→ Television Theatre, London, for The Beatles' second appearance on national BBC TV. They shared the bill with a glove puppet, Lenny the Lion, The Raindrops and Patsy Ann Noble on children's programme *Pops And Lenny* which went out live before an invited audience. With the puppet, The Beatles performed 'From Me To

1963

You', a short version of 'Please Please Me' and then joined Lenny The Lion and the rest of the cast for a version of 'After You've Gone'.

17 May
→ Grosvenor Rooms, Norwich.

18 May
→ Adelphi Cinema, Slough, on tour with Gerry & The Pacemakers, Tony Marsh, Erkey Grant, Ian Crawford, The Terry Young Six, Daiv Macbeth, Louise Cordet and, heading the bill, Roy Orbison.
→ The Beatles' set for this tour was 'Some Other Guy', 'Do You Want To Know A Secret?', 'Love Me Do', 'From Me To You', 'Please Please Me', 'I Saw Her Standing There' and 'Twist And Shout'.
→ The Roy Orbison tour itinerary included: 19 May: Gaumont Cinema, Hanley, Staffordshire; 20 May: Gaumont Cinema, Southampton; 22 May: Gaumont Cinema, Ipswich; 23 May: Odeon Cinema, Nottingham; 24 May: Granada Cinema, Walthamstow, London. The Beatles were now officially billed as the headliners for the tour, Roy Orbison having graciously bowed to public opinion.
→ 25 May: City Hall, Sheffield; 26 May: Empire Theatre, Liverpool; 27 May: Capitol Cinema, Cardiff; 28 May: Gaumont Cinema, Worcester; 29 May: Rialto Theatre, York; 30 May: Odeon Cinema, Manchester; 31 May: Odeon Cinema, Southend-on-Sea; 1 June: Granada Cinema, Tooting, London; 2 June: Hippodrome Theatre, Brighton; 3 June: Granada Cinema, Woolwich, London; 4 June: Town Hall, Birmingham; 5 June: Odeon Cinema, Leeds; 7 June: Odeon Cinema, Glasgow; 8 June: City Hall, Newcastle-upon-Tyne; 9 June: King George's Hall, Blackburn.

21 May
→ Playhouse Theatre, London, to record the BBC Light Programme's *Saturday Club*. They were interviewed by presenter Brian Matthew and performed 'I Saw Her Standing There', 'Do You Want To Know A Secret?', 'Boys', 'Long Tall Sally', 'From Me To You' and 'Money (That's What I Want)'.
→ They also recorded a session for a new radio programme *Steppin' Out*, for

which they did 'Please Please Me', 'I Saw Her Standing There', 'Roll Over Beethoven', 'Thank You Girl' and 'From Me To You' before a live audience.

24 May
→ Studio Two, Aeolian Hall, London, to record the first programme in The Beatles' own BBC Light Programme series: *Pop Go The Beatles*. The programme began and closed with a rocked-up version of 'Pop Goes The Weasel' recorded by The Beatles with the aid of their guests for this programme, The Lorne Gibson Trio. The Beatles performed 'From Me To You', 'Everybody's Trying To Be My Baby', 'Do You Want To Know A Secret?', 'You Really Got A Hold On Me', 'Misery' and 'The Hippy Hippy Shake'.

27 May
→ 'From Me To You'/ 'Thank You Girl' was released in US as Vee Jay VJ 522, where it competed with Del Shannon's recently issued cover version of the A-side.

1 June
→ BBC Paris Studio, London. The Beatles recorded the second and third *Pop Go The Beatles*. On the second programme they sang 'Too Much Monkey Business', 'I Got To Find My Baby', 'Youngblood', 'Baby It's You', 'Till There Was You' and 'Love Me Do'. Their guests were The Countrymen. For the third programme they performed 'A Shot Of Rhythm And Blues', 'Memphis, Tennessee', 'A Taste Of Honey' and 'Sure To Fall (In Love With You)' with Carter-Lewis & The Southerners as their guests.

10 June
→ The Pavilion, Bath.

12 June
→ Grafton Rooms, Liverpool. Free charity benefit for the NSPCC.

13 June
→ Palace Theatre Club, Stockport, and Southern Sporting Club, Manchester.

14 June
→ Tower Ballroom, Wallasey. Another of Brian Epstein's 'Mersey Beat Showcase' promotions.

Above and opposite: The Beatles pictured backstage in yet another dressing room – their only sanctuary from hordes of screaming fans.

15 June
→ City Hall, Salisbury.

16 June
→ Odeon Cinema, Romford. The last of the 'Mersey Beat Showcase' concerts.

17 June
→ BBC Maida Vale Studios, London, to record the fourth of the *Pop Go The Beatles* programmes. The Beatles performed 'I Saw Her Standing There', 'Anna (Go To Him)', 'Boys', 'Chains', 'P.S. I Love You' and 'Twist And Shout'.
→ Dezo Hoffmann photographed the session and did a separate photo shoot outside the studio on Delaware Road where John, George and Ringo gave Paul 'the bumps' ahead of his 21st birthday.

18 June
→ Paul's 21st birthday party was held in a marquee in the back garden of his Aunt Jin's house at 147 Dinas Lane, Huyton. The Beatles' old friend Bob Wooler teased John about his recent trip to Spain with Brian Epstein but

1963

Lennon was drunk and in a belligerent mood. He leapt on Wooler and beat him up.

John said, "He called me a queer so I battered his bloody ribs in."

Next John attacked a woman who was standing nearby. Two days later, on orders from Brian Epstein, John sent Wooler a telegram reading:

19 June
→ Playhouse Theatre, London to record The Beatles' second appearance on BBC Radio's *Easy Beat* before a live, screaming audience. The group performed 'Some Other Guy', 'A Taste Of Honey', 'Thank You Girl' and 'From Me To You'.

20 June
→ The Beatles Limited was formed, as a corporate device to handle the group's legal and business affairs.

"Really sorry Bob. Terribly worried to realise what I had done. What more can I say?"

21 June
→ Odeon Cinema, Guildford.

22 June
→ Television Theatre, London: John taped a BBC TV *Juke Box Jury*, hosted by David Jacobs, with fellow jurors Katie Boyle, Bruce Prochnik and Caroline Maudling. Unbowed by his villainous role in the previous day's press (over the Bob Wooler incident at Paul's 21st), John outspokenly voted every one of the records presented as a 'miss'.
→ Afterwards he was driven to the Battersea Heliport where he flew by specially chartered helicopter to join the others in Wales.
→ Ballroom, Town Hall, Abergavenny.

23 June
→ Alpha TV Studios, Birmingham, to tape a session for *Summer Spin* – the summer name for *Thank Your Lucky Stars*. The whole show was a celebration of the Mersey scene. The Beatles mimed 'From Me To You' and 'I Saw Her Standing There'.

24 June
→ Playhouse Theatre, London, recording another session for BBC Radio's *Saturday Club*. The Beatles sang 'I Got To Find My Baby', 'Memphis, Tennessee', 'Money (That's What I Want)', 'Till There Was You', 'From Me To You' and 'Roll Over Beethoven'.

25 June
→ Astoria Ballroom, Middlesbrough.

26 June
→ Majestic Ballroom, Newcastle-upon-Tyne.
→ Before this show Paul and John began to write their next single, 'She Loves You', in their room at Turk's Hotel.

28 June
→ Queen's Hall, Leeds, with Acker Bilk and his Paramount Jazz Band to an audience of 3,200.

30 June
→ ABC Cinema, Great Yarmouth.
→ The first of a 10-week series of seaside concerts. The Beatles played 'Some Other Guy', 'Thank You Girl', 'Do You Want To Know A Secret?', 'Misery', 'A Taste Of Honey', 'I Saw Her Standing There', 'Love Me Do', 'From Me To You', 'Baby It's You', 'Please Please Me' and 'Twist And Shout'.

1 July
→ Abbey Road. The Beatles recorded their next single, 'She Loves You'/'I'll Get You' and posed for another official EMI photographic session.

2 July
→ Maida Vale Studios, London, to record the first of 11 new *Pop Go The Beatles* programmes, this time presented by Rodney Burke. The Beatles performed 'That's All Right (Mama)', 'Carol', 'Soldier Of Love (Lay Down Your Arms)', 'Lend Me Your Comb', 'Clarabella' and 'There's A Place'.

3 July
→ Playhouse Theatre to record a

session for BBC Light Programme's *The Beat Show*. The Beatles performed 'From Me To You', 'A Taste Of Honey' and 'Twist And Shout'.

5 July
→ Plaza Ballroom, Old Hill, Dudley.

6 July
→ Northwich Carnival, Verdin Park. That afternoon, Paul crowned the Carnival Queen.
→ The Victory Memorial Hall, Northwich.

7 July
→ ABC Theatre, Blackpool.

8 – 13 July
→ Winter Gardens, Margate. Six-day residency.
→ The Beatles' set: 'Roll Over Beethoven', 'Thank You Girl', 'Chains', 'Please Please Me', 'A Taste Of Honey', 'I Saw Her Standing There', 'Baby It's You', 'From Me To You' and 'Twist And Shout'.

10 July
→ Aeolian Hall, London, to record two more *Pop Go The Beatles* shows. For the sixth programme they performed 'Sweet Little Sixteen', 'A Taste Of Honey', 'Nothin' Shakin (But The Leaves On The Trees)', 'Love Me Do', 'Lonesome Tears In My Eyes' and 'So How Come (Nobody Loves Me)'
→ For the seventh programme they recorded 'Memphis, Tennessee', 'Do You Want To Know A Secret?', 'Till There Was You', 'Matchbox', 'Please Mister Postman' and 'The Hippy Hippy Shake' After the recording session they drove back to Margate in time for the first house.
→ Winter Gardens, Margate.

12 July
→ The EP *Twist And Shout* was released in the UK as Parlophone GEP 8882 (mono only): Side A: 'Twist And Shout', 'A Taste Of Honey'; Side B: ' Do You Want To Know A Secret?', 'There's A Place'.
→ As a spoiler for this release, Polydor chose the same day to issue *My Bonnie*, a four-track EP taken from The Beatles' Hamburg sessions with Tony Sheridan. The EP was released as Polydor H 21-610 (mono only): Side A:

'My Bonnie', 'Why'. Side B: 'Cry For A Shadow', 'The Saints'.

14 July
→ ABC Theatre, Blackpool.

16 July
→ BBC Paris Studio, London. Programmes eight, nine and 10 of *Pop Go The Beatles* were recorded and stockpiled in one long session. For programme eight they recorded 'I'm Gonna Sit Right Down And Cry (Over You)', 'Crying, Waiting, Hoping', 'Kansas City'/'Hey-Hey-Hey-Hey!', 'To Know Her Is To Love Her', 'The Honeymoon Song' and 'Twist And Shout'.
→ The ninth programme featured 'Long Tall Sally', 'Please Please Me', 'She Loves You', 'You Really Got A Hold On Me', 'I'll Get You' and 'I Got A Woman'.
→ Programme 10 featured 'She Loves You', 'Words Of Love', 'Glad All Over', 'I Just Don't Understand', '(There's A)

Devil In Her Heart' and 'Slow Down'.

17 July
→ Playhouse Theatre, London, to record the BBC Light Programme's *Easy Beat*. The Beatles performed four numbers before the usual live teenage audience: 'I Saw Her Standing There', 'A Shot Of Rhythm And Blues', 'There's A Place' and 'Twist And Shout'.

18 July
→ Abbey Road. The Beatles worked on material for their second album: 'You Really Got A Hold On Me', 'Money (That's What I Want)', '(There's A) Devil In Her Heart' and 'Till There Was You'.

19-20 July
→ Ritz Ballroom, Rhyl.

21 July
→ Queen's Theatre, Blackpool.
→ 4,000 fans blocked the streets of Blackpool before the concert, an early

intimation of Beatlemania to come.

22-27 July
→ Six-night engagement at the Odeon Cinema, Weston-super-Mare.
→ Dezo Hoffmann spent the day with the group on the beach at Bream Down, where he got them to pose in Victorian swimming costumes and ride donkeys.

26 July
→ The album *Introducing The Beatles* was released in the US as Vee Jay VJLP 1062 (mono) and SR 1062 (stereo). Side A: 'I Saw Her Standing There', 'Misery', 'Anna (Go To Him)', 'Chains', 'Boys', 'Love Me Do'; Side B: 'P.S. I Love You', 'Baby It's You', 'Do You Want To Know A Secret?', 'A Taste Of Honey', 'There's A Place', 'Twist And Shout'.

28 July
→ ABC Cinema, Great Yarmouth.

30 July

→ Abbey Road. The Beatles recorded 'Please Mister Postman' and 'It Won't Be Long' in a morning session.

→ Playhouse Theatre, London, for two BBC Light Programme recordings: an interview with Phil Tate for the 'Pop Chat' spot on *Non Stop Pop*, and a session for *Saturday Club* where they played 'Long Tall Sally', 'She Loves You', 'Glad All Over', 'Twist And Shout', 'You Really Got A Hold On Me' and 'I'll Get You'.

→ Back at Abbey Road for an evening session, The Beatles worked on 'Till There Was You', 'Roll Over Beethoven', 'It Won't Be Long' and 'All My Loving'.

31 July

→ Imperial Ballroom, Nelson.

1 August

→ Playhouse Theatre, Manchester, to record two more sessions for the BBC Light Programme's *Pop Go The Beatles*. For the 11th show in the series, they recorded 'Ooh! My Soul', 'Don't Ever Change', 'Twist And Shout', 'She Loves You', 'Anna (Go To Him)' and 'A Shot Of Rhythm & Blues'.

→ The 12th show featured Brian Poole & The Tremeloes as guests and The Beatles playing 'From Me To You', 'I'll Get You', 'Money (That's What I Want)', 'There's A Place', 'Honey Don't' and 'Roll Over Beethoven'.

→ The first issue of *The Beatles Book* was published by Beat Publications Ltd.

2 August

→ Grafton Rooms, Liverpool.

3 August

→ Cavern Club.

→ The Beatles' last performance at the club – documented by the Cavern management as their 292nd appearance.

4 August

→ Queen's Theatre, Blackpool.

→ The Beatles had to enter the theatre through a trap door on the roof, reached through scaffolding in the next door builder's yard, because the normal entrances were totally blocked by fans.

5 August

→ Urmston Show.

Above: The Beatles receive an award for Best Vocal Group of the Year at the Variety Club luncheon, 10 September. Opposite: The Beatles appearance on ITV's *Sunday Night At The London Palladium* marked the official beginning of Beatlemania in Britain.

→ An annual bank holiday show held in a giant marquee. The Beatles topped a four-act bill.

6-7 August

→ Springfield Ballroom, St Saviour, Jersey.

8 August

→ Auditorium, Candie Gardens, Guernsey.

9-10 August

→ Springfield Ballroom, St Saviour, Jersey.

11 August

→ ABC Theatre, Blackpool.

→ Roadie Mal Evans met the group when they arrived at Manchester Airport after their week in the Channel Islands. It was his first day as a full-time employee of the group.

12-17 August

→ Odeon Cinema, Llandudno.

→ The first night of a six-night season at the seaside, with two houses each night.

14 August

→ In the morning the Beatles drove to Granada TV Centre, Manchester, to record two songs; 'Twist And Shout' and 'She Loves You' for *Scene At 6:30*.

18 August

→ Alpha TV Studios, Birmingham, to pre-record an appearance for the following week's ABC TV's *Lucky Stars (Summer Spin)*. They mimed 'She Loves You' and 'I'll Get You', the 'A' and B-sides to their next single

→ Princess Theatre, Devon.

19-24 August

→ Gaumont Cinema, Bournemouth, with Billy J. Kramer & The Dakotas and Tommy Quickly. Another summer seaside residency.

22 August

→ While in Bournemouth, The Beatles stayed at the Palace Court Hotel where, probably on this day, Robert Freeman shot the famous monochrome photograph for the *With The Beatles* album, which was based on Astrid Kirchherr's Hamburg photos.

→ After lunch, The Beatles drove to the Southern ITV Centre, Southampton, where they recorded an appearance on the *Day By Day* programme, miming 'She Loves You', which was broadcast that evening.

23 August

→ The single, 'She Loves You'/'I'll Get You' was released in the UK as Parlophone R 5055. Demand for the new single was so great that EMI pressed over a quarter of a million copies in the four weeks before its official release.

25 August

→ ABC Theatre, Blackpool.

26-31 August

→ Odeon Cinema, Southport.

→ Another seaside residency. The Beatles set consisted of 'Roll Over Beethoven', 'Thank You Girl', 'Chains', 'A Taste Of Honey', 'She Loves You', 'Baby It's You', 'From Me To You', 'Boys', 'I Saw Her Standing There' and 'Twist And Shout'.

27 August

→ The Beatles were filmed playing 'Twist And Shout' and 'She Loves You' on stage, but with no audience, at The Little Theatre in Southport as part of an upcoming BBC TV special entitled *The Mersey Sound*.

28 August

The Beatles were interviewed at the BBC's Manchester studios.

1 September

→ ABC TV's Didsbury Studio Centre, Manchester. The group recorded an appearance on the variety show *Big Night Out* presented by comedians Mike and Bernie Winters. They mimed 'From Me To You', 'She Loves You', 'Twist And Shout' and 'I Saw Her Standing There' before a studio audience of 600.

3 September

→ Aeolian Hall, London, to record the last three programmes in the *Pop Go The Beatles* series. For the 13th edition The Beatles recorded 'Too Much Monkey Business', 'Love Me Do', 'She Loves You', 'Till There Was You', 'I'll Get You' and 'The Hippy Hippy Shake'. Their guests were Johnny Kidd & The Pirates.

→ For the 14th they played 'Chains', 'You Really Got A Hold On Me', 'Misery', 'A Taste Of Honey' (which was later edited into the preceding programme), 'Lucille' and 'From Me To You'. For the 15th and final session they played 'She Loves You', 'Ask Me Why' '(There's A) Devil In Her Heart', 'I Saw Her Standing There', 'Sure To Fall (In Love With You)' and 'Twist And Shout'.

4 September

→ Gaumont Cinema, Worcester.

5 September

→ Gaumont Cinema, Taunton.

6 September

→ Odeon Cinema, Luton.

→ The EP *The Beatles' Hits* was released in the UK as Parlophone GEP 8880 (mono only). Side A: 'From Me To You', 'Thank You Girl'; Side B: 'Please Please Me', 'Love Me Do'.

7 September

→ Playhouse Theatre, London, to record a session for the BBC Light Programme's fifth birthday edition of *Saturday Club*. The Beatles performed 'I Saw Her Standing There', 'Memphis, Tennessee', 'Happy Birthday Saturday Club', which was

John and Paul write for the Stones: 10 September

After the Variety Club lunch, John and Paul were taking a taxi along Jermyn Street when they encountered Andrew 'Loog' Oldham, who had previously worked in promoting The Beatles for Brian Epstein and was now manager of the Rolling Stones. Oldham said he was looking for the right song for the Stones to record as their second single release after 'Come On'. John and Paul immediately suggested that he might like to hear one that they were working on called 'I Wanna Be Your Man'. They returned with Andrew to meet the Stones, who were rehearsing at Ken Colyer's Studio 51 in Great Newport Street, Soho. Lennon and McCartney

asked to borrow a couple of guitars from Brian Jones and Keith Richards and launched into the number. There was only one problem: the song didn't have a middle eight.

After a quick conference John and Paul told them that if they really liked the song, they would finish it off for them. They disappeared into a side room and reappeared a few minutes later. 'Forget something?' asked Bill Wyman. 'No,' said Paul. 'We've just finished the middle eight. How does this sound?'

The Stones released the song on 1 November and it became the group's first Top 20 hit. Ringo sang it on The Beatles' second LP.

written especially for the occasion by John, 'I'll Get You', 'She Loves You', and 'Lucille'.

→ After the recording, Paul did an interview with Rosemary Hart for the BBC Home Service series *A World Of Sound*.

→ Fairfield Hall, Croydon.

→ 'She Loves You' reached number one in the charts where it stayed for seven weeks.

8 September

→ ABC Theatre, Blackpool.

10 September

→ The Beatles attended a Variety Club of Great Britain luncheon at the Savoy Hotel where they received the award for 'Top Vocal Group of the Year'.

11 September

→ Abbey Road, to continue work on the *With The Beatles* album. The Beatles

Below: The Beatles win over royalty on 4 November. Opposite: The Beatles dressed in boaters and blazers to perform 'Moonlight Bay' on *The Morecambe And Wise Show*, 2 December.

worked on 'I Wanna Be Your Man', 'Little Child', 'All I've Got To Do' and 'Not A Second Time'. Finally, they made a number of takes of George's 'Don't Bother Me'.

12 September
→ Abbey Road. They continued work on 'Hold Me Tight', 'Don't Bother Me', 'Little Child' and 'I Wanna Be Your Man'.

13 September
→ Public Hall, Preston. After the show Paul drove to Nelson to take his place on the panel of judges at the 'Miss Imperial 1963' contest at the Imperial Ballroom, Nelson, Lancashire.

14 September
→ The Victory Memorial Hall, Northwich.

15 September
→ Royal Albert Hall, London.
→ The annual 'Great Pop Prom' promoted by *Valentine, Marilyn* and *Roxy* magazines. The Beatles appeared with 11 other acts.
→ The single, 'She Loves You'/ 'I'll Get You' was released in the US as Swan 4152.

16 September
→ John and Cynthia flew to Paris on holiday. George and his brother Peter visited their sister Louise in Benton,

Illinois, USA – George thereby becoming the first of the Beatles to travel to America. Paul, Jane, Ringo and Maureen went to Greece.

3 October
→ Abbey Road. Ringo overdubbed his vocal on 'I Wanna Be Your Man' and John and Paul put theirs on 'Little Child'.

4 October
→ Associated-Rediffusion's studios at Television House, London, to record their first appearance on *Ready, Steady, Go!* They mimed 'Twist And Shout', 'I'll Get You' and 'She Loves You' live and were interviewed by Keith Fordyce and Dusty Springfield.

5 October
→ Town Hall, Glasgow.

6 October
→ Carlton Theatre, Kirkaldy.

7 October
→ Caird Hall, Dundee.

9 October
→ BBC Paris Studio, London, to record 'She Loves You' for the BBC Light Programme comedy show, *The Ken Dodd Show*.

11 October
→ Ballroom, Trentham.

13 October
→ The Beatles topped the bill on ATV's *Val Parnell's Sunday Night At The London Palladium*, transmitted live from the Palladium theatre to an audience of 15 million viewers. They played 'From Me To You', 'I'll Get You', 'She Loves You' and 'Twist And Shout', and joined the other acts, to wave goodbye to the audience and viewers from the revolving stage which traditionally ended the show.

16 October
→ Playhouse Theatre, London, to record a final session for the BBC Light Programme's *Easy Beat*. They played 'I Saw Her Standing There', 'Love Me Do', 'Please Please Me', 'From Me To You' and 'She Loves You'.
→ The Beatles were also interviewed about their forthcoming Royal Variety Show appearance by Peter Woods for the BBC Light Programme's *Radio Newsreel*.

17 October
→ Abbey Road. The Beatles recorded both sides of their next single – 'I Want To Hold Your Hand' and 'This Boy'. They also worked on 'You Really Got A Hold On Me', and made 'The Beatles' Christmas Record' for their fan club members.
→ Fans blocked Bond Street when Paul arrived to take a girl out to lunch who had won a 'Why I Like The Beatles' magazine competition.

18 October
→ Granada Television Centre, Manchester, to mime 'She Loves You' for that evening's edition of *Scene At 6.30*.

19 October
→ Pavilion Gardens Ballroom, Buxton. The performance was preceded by another frenetic struggle between fans and police.

20 October
→ Alpha TV Studios, Birmingham, to record a headline appearance on ABC TV's *Thank Your Lucky Stars*. They mimed 'All My Loving', 'Money (That's What I Want)' and 'She Loves You' while 3,000 fans blocked the street outside and attempted to storm the studios.

23 October
→ Abbey Road. The Beatles completed work on 'I Wanna Be Your Man'.
→ That afternoon The Beatles flew BEA to Arlanda Airport, Stockholm, arriving to a scene of screaming fans and uncharacteristic Swedish chaos.

24 October
→ Karlaplansstudion, Stockholm, to record an interview and a live set for Klas Burling's Sveriges Radio show, *Pop '63*, which for this edition was renamed *The Beatles pupgrupp från Liverpool på besök i Stockholm* (The Beatles pop group from Liverpool visiting Stockholm). The group played a lively seven numbers: 'I Saw Her Standing There', 'From Me To You', 'Money (That's What I Want)', 'Roll Over Beethoven', 'You Really Got A Hold On Me', 'She Loves You' and 'Twist And Shout'.

25 October
→ Nya Aulan, Karlstad. The Beatles played two performances of their standard set for the tour: 'Long Tall Sally', 'Please Please Me', 'I Saw Her Standing There', 'From Me To You', 'A Taste Of Honey', 'Chains', 'Boys', 'She Loves You' and 'Twist And Shout'. As in England, their performance was almost entirely drowned by screams.

26 October
→ Kungliga Tennishallen, Stockholm, where The Beatles were second billed to Joey Dee & The Starlighters for the two shows. The audience clearly thought otherwise.

27 October
→ Cirkus, Gothenburg. The Beatles played an afternoon show as well as two houses in the evening.

29 October
→ Sporthallen, Eskilstuna.

30 October
→ Narren-teatern, Stockholm, to record an appearance on the Sveriges Television show *Drop In* before a live audience. They performed 'She Loves You', 'Twist And Shout', 'I Saw Her Standing There' and 'Long Tall Sally'.

31 October

→ The Beatles flew SAS back to London where hundreds of screaming teenage girls had gathered on the roof of the Queen's Building at Heathrow Airport to welcome them back to Britain. The scenes were broadcast on national TV news, heightening the media frenzy about 'Beatlemania'. By coincidence, Ed Sullivan happened to be passing through London airport at that time and witnessed the scene. Impressed, it led him to book The Beatles for his show when they were still virtually unknown in the USA.

1 November

→ Odeon Cinema, Cheltenham.

→ The first night of The Beatles' autumn tour, their first series of concerts as unchallenged headliners, with support from The Rhythm & Blues Quartet, The Vernons Girls, The Brook Brothers, Peter Jay & The Jaywalkers, and The Kestrels. The compere was Frank Berry.

→ The Beatles' standard set for the tour was 'I Saw Her Standing There', 'From Me To You', 'All My Loving', 'You Really Got A Hold On Me', 'Roll Over Beethoven', 'Boys', 'Till There Was You', 'She Loves You', 'Money (That's What I Want)' and 'Twist And Shout'.

→ The tour continued as follows: 2 November: City Hall, Sheffield; 3 November: Odeon Cinema, Leeds; 5 November: Adelphi Cinema, Slough; 6 November: ABC Cinema, Northampton; 7 November: Adelphi Cinema, Dublin, the Beatles' only appearance in Eire. They were accompanied by playwright Alun Owen, who remained with them for three days, making notes for their projected first film.

→ 9 November: Granada Cinema, East Ham, London; 10 November: Hippodrome Theatre, Birmingham. The Beatles had to don police uniforms to make their way into the theatre; 13 November: ABC Cinema, Plymouth; 14 November: ABC Cinema, Exeter; 15 November: Colston Hall, Bristol; 16 November: Winter Gardens, Bournemouth. The three rival American television networks – NBC, CBS and ABC – were permitted to film the hysterical audience and part of the show.

→ 17 November: Coventry Theatre, Coventry; 19 November: Gaumont Cinema, Wolverhampton; 20 November: ABC Cinema, Manchester; Backstage were news crews from Pathé News, Granada TV and BBC Radio. 21 November: ABC Cinema, Carlisle; 22 November: Globe Cinema, Stockton-on-Tees; 23 November: City Hall, Newcastle-upon-Tyne; 24 November: ABC Cinema, Hull; 26 November: Regal Cinema, Cambridge; 27 November: Rialto Theatre, York; 28 November: ABC Cinema, Lincoln; 29 November: ABC Cinema, Huddersfield; 30 November: Empire Theatre, Sunderland; 1 December: De Montfort Hall, Leicester; 3 December: Guildhall, Portsmouth; 7 December: Empire Theatre, Liverpool; 8 December: Odeon Cinema, Lewisham, London; 9 December: Odeon Cinema, Southend-on-Sea; 10 December: Gaumont Cinema, Doncaster; 11 December: Futurist Theatre, Scarborough; 12 December: Odeon Cinema, Nottingham; 13 December: Gaumont Cinema, Southampton.

→ The EP *The Beatles (No.1)* was released in the UK as Parlophone GEP 8883 (mono only). Side A: 'I Saw Her Standing There', 'Misery'; Side B: 'Anna (Go To Him)', 'Chains'.

→ The single 'I Wanna Be Your Man' by The Rolling Stones, written by Lennon & McCartney, was released in the UK as Decca F 11764.

4 November

→ Prince Of Wales Theatre, London, for the Royal Command Performance, in the presence of their Majesties the Queen Mother and Princess Margaret, accompanied by Lord Snowdon. The Beatles performed 'From Me To You', 'She Loves You' and 'Till There Was You' Introducing their last number, 'Twist And Shout', John asked the audience:

5 November

→ EMI claimed that 500,000 advance orders had been received for The Beatles' forthcoming single, 'I Want To Hold Your Hand', in a single day.

8 November

→ The Beatles filmed an interview with Jimmy Robinson of Ulster TV near the Irish border which was

> ## "Would the people in the cheaper seats, clap your hands. And the rest of you, if you'd just rattle your jewellery."

included in that evening's edition of *Ulster News*.

13 November

→ Westward TV Studios, Plymouth. The Beatles were interviewed for *Move Over, Dad*, a local teenagers' programme.

18 November

→ EMI House, London, to receive silver discs for *Please Please Me* and the not yet released *With The Beatles* album from EMI Chairman Sir Joseph Lockwood. They also received silver EPs (250,000 sales) for *Twist And Shout* from George Martin.

22 November

→ *With The Beatles* was released in the UK as Parlophone PMC 1206 (mono) and PCS 3045 (stereo). Side A: 'It Won't Be Long', 'All I've Got To Do', 'All My Loving', 'Don't Bother Me', 'Little Child', 'Till There Was You', 'Please Mister Postman'; Side B: 'Roll Over Beethoven', 'You Really Got A Hold On Me', 'I Wanna Be Your Man', '(There's A) Devil In Her Heart', 'Not A

Second Time', 'Money (That's What I Want)'.

25 November
→ Granada TV Centre, Manchester. The Beatles mimed 'I Want To Hold Your Hand' and 'This Boy' and were later interviewed for Granada's *Scene* and *Late Scene Extra* programmes.

26 November
→ Regal Cinema, Cambridge. The Beatles were interviewed in their dressing room for the local BBC TV show *East At Six Ten*.

29 November
→ The single 'I Want To Hold Your Hand'/ 'This Boy' was released in the UK as Parlophone R 5084. Advance sales passed the million mark before it was released, the first time this had ever happened in Britain.

2 December
→ Elstree Studio Centre, Borehamwood, to record an appearance on ATV's *The Morecambe And Wise Show*. The group sang 'This Boy', 'All My Loving' and 'I Want To Hold Your Hand' live before a small studio audience and did a comedy sketch with Eric and Ernie.
→ The Ballroom, Grosvenor House Hotel, Park Lane, in aid of a charity for spastics. The group was part of a cabaret-style floor show and the audience wore evening dress – which didn't prevent them rushing the stage as The Beatles' performance ended.

7 December
→ The Beatles comprised the entire panel for a special edition of BBC-TV's *Juke Box Jury* before an audience of 2,500 members of The Beatles' Northern Area Fan Club.
→ Next, the Fan Club audience saw a special concert, shown later the same day as *It's The Beatles!* For this they played 'From Me To You', 'I Saw Her Standing There', 'All My Loving', 'Roll Over Beethoven', 'Boys', 'Till There Was You', 'She Loves You', 'This Boy', 'I Want To Hold Your Hand', 'Money (That's What I Want)', 'Twist And Shout' and 'From Me To You' (instrumental outro).
→ The BBC Light Programme then recorded a two-minute interview to

Above: On the all-Merseyside edition of ITV's *Thank Your Lucky Stars*, 15 December. Opposite: The Beatles Christmas Show photocall, 24 December.

use on their Christmas Day special *Top Pops Of 1963*.

14 December
→ Wimbledon Palais.
→ The Beatles' Southern Area Fan Club concert. An afternoon performance, after which The Beatles sat behind the Palais bar and shook hands with 3,000 of their SFC members. A few girls fainted. They very soon had to stop giving autographs as the line grew too long.

15 December
→ Alpha TV Studios, Birmingham, to record the second all-Merseyside edition of ABC TV's *Thank Your Lucky Stars*. The Beatles mimed 'I Want To Hold Your Hand', 'All My Loving', 'Twist And Shout' and 'She Loves You' and were presented with two gold discs by George Martin.
→ The Beatles' Christmas flexi-disc was sent out to the 28,000 members of their fan club.

17 December
→ Playhouse Theatre, London, to record a Christmas edition of *Saturday Club* for the BBC Light Programme. The Beatles played 'All My Loving', 'This Boy', 'I Want To Hold Your Hand', 'Till There Was You', 'Roll Over Beethoven' and 'She Loves You'. They parodied Dora Bryan's recent hit 'All I Want For Christmas Is A Beatle' with 'All I Want

For Christmas Is A Bottle', followed by a half-minute medley entitled 'The Chrimble Mudley' which combined 'Love Me Do', 'Please Please Me', 'From Me To You', 'I Want To Hold Your Hand' and 'Rudolph The Red-Nosed Reindeer'.

18 December
→ BBC Paris Studio, London, to record *From Us To You*, a two-hour Beatles Boxing Day bank holiday special for the Light Programme. 'From Me To You' was recorded as 'From Us To You' as the signature tune to begin and end the programme. The Beatles and Rolf Harris joined together for a parody version of his 'Tie Me Kangaroo Down, Sport' hit and The Beatles performed 'She Loves You', 'All My Loving', 'Roll Over Beethoven', 'Till There Was You', 'Boys', 'Money (That's What I Want)', 'I Saw Her Standing There' and 'I Want To Hold Your Hand'.

21 December
→ Gaumont Cinema, Bradford.
→ The first of two special previews of 'The Beatles' Christmas Show', performed as a concert without costume or comedy sketches.

22 December
→ Empire Theatre, Liverpool.
→ Second of the 'The Beatles' Christmas Show' previews.

24 December -11 January
→ Astoria Cinema, Finsbury Park, London. 'The Beatles' Christmas Show' with The Barron Knights & Duke D'Mond, Tommy Quickly, The Fourmost, Billy J. Kramer & The Dakotas, Cilla Black and Rolf Harris. The show ran for 16 nights, with two houses per night, finishing on January 11, 1964, and was seen by almost 100,000 people. As well as appearing in sketches they played 'Roll Over Beethoven', 'All My Loving', 'This Boy', 'I Wanna Be Your Man', 'She Loves You', 'Till There Was You', 'I Want To Hold Your Hand', 'Money (That's What I Want)' and ended, as usual, with 'Twist And Shout'.

26 December
→ The single 'I Want To Hold Your Hand'/ 'I Saw Her Standing There' was released in the US as Capitol 5112.

Please Please Me

Words & Music by John Lennon
& Paul McCartney
© Copyright 1962 Dick James Music
Limited, 47 British Grove, London W4
All Rights Reserved.
International Copyright Secured.

1. Last night I said these words to my____ girl,

(Verse 2 see block lyrics)

"I know you nev-er e-ven try____ girl. Come

on, come on, come on, come on. Please

please me, whoa yeah, like I please you."

I don't want to sound com-plain-ing, but you know there's al-ways rain in

Verse 2:
You don't need me to show the way love.
Why do I always have to say love,
"Come on, come on, come on, come on.
Please please me, whoa yeah, like I please you"?

I Saw Her Standing There

Words & Music by John Lennon
& Paul McCartney

1. Well, she was just sev-en-teen,___ and you know what I mean,___ and the

(Verse 2 see block lyrics)

way she looked___ was way be-yond com - pare.___ So

how could I dance___ with an-oth - er,___ oh,___ when I

saw her stand - ing there.

2. Well,

Well, my heart went boom when I crossed that

room,   and   I   held   her   hand   in   mine._____

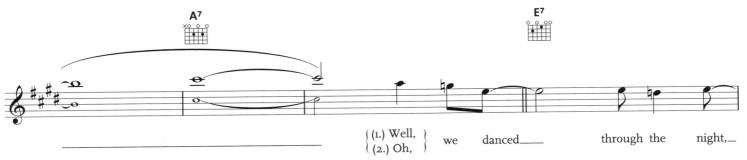

_____   ((1.) Well,) we danced_____ through the   night,___
                                   ((2.) Oh,)

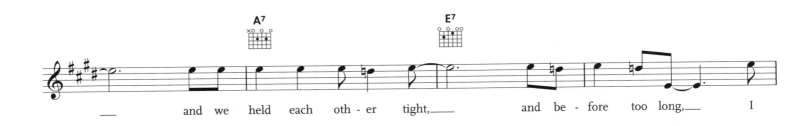

___   and we   held   each   oth - er   tight,___   and be - fore too long,___   I

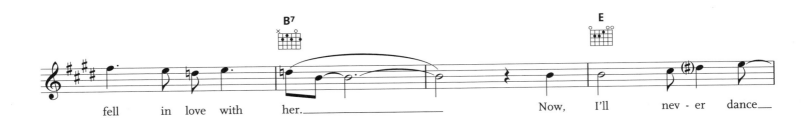

fell   in   love   with   her._____   Now,   I'll   nev - er   dance___

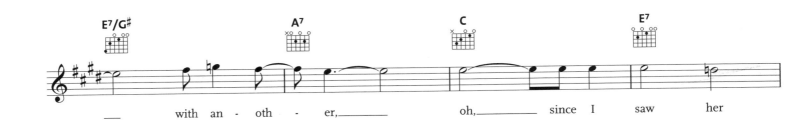

___   with an - oth - er,_____   oh,_____ since I   saw   her

To Coda ⊕

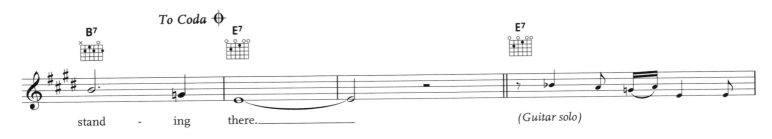

stand - ing   there._____   *(Guitar solo)*

Verse 2:
Well, she looked at me, and I, I could see,
That before too long I'd fall in love with her.
She wouldn't dance with another, oh,
When I saw her standing there.

Do You Want To Know A Secret

Words & Music by John Lennon
& Paul McCartney

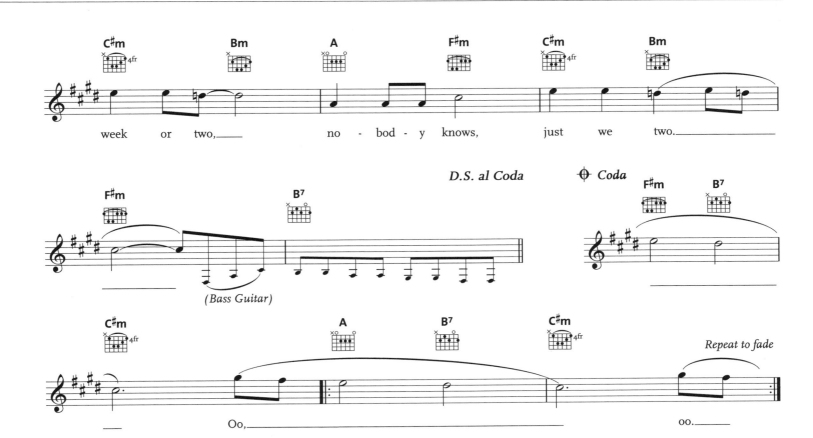

week　or　two,＿＿＿　no - bod - y　knows,　just　we　two.＿＿＿＿＿

D.S. al Coda　　　　⊕ *Coda*

(Bass Guitar)

Oo,＿＿＿＿＿＿＿＿＿＿＿＿＿＿＿＿＿＿＿＿

Repeat to fade

oo.＿＿＿

From Me To You

♩ = 138

Da da da da da dum dum da. Da da da da da dum dum da. 1. If there's

an - y - thing that you want, if there's an - y - thing I can do, just

call on me___ and I'll send it a - long,___ with love___ from me___ to you.___ 2. I've got

ev - 'ry - thing that you want, like a heart___ that's oh so true. (2, 4.) Just

4. *Harmonica solo (4 bars)*

call on me___ and I'll send it a - long,___ with love___ from me___ to you.___ I got

arms that long to hold___ you,_____ and keep you by my side. I got

lips that long to kiss___ you,_____ and keep you sat - is - fied. 3, 5. If there's

an - y - thing that you want, if there's an - y - thing I can do, just

call on me___ and I'll send it a - long,___ with love___ from me___ to you.___

1.

2.

___ to you,___ to you,___ to you.___

She Loves You

Words & Music by John Lennon
& Paul McCartney

She loves you, yeah, yeah, yeah. She loves you, yeah, yeah, yeah. She

loves you, yeah, yeah, yeah, yeah! 1. You

think you've lost your love, well, I saw her yes - ter - day - ee - ay. It's
(Verses 2 & 3 see block lyrics)

you she's think - ing of, and she told me what to say - ee - ay. She says she

loves you, and you know that can't be bad; yes, she loves you, and you

1.

know you should be glad. 2. She

2, 3.

Oo. She

loves you, yeah, yeah, yeah. She loves you, yeah, yeah, yeah, and with a

love like that, you know you should be glad.

To Coda

D.S. al Coda
(to 3rd time bar)

3. You

Coda

With a love like that, you know you should be glad,

with a love like that, you know you should be

A tempo

glad. Yeah, yeah, yeah,

yeah, yeah, yeah, yeah.

Verse 2:
She said you hurt her so,
She almost lost her mind;
But now she says she knows,
You're not the hurting kind.
She says she loves you,
And you know that can't be bad;
Yes, she loves you,
And you know you should be glad, oo.

She loves you, yeah, yeah, yeah...

Verse 3:
You know it's up to you,
I think it's only fair.
Pride can hurt you too,
Apologise to her.
Because she loves you,
And you know that can't be bad;
She loves you,
And you know you should be glad, oo.

She loves you, yeah, yeah, yeah...

93

It Won't Be Long

Words & Music by John Lennon
& Paul McCartney
© Copyright 1963 Northern Songs.
All Rights Reserved.
International Copyright Secured.

♩ = 138

It won't be long, yeah, yeah, yeah. It won't be long,— yeah, yeah,
(Yeah, yeah, yeah.) (Yeah,

yeah. It won't be long, yeah, till I be-long to you.———
yeah, yeah.) (Yeah.)

— 1. Ev-'ry night, when ev-'ry-bod-y has fun,
(Verses 2 & 3 see block lyrics)

here am I, sit-ting all— on my own. It won't be

long, yeah, yeah, yeah. It won't be long,— yeah, yeah, yeah. It won't be
(Yeah, yeah, yeah.) (Yeah, yeah, yeah.)

To Coda

long, yeah, till I be-long to you.——— Since you
(Yeah.)

Baug **Bm** **C#7**

left me, I'm so a-lone.__ Now you're com-ing,__ you're com-ing on home.__

A **B7** **C#m** **F#7** **1. B7**

I'll be good like I know__ I should,__ you're com-ing home,__ you're com-ing home.____

2. B7 *D.S. al Coda* **rit.** ⊕ *Coda* **A** **F#7** **N.C.** **G6** **F#7** **Fmaj7** **Emaj7**

home.____ I be-long to__ you.

Verse 2:
Every night, the tears come down from my eyes,
Every day, I've done nothing but cry.

It won't be long...

Verse 3:
Every day, we'll be happy, I know,
Now I know that you won't leave me no more.

It won't be long...

All I've Got To Do

Words & Music by John Lennon
& Paul McCartney

just got-ta call on me._____   3. And when

⊕ *Coda*

And the same goes for me, when-ev-er you want me at all,_____ I'll be

here, yes I will, when-ev-er you call._____ You just got-ta call on me,__

_____ yeah,_____ you just got-ta call on me._____ Oh,_____ you

just got-ta call on me._____   Mm,_____

mm,__ mm,__ mm,_____ mm,_____ mm.   *Repeat to fade*   Mm,_____

Verse 2:
And when I, I wanna kiss you, yeah,
All I gotta do is whisper in your ear
The words you long to hear,
And I'll be kissing you.

Verse 3:
And when I, I wanna kiss you, yeah,
All I gotta do is call you on the phone,
And you'll come running home, yeah,
That's all I gotta do.

All My Loving

Words & Music by John Lennon
& Paul McCartney
© Copyright 1963 Northern Songs.

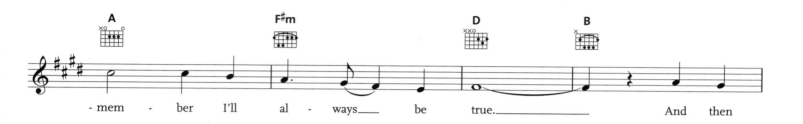

1,3. Close your eyes and I'll kiss___ you,___ to - mor - row I'll miss___ you; re -
(Verse 2 see block lyrics)

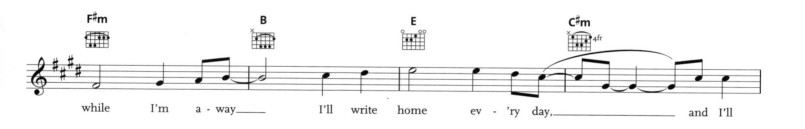

- mem - ber I'll al - ways___ be true.___ And then

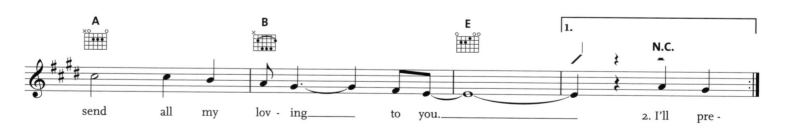

while I'm a - way___ I'll write home ev - 'ry day,_____ and I'll

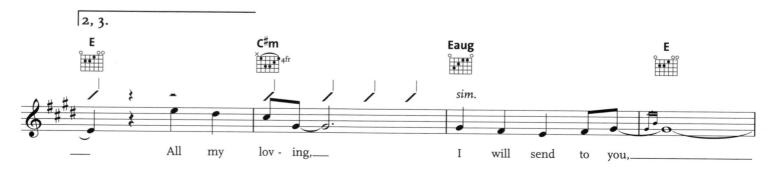

send all my lov - ing_____ to you._____ 2. I'll pre -

___ All my lov - ing,___ I will send to you,_____

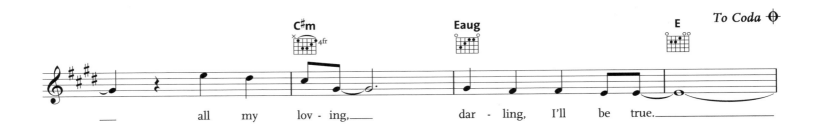

all my lov-ing,____ dar-ling, I'll be true._____

____ *(Guitar)* *(Guitar solo)*

D.S. al Coda
(to 3rd time bar)

3. Close your

⊕ *Coda*

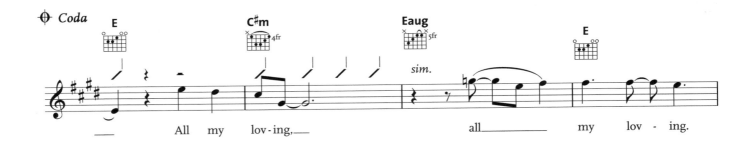

____ All my lov-ing,____ all_____ my lov-ing.

Oo,____ all my__ lov-ing,_____ I will send__ to you.

Verse 2:
I'll pretend that I'm kissing
The lips I am missing,
And hope that my dreams will come true.
And then while I'm away
I'll write home every day,
And I'll send all my loving to you.

I Wanna Be Your Man

Words & Music by John Lennon
& Paul McCartney
© Copyright 1963 Northern Songs.
All Rights Reserved.
International Copyright Secured.

1, 3. I wan-na be your lov-er, ba-by, I wan-na be your man._____
(*Verse 2 see block lyrics*)

I wan-na be your lov-er, ba-by, I wan-na be your man._____

Love you like no oth-er, ba-by, like no oth-er can._____

Love you like no oth-er, ba-by, like no oth-er can._____

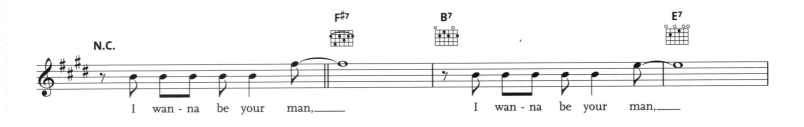

I wan-na be your man,_____ I wan-na be your man,_____

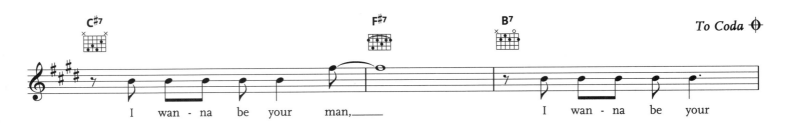

I wan-na be your man,_____ I wan-na be your

Verse 2:
Tell me that you love me, baby,
Let me understand.
Tell me that you love me, baby,
I wanna be your man.

I wanna be your lover, baby,
I wanna be your man.
I wanna be your lover, baby,
I wanna be your man.

I wanna be your man...

I Want To Hold Your Hand

Words & Music by John Lennon
& Paul McCartney
© Copyright 1963 Northern Songs.
All Rights Reserved.
International Copyright Secured.

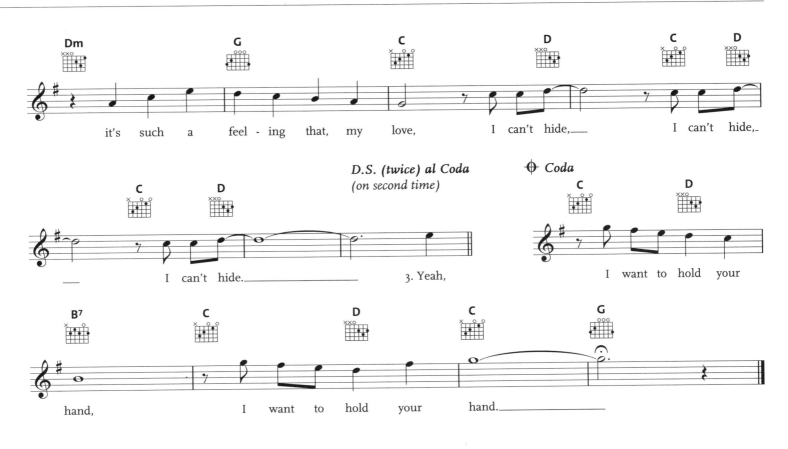

it's such a feel-ing that, my love, I can't hide,___ I can't hide,_

D.S. (twice) al Coda
(on second time)

⊕ *Coda*

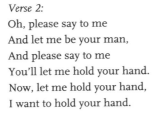

_ I can't hide._____ 3. Yeah, I want to hold your

hand, I want to hold your hand._____

Verse 2:
Oh, please say to me
And let me be your man,
And please say to me
You'll let me hold your hand.
Now, let me hold your hand,
I want to hold your hand.

Verses 3 & 4:
Yeah, you got that something,
I think you'll understand,
When I say that something,
I want to hold your hand.
I want to hold your hand,
I want to hold your hand, I want to hold your hand.

This Boy

Words & Music by John Lennon
& Paul McCartney
© Copyright 1963 Northern Songs.
All Rights Reserved.
International Copyright Secured.

Verse 2:
That boy isn't good for you,
Though he may want you too;
This boy wants you back again.

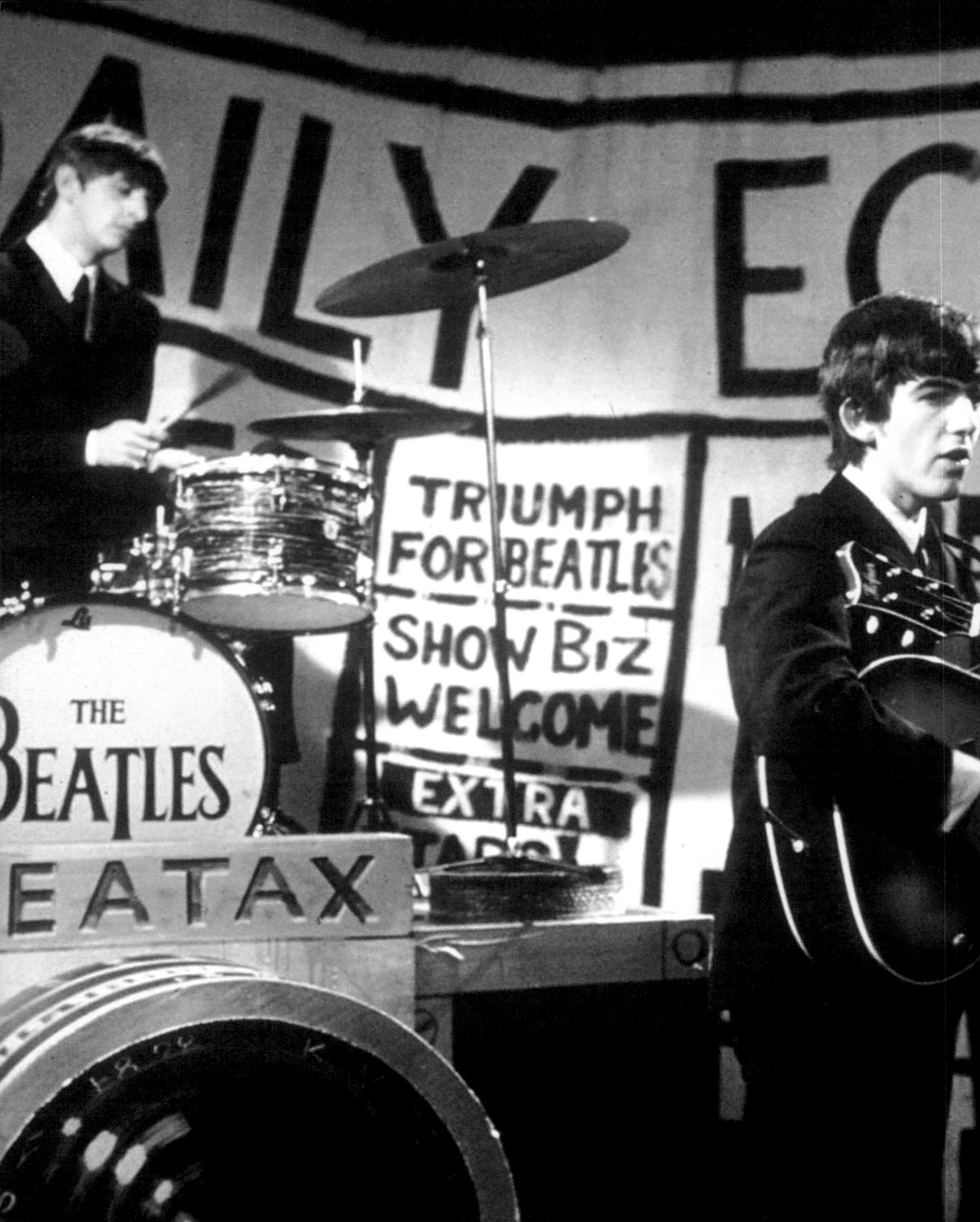
TRIUMPH FOR BEATLES
SHOW BIZ WELCOME
EXTRA
THE BEATLES

1964

1 January
→ A BBC clip of The Beatles singing 'She Loves You' was shown on American TV's *The Jack Paar Show*, the first film of The Beatles shown to US television audiences.

4 January
→ George and Ringo recorded an interview for the BBC Light Programme magazine *The Public Ear* at their Green Street flat.

7 January
→ The Beatles recorded an appearance for *Saturday Club* at the Playhouse Theatre, London. They performed 'All My Loving', 'Money (That's What I Want)', 'The Hippy Hippy Shake', 'I Want To Hold Your Hand', 'Roll Over Beethoven', 'Johnny B. Goode' and 'I Wanna Be Your Man'.

11 January
→ 'I Want To Hold Your Hand' entered the American *Cashbox* charts at number 80.

12 January
→ London Palladium.
The Beatles appeared for the second time on the ATV television variety show *Val Parnell's Sunday Night At The London Palladium*. They performed 'I Want To Hold Your Hand', 'This Boy', 'All My Loving', 'Money (That's What I Want)' and 'Twist And Shout'. As before, they appeared on the carousel at the end of the show where, by tradition, all the featured artists stood and waved goodbye as it slowly revolved.

15 January
→ Prior to their three week residency at the Paris Olympia, the Beatles did a try-out concert at the Cyrano Theatre in Versailles with all the other artists who would be appearing on the Olympia bill.

16 January - 4 February
→ John and Paul shared a suite at the George V because they were committed to writing six new songs for their forthcoming film, a song for Billy J. Kramer and one for Tommy Quickly. They had a piano brought in and got to work.

17 January
→ That evening a telephone call brought the news that 'I Want To Hold Your Hand' had reached number one in America. It had taken only three weeks to reach the top position. The Beatles celebrated until 5am.
→ Up until now, only a handful of British acts had ever made the charts in the US; The Beatles changed all that and opened the door for a tidal wave of British acts which transformed the face of American popular music for ever.

20 January
→ The album *Meet The Beatles* was released in the US as Capitol ST 2047, the first of 33 Beatles records issued in America during 1964.
→ Side A: 'I Want To Hold Your Hand', 'I Saw Her Standing There', 'This Boy', 'It Won't Be Long', 'All I've Got To Do', 'All My Loving'; Side B: 'Don't Bother Me', 'Little Child', 'Till There Was You', 'Hold Me Tight', 'I Wanna Be Your Man', 'Not A Second Time'.

24 January
→ The Beatles recorded an interview for American Forces Network (AFN) in their Paris studio.

27 January
→ The single 'My Bonnie'/'The Saints' by Tony Sheridan & The Beatles was re-released in the US as MGM K 13213.
→ The album *Introducing The Beatles* was re-released in the US as Vee Jay VJLP 1062, with two tracks substituted in the original track listing of the LP.

Beatles win over Paris: 16 January 4 February

A three week residency commenced at L'Olympia with Trini Lopez, Sylvie Vartan and a full music hall variety act including a juggler. Lopez closed the first half. Sylvie Vartan preceded The Beatles, an unenviable position. In France they drew a male crowd rather than female, and because there was much less screaming they could actually hear the music. French fans danced in the aisles and chanted for 'Les Beat-les!'.

Below: Posing with Sylvie Vartan backstage at the Paris Olympia. Opposite: The Beatles return to the London Palladium, 12 January.

Side A: 'I Saw Her Standing There', 'Misery', 'Anna (Go To Him)', 'Chains', 'Boys', 'Ask Me Why'; Side B: 'Please Please Me', 'Baby It's You', 'Do You Want To Know A Secret?', 'A Taste Of Honey', 'There's A Place', 'Twist And Shout'.

29 January
→ At the Pathé Marconi Studio in Paris, The Beatles recorded 'Can't Buy Me Love' and German language versions of 'I Want To Hold Your Hand' and 'She Loves You'. Despite regular attempts in later years to persuade EMI to let them record in the US, this proved to be The Beatles' only studio session outside the UK.

30 January
→ The single 'Please Please Me'/'From Me To You' was released in the US as Vee Jay VJ 581.

5 February
→ The Beatles returned to London from Paris.

7 February
→ The EP *All My Loving* was released in the UK as Parlophone GEP 8891. Side A: 'All My Loving', 'Ask Me Why'; Side B: 'Money (That's What I Want)', 'P.S. I Love You'.
→ The Beatles flew to New York on Pan Am flight 101, where 3,000 fans were waiting at JFK airport. Their party consisted of John's wife Cynthia plus Neil Aspinall, Mal Evans, publicist Brian Sommerville, Brian Epstein, and record producer Phil Spector. Ed Sullivan had

1964

"We love you Beat-les, oh yes we dooo! We love you Beatles and we'll be true!" interspersed with shouts of "We want The Beatles!"

already received 50,000 applications for tickets to his show which only seated 728, and fans had been gathering at JFK since the previous afternoon. The Beatles' Boeing 707 touched down at 1:20 pm to scenes never before witnessed at Kennedy. The fans were crowded four deep on the upper arcade of the arrivals building, waving 'We Love You Beatles' placards and home-made banners welcoming the group to America. In addition to the screaming teenagers, they were met by over 200 reporters and photographers from radio, television, magazines and newspapers.

→ Over 100 yelling journalists were waiting for the group as they emerged from immigration, and at first they couldn't see for the flash bulbs.

"So this is America," said Ringo. "They all seem to be out of their minds."

→ The scene at the Plaza, New York's grandest hotel, was chaotic with hundreds of fans being held at bay by police barricades and 20 mounted police. They kept up a constant mantra-like chant:

→ 100,000 fan letters were waiting for them when they arrived in New York.

8 February

→ John, Paul and Ringo went for a photo-opportunity walkabout in Central Park followed by about 400 girls (George was ill with a sore throat). At 1:30 pm The Beatles travelled by limousines to CBS studios at 53rd Street for a sound check. On the way,

Ed Sullivan Show: 9 February

Studio 50, West 53rd Street. At rehearsals for The *Ed Sullivan Show* took up the morning. In the afternoon The Beatles recorded numbers for another *Ed Sullivan Show* to be broadcast on 23 February, after they had left the country. This would be their third show – their first was to be done live that evening and the second was to be a live show from Florida on February 16. For the 'third' show, they recorded 'Twist And Shout', 'Please Please Me' and 'I Want To Hold Your Hand'. There was a different audience for the third show recording

than that which attended the live transmission that evening.

For the 8 pm live show, The Beatles performed 'All My Loving', 'Till There Was You' and 'She Loves You' and the show closed with 'I Saw Her Standing There' and 'I Want To Hold Your Hand'. Thirteen-and-a-half minutes of television changed the face of American popular music. The Nielsen ratings showed that 73,700,000 people had watched The Beatles on *Ed Sullivan*, not just the largest audience that Sullivan had ever had, but the largest audience in the history of television.

Opposite and above: The Beatles first appearance on *The Ed Sullivan Show* on 9 February marked America's capitulation to Beatlemania. Right: George celebrates his 21st birthday, 25 February.

fans charged at the cars en masse and it was up to mounted police to get them through. The studios themselves were guarded by 52 police officers and 10 mounted police.

10 February

→ The day was taken up with press interviews and presentations at the Plaza. At one ceremony, Capitol Records president Alan Livingstone presented The Beatles with golden discs to mark the sale of a million copies of 'I Want To Hold Your Hand' and a million dollars worth of sales of the album *Meet The Beatles*. The evening was spent at clubs. Once again, they returned to the Plaza at 4 am.

11 February

→ Washington Coliseum, Washington DC.
→ The party checked into The Shoreham Hotel, taking the whole of the seventh floor which was sealed off from fans. At the concert they were protected by 362 police officers. The Beatles' set consisted of: 'Roll Over Beethoven', 'From Me To You', 'I Saw Her Standing There', 'This Boy', 'All My Loving', 'I Wanna Be Your Man', 'Please Please Me', 'Till There Was You', 'She

Loves You', 'I Want To Hold Your Hand', 'Twist And Shout' and 'Long Tall Sally'.

12 February

→ Carnegie Hall, New York. Lincoln's birthday, a public holiday, so school was out and 10,000 fans were waiting at Penn Station for the Beatles to return from Washington.

13 February

→ At Miami there were 7,000 fans waiting, but The Beatles leapt straight from the plane into a waiting limousine and were off to the Deauville Hotel in Miami Beach. Their convoy of three black limousines had motorcycle outriders front and back and made the eight miles of expressway into the city in record time, going through red lights, driving on the wrong side of the road, as fans lining the streets cheered and waved.

14 February

→ A short rehearsal for *The Ed Sullivan Show*.

15 February

→ The group, wearing swimming trunks, rehearsed in the hotel's Napoleon Room. At 2 pm The Beatles did a dress rehearsal for *The Ed Sullivan Show* before an audience of 2,500, many of whom had queued outside since early morning. The rest of the day was spent fishing.
→ ABC TV's *Dick Clark's American Bandstand* broadcast a telephone interview with the group. The Beatles never personally appeared on his show.

16 February

→ *The Ed Sullivan Show* was transmitted from the Deauville Hotel. CBS gave out 3,500 tickets when the hall only held 2,600. The police had to deal with riots when fans holding perfectly valid tickets were turned away. The group played 'She Loves You', 'This Boy', 'All My Loving', 'I Saw Her Standing There', 'From Me To You' and 'I Want To Hold Your Hand'. 70,000,000 viewers tuned in to watch The Beatles.

18 February

→ The Beatles visited Cassius Clay's training camp where he was preparing for his rematch with the champion,

Sonny Liston. The photographers went crazy as ex-heavyweight champ Clay picked up Ringo as if he weighed only a few ounces.

22 February

The Beatles arrived back in London at 8:10 am from Miami via New York to a tumultuous welcome. They gave a press conference at the airport which was shown by BBC TV later as part of the sports programme *Grandstand*. News of their return was also featured on radio news and other programmes.

23 February

→ ABC TV's Teddington Studio Centre. Without even a day off to get over jet-lag, The Beatles taped an appearance for Mike & Bernie Winters' variety show *Big Night Out* before a live audience. They appeared in various skits, including a river cruise which was also filmed by ITN and used in its news bulletin that evening. They mimed to 'All My Loving', 'I Wanna Be Your Man', 'Till There Was You', 'Please Mister Postman', 'Money (That's What I Want)' and 'I Want To Hold Your Hand'.

25 February

→ Abbey Road. The Beatles finished 'Can't Buy Me Love', recorded 'You Can't Do That' (featuring John on lead guitar for the first time on record) and began work on Paul's 'And I Love Her' and John's 'I Should Have Known Better'.
→ George's 21st birthday. He received

52 mail-sacks holding about 30,000 cards.

26 February

➔ Abbey Road. Further work on 'And I Love Her' and 'I Should Have Known Better'.

➔ The album *Jolly What! The Beatles And Frank Ifield On Stage* was released in the US as Vee Jay VJLP 1085. Despite its title, it featured regular studio recordings by both artists, allowing Vee Jay to extract yet more mileage from the dozen Beatles tracks which they had under licence. This LP featured eight Ifield songs, plus 'Please Please Me', 'From Me To You', 'Ask Me Why' and 'Thank You Girl'.

27 February

➔ Abbey Road. 'And I Love Her' was finished, plus complete recordings made of John's 'Tell Me Why' and 'If I Fell'.

28 February

➔ BBC Studios at 201 Piccadilly. The Beatles recorded a second *From Us To You* Easter bank holiday special for the Light Programme. The group was interviewed by Alan ('Fluff') Freeman and taped 'You Can't Do That', 'Roll Over Beethoven', 'Till There Was You', 'I Wanna Be Your Man', 'Please Mister Postman', 'All My Loving', 'This Boy' and 'Can't Buy Me Love'. As before they taped their own version of the show's theme tune 'From Us To You' to open and close the programme.

➔ The single 'Why'/'Cry For A Shadow' by Tony Sheridan & The Beatles (A-side) and The Beatles (B-side) was released in the UK as Polydor NH 52-275.

1 March

➔ Abbey Road. 'I'm Happy Just To Dance With You' was recorded, specially written for George who was not yet writing songs regularly. This was followed by 'Long Tall Sally' with Paul in fine Little Richard form, and 'I Call Your Name'.

5 March

➔ The single 'Komm, Gib Mir Deine Hand'/'Sie Liebt Dich' was released in Germany as Odeon 22671.

➔ The single 'Twist And Shout'/

'There's A Place' was released in the US as Tollie 9001.

9 March

➔ Filming on location, between London and Newton Abbott, Devon.

➔ NEMS Enterprises Limited moved from Liverpool to new headquarters on the fifth floor of Sutherland House, 5 & 6 Argyll Street, London.

➔ NEMS then managed The Beatles, Gerry & The Pacemakers, Billy J. Kramer, The Dakotas, Cilla Black, The Fourmost, Tommy Quickly, Sounds Incorporated and The Remo Four.

10 March

➔ AHDN filming at The Turk's Head, Twickenham.

11 March

➔ *AHDN* filming at Twickenham Film Studios, miming to 'I Should Have Known Better' in a mock-up of the train's guard's van.

12 March

➔ *AHDN* filming at Twickenham: hotel room sequences

13 March

➔ The movie's closing sequence was filmed with a helicopter at Gatwick Airport.

16 March

➔ Ringo filmed his canteen sequence at Twickenham Studios.

➔ The single 'Can't Buy Me Love'/'You Can't Do That' was released in the US as Capitol 5150.

17 March

➔ *AHDN* filming at Les

Beatles begin filming: 2-6 March

Directed by Richard Lester, produced by Walter Shenson with a screenplay written by Alun Owen, filming began on 2 March for *A Hard Day's Night* at 8:30 am on Paddington Station, with The Beatles hurriedly joining Equity minutes before boarding the train. The first week was spent filming on a specially hired train going from Paddington to Minehead and back, covering 2,500 miles in six days. After the crowds on the first day, they boarded the train at Acton station to avoid Paddington. One of the actresses playing a schoolgirl on the train was Patti Boyd, with whom George struck up an immediate friendship. They married in 1966.

Opposite: The Beatles on the set of their first movie, *A Hard Day's Night*. Television actor Wilfred Brambell, of *Steptoe And Son*, (seen seated) played Paul's troublesome grandfather in the film. **Below: The girl tending George's hair was model and actress Patti Boyd.** The two began dating and were married in 1966.

Ambassadeurs Club.

➔ John recorded an interview with Jack de Manio for the BBC Home Service programme *Today* to promote his forthcoming book *In His Own Write*.

18 March

➔ *AHDN* filming at Twickenham.

➔ While on the set they recorded an interview for the BBC Light Programme show *The Public Ear* in which they interviewed each other.

19 March

➔ The Variety Club of Great Britain 12th Annual Show Business Awards were presented at a luncheon at the Dorchester Hotel. Harold Wilson, Leader of the Opposition, presented The Beatles with their awards for 'Show Business Personalities of 1963'.

➔ The Beatles were filming that morning at Twickenham and returned to the set directly after the luncheon. Later that evening they recorded their first *Top Of The Pops* programme for the BBC. They mimed to 'Can't Buy Me Love' and 'You Can't Do That'.

20 March

➔ *AHDN* filming at Twickenham.

➔ Ringo was interviewed on the set by Peter Nobel for the BBC radio programme *Movie-Go-Round*.

➔ In the late afternoon The Beatles drove to the London studios of Associated Rediffusion on Kingsway and appeared live on *Ready, Steady, Go!* miming to 'It Won't Be Long', 'You Can't Do That' and 'Can't Buy Me Love'.

➔ The single 'Can't Buy Me Love'/'You Can't Do That' was released in the UK as Parlophone R 5114.

23-26 March

➔ *AHDN* filming at the Scala Theatre, Charlotte Street, London, where they were to remain all week.

➔ *In His Own Write* by John Lennon was published by Jonathan Cape. To promote the book, John appeared live on the BBC television *Tonight* programme broadcast from Lime Grove. He was interviewed by Kenneth Allsop and read selections from the book, many of which first saw print in John's 'Beatcomber' column in *Mersey Beat*.

➔ The Duke of Edinburgh presented

The Beatles with the Carl-Alan Award for Musical Achievement in 1963 at a ceremony at the Empire Ballroom in Leicester Square as part of the annual Carl-Alan Ballroom Dancing Awards.

→ The single 'Do You Want To Know A Secret?'/'Thank You Girl' was released in the US as Vee Jay VJ 587.

→ The EP *The Beatles* was released in the US as Vee Jay VJEP 1-903. Side A: 'Misery', 'A Taste Of Honey'; Side B: 'Ask Me Why', 'Anna (Go To Him)'. The EP format was unusual in the US, but Vee Jay only had a few tracks to play with and so they released them in every possible format.

24 March

→ John did an interview to promote his new book for *Dateline London*, a BBC Overseas Service magazine programme.

31 March

→ The group filmed a live concert at the Scala Theatre, Charlotte Street, London, for *A Hard Day's Night*. They mimed to 'Tell Me Why', 'And I Love Her', 'I Should Have Known Better' and 'She Loves You'. 13-year old Phil Collins was in the audience as one of the 350 paid extras.

→ That evening, The Beatles recorded a session for the BBC Light Programme's *Saturday Club*. They performed 'Everybody's Trying To Be My Baby', 'I Call Your Name', 'I Got A Woman', 'You Can't Do That', 'Can't Buy Me Love', 'Sure To Fall (In Love With You)' and 'Long Tall Sally'.

→ John was interviewed about his book by Brian Matthew for the BBC Home Service programme *A Slice of Life*.

1-2 April

→ *AHDN* filming at the Scala Theatre, Charlotte Street, London.

→ A meeting was arranged at the London offices of NEMS between John and his father, Freddie. It lasted 20 minutes and George and Ringo were also present. Father and son had not seen each other for 17 years.

3 April

→ *AHDN* filming at Twickenham Film Studios.

→ The Beatles filmed answers to viewers' questions for the Tyne Tees

Television programme *Star Parade*.

4 April

➔ In the *Billboard* 'Hot 100' chart for the week of April 4, The Beatles occupied no fewer than 12 places, including the top five, an unprecedented achievement that is unlikely ever to be equalled. 'Can't Buy Me Love' was at number 1, followed by 'Twist And Shout' (2), 'She Loves You' (3), 'I Want To Hold Your Hand' (4), 'Please Please Me' (5), 'I Saw Her Standing There' (31), 'From Me To You' (41), 'Do You Want to Know A Secret?' (46), 'All My Loving' (58), 'You Can't Do That' (65), 'Roll Over Beethoven' (68) and 'Thank You Girl' (79). A week later two more singles entered the chart – 'There's A Place' (74) and 'Love Me Do' (81).

5 April

➔ Filming the opening chase sequence for *AHDN* at Marylebone Railway Station.

6-7 April

➔ *AHDN* filming at Twickenham.

9 April

➔ Ringo filmed his solo spot for the film on the towpath of the Thames at Kew.

10 April

➔ *AHDN* filming at Twickenham.
➔ *The Beatles' Second Album* was released in the US as Capitol ST 2080. Side A: 'Roll Over Beethoven', 'Thank You Girl', 'You Really Got A Hold On Me', 'Devil In Her Heart', 'Money (That's What I Want)', 'You Can't Do That'; Side B: 'Long Tall Sally', 'I Call Your Name', 'Please Mister Postman', 'I'll Get You', 'She Loves You'.
➔ Despite its title, the LP was technically the group's third album release in the US, though only their second on Capitol.

12 April

➔ *AHDN* filming at Marylebone Station which was closed on Sundays.

13 April

➔ *AHDN* filming at Twickenham.
➔ With *A Hard Day's Night* confirmed as the title of their film, John announced his intention to write a

title tune to order – which he did that evening.

14 April

➔ *AHDN* filming at Twickenham.
➔ John arrived for the day's filming with his song 'A Hard Day's Night', quickly taught it to Paul, who tidied up the middle section, and the pair then played it to film producer Walter Shenson for the first time.

15 April

➔ *AHDN* filming outside shots at the Scala Theatre, Charlotte Street, London.
➔ Paul was interviewed by David Frost for the BBC television show, *A Degree Of Frost*.

16 April

➔ *AHDN* filming chase scenes in Notting Hill Gate.
➔ Abbey Road. Recording 'A Hard Day's Night'.

17 April

➔ *AHDN* filming at Les Ambassadeurs.
➔ The group were interviewed by Ed Sullivan in the club's walled garden during a break in filming.
➔ The title *A Hard Day's Night* was announced as the name of The Beatles' first film.

18 April

➔ The morning was spent at Twickenham Film Studios working on *AHDN*.
➔ The afternoon was spent in rehearsal at The Hall Of Remembrance, Flood Street, Chelsea, for a TV special for Rediffusion called *Around The Beatles*.

19 April

➔ IBC Studios, Portland Place, with engineer Glyn Johns, recording their contribution to *Around The Beatles*. The Beatles recorded (the tape of which they would mime to on the actual show): 'Twist And Shout', 'Roll Over Beethoven', 'I Wanna Be Your Man', 'Long Tall Sally', 'Boys' (omitted from the final broadcast), 'Can't Buy Me Love' and a greatest hits medley: 'Love Me Do'/'Please Please Me'/'From Me To You'/'She Loves You'/'I

Want To Hold Your Hand' and a version of The Isley Brothers' 'Shout' to close the special.

20-21 April
→ Paul was filmed at the Jack Billings TV School of Dance, Notting Hill, in a solo spot that was ultimately cut from the final of *AHDN*.

22 April
→ *AHDN* outdoor locations shots were filmed at the Hammersmith Odeonand in Notting Hill and Shepherd's Bush.

23 April
→ *AHDN* filming at Thornbury Playing Fields, Isleworth, Middlesex.
→ John cut short his day's filming in order to attend a Foyle's Literary Luncheon, given in his honour, at the Dorchester Hotel. Christina Foyle was put out when the severely hungover Lennon restricted his speech to the words,

"Thank you very much and God bless you. You've got a lucky face".

24 April
→ Ringo's Sir Walter Raleigh puddle sequence in *AHDN* was filmed in West Ealing. As it was the final day of shooting, The Beatles, the entire crew, and Murray the K, who was visiting, trooped across the road from the studios to The Turk's Head pub nearby where food and drinks had been laid on in a private room at the back.

25 April
→ Rehearsals for *Around The Beatles* continued at The Hall of Remembrance, Flood Street, Chelsea.

26 April
→ The Beatles topped the bill at the *New Musical Express* 1963-4 Annual Poll Winners' All-Star Concert held at Empire Pool, Wembley, in the afternoon. 10,000 fans saw them receive their awards from Roger Moore and perform 'She Loves You', 'You Can't Do That', 'Twist And Shout', Long Tall Sally' and 'Can't Buy Me Love'.

27 April
→ The Beatles attended a full dress

Opposite: Filming scenes for *A Hard Day's Night* with director Dick Lester.
Above: In Shakespearian garb in a scene from *A Midsummer Night's Dream* for the *Around The Beatles* TV special, 27 April.

rehearsal before a live audience for the *Around The Beatles* TV special at Rediffusion's Wembley studios.
→ The single 'Love Me Do'/'P.S. I Love You' was released in the US as Tollie 9008.
→ The single 'Why'/'Cry For A Shadow' by Tony Sheridan & The Beatles (A- side) and The Beatles (B-side) was released in the US as MGM K 13227.
→ John's *In His Own Write* was published in the US by Simon & Schuster.
→ NEMS Enterprises increased its share capital to 10,000 £1 shares. Brian Epstein gave The Beatles 250 shares each.

28 April
→ The *Around The Beatles* TV Special

was taped at Rediffusion's Wembley Studio. As well as the numbers they had already recorded, The Beatles played 'Act V Scene 1' of Shakespeare's *A Midsummer Night's Dream* with John taking the female role of Thisbe, Paul as Pyramus, George as Moonshine and Ringo as Lion. Paul later named his cat Thisbe.

29 April
→ ABC Cinema, Edinburgh.

30 April
→ Odeon Cinema, Glasgow. Two sets. The group was interviewed in the afternoon by BBC Scotland for the news programme *Six Ten*, they then recorded an interview at the Theatre Royal for STV's *Roundabout* programme.

1 May

→ BBC's Paris Studio to record their third *From Us To You* bank holiday special for the BBC Light Programme. The Beatles played: 'I Saw Her Standing There', 'Kansas City'/'Hey, Hey, Hey, Hey', 'I Forgot To Remember To Forget', 'You Can't Do That', 'Sure To Fall (In Love With You)', 'Can't Buy Me Love', 'Matchbox' and 'Honey Don't'.

2 May

→ Travelling under pseudonyms John and Cynthia, and George and Patti flew to Honolulu on holiday but the pressure from the press was relentless and they were forced to leave. They flew on to Papeeti, in Tahiti. When a reporter asked,

"Why are you leaving Hawaii so soon?" George snapped back at him, "Why didn't you leave us alone? How would you like a microphone always stuck in your face when you are on holiday?"

→ Paul and Jane, and Ringo and Maureen, took a holiday in St Thomas, in the Virgin Islands. also travelling under aliases. They left from Luton Airport and flew to Paris. From there they flew to Lisbon, where they spent the night at the Ritz Hotel.

→ An exhibition of Stuart Sutcliffe's paintings opened at the Walker Art Gallery in Liverpool.

3 May

→ From Lisbon, Paul and Jane, and Ringo and Maureen, flew to Puerto Rico and from there to the Virgin Islands – a convoluted route designed to avoid the press. In St Thomas, they hired a yacht, complete with crew. The fact that The Beatles and their girlfriends were holidaying out of wedlock brought press criticism.

8 May

→ The album *Let's Do The Twist, Hully Gully, Slop, Surf, Locomotion, Monkey* was released in the US: despite being credited to The Beatles, it only featured four songs on which they performed, three of them as support group for Tony Sheridan.

Paul: "There was something about the atmosphere there that made me get quite keen on writing new songs in the evenings. I did a couple while I was there which we recorded when we got back, 'The Things We Said Today' and 'Always And Only' ('It's For You')."

11 May

→ The EP *Four By The Beatles* was released in the US as Capitol EAP 2121.

→ Side A: 'Roll Over Beethoven', 'All My Loving'; Side B: 'This Boy', 'Please Mister Postman'.

21 May

→ The German-language single 'Sie Liebt Dich'/'Komm, Gib Mir Deine Hand' was released in the US as Swan 4182.

24 May

→ The Beatles' interview with Ed Sullivan was screened along with a clip filmed at the Scala for *A Hard Day's Night*, but not used in the film, of the group miming to 'You Can't Do That'.

26 May

→ John, Cynthia, George and Patti returned to London from their holiday followed the next day by Paul, Jane, Ringo and Maureen.

29 May

→ The single 'Ain't She Sweet'/'If You Love Me Baby', the A-side by The Beatles and B-side by Tony Sheridan & The Beatles, was released in the UK as Polydor NH 52-317.

30 May

→ The Beatles gave a press conference to discuss their world tour at NEMS' London offices presided over by Derek Taylor, their new press representative.

31 May

→ Prince of Wales Theatre, London. The Beatles performed two sets, playing 'Can't Buy Me Love', 'All My Loving', 'This Boy', 'Roll Over Beethoven', 'Till There Was You', 'Twist And Shout' and 'Long Tall Sally'.

June

→ Paul bought a steel blue Aston Martin DB5 just before leaving for The Beatles world tour.

1 June

→ Abbey Road. The Beatles worked on songs intended to be used on the *A Hard Day's Night* album: 'Matchbox', 'I'll Cry Instead' and 'Slow Down'. Carl Perkins, the composer of 'Matchbox', was in the studio to watch them.

Opposite: John and wife Cynthia return to London from a holiday in Tahiti, 26 May. Above: "Flew into London Airport BOAC..." George got his mop combed by Liverpudlian air hostess Anne Creech when The Beatles returned from Holland, 7 June. Stand-in drummer Jimmy Nicol (far right) looks on.

→ The single 'Sweet Georgia Brown'/ 'Take Out Some Insurance On Me Baby' by Tony Sheridan & The Beatles was released in the US as Atco 6302.

2 June
→ Abbey Road. John's 'Any Time At All' and 'When I Get Home', and Paul's 'Things We Said Today' were recorded.
→ At the studio The Beatles recorded an interview with Bob Rogers for Australian television ATN 7.

3 June
→ Ringo collapsed during a morning photo session in Barnes for *The Saturday Evening Post* and was taken to University College Hospital suffering

from acute tonsillitis and pharyngitis, requiring complete rest and quiet. With The Beatles due to leave on a world tour the next morning, a substitute drummer was urgently required. George Martin suggested Jimmy Nicol, who suddenly found himself a temporary member of the most famous group on earth. The Beatles cancelled a recording session and spent the time at Abbey Road rehearsing with Nicol instead.
→ That evening, the remaining Beatles recorded demo versions of their own compositions: George did 'You'll Know What To Do' (unreleased until *Beatles Anthology 1*), Paul did a demo of 'It's For You' to

give to Cilla Black and John recorded 'No Reply' (also released on *Anthology 1*) which he gave to Tommy Quickly for a single before The Beatles recorded it.

4 June
→ John, Paul, George and Jimmy Nicol flew to Denmark. Over 6,000 fans were waiting at Kastrup Airport, Copenhagen and fans attempted to storm the doors of the Royal Hotel, opposite the Tivoli Gardens, when they checked in. The crowd of 10,000 fans, who brought the centre of Copenhagen to a standstill, were controlled by Danish police assisted by visiting members of the British Royal Fusiliers.

→ The group had to rehearse their repertoire for Jimmy Nicol, Ringo's stand-in, and Mal Evans introduced a new way of getting them to remember the playlist – he taped it onto their guitars.

→ They played two shows at the KB Hallen with 4,400 fans in each. The first set consisted of: 'I Want To Hold Your Hand', 'I Saw Her Standing There', 'You Can't Do That', 'All My Loving', 'She Loves You', 'Till There Was You', 'Roll Over Beethoven', Can't Buy Me Love', This Boy' and 'Long Tall Sally'. For the second set, and the rest of the tour, the order of the first two numbers was switched round. Ringo's 'I Wanna Be Your Man' was left out of the set.

Above: Ringo gets lei'd in Honolulu on his way to Australia, 13 June.

5 June

→ The Beatles arrived at Amsterdam's Schiphol Airport at 1 pm and after the usual press conference they went straight to Hillegom, 26 miles outside Amsterdam, to rehearse and record a television show for VARA TV at the Treslong café-restaurant. The group (with Jimmy Nicol) mimed to 'Twist And Shout', 'All My Loving', 'Roll Over Beethoven', 'Long Tall Sally', 'She Loves You' and 'Can't Buy Me Love', but before they could complete the last number, they were engulfed by fans, mostly boys.

→ After the concert that evening they toured Amsterdam's red-light district, the Walletjes.

John: "When we hit town, we hit it, we were not pissing about. You know, there's photographs of me grovelling about, crawling about in Amsterdam on my knees, coming out of whore houses and things like that, and people saying, 'Good morning, John...' The police escorted me to the places because they never wanted a big scandal."

6 June

→ The Beatles made a highly publicised tour of the Amsterdam canals in one of the glass-topped tourist boats. Some fans dived into the canal and the police used very rough tactics in getting them out. All police leave was cancelled and 15,000 police were on duty for the canal trip, watched by 50,000 fans.

→ The Dutch concerts were held at the Exhibition Hall in Blokker, about 36 miles from Amsterdam. The Beatles travelled there in two white Cadillacs with motorcycle outriders.

7 June

→ The 10:15 am BEA flight to Hong Kong from London, Heathrow, was held up for an hour to enable The Beatles to make the connection from their flight from Amsterdam, which caused some grumbles in the British press. The plane stopped to refuel at Zürich, Beirut, Karachi, Calcutta and Bangkok. In Beirut, police turned fire fighting foam on the hundreds of fans who invaded the runway. In Karachi Paul attempted to buy a few souvenirs at the airport but even at 2 am shrieking fans appeared from nowhere and he was forced back on to the plane. At Bangkok about 1,000 fans, mostly in school uniforms, rampaged through the airport chanting, 'Beatles come out!' They did go down the ramp to sign autographs and be kissed.

8 June

→ The Beatles arrived at Kai Tak Airport in Hong Kong and were quickly transferred to the 15th floor of the President Hotel in Kowloon, by-passing customs and immigration formalities. Paul and Neil ordered a couple of the famous 24-hour tailored suits. That evening, tired and jet-lagged, The Beatles were expected to attend the Miss Hong Kong Pageant, held in the hotel. When they refused

The Beatles arrival in Sydney: 11 June

The Beatles flew to Sydney, stopping for fuel in Darwin where, at 2:35 in the morning, 400 fans stood waiting at the airport for a glimpse of the group. The Beatles went through customs and immigration and met the press. It was raining heavily and very cold when they arrived at Sydney's Mascot International Airport, despite which 2,000 fans managed to give them a damp welcome. The Beatles were paraded around the airport in an open-topped milk truck so by the time they reached the Sheraton Hotel in King's Cross, they were soaked to the skin.

Once they had dried off and warmed up, they launched straight into a press conference, attended by representatives from the country's media.

there were so many tears that John went down to the Convention Hall to make an appearance. He shook the contestants' hands and made a few choice remarks about the beauty of oriental girls.

9 June
→ Princess Theatre, Kowloon, Hong Kong. The Beatles played two shows, but since the Chinese promoter had charged outrageous ticket prices, not all the seats were full, and many of the thousands of fans who greeted them at the airport could not afford to see the shows. A ticket cost the equivalent of one week's pay.

12 June
→ Ringo, accompanied by Brian Epstein, flew to Australia via San Francisco, Honolulu and Fiji. He forgot his passport and the plane was delayed. Eventually he left without it. His passport finally arrived at the airport and was put on another plane to be given to him during his stopover in San Francisco.
→ That evening, The Beatles played two sets at Centennial Hall. More than 50,000 applications had been made for the four concerts at this 3,000 seater hall. Their set was the same as in Denmark and Holland: 'I Saw Her Standing There', 'I Want To Hold Your Hand', 'You Can't Do That', 'All My Loving', 'She Loves You', 'Till There Was You', 'Roll Over Beethoven', 'Can't Buy Me Love', 'This Boy' and 'Long Tall Sally'.

The Adelaide reception: 12 June

The Beatles flew from Sydney to Adelaide in a chartered Ansett ANA jet, arriving at 11:57 am.

Police estimated that 200,000 people lined the 10 mile route of their motorcade from the airport to the city centre – the biggest welcome the Beatles received anywhere in the world throughout their career. Around 30,000 blocked the area near the City Hall where the group met city officials and their families and received toy koala bears as gifts.

George: "The best flight I remember was the one to Hong Kong. It took several hours and I remember them saying, 'Return to your seats because we're approaching Hong Kong' and I thought, 'We can't be there already.' We'd been sitting on the floor drinking and taking Preludins for about 30 hours and so it seemed like a ten-minute flight."

→ That night, The Beatles had a private party in their hotel suite, ignoring a society extravaganza held in their honour in the Adelaide Hills.

13 June
→ In the afternoon Ringo arrived in San Francisco and gave a press conference at the airport while changing planes. The conference turned into chaos as reporters scrambled to get autographs, and Ringo was hurried away to board a Qantas flight to Sydney.
→ Meanwhile, 4,000 fans were still camped outside the South Australia Hotel in Adelaide, when The Beatles woke up just after noon. The group held a small reception for their Fan Club organisers before the show.
→ Centennial Hall, Adelaide. Two sets.
→ The Beatles again held a private party in their suite.

14 June
→ Ringo arrived in Sydney to the usual shrieking fans and clamouring pressmen. After 90 minutes in Sydney, Ringo and Brian Epstein flew on to Melbourne where the crowd at the

airport was already large, waiting to greet the other members of the group due to arrive five hours later. When Brian and Ringo arrived at the Southern Cross Hotel, a crowd of 3,000 fans were already gathered outside.

→ The other Beatles left the South Australia hotel at 12:15 pm and flew from Adelaide to Melbourne in a chartered Ansett ANA Fokker Friendship. They arrived at Essendon Airport to a frenzied welcome from a crowd of 5,000. The crowd outside the hotel was so large that army and navy units had been called in as reinforcements when steel barriers were knocked down and casualties began to mount up. Their route into the city was lined by 20,000 fans, most of whom moved on to the Southern Cross Hotel which was under a state of siege.

→ Protected by 12 motorcycle outriders, the group neared the hotel at 4 pm and were driven into a garage entrance while a dummy police car with siren blaring pulled up at the hotel's front door as a diversion. In front of the hotel, 300 police and 100 military battled with the crowd, cars were crushed, people broke bones, fell from trees and more than 150 girls fainted. Some 50 people, many of them adults, were taken to hospital with injuries sustained in the crush. Scores of girls had their sweaters torn off and many lost their shoes.

→ To relieve the crush, The Beatles were asked to show themselves, and all five appeared on the first floor balcony. The roar of the crowd was like that at a Nuremburg rally, prompting John to give a Nazi salute and shout 'Sieg Heil', holding his finger to his upper lip as a moustache.

→ Once The Beatles had been properly reunited there was a press conference with all five, after which Nicol's services were no longer needed. The Beatles celebrated their reunion with a party attended by local girls.

15 June

→ Jimmy Nicol slipped out of The Beatles' Melbourne hotel on Bourke Street at 8 am in the morning accompanied by Brian Epstein. At the airport Brian paid him his agreed fee

of £500 and gave him a gold watch, engraved,

"To Jimmy, with appreciation and gratitude – Brian Epstein and The Beatles."

→ Festival Hall, Melbourne, two sets, after which The Beatles attended a private party given by Melbourne socialites in the rich suburb of Toorak.

16 June

→ The Beatles attended a civic reception at Melbourne Town Hall. Police closed several streets as 15,000 fans took the day off school to catch a glimpse of the group on the Town Hall balcony. They arrived half an hour late because the ticker tape reception slowed their car down. Mayor Leo Curtis had foolishly given tickets for the reception to any fan who wrote in and the reception, planned for 150 people, had swelled to 350. Ringo was asked to speak and gave them a classic Ringo line:

"I wish you'd had this reception a little earlier instead of dragging me out of bed at this early hour."

(It was 1:15 pm.) The Mayor then asked for autographs, prompting a melée as fans and dignitaries scrambled to touch the group. Ringo demanded that they leave immediately and the Mayor took them to his wife's chambers on the second floor.

Jimmy Nicol: "The boys were very kind but I felt like an intruder. They accepted me, but you can't just get into a group like that – they have their own atmosphere, their own sense of humour. It's a little clique and outsiders just can't break in."

→ Festival Hall, Melbourne (two sets).

17 June

→ Festival Hall, Melbourne (two sets). Channel Nine filmed one of the Melbourne concerts for a TV show: *The Beatles Sing For Shell* (the oil company).

18 June

→ The Beatles flew into Sydney at 11.40 am, where a relatively small crowd of 1,200 fans were waiting, guarded by 300 police. The group were rapidly transferred to their previous suite in the Sheraton before the usual press conference. That evening the Beatles played two sets at Sydney Stadium.

John: "You know, The Beatles' tours were like Fellini's Satyricon. I mean, we had that image, but man, our tours were like something else. If you could get on our tours, you were in... Australia, just everywhere. Just think of Satyricon with four musicians going through it. Wherever we went there was always a whole scene going on. We had our four bedrooms separate from... tried to keep them out of our room. And Derek's and Neil's rooms were always full of fuck knows what, and policemen and everything... they didn't call them groupies then, they called it something else. If we couldn't get groupies, we would have whores and everything, whatever was going."

19 June

→ Sydney Stadium, Sydney (two sets).

→ The EP *Long Tall Sally* was released in the UK as Parlophone GEP 8913. Side A: 'Long Tall Sally', 'I Call Your Name'; Side B: 'Slow Down', 'Matchbox'.

20 June

→ Sydney Stadium, Sydney (two sets).

→ The Beatles did a telephone

interview with Colin Hamilton for the BBC Light Programme show *Roundabout*.

21 June

→ As they were packing to leave in the early hours of the morning, a tapping on the window of suite 801 revealed 20-year-old Peter Roberts, an 'exile' from Netherton, Liverpool, who had scaled the drainpipes of the hotel in total darkness to say hello.

→ 10,000 fans saw The Beatles off at Sydney airport, the biggest turn-out yet. They flew the 1,500 miles to Wellington, New Zealand, where 7,000 screaming fans were waiting at the airport.

22 - 23 June

→ Town Hall, Wellington, North Island, NZ (two sets per night).

→ The sound system was so primitive that as The Beatles came off stage after the first show, John screamed,

"What the fucking hell is going on here?"

The second house was considerably louder but the sound quality was still bad. After one concert, Mal Evans had to use his muscle to clear a way through to the hotel because the local police thought that two men would be enough to control a crowd of 5,000 fans.

24 – 25 June

→ Town Hall, Auckland, North Island, NZ (two sets per night).

→ When arriving on the 24th, The Beatles' Cadillac was stuck 30 feet from the Royal International Hotel where they were staying because so few police were on duty. Mal, Neil and Lloyd Ravenscroft had to lock The Beatles in the car and push it to the garage door, fighting off fans all the way. It took 20 minutes and about 200 fans managed to get into the garage with them. They then had to throw the fans out one by one before The Beatles could go to their rooms.

→ After this incident John lost his temper and refused to play any more unless more police were provided. Auckland Chief Constable, Superintendent Quinn, had initially refused a police escort for The Beatles between their hotel and the Town Hall because:

"We provide such escorts only

John: "I knew before he opened his mouth where he was from because I knew nobody else would be climbing up eight floors...
I gave him a drink because he deserved one and then I took him around to see the others."

for royalty and other important visitors."

This smug attitude by the authorities caused problems throughout New Zealand.

26 June

→ Town Hall, Dunedin, South Island, NZ. (Two sets)

→ The local police only allocated three policemen to control the thousands of fans who gathered outside the New City Hotel. When they arrived the police had only left a three-foot hole in their barrier outside the hotel through which The Beatles literally had to fight their way as fans easily overwhelmed the three Dunedin constables. Paul's face was scratched and John lost some of his hair as Mal and Neil fought back the crowd to get the group through. John Lennon's expressed opinion of the Dunedin local authorities was rich

Buy Me Love', 'A Hard Day's Night'
(by George Martin & Orchestra).

27 June

→ Majestic Theatre, Christchurch, South Island, NZ. (Two sets)

→ A crowd of 5,000 fans turned out to watch the group land and drive to the Clarendon Hotel in the city centre. The first incident of egg throwing occurred when the Beatles made a balcony appearance.

28 June

→ The group flew to Brisbane, via Auckland and Sydney. They arrived in Sydney on a TEAL flight at 9:35 pm. A crowd of 4,000 fans watched them walk a short distance to their chartered Ansett ANA Fokker Friendship aircraft and half an hour later they were gone.

29 June

→ The Beatles arrived in Brisbane just after midnight where 8,000 fans were waiting. The group were driven past the crowd in an open-topped truck. Eggs and other missiles were thrown though most landed away from The Beatles.

→ Festival Hall, Brisbane. Two houses of 5,500 each. That night The Beatles and 20 Brisbane girls partied till the early hours, dancing to Motown records.

30 June

→ Festival Hall, Brisbane. (Two sets)

1 July

→ Early in the morning a Rolls Royce delivered the group to Brisbane airport to catch a plane for Sydney. Then began the long Qantas-V flight home, refuelling in Singapore – where Paul and Ringo disembarked to wave to the 600 waiting fans – and Frankfurt.

2 July

→ The Beatles arrived at Heathrow Airport, London, at 11.10 am.

→ Paul played piano and John observed as Cilla Black recorded 'It's For You' at Abbey Road.

3 July

→ Former Beatles drummer Pete Best

A Hard Day's Night film premiere: 6 July

The Beatles and their wives and girlfriends were present at the royal gala world premiere of *A Hard Day's Night*, attended by Princess Margaret and her husband Lord Snowdon, at the London Pavilion. 12,000 fans filled Piccadilly Circus, which had been closed to traffic for the occasion, hoping just for a glimpse of The Beatles.

Afterwards, The Beatles and their guests, including the royal party, adjourned to the Dorchester Hotel for a champagne supper party. Brian Jones and Keith Richards of the Rolling Stones were initially refused admittance. The group ended the night at the Ad Lib Club, staying there long enough to read the reviews of *A Hard Day's Night* in the first editions of the morning papers.

and colourful and he refused to attend the afternoon's press conference.

→ The album *A Hard Day's Night (Original Soundtrack Album)* was released in the US as United Artists UAS 6366. Side A: 'A Hard Day's Night', 'Tell Me Why', 'I'll Cry Instead', 'I Should Have Known Better' (by George Martin & Orchestra), 'I'm Happy Just To Dance With You', 'And I Love Her' (by George Martin & Orchestra); Side B: 'I Should Have Known Better', 'If I Fell', 'And I Love Her', 'Ringo's Theme (This Boy)' (by George Martin & Orchestra), 'Can't released his single, 'I'm Gonna Knock On Your Door' by The Pete Best Four.

6 July
→ The single 'Ain't She Sweet'/ 'Nobody's Child' by The Beatles on the A-side and Tony Sheridan & The Beatles on the B-side was released in the US as Atco 6308.

7 July
→ Ringo's 24th birthday. The Beatles mimed 'A Hard Day's Night', 'Things We Said Today' and 'Long Tall Sally' for BBC TV's *Top Of The Pops* at Lime Grove Studios, London.
→ After this, they went to Rediffusion's studios at Television House to record an interview about the film, which was broadcast that evening on Granada Television's *Scene At 6:30*.
→ John was interviewed by journalist Chris Hutchins about *A Hard Day's Night* for the BBC Light Programme's *The Teen Scene*.

10 July
→ 3,000 screaming fans were waiting in the bright sunshine at Speke Airport when The Beatles flew from London to attend the Northern premiere of *A Hard Day's Night* and appear as guests of honour at a civic reception. After struggling through the crowd of photographers, The Beatles held a brief press conference.

They were then driven to the Town Hall in a police cavalcade led by motorcycle police, while an estimated 200,000 people (a quarter of the entire population of Liverpool) lined the route, restrained by hundreds of police officers. On a dozen occasions the screaming girls managed to break through the police cordons and bring their motorcade to a screeching halt.
→ The Beatles arrived at the Town Hall at 6.55 pm, 25 minutes behind schedule, where an estimated 20,000 fans had gathered to see them. They were welcomed by Elizabeth 'Bessie' Braddock, MP for Liverpool's Exchange Division, wearing her Cavern Club membership badge.

younger brethren in the stalls for a night out with the city's favourite sons."

→ After the premiere, the group returned by limousine to Speke Airport, for another round of civic ceremonies, and finally the return flight to London.

→ BBC1's *Look North* news programme broadcast part of their press conference and an interview with the group conducted by Gerald Harrison.

→ Granada Televsion's *Scene At 6:30* broadcast their own interview, done at the airport, as well as film of the balcony ceremony.

→ The single 'A Hard Day's Night'/ 'Things We Said Today' was released in the UK as Parlophone R 5160.

→ The album *A Hard Day's Night* was released in the UK as Parlophone PCS 3058. Side A: 'A Hard Day's Night', 'I Should Have Known Better', 'If I Fell', 'I'm Happy Just To Dance With You', 'And I Love Her', 'Tell Me Why', 'Can't Buy Me Love'; Side B: Any Time At All', 'I'll Cry Instead', 'Things We Said Today', 'When I Get Home', 'You Can't Do That', 'I'll Be Back'.

11 July

→ The Beatles flew from Liverpool to London in the early hours of the morning to appear live on ABC TV's *Lucky Stars (Summer Spin)*. They mimed to 'A Hard Day's Night', 'Long Tall Sally', 'Things We Said Today' and 'You Can't Do That'. The appearance took place at ABC's Teddington Film Studios, where hundreds of fans were awaiting their arrival by boat which was documented by photographer John 'Hoppy' Hopkins.

12 July

→ Hippodrome Theatre, Brighton.

13 July

→ The single 'A Hard Day's Night'/'I Should Have Known Better' was released in the US as Capitol 5222.

14 July

→ Broadcasting House, Portland Place, London, to appear on the first edition of *Top Gear*, the BBC's new rock programme. The Beatles played 'Long Tall Sally', 'Things We Said Today', 'A

After a meal The Beatles and the Mayor and Mayoress made an appearance on the balcony overlooking Castle Street to be greeted by screaming crowds and the Liverpool City Police Band playing 'Can't Buy Me Love'. John enlivened proceedings by making a series of Hitler salutes to the crowd.

→ The Lord Mayor presented them with the keys to the city.

→ John was quoted in the *Liverpool Echo* as saying,

→ Shortly before 9 pm they left in an Austin Princess limousine for the Odeon Cinema for the charity premiere of *A Hard Day's Night*. The *Echo* said,

"The Odeon Cinema last night had more of the atmosphere of a big family show than a glittering premiere. It was an occasion when the distinguished relatives in the dress circle joined their

"This is the proudest moment of our lives. We never expected so many people would turn out. We thought there would only be a few people standing on the odd street corner."

Opposite: The Beatles record a radio session for the BBC in July.
Below: The Beatles rehearsing with fellow guest Zsa Zsa Gabor for The Night Of A Hundred Stars spectacular, 23 July.

Hard Day's Night', 'And I Love Her', 'I Should Have Known Better', 'If I Fell' and 'You Can't Do That'.

→ Paul was interviewed by Michael Smee for the BBC Overseas Service programme *Highlight*.

15 July
→ John and Cynthia bought 'Kenwood' in St. George's Hill, Surrey. The mock-Tudor mansion in a private estate next to the golf course cost him £20,000, and allowed the couple to escape from their virtual imprisonment at their Kensington flat, which had been under constant siege from fans and the media.

17 July
→ The Beatles recorded their fourth bank holiday special *From Us To You* for the BBC Light Programme. They played 'Long Tall Sally', 'If I Fell', 'I'm Happy Just To Dance With You', 'Things We Said Today', 'I Should Have Known Better', 'Boys', 'Kansas City'/'Hey-Hey-Hey-Hey'. John read the closing credits.

18 July
→ The Beatles flew to Blackpool to spend the day rehearsing for the next day's live broadcast of Mike and Bernie Winters' *Big Night Out* from the ABC Theatre, Blackpool.

19 July
→ ABC Theatre, Blackpool.
→ The Beatles appeared in a live transmission of Mike and Bernie Winters' *Big Night Out*. They played 'A Hard Day's Night', 'And I Love Her', 'If I Fell', 'Things We Said Today' and 'Long Tall Sally' as well as participating in various sketches with Mike and Bernie.

20 July
→ The single 'I'll Cry Instead'/'I'm Happy Just To Dance With You' was released in the US as Capitol 5234.
→ The single 'And I Love Her'/'If I Fell' was released in the US as Capitol 5235.
→ The album *Something New* was released in the US as Capitol ST 2108. Side A: 'I'll Cry Instead', 'Things We Said Today', 'Any Time At All', 'When I Get Home', 'Slow Down', 'Matchbox'; Side B: 'Tell Me Why', 'And I Love Her', 'I'm Happy Just To Dance With

You', 'If I Fell', 'Komm, Gib Mir Deine Hand'.

23 July
→ The Night Of A Hundred Stars, London Palladium, with Judy Garland, Sir Laurence Olivier, et al. The Beatles took part in a sketch and played a brief set for this benefit concert in aid of the Combined Theatrical Charities Appeals Council.

25 July
→ BBC Television Centre, Shepherd's Bush. George and Ringo each taped appearances as members of the *Juke Box Jury* panel.

26 July
→ Opera House, Blackpool.

28 July
→ The Beatles flew to Stockholm, Sweden, on the 11:10 am flight from Heathrow Airport, London. Despite the fact that Arlanda airport was situated more than 25 miles from the centre of Stockholm, more than 3,000 fans assembled to welcome the group to Sweden.
→ Johanneshovs Isstadion, Stockholm. The group did two houses each night in the ice hockey stadium.

29 July
→ Johanneshovs Isstadion, Stockholm.

30 July
→ The Beatles flew from Stockholm back to London, arriving mid-afternoon.

2 August
→ Gaumont Cinema, Bournemouth.

3 August
→ Beatles producer George Martin released an album of instrumental interpretations of The Beatles' music, *Off The Beatle Track*.

9 August
→ Futurist Theatre, Scarborough.

10 August
→ The single 'Do You Want To Know A Secret?'/'Thank You Girl' was released in the US as Oldies 45 OL 149.

Above and following pages: Scenes from The Beatles' first concert tour of America, August-September.

→ The single 'Please Please Me'/'From Me To You' was released in the US as Oldies 45 OL 150.
→ The single 'Love Me Do'/'P.S. I Love You' was released in the US as Oldies 45 OL 151.
→ The single 'Twist And Shout'/ 'There's A Place' was released in the US as Oldies 45 OL 152.

11 August
→ Abbey Road. The Beatles began work on what was to be the *Beatles For Sale* album, recording 'Baby's In Black'.

12 August
→ The film *A Hard Day's Night* opened simultaneously in 500 American cinemas.
→ Ringo was interviewed by Chris Hutchins for the BBC Light Programme's *The Teen Scene*, during one of Brian Epstein's 'At Home' parties at his flat in Whaddon House, William Mews. All four Beatles attended the party, alongside Judy Garland, members of The Rolling Stones, Cilla Black and Lionel Bart.

14 August
→ Abbey Road. The Beatles worked on 'I'm A Loser', 'Mr Moonlight' and 'Leave My Kitten Alone', which was not officially released until the 1995 *Anthology 1* CD.

16 August
→ Opera House, Blackpool.
→ Among the support acts were The Who, then known as The High Numbers, and The Kinks, who had just released 'You Really Got Me'.

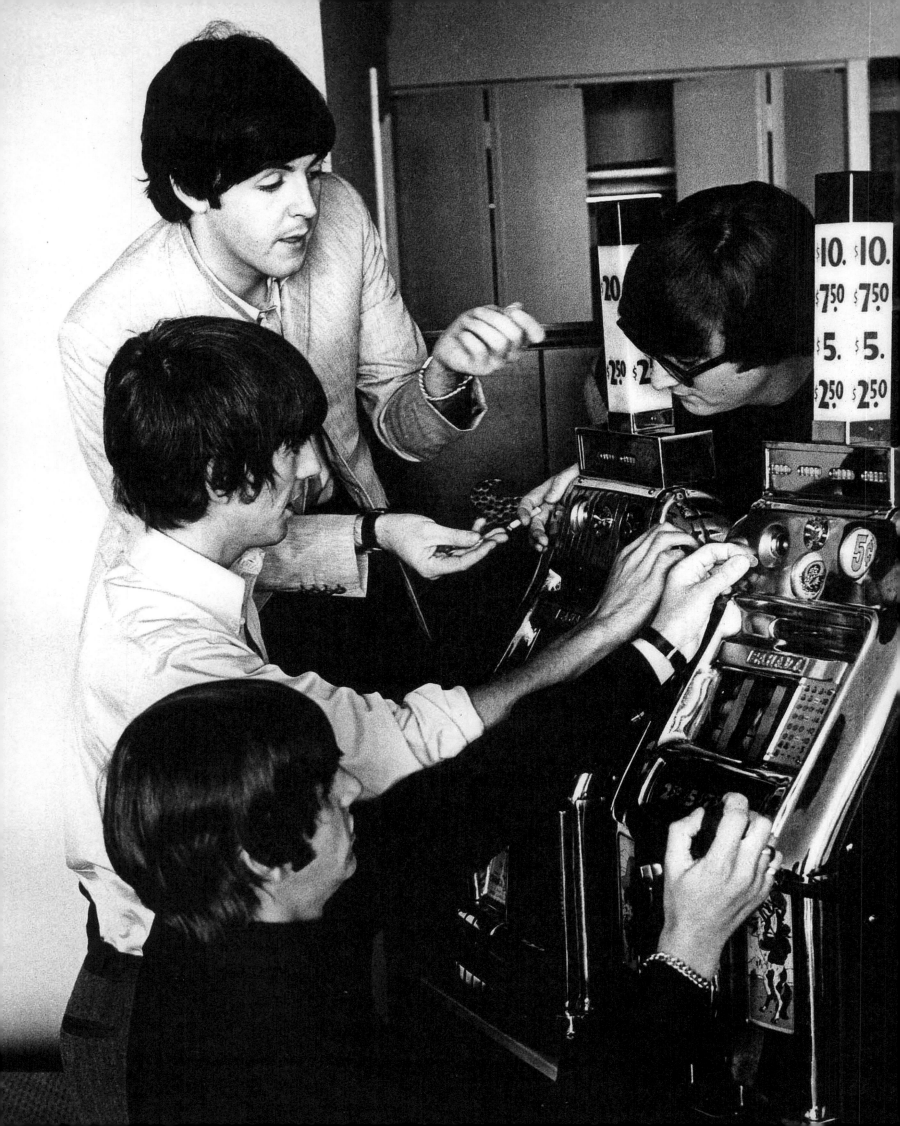

1964

morning in their penthouse suite on the 18th floor of the hotel while fans attempted to scale the walls, climb the garbage shoot and use the freight elevator. The group left for the 8,000-seater Convention Center at 2:30 for a soundcheck. The afternoon show opened at 4 pm but it was not until 5:30 that The Beatles took the stage. After the concert the police used brutal tactics to force the fans away from the backstage exit when The Beatles departed.

21 August
→ Seattle Center Coliseum, Seattle, Washington.
→ The Beatles stayed at the Edgewater Inn. When the group hit the stage at 9:25 pm, all 14,720 girls in the audience seemed to have brought their cameras. The auditorium was illuminated with sheet lightning from the flash bulbs. The Beatles played their final note, dropped their instruments, leaped to the back of the stage and out through the door. Hundreds of teenagers swept down the ramps straight into the cordon of United States Navy officers, standing with locked arms. The car that was to have taken The Beatles back to the hotel was so badly damaged by fans that it had to be abandoned and it was another hour before the crowds had thinned enough for the group to be spirited out of the building in an ambulance.

August 19
→ Cow Palace, San Francisco, California, with The Bill Black Combo, The Exciters, The Righteous Brothers and Jackie DeShannon.
→ The Beatles standard set for the tour was 'Twist And Shout', 'You Can't Do That', 'All My Loving', She Loves You', Things We Said Today', Roll Over Beethoven', 'Can't Buy Me Love', 'If I Fell', 'I Want To Hold Your Hand', 'Boys', 'A Hard Day's Night' and 'Long Tall Sally'. Sometimes they would open with 'I Saw Her Standing There' and close with 'Twist And Shout'.
→ The Beatles played a total of 29 minutes. The gross was $91,670, the net take $49,800. They left behind an astonished populace; 17,130 delirious fans, 19 schoolgirls so overcome with emotion that first aid was necessary with one boy suffering a dislocated shoulder.
→ On the 15th floor of the hotel, 35 girls were rounded up all together trying to sneak past the guards. Some of the girls were dressed as maids. The Beatles did not stay to party, but flew straight to their next venue instead.

20 August
→ At one am, The Beatles' chartered plane touched down at Old McCarran Field in Las Vegas, Nevada. The Beatles were promptly driven to the Sahara Hotel where, despite a curfew, 2,000 fans were waiting to scream a welcome. The fans were dispersed by police using dogs. The group spent the

Beatles US tour starts: 18 August

The Beatles flew from London to start their 25-date North American tour. Their Clipper took them first to Winnipeg, Canada, where 500 fans stood screaming on the airport roof as the group did a couple of 'Hello America' radio interviews from the steps of the plane. The plane stopped again in Los Angeles, where there were 2,000 fans and even more interviews. Finally, at 6:24 pm The Beatles touched down at San Francisco International Airport to mass hysteria from 9,000 screaming West Coast fans.

Opposite: The Beatles try their luck with the one-armed-bandits at The Sahara Hotel, Las Vegas, 20 August.

22 August
→ Empire Stadium, Vancouver, British Columbia, Canada.
→ The show began at 8:14 and The Beatles came on at 9:23. Their exit was timed to perfection. They completed 'Long Tall Sally', bowed low while unstrapping their guitars, bolted from the stage into waiting limousines and with motorcycle outriders, they were out of the stadium fewer than 30 seconds from their last note. The Beatles drove straight to the airport where they caught a plane to Los Angeles.
→ Thousands of teenagers left their seats and rushed the stage, crushing hundreds of young girls against the restraining fence. Dozens of girls suffered broken ribs and hundreds were treated for hysteria and shock.

23 August

→ The Hollywood Bowl, Hollywood, California.

→ 18,700 people filled the Bowl, which sold out four months earlier, for their concert, which was recorded for posterity by a team of engineers representing Capitol Records. Outside 600 teenagers who were unable to get tickets shrieked, shouted and pushed to get in. Police made several arrests. A car was parked alongside the stage in which the group made their getaway as the concert ended at 10 pm.

→ The Beatles stayed in a rented house at 356 St. Pierre Road, in Brown Canyon, Bel Air. That night, West Los Angeles police took more than 50 adolescents into technical custody for violating a 10 pm curfew as over 400 fans milled around at the junction of Sunset Boulevard and Bel Air Road hoping to see The Beatles. St. Pierre Road itself was blocked by police. Over $5,000 worth of damage was done to shrubs and flowers by the fans and many residents turned on their sprinkler systems to try and ward off the teenagers but to no avail.

24 August

→ The single 'Slow Down'/'Matchbox' was released in the US as Capitol 5255.

25 August

→ That evening John and Jayne Manfield went to the Whiskey A-Go-Go. When no-one could see, Jayne put her hand on John's thigh and startled him.

26 August

→ Red Rocks Amphitheater, Denver, Colorado.

→ Though 2,000 seats remained empty, the 7,000 fans who bought tickets created a box-office record for this open-air stadium.

27 August

→ Cincinnati Gardens, Cincinnati, Ohio.

→ Of the 17,000 in the audience, girls fainted and one went into convulsions. As usual, the show itself was drowned out by screaming. The Beatles ran from the stage, straight to their Cadillac limousines and headed to Lunken Airport where their chartered plane

was waiting to take them to New York. They took off shortly after midnight.

28 August

→ Forest Hills Tennis Stadium, Forest Hills, New York.

→ When the Beatles' plane touched down at 3:02 am at Kennedy Airport, 3,000 fans were waiting for them, and another few hundred were stationed outside The Delmonico, at Park Avenue and 59th Street, where they were staying, even though their hotel was supposed to be a secret. By the next morning there were thousands of fans outside, who stayed there until 4 am. Many of them carried portable radios tuned in to various Beatles stations. The girls were restrained by police barricades erected on the other side of Park Avenue, but anyone appearing at a window caused screams and chaos as the girls spilled out into the street, disrupting the traffic. Police used bullhorns to ask hotel guests to stay away from the windows. The crowd was encouraged by radio reporters who thrust microphones in front of their faces and yelled, - - - - - -

"Okay, let's hear it for The Beatles!"

→ The stadium's 15,983 seats were sold out and extra field seats were added at $6.50 each, a steep price in those days. The fans were kept from The Beatles by an eight-feet-high fence topped with barbed wire. The group flew to the stadium by helicopter from the Wall Street heliport.

→ Bob Dylan, accompanied by journalist Al Aronowitz, visited the group at their hotel after the show, and turned The Beatles and Brian Epstein on to marijuana for the first time.

30 August

→ Convention Hall, Atlantic City, New Jersey.

→ The Beatles stayed at the Lafayette Motel in Atlantic City. At 2:15 pm, in order to get through the crowds of fans, the group had to sneak out of the motel in the back of a fish truck. Six miles west of Atlantic City they transferred to the tour bus which took them straight to the Philadelphia Convention Hall.

31 August

→ The group spent their rest day holed up at the Lafayette Motel.

2 September

→ Convention Hall, Philadelphia, Pennsylvania, before an audience of 13,000.

3 September

→ State Fair Coliseum, Indianapolis, Indiana.

→ The Beatles spent two nights in Indianapolis in all, staying at the Speedway Motel on West 16th Street. When The Beatles boarded their chartered plane at Weir Cook Municipal Airport, they were $85,231.93 the richer. ($1,719.02 had already been deducted for state gross income tax. There was some debate in the press as to whether The Beatles (NEMS Ltd) counted as a foreign corporation – if not, then they owed the federal government a further $42,000.)

4 September

→ Milwaukee Auditorium, Milwaukee, Wisconsin.

5 September

→ International Amphitheater, Chicago, Illinois.

→ The Beatles' plane flew into the rarely used Midway Airport an hour late. They were due at 3:40 pm but by the time they arrived over 5,000 fans were waiting for them. The girls were kept behind a chain-link fence as the group were bundled into a long black limousine and roared off to the Stock Yard Inn attached to the amphitheater at 42nd Street and Halsted. The crowds outside were so thick that the group had to enter through the kitchens.

→ After the show, The Beatles hurried into waiting cars and drove straight back to the airport where they flew on to Detroit. A police guard was mounted on their hotel room to prevent fans from tearing it apart for souvenirs.

6 September

→ Olympic Stadium, Detroit, Michigan.

→ Two shows in the home of Tamla Motown. The sheets used by The Beatles at the Whittier Hotel in Detroit were bought by a radio station, cut into thousands of small squares, and then sold to avid fans.

7 September

→ Maple Leaf Gardens, Toronto, Canada.

→ The Beatles flew in on board their charter Electra and parked at the old airport terminal. The first people on board were two immigration nurses who were only interested in getting the group's autographs. They were followed by an immigration officer who had the same thought in mind. George told a reporter from the *Toronto Daily Star,*

→ When travelling into the city the group barely made it inside the King Edward Hotel. Paul's shirt was ripped and torn:

"I thought I was for it, but an immense copper lifted me up and shoved me into the elevator."

John: "The best view of the country is over the blue shoulder of a policeman."

→ There were 35,522 paying customers at the two shows, which resulted in a

"We don't like being asked for autographs by the officials. Everywhere we go it's always the police guarding us, or the journalists or the relatives of the promoters who ask us to sign."

cheque for $93,000 for the group. Some 4,000 men and women police and Mounties were on duty at the Maple Leaf Gardens and a five block area around the Gardens was roped off and patrolled for 12 hours before the group was due to arrive.

8 September

→ The Forum, Montreal, Quebec, Canada. The two shows were seen by 21,000 fans.

1964

9 September
→ The Beatles' plane was re-routed by Hurricane Dora, and landed instead at Key West at 3:30 am. Even in the middle of the night hundreds of teenagers were waiting to scream a welcome.

10 September
→ During their rest day, The Beatles played a jam session at their hotel with New Orleans R&B star Clarence 'Frogman' Henry, and members of The Bill Black Combo and The Exciters.

11 September
→ The Gator Bowl, Jacksonville, Florida.
→ In Jacksonville the band had a hard time reaching The Gator Bowl. Two dozen police battled about 500 Beatles fans for 15 minutes in the George Washington hotel's parking garage trying to get The Beatles out of the elevator and into their limousine. It took the group 15 minutes to move 25 feet. Eventually the police drove a flying wedge through the crowd with motorcycle outriders and managed to transfer the group to their trailer at the Gator Bowl by 7:15.
→ Despite the screaming girls, The Beatles had to refuse to go on until newsreel and television cameramen had left the arena. Newsreel footage, and particularly footage of the group playing, was a valuable commodity and the cameramen refused to leave. Eventually Derek Taylor issued an ultimatum.

"The Beatles are 100 feet away," he said. **"They came thousands of miles to be here. The only thing preventing their appearance is cine cameramen."**

He said that the film made as newsreels was ultimately sold and shown in cinemas with no royalties paid to The Beatles.
→ Police officers physically restrained eight cameramen, covered their camera lenses with their hands and led them by the arm from the performance area.

12 September
→ Boston Garden, Boston, Massachusetts.

13 September
→ Civic Center, Baltimore, Maryland.

14 September
→ Civic Arena, Pittsburgh, Pennsylvania.
→ The Beatles' Lockheed Electra arrived at Greater Pittsburgh Airport half an hour late at 4:36 pm to the screams of 4,000 fans, mostly girls, some of whom had been waiting since 9:00 am. 5,000 fans surrounded the Civic Arena where The Beatles gave a press conference, then ate a catered meal before showtime.

15 September
→ Public Hall, Cleveland, Ohio.
→ The Beatles stayed at the Sheraton-Cleveland which, as usual, was inundated with fans. On Public Square outside the only time the police cordons broke was when The Beatles appeared at a window and waved. Traffic was restricted to one mile an hour in case fans surged forward.
→ Shortly after The Beatles took the stage, a great wave of teenagers began pushing to the front, slowly taking the police line with them. More than 100 police leaned into the crowd but they were steadily forced back towards the stage, threatening the safety of the group. Inspector Michael Blackwell and Deputy Inspector Carl C. Bare panicked and decided to stop the show.
→ Bare charged out of the wings onto the stage, shouldered The Beatles aside, grabbed a microphone and bellowed,

"Sit down! The show is over!"

The Beatles, however, were in the middle of 'All My Loving' and carried on playing. Bare turned and walked towards John, who instead of stopping, did a little dance and made a face at him. Then Inspector Blackwell came storming out, gesturing to the group to get off the stage. He grabbed George by the elbow and steered him to the wings. George turned on him,

The crowd shouted in protest but the music stopped and The Beatles slowly left the stage. The steel safety curtain came down and Blackwell and Bare stared down the booing fans.

"What the hell do you think you are doing? Get your hands off me!"

Opposite: 'Sheriff McCartney', Dallas, 18 September.
Below: The Beatles backstage with Clarence 'Frogman' Henry (third left) and press agent Derek Taylor (far right), New Orleans, 16 September.

"This had never happened to us before," said John. "These policemen are a bunch of amateurs."

After lecturing the audience, Blackwell allowed the show to continue after a 10-minute delay, but only on condition that the audience remained in their seats and that the house lights stayed up.

16 September
→ City Park Stadium, New Orleans, Louisiana.
→ At the concert some 700 teenagers broke away from the stand and attempted to crash through the barriers keeping them from the stage. It took 225 New Orleans police more than 20 minutes to restore order. Mounted police patrolled the area around the stage while the fans who broke through onto the football field were roped off to one side. More than 200 collapsed and had to be revived with smelling salts.

17 September
→ Municipal Stadium, Kansas City, Missouri.
→ The Beatles added 'KansasCity'/ 'Hey-Hey-Hey-Hey' to their repertoire, which the local fans loved. Excitement ran so high that the concert had to be stopped, with a threat of cancellation, if the audience did not calm down. They did and The Beatles played on.
→ The Muehlebach Towers sold the group's bed linen – 16 sheets and eight pillow cases – to a Chicago man for $750. As in Detroit a few days earlier, these were later chopped into small pieces and turned into instant souvenirs.

18 September
→ Memorial Coliseum, Dallas, Texas.

20 September
→ Paramount Theater, Broadway, NewYork City, 'An Evening With The Beatles' with Steve Lawrence and Eydie Gorme.
→ One of the few charity concerts The Beatles gave - on behalf of the United Cerebral Palsy Fund of New York - this performance was attended by 3,682 members of society, who paid up to $100 a ticket.

21 September
→ The Beatles' Flight BA 510 landed at Heathrow Airport, London, at 9:30 pm by which time thousands of fans had gathered on the roof of the Queen's Building to greet them.

27 September
→ Prince Of Wales Theatre, London. Ringo acted as one of a panel of celebrity judges in the final of the National Beat Group Competition, a charity event in aid of Oxfam. The second half of the show was broadcast live by BBC2 as *It's Beat Time*.

29-30 September
→ Abbey Road. The Beatles recorded 'Every Little Thing', 'I Don't Want To Spoil The Party' and 'What You're Doing'.

1 October
→ Vee Jay Records re-released the *Introducing The Beatles* LP alongside a collection of hits by The Four Seasons, as part of a two-record package, imaginatively titled *The Beatles Vs. The Four Seasons* (VJDX 30).

2 October
→ Rehearsals at the Granville Theatre, Fulham, for the American TV show *Shindig!* produced by Jack Good, also featuring Sandie Shaw among others.
→ That evening Paul attended an Alma Cogan recording session, playing tambourine on the track 'I Knew Right Away' (the B-side of her single 'It's You').

3 October
→ *Shindig!* was recorded live before a lively audience of Beatles Fan Club members at the Granville Theatre, Fulham. The Beatles performed 'Kansas City'/'Hey-Hey-Hey-Hey', 'I'm A Loser' and 'Boys'. They also took part in the finale with the Karl Denver Trio.

5 October
→ The *Ain't She Sweet* album is released in the US as Atco SD 33-169. Despite being credited to The Beatles, it actually contains eight songs by The Swallows, and only four of The Beatles' Hamburg recordings, 'Ain't She Sweet', 'Sweet Georgia Brown', 'Take Out Some Insurance On Me Baby' and 'Nobody's Child'.

Opposite: Ciggie break during rehearsals for *Shindig!* TV show, 3 October.

6 October
→ Abbey Road. The entire session was spent recording 'Eight Days A Week'.

8 October
→ Abbey Road. The Beatles recorded Paul's 'She's A Woman', which he had begun to write that morning and then finished before leaving for the studio.

9 October
→ Gaumont Cinema, Bradford.
→ Opening night of The Beatles' autumn British tour on John's 24th birthday. The group were delayed by heavy traffic and by police on the A1 who flagged them down in order to get autographs, which caused them to arrive in Bradford two hours late. Also on the bill were The Rustiks, Sounds Incorporated, Michael Haslam, The Remo Four, Tommy Quickly and Mary Wells. The MC was Bob Bain.
→ The Beatles' set for this tour consisted of 'Twist And Shout', 'Money (That's What I Want)', 'Can't Buy Me Love', 'Things We Said Today', 'I'm Happy Just To Dance With You', 'I Should Have Known Better', 'If I Fell', 'I Wanna Be Your Man', 'A Hard Day's Night' and 'Long Tall Sally'. 60 police guarded the stage area, and there were 40 firemen and 60 St John Ambulance men and nurses on hand to deal with fainting fans.
→ The four-week tour itinerary took them to: 10 October: De Montfort Hall, Leicester; 11 October: Odeon Cinema, Birmingham; 13 October: ABC Cinema,Wigan; 14 October: ABC Cinema, Ardwick, Manchester; 15 October: Globe Theatre, Stockton-on-Tees; 16 October: ABC Cinema, Hull; 19 October: ABC Cinema, Edinburgh; 20 October: Caird Hall, Dundee; 21 October: Odeon Cinema, Glasgow; October 22: Odeon Cinema, Leeds; 23 October: Gaumont State Cinema, Kilburn; 24 October: Granada Cinema, Walthamstow, London; 25 October: Hippodrome Theatre, Brighton; 28 October: ABC Cinema, Exeter; 29 October: ABC Theatre, Plymouth; 30 October: Gaumont Cinema, Bournemouth; 31 October: Gaumont Theatre, Ipswich; 1 November: Astoria Theatre, Finsbury Park, London; 2 November: King's Hall, Belfast; 4

November: Ritz Cinema, Luton; 5 November: Odeon Cinema, Nottingham; 6 November: Gaumont Cinema, Southampton; 7 November: Capitol Cinema, Cardiff; 8 November: Empire Theatre, Liverpool; 9 November: City Hall, Sheffield; 10 November: Colston Hall, Bristol.

12 October
The album *Songs, Pictures And Stories Of The Fabulous Beatles* was released in the US as Vee Jay VJLP 1092. Side A: 'I Saw Her Standing There', 'Misery', 'Anna (Go To Him)', 'Chains', 'Boys', 'Ask Me Why'; Side B: 'Please Please Me', 'Baby, It's You', 'Do You Want To Know A Secret?', 'A Taste Of Honey', 'There's A Place', 'Twist And Shout'.
→ This album, effectively a reissue of *Introducing The Beatles*, brought to an end Vee Jay's merciless recycling of The Beatles' early recordings, which they had now released on five separate LPs.

14 October
→ The group spent the afternoon at Granada Television studios in Manchester miming 'I Should Have Known Better' and conducting an interview for the show *Scene At 6:30*.
→ The Beatles were also interviewed for BBC1 news magazine *Look North*.

18 October
→ Abbey Road. The Beatles finished 'Eight Days A Week'. They then worked on 'Kansas City'/'Hey-Hey-Hey-Hey', followed by 'Mr Moonlight', 'I Feel Fine' and Paul's 'I'll Follow The Sun'. George sang Carl Perkins' 'Everybody's Trying To Be My Baby' which they followed with 'Rock And Roll Music' and 'Words Of Love'.

26 October
→ Abbey Road. Ringo recorded his vocal for 'Honey Don't'. During the evening session, the group recorded some material for their Christmas flexi-disc.

4 November
→ The EP *Extracts From The Film A Hard Day's Night* was released in the UK as Parlophone GEP 8920. Side A: 'I Should Have Known Better', 'If I Fell'; Side B: 'Tell Me Why', 'And I Love Her'.

Left: The Beatles with supporting cast, 'Another Beatles Christmas Show', 24 December.

6 November
→ The Beatles were interviewed for the Southern Television programme *Day By Day*, broadcast that evening.
→ The EP *Extracts From The Film A Hard Day's Night (Volume Two)* was released in the UK as Parlophone GEP 8924. Side A: 'Any Time At All', 'I'll Cry Instead'; Side B: 'Things We Said Today', 'When I Get Home'.

14 November
→ At Television Studios, Teddington, The Beatles recorded a *Thank Your Lucky Stars* show, renamed *Lucky Stars Special* in their honour, presented by Brian Matthew. They mimed to 'I Feel Fine', 'She's A Woman', 'I'm A Loser' and 'Rock And Roll Music'.

16 November
→ The Beatles recorded 'I Feel Fine' and 'I'm A Loser' at Riverside Studios, London, for an edition of BBC TV's *Top Of The Pops*. They mimed to both sides of their new single: 'I Feel Fine' and 'She's A Woman'.

17 November
→ The Beatles recorded a *Top Gear* show for the BBC Light Programme at the Playhouse Theatre, London. They recorded 'I'm A Loser', 'Honey Don't', 'She's A Woman', 'Everybody's Trying To Be My Baby', 'I'll Follow The Sun' and 'I Feel Fine'.

20 November
→ John filmed a surreal film sequence with Dudley Moore and Norman Rossington on Wimbledon Common, to accompany a reading from *In His Own Write* on Moore's new BBC2 programme *Not Only... But Also*.

23 November
→ Wembley studios. A pre-taped appearance on *Ready Steady Go!* to promote The Beatles new recordings. The group mimed to 'I Feel Fine', 'She's A Woman', 'Baby's In Black' and 'Kansas City'/'Hey, Hey, Hey, Hey' and were interviewed by Keith Fordyce and Cathy McGowan.
→ The single 'I Feel Fine'/'She's A Woman' was released in the US as Capitol 5327.
→ The album *The Beatles' Story* was released in the US as Capitol STBO 2222 (a 48-minute documentary double album containing one previously unreleased live cut recorded August 23, 1964 at the Hollywood Bowl). Side A: 'On Stage With The Beatles', 'How Beatlemania Began', 'Beatlemania In Action', 'The Man Behind The Beatles – Brian Epstein', 'John Lennon', 'Who's A Millionaire?'; Side B: 'Beatles Will Be Beatles', 'Man Behind The Music – George Martin', 'George Harrison'; Side C: 'A Hard Day's Night – Their First Movie', 'Paul McCartney', 'Sneaky Haircuts And More About Paul'; Side D: 'Twist And Shout' (live), 'The Beatles Look At Life', 'Victims of Beatlemania', 'Beatle Medley', 'Ringo Starr', 'Liverpool And All The World!'.

25 November
→ The Beatles recorded a Boxing Day special edition of BBC Light Programme's *Saturday Club* show. The broadcast consisted of six songs: 'Rock And Roll Music', 'I'm A Loser', 'Everybody's Trying To Be My Baby', 'I Feel Fine', 'Kansas City'/'Hey-Hey-Hey-Hey' and 'She's A Woman', but four of these, all except 'Rock And Roll Music' and 'Kansas City' were previously recorded versions.

27 November
→ 'I Feel Fine'/'She's A Woman' was released in the UK as Parlophone R 5200.

28 November
→ Chris Hutchins visited John at his home in Weybridge to interview him for the BBC Light Programme's *Teen Scene*.

29 November
→ Before a live TV studio audience, John read from his book *In His Own Write* as part of Dudley Moore's BBC2 programme *Not Only... But Also*.

1-10 December

→ Ringo went into University College Hospital to have his tonsils removed.

4 December

→ *Beatles For Sale* was released in the UK as Parlophone PCS 3062. Side A: 'No Reply', 'I'm A Loser', 'Baby's In Black', 'Rock And Roll Music', 'I'll Follow The Sun', 'Mr Moonlight', 'KansasCity'/'Hey-Hey-Hey-Hey'; Side B: 'Eight Days A Week', 'Words Of Love', 'Honey Don't', 'Every Little Thing', 'I Don't Want To Spoil The Party', 'What You're Doing', 'Everybody's Trying To Be My Baby'.

15 December

→ The album *Beatles '65* was released in the US as Capitol ST 2228. Side A: 'No Reply', 'I'm A Loser', 'Baby's In Black', 'Rock And Roll Music', 'I'll Follow The Sun', 'Mr. Moonlight'; Side B: 'Honey Don't', 'I'll Be Back', 'She's A Woman', 'I Feel Fine', 'Everybody's Trying To Be My Baby'.

18 December

→ The flexi-disc, *Another Beatles' Christmas Record*, was sent out free to members of The Beatles Fan Club.

21-23 December

→ Rehearsals for 'Another Beatles' Christmas Show' at the Hammersmith Odeon.

24, 26, 28-31 December 1964; 1, 2, 4-9, 11-16 January 1965

→ 'Another Beatles' Christmas Show' at the Hammersmith Odeon, London. Chris Dreja (The Yardbirds guitarist): "It was fascinating to observe how the Beatles were basically imprisoned while they were at the Hammersmith Odeon. They couldn't go out so everything had to come to them.

→ "I remember them standing in the back yard there watching as various people from different car companies drove around and John Lennon was saying 'yes' or 'no' to all these Rolls-Royce's and Porsche's that were driving past him in a kind of circus procession.

→ "The other thing I recall is that Paul McCartney kept trying to sell us this song he'd just written but we didn't think it was suited to our style. The song turned out to be 'Yesterday'!"

Another Beatles' Christmas Show: 24 December

The show was compered by Jimmy Savile. The Mike Cotton Sound playing Georgie Fame's 'Yeh, Yeh!' opened. They were joined by Michael Haslem, a Brian Epstein protégé – to sing 'Scarlet Ribbons'. The Yardbirds were followed by a pantomime sketch involving The Beatles dressed as Antarctic explorers looking for the Abominable Snowman, compered by Liverpudlian Ray Fell. So excruciating was this section of the show, both for the group and their fans, that The Beatles resolved never to take part in a similar enterprise again. The first half ended with Freddie and The Dreamers.

The second half opened with Elkie Brooks, followed by Sounds Incorporated, then finally Jimmy Saville introduced The Beatles dressed in blue mohair suits. Their set included 'She's A Woman', 'I'm A Loser', 'Everybody's Trying To Be My Baby', 'Baby's In Black', 'Honey Don't', 'A Hard Day's Night', 'I Feel Fine', with 'Long Tall Sally' as the finale.

Can't Buy Me Love

Words & Music by John Lennon
& Paul McCartney

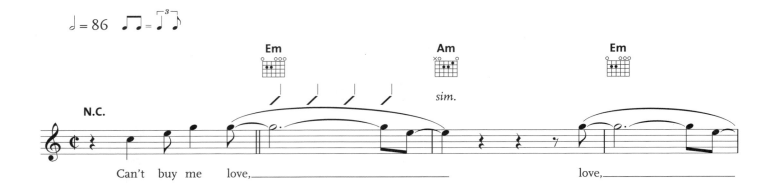

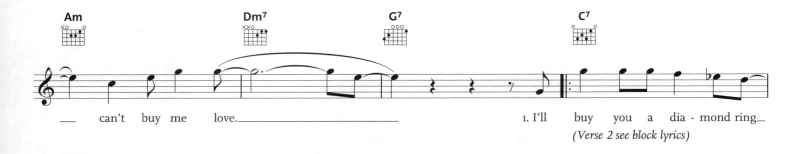

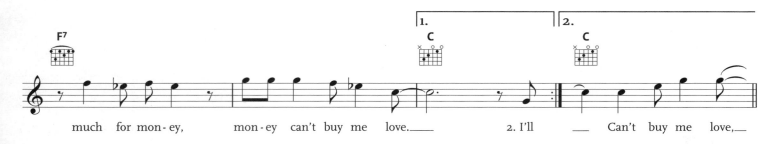

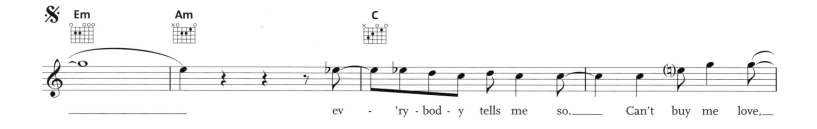

ev - 'ry-bod - y tells me so.___ Can't buy me love,___

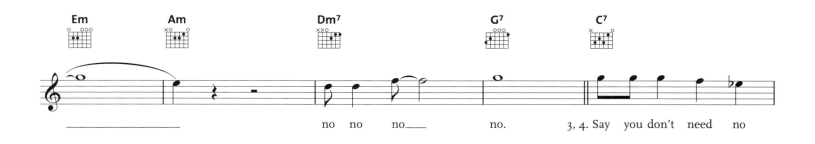

no no no___ no. 3, 4. Say you don't need no

dia-mond rings, and I'll be sat - is - fied.___ Tell___ me that you want the

kind of things that mon - ey just___ can't buy.___ I___ don't care too

To Coda ⊕

much for mon - ey; mon - ey can't buy me love.___

(Guitar solo)

D.S al Coda

Buy me love,____

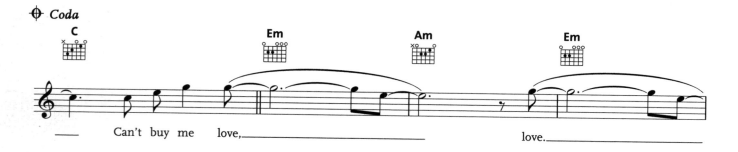

____ Can't buy me love,_____ love._____

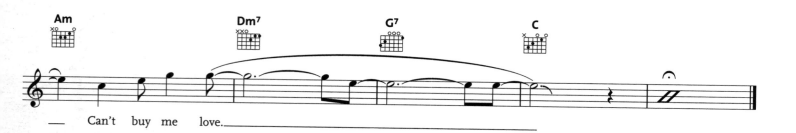

____ Can't buy me love._____

Verse 2:
I'll give you all I've got to give
If you say you love me too.
I may not have a lot to give,
But what I got I'll give to you.
I don't care too much for money,
Money can't buy me love.

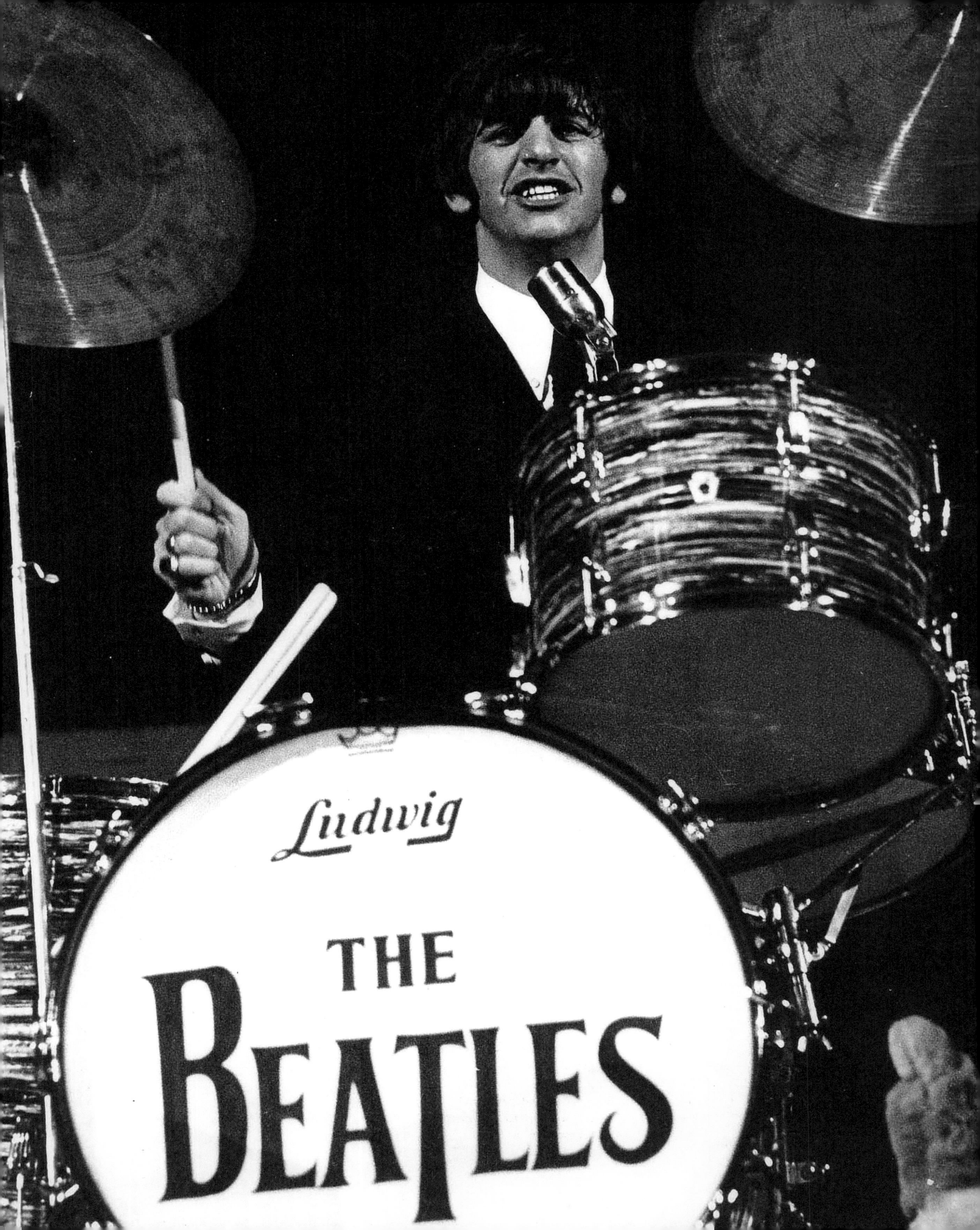
Ludwig
THE
BEATLES

You Can't Do That

Words & Music by John Lennon
& Paul McCartney
© Copyright 1964 Northern Songs.
All Rights Reserved.
International Copyright Secured.

* B major on studio recording in Verse 1

laugh in my face.____ 3. So, please lis-ten to me if you wan-na stay mine.. I can't help my feel-ings, I'll go

out of my mind. I'm gon-na let you down____ (Let you down, and leave you flat.
(Backing vocals)

leave you flat.)____ Be-cause I told you be-fore,__ oh,__ you can't do that.____ *(Guitar)*

To Coda ⊕

You can't do that.____ You

can't do that.____ You can't do that.____ You

can't do that.____ You can't do that.____

D.S. al Coda   ⊕ *Coda*   *rit.*

Ev-'ry-bod-y's green____   that._____   *(Guitar)*

Verse 2:
Well it's the second time I've caught you talking to him.
Do I have to tell you one more time I think it's a sin?
I think I'll let you down and leave you flat.
Because I've told you before,
Oh, you can't do that.

A Hard Day's Night

Words & Music by John Lennon
& Paul McCartney
© Copyright 1964 Northern Songs.
All Rights Reserved.
International Copyright Secured.

1, 3. It's been a hard day's night,___ and I've been work-ing___ like a dog._

(Verse 2 see block lyrics)
(Verse 4: Instrumental for 8 bars)

___ It's been a hard day's night,___ I should be sleep-ing___ like a log._

___ But when I get home to you___ I find the things that you do___ will make me

4. So why on earth should I moan,___ 'cause when I get you a-lone,___ you know I'll

1, 3.
feel___ all right.   2. You know I   (2.) - kay.
be___ o -   4. Instrumental   (4.) - kay.

2, 4.
When I'm home,___

ev - 'ry - thing seems___ to be___ right.   When I'm home,___

feel - ing you hold - ing me tight,   tight,   yeah.___   3. It's been a
                                                                   5. It's been a

hard day's night,____ and I've been work-ing____ like a dog.____

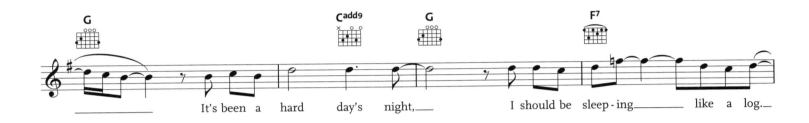

____ It's been a hard day's night,____ I should be sleep-ing____ like a log.____

____ But when I get home to you____ I find the things that you do____ will make me

feel____ all right. You know I feel____ al - right, you know I

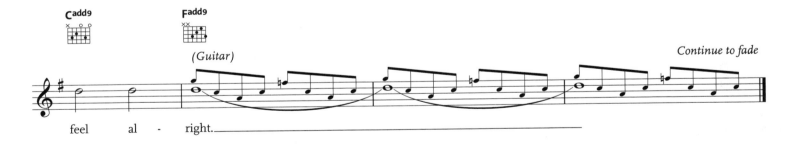

(Guitar)

Continue to fade

feel al - right.____

Verse 2:
You know I work all day,
To get you money to buy you things.
And it's worth it just to hear you say,
You're gonna give me everything.
So why on earth should I moan,
'Cause when I get you alone,
You know I'll feel okay.

If I Fell

Words & Music by John Lennon
& Paul McCartney

♩ = 108

If I fell in love with you, would you prom-ise to be true, and

help me un-der-stand?__ 'Cause I've been in love be-fore and I

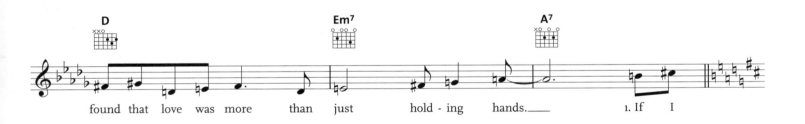

found that love was more than just hold-ing hands.__ 1. If I

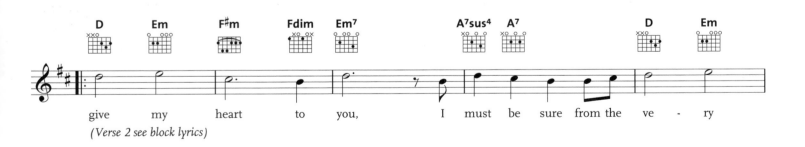

give my heart to you, I must be sure from the ve - ry

(Verse 2 see block lyrics)

1.

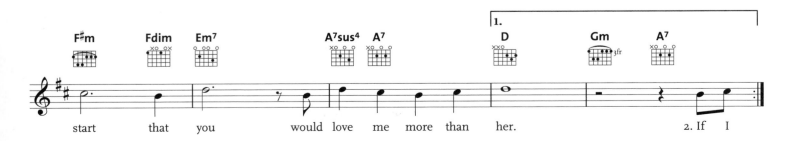

start that you would love me more than her. 2. If I

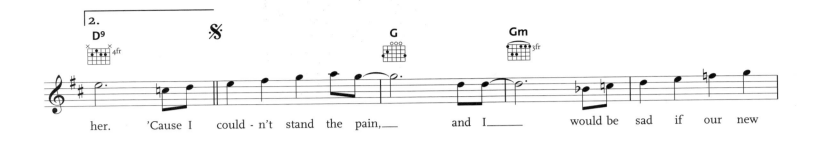

her. 'Cause I could-n't stand the pain,___ and I___ would be sad if our new

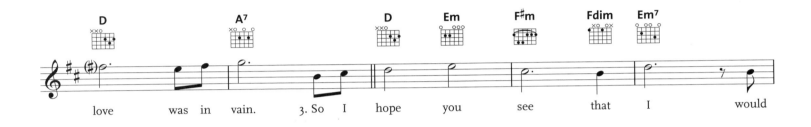

love was in vain. 3. So I hope you see that I would

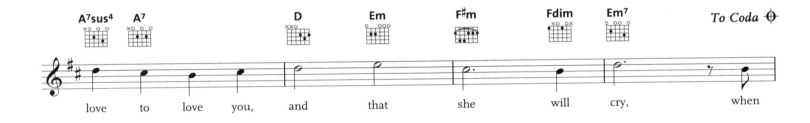

To Coda

love to love you, and that she will cry, when

D.S. al Coda   Coda

she learns we are two.___ 'Cause I   she learns we are two;

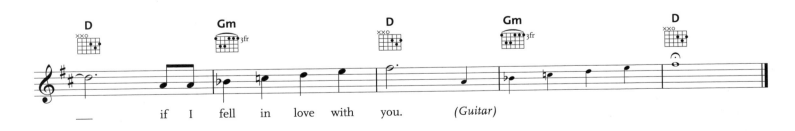

___ if I fell in love with you. *(Guitar)*

Verse 2:
If I trust in you, oh please, don't run and hide;
If I love you too, oh please, don't hurt my pride like her.

And I Love Her

Words & Music by John Lennon
& Paul McCartney
© Copyright 1964 Northern Songs.

(Guitar)

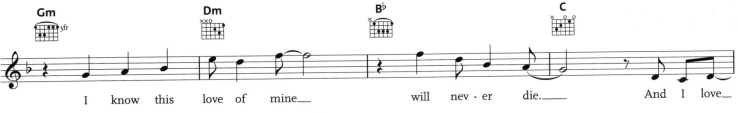

4. Bright are the stars that shine,____ dark is the sky,____

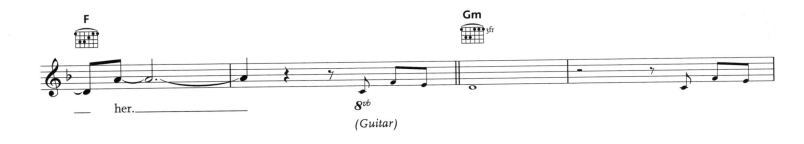

I know this love of mine____ will nev - er die.____ And I love____

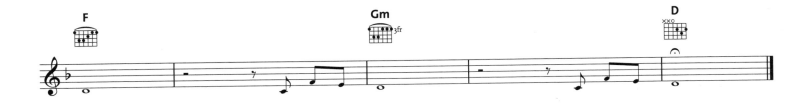

____ her._____

8vb

(Guitar)

Verse 2:
She gives me everything, and tenderly,
The kiss my lover brings, she brings to me.
And I love her.

Verse 3:
Bright are the stars that shine, dark is the sky,
I know this love of mine will never die.
And I love her.

Any Time At All

Words & Music by John Lennon
& Paul McCartney
© Copyright 1964 Northern Songs.
All Rights Reserved.
International Copyright Secured.

A - ny time at all, a - ny time at all, a - ny time at all, all you've got to do is call and I'll be there.

1. If you need some -
(Verse 2 see block lyrics)

- bod - y to love, just look in - to my eyes: I'll be there to make you feel right. If you're feel - ing sor - ry and sad, I'd real - ly sym - path - ise.

Don't you be sad, just call me to - night. A - ny time at

Verse 2:
If the sun has faded away,
I'll try to make it shine;
There is nothing I won't do.
If you need a shoulder to cry on,
I hope it will be mine.
Call me tonight and I'll come to you.

Things We Said Today

Words & Music by John Lennon
& Paul McCartney
© Copyright 1964 Northern Songs.
All Rights Reserved.
International Copyright Secured.

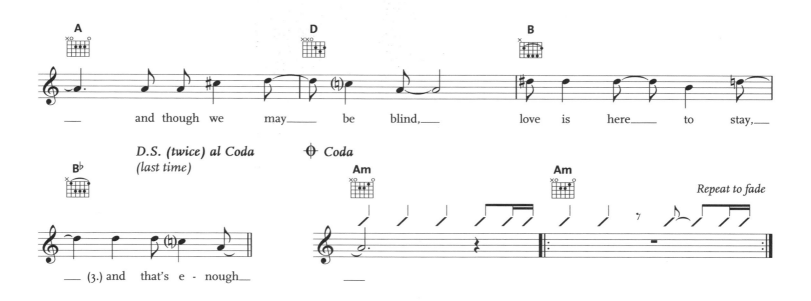

and though we may be blind, love is here to stay,

D.S. (twice) al Coda
(last time)

✛ **Coda**

Repeat to fade

(3.) and that's e - nough

Verse 2:

You say you'll be mine, girl,
'Til the end of time.
These days, such a kind girl
Seems so hard to find.
Someday, when we're dreaming,
Deep in love, not a lot to say,
Then we will remember
Things we said today.

Verses 3 & 4:

...And that's enough to make you mine, girl,
Be the only one.
Love me all the time, girl,
We'll go on and on.
Someday, when we're deaming,
Deep in love, not a lot to say,
Then we will remember
Things we said today.

I'll Be Back

Words & Music by John Lennon
& Paul McCartney
© Copyright 1964 Northern Songs.
All Rights Reserved.
International Copyright Secured.

(Guitar)　　　　　　　　　　　　　　　　　　　　　　　　1. You know,__

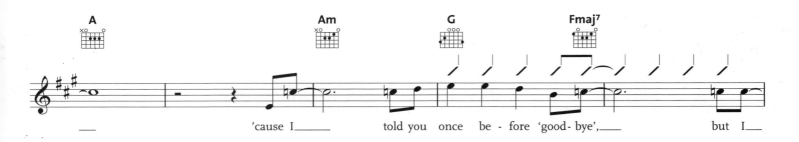

__　if you break my heart I'll go,__　but I'll__ be back a-gain;__

(Verses 2 & 3 see block lyrics)

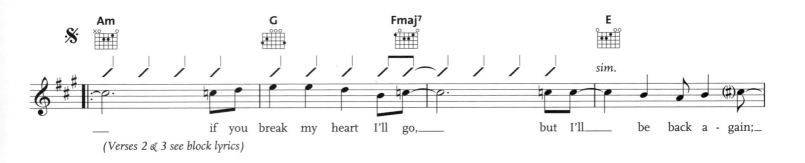

__　'cause I__ told you once be-fore 'good-bye',__　but I__

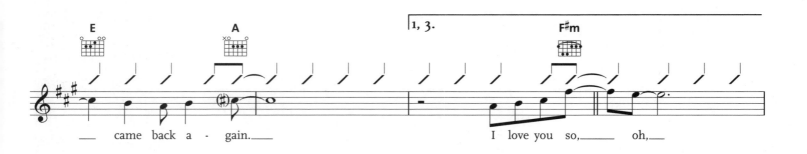

__ came back a-gain.__　I love you so,__ oh,__

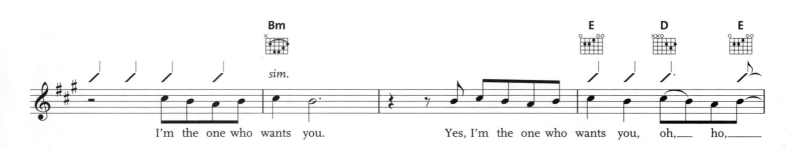

I'm the one who wants you.　　Yes, I'm the one who wants you,　oh,__ ho,__

Verse 2:
Oh, you could find better things to do,
Than to break my heart again.
This time, I will try to show that I'm
Not trying to pretend.

I thought that you would realise...

Verse 3:
Oh, you could find better things to do,
Than to break my heart again.
This time, I will try to show that I'm
Not trying to pretend.
I wanna go, but I hate to leave you,
You know I hate to leave you, oh, ho, oh, ho.

Oh, you, if you break my heart, I'll go,
But I'll be back again.

I Feel Fine

Words & Music by John Lennon
& Paul McCartney
© Copyright 1964 Northern Songs.
All Rights Reserved.
International Copyright Secured.

1. Ba - by's good to me,___ you know, she's hap - py as can be,___ you know, she said___
(Verses 2 & 4 see block lyrics)

___ so; I'm in love___ with her___ and I___ feel___ fine.___

___ I'm so glad that

she's my lit - tle girl;_____ she's so glad, she's

tell - ing all the world___ 3, 5. that her ba - by buys her things,___ you know, he buys___

_her dia - mond rings,___ you know,___ she said___ so;___

To Coda ⊕

(Guitar)

She's in love___ with me___ and I___ feel___ fine.___

(Guitar solo)

N.C.

D.S. al Coda
(without repeat)

⊕ **Coda**

sim.

She's in love___ with me___

___ and I___ feel___ fine.___

(Guitar)

Verses 2 & 4:
Baby says she's mine,
You know, she tells me all the time,
You know, she said so;
I'm in love with her and I feel fine.

She's A Woman

Words & Music by John Lennon
& Paul McCartney
© Copyright 1964 Northern Songs.
All Rights Reserved.
International Copyright Secured.

(Guitar)

(+ rhythm)

1, 3 & 4. My love don't give me pres-ents.
(Verse 2 see block lyrics)

I know that she's no peas-ant.

On-ly ev-er has__ to give__ me love for-ev-er and for-ev-er. My__

__ love__ don't give me pres-ents.

Turn me on___ when I___ get lone - ly; peo - ple tell me that___ she's on - ly

fool - in':___ I know she is - n't.

She's a wo - man who un - der - stands;___

she's a wo - man who loves___ her man.___ Woo,___

(Guitar solo)

woo.

Verse 2:
She don't give boys the eye.
She hates to see me cry.
She is happy just to hear me
Say that I will never leave her.
She don't give boys the eye,
She will never make me jealous;
Gives me all her time as well as
Lovin', don't ask me why.

No Reply

Words & Music by John Lennon
& Paul McCartney
© Copyright 1964 Northern Songs.
All Rights Reserved.
International Copyright Secured.

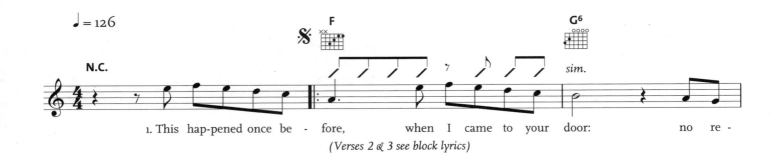

1. This hap-pened once be - fore, when I came to your door: no re -

(Verses 2 & 3 see block lyrics)

- ply._____ They said it was - n't you, but I saw you peep through your

win - dow.___ I saw the light,___ I saw the light;_

___ I know that you saw me, 'cause I looked up to see your

face.___ 2. I tried to tel - e - If I were you, I'd

Verses 2 & 3:
I tried to telephone,
They said you were not home:
That's a lie.
'Cause I know where you've been,
I saw you walk in your door.

I nearly died, I nearly died,
'Cause you walked hand in hand
With another man in my place.

I'm A Loser

Words & Music by John Lennon
& Paul McCartney

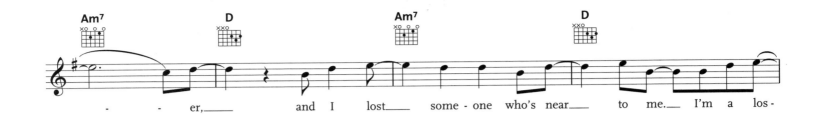

- - er,_____ and I lost_____ some-one who's near_____ to me.____ I'm a los-

To Coda ✛

1.

- - er,_____ and I'm not what I ap-pear____ to be.____

2.

Instrumental

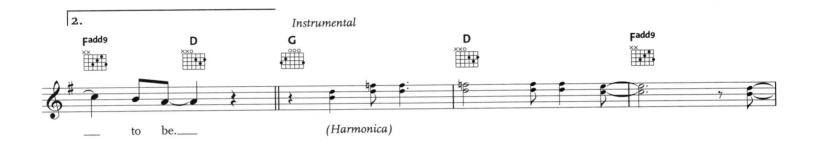

___ to be.____ *(Harmonica)*

(Guitar)

D.S. al Coda   ✛ **Coda**

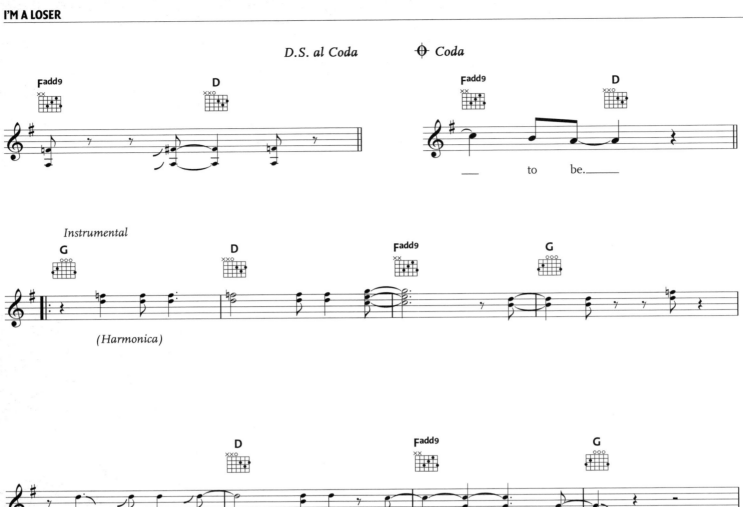

(Harmonica)

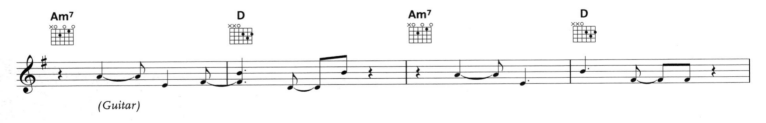

(Guitar)

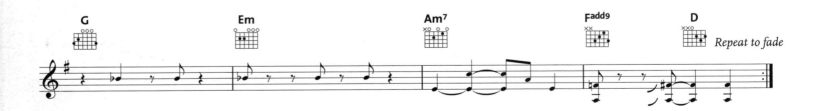

Repeat to fade

Verse 2:

Although I laugh and I act like a clown,
Beneath this mask I am wearing a frown.
My tears are falling like rain from the sky,
Is it for her or myself that I cry?

Verse 3:

What have I done to deserve such a fate?
I realise I have left it too late.
And so it's true, pride comes before a fall;
I'm telling you so that you won't lose all.

I'll Follow The Sun

Words & Music by John Lennon
& Paul McCartney

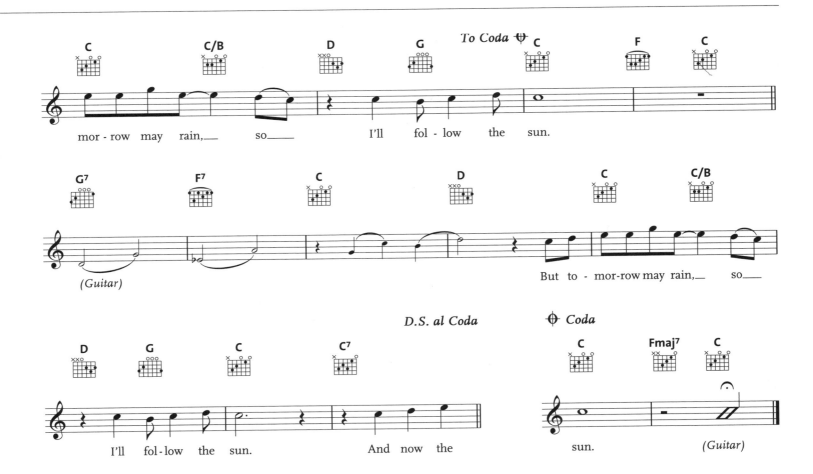

C	C/B	D	G	*To Coda* ⊕ C	F	C

mor - row may rain,___ so___ I'll fol - low the sun.

G⁷	F⁷	C	D	C	C/B

(Guitar)

But to - mor-row may rain,___ so___

D.S. al Coda   ⊕ *Coda*

D	G	C	C⁷	C	Fmaj⁷	C

I'll fol - low the sun.   And now the   sun.   *(Guitar)*

Verse 2:
Some day you'll know
I was the one,
But tomorrow may rain,
So I'll follow the sun.

Eight Days A Week

Words & Music by John Lennon
& Paul McCartney
© Copyright 1964 Northern Songs.

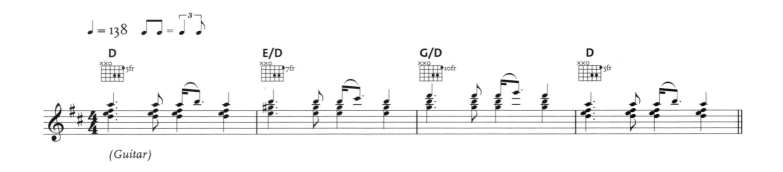

(Guitar)

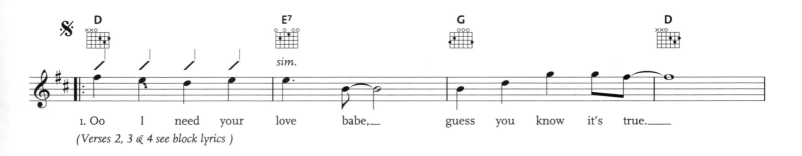

1. Oo I need your love babe,__ guess you know it's true.__
(Verses 2, 3 & 4 see block lyrics)

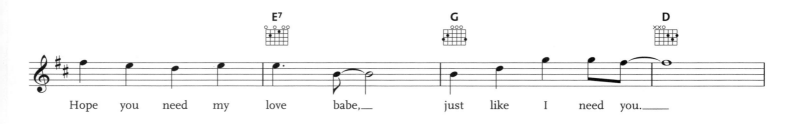

Hope you need my love babe,__ just like I need you.__

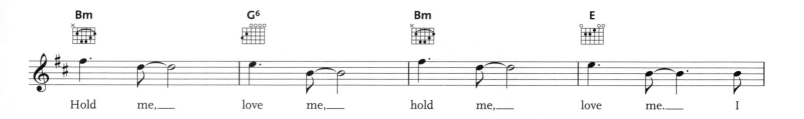

Hold me,__ love me,__ hold me,__ love me.__ I

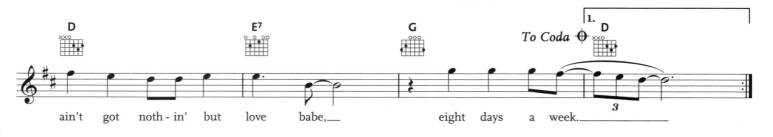

ain't got noth-in' but love babe,__ eight days a week.__

Eight days a week, I love

you. Eight days a week is not e - nough to

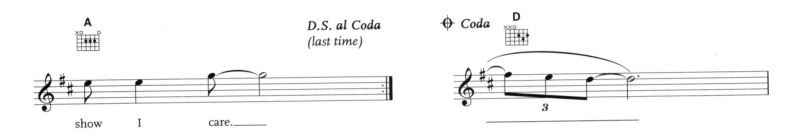

D.S. al Coda
(last time)

☩ *Coda*

show I care.

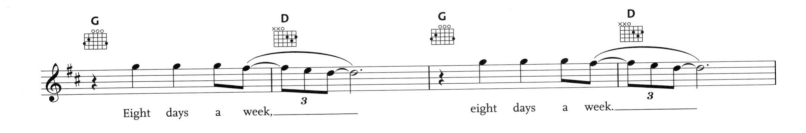

Eight days a week, eight days a week.

(Guitar)

Verse 2:
Love you every day girl, always on my mind.
One thing I can say girl, love you all the time.
Hold me, love me, hold me, love me.
I ain't got nothin' but love, girl, eight days a week.

Verse 3:
Oo, I need your love babe, guess you know it's true.
Hope you need my love babe, just like I need you.
Hold me, love me, hold me, love me.
I ain't got nothin' but love, girl, eight days a week.

Verse 4:
Love you every day girl, always on my mind.
One thing I can say girl, love you all the time.
Hold me, love me, hold me, love me.
I ain't got nothin' but love, babe, eight days a week.

Every Little Thing

Words & Music by John Lennon
& Paul McCartney
© Copyright 1964 Northern Songs.

(Guitar)

1. When I'm walk-ing be - side her,
(Verse 2 see block lyrics)

peo - ple tell me I'm luck - y. Yes, I know I'm a luck - y guy;

I re - mem - ber the first time I was lone - ly with - out her.

Can't stop think - ing a - bout her now. Ev - 'ry lit - tle thing she does,

she does for me, yeah. And you know the things she does,

she does for me, woo. (Guitar solo)

To Coda

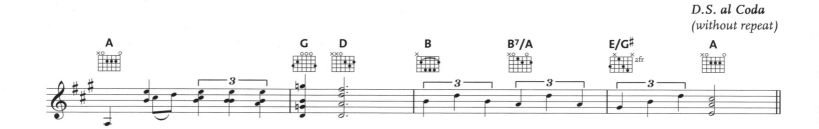

D.S. al Coda
(without repeat)

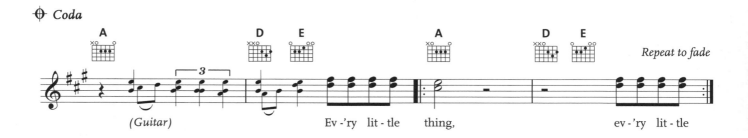

(Guitar)

Ev -'ry lit - tle thing,

ev -'ry lit - tle

Verse 2:
When I'm with her I'm happy
Just to know that she loves me.
Yes, I know that she loves me now;
There is one thing I'm sure of:
I will love her for ever,
For I know love will never die.

Every little thing she does...

1965

27 January
→ The music publishing company Maclen Limited was formed with John, Paul and Brian Epstein as directors

1 February
→ The EP *4 By The Beatles* was released in the US as Capitol R 5365. Side A: 'Honey Don't', 'I'm A Loser'; Side B: 'Mr. Moonlight', 'Everybody's Trying To Be My Baby'.

11 February
→ Having proposed the previous month at the Ad Lib Club, Ringo married hairdresser Maureen Cox at Caxton Hall Register Office, London; registrar Mr D.A. Boreham. John, George and Brian Epstein attended but Paul was on holiday in North Africa.

12 February
→ Ringo and Maureen gave a press conference in David Jacobs' back garden in Hove, Sussex.

15 February
→ Abbey Road. The group arrived at 2:30 and spent the afternoon recording John's 'Ticket To Ride'. The evening session was spent recording Paul's 'Another Girl' and George's 'I Need You'.
→ A single, 'Eight Days A Week'/ 'I Don't Want To Spoil The Party' was released in the US as Capitol 5371.

16 February
→ Abbey Road. An afternoon session completing 'I Need You' and 'Another Girl' followed by John's 'Yes It Is'.

17 February
→ Abbey Road. An afternoon session was spent recording Paul's 'The Night Before', after which they worked on George's 'You Like Me Too Much'.

18 February
→ Abbey Road. The Beatles spent the morning mixing. John's 'You've Got To Hide Your Love Away' was recorded

Below: Filming *Help!* **in the Bahamas**

during the afternoon session. 'If You've Got Trouble' was recorded during the evening session but John and Paul, who wrote the song specifically for Ringo, were not happy with the results and the track was not used (it was officially released on *Anthology 2* in 1996). The remainder of the evening session was spent recording Paul's 'Tell Me What You See'.
→ Northern Songs was launched on the stock exchange. Two million of the company's five million shares were made available to the public, at seven shillings and ninepence apiece (39p). The share price immediately dropped to below six shillings (30p), but soon recovered to 14 shillings (70p).

19 February
→ Abbey Road. John's 'You're Going To Lose That Girl' was recorded in a three-hour afternoon session.

20 February
→ Abbey Road. The group recorded 'That Means A Lot' (a version which wasn't released until *Anthology 2*).

22 February
→ The Beatles flew to the Bahamas from Heathrow in a chartered Boeing 707 to begin filming *Help!*; 1,400 fans waved goodbye. Actress Eleanor Bron, the female lead in the movie, travelled with the group. There was a refuelling stopover in New York en route but The Beatles did not leave the aircraft, despite US Customs and Immigration insisting that they should pass through US Customs. They lit up immediately after take-off and didn't stop giggling until the plane landed. In the Bahamas they stayed in a house in the grounds of the Balmoral Club near Cable Beach. The Beatles' arrival in Nassau was seen by thousands of local fans.

23-28 February, 1-9 March
→ *Help!* filming on New Providence Island, Bahamas.

10 March
→ The Beatles began the journey back to London, arriving 7.05am the next day.

13 March
→ The Beatles took the 11 am flight to Salzburg, Austria to continue filming

1965

Help! At Salzburg Airport, 4,000 fans were waiting to greet them, as well as the press. They gave a press conference in a nearby hotel before checking into the Hotel Edelweiss in Obertauern.

→ 'Eight Days A Week' reached number one in the US charts.

14 – 20 March

→ Help! filming in the Alps.

→ *Eight Arms To Hold You* was announced by United Artists as the working title for The Beatles' new film.

18 March

→ Hayling Supermarkets Limited was incorporated to control a supermarket on Hayling Island, Hampshire, run by John's old school friend Pete Shotton. The directors were Shotton, John Lennon and George Harrison.

22 March

→ The Beatles flew back to London from Austria.

→ The album *The Early Beatles* was released in the US as Capitol T-2309 (mono) and ST-2309 (stereo). Side A: 'Love Me Do', 'Twist And Shout', 'Anna (Go To Him)', 'Chains', 'Boys', 'Ask Me Why'; Side B: 'Please Please Me', 'P.S. I Love You', 'Baby, It's You', 'A Taste Of Honey', 'Do You Want To Know A Secret?'

24-26 March

→ With the location shooting completed, The Beatles continued to film *Help!* at Twickenham film studios.

27 March

→ Around this date, John and Cynthia were introduced to the chemical stimulus of LSD by their dentist, who spiked their late-night cups of coffee with impregnated sugar cubes. The now hallucinating party made their way from the dentist's home to The Pickwick Club in central London, where John interpreted a red light bulb as being the site of a raging inferno of fire, and then on to George's house in Surrey. There John drew his first psychedelic cartoons, portraying The Beatles as a hydra-like creature, with each head pronouncing: 'We all agree with you'.

Above: The Beatles plug their latest single 'Ticket To Ride'/'Yes It Is' on *The Eamonn Andrews Show*, 11 April.

28 March

→ Alpha Studios at Aston in Birmingham, to record their final in-studio appearance on the ABC TV show *Thank Your Lucky Stars*. They were interviewed by Brian Matthew and mimed to 'Eight Days A Week', 'Yes It Is', and 'Ticket To Ride'.

29-31 March, 1, 2, 5-9, 12 April

→ *Help!* filming at Twickenham.

30 March

→ Abbey Road in an evening session where The Beatles attempted five more (unreleased) takes of Paul's 'That Means A Lot'. The song was eventaully given to singer P.J Proby to cover.

1 April

→ Brian Epstein took a lease on the Saville Theatre on Shaftesbury Avenue to use as a showcase for his many showbusiness interests, eventually opening it as a rock venue late the following year on Sunday evenings.

5 April

→ The Beatles filmed the 'Rajahama' Indian restaurant sequence in *Help!* at Twickenham.

6 April

→ The *Beatles For Sale* EP was released in the UK as Parlophone GEP 8931 (mono only): Side A: 'No Reply', 'I'm A Loser'; Side B: 'Rock And Roll Music', 'Eight Days A Week'

9 April

→ 'Ticket To Ride'/'Yes It Is' was released in the UK as Parlophone R 5265.

10 April

→ A filmed insert of the group performing 'Ticket To Ride' and 'Yes It Is' was filmed at Riverside Studios for use on the BBC's *Top Of The Pops*.

11 April

→ The Beatles topped the bill at the Empire Pool, Wembley, for the *New Musical Express* Poll Winners show. They played 'I Feel Fine', 'She's A Woman', 'Baby's In Black', 'Ticket To Ride' and 'Long Tall Sally' to an audience of 10,000 people, and received their awards from Tony Bennett.

→ Afterwards the group drove to the ABC Television studios at Teddington to appear live on *The Eamonn Andrews Show*, chatting and miming to both sides of their new single.

13 April

→ At Twickenham where they were filming The Beatles did a live interview for BBC Light Programme's *Pop Inn* to promote 'Ticket To Ride'. This was followed by a late-night session at Abbey Road to record 'Help!'

→ Paul bought a three-storey Regency house at 7 Cavendish Avenue in St Johns Wood, London, for £40,000.

14 April

→ Location filming for *Help!* in Ailsa Avenue, not far from the Old Deer Park in Twickenham.

→ *Help!* was announced as the title of the new film, replacing *Eight Arms To Hold You*.

16 April

→ John and George were surprise guests, interviewed live by Cathy McGowan on *Ready, Steady, Goes Live!* at the Rediffusion Television Studios, Wembley.

19 April

→ 'Ticket to Ride'/'Yes It Is' was released in the US as Capitol 5407.

20-30 April

→ *Help!* filming at Twickenham.

29 April

→ Chris Denning interviewed all four Beatles for his weekly Radio Luxembourg show, *The Beatles*.

3-5 May

→ *Help!* filming on Salisbury Plain with the assistance of the British Army's Third Tank Division. The Beatles, Eleanor Bron (with whom John had struck up a strong rapport), Victor Spinetti, Roy Kinnear, Leo McKern and the other actors and film crew all stayed at The Antrobus Arms in nearby Amesbury.

6-7 May

→ *Help!* filming at Twickenham.

9 May

→ *Help!* filming in New Bond Street; John and Ringo filming at Twickenham.

May 10

→ *Help!* filming at Cliveden House,

near Maidenhead, Berkshire.

→ Abbey Road. The Beatles recorded two old Larry Williams rock'n'roll numbers, 'Dizzy Miss Lizzy' and 'Bad Boy', aimed at the American market.

11 May

→ *Help!* filming continued at Cliveden House for the 'Buckingham Palace' scenes in the movie.

18 May

→ Twickenham for post synchronisation work on the soundtrack to *Help!*

22 May

→ 'Ticket To Ride' reached number one in the US charts.

→ A brief *Top Of The Pops* clip of The Beatles singing 'Ticket To Ride' (from 10 April) appeared in an episode of BBC TV's *Doctor Who*.

25 May

→ John and Cynthia returned to London from Cannes, where they had attended the Film Festival. That afternoon, before leaving, John recorded an interview with Martin Ogronsky for CBS-TV's *The Merv Griffin Show*.

26 May

→ The Beatles drove to the BBC's Piccadilly Studios where they recorded their last radio show for the BBC, a Bank Holiday special. They insisted that the name be changed from the usual *From Us To You*, to *The Beatles (Invite You To Take A Ticket To Ride)* which they thought was more suitable for their maturing image. They recorded live versions of 'Ticket To Ride', 'Everybody's Trying To Be My Baby', 'I'm A Loser', 'The Night Before', 'Honey Don't', 'Dizzy Miss Lizzy' and 'She's A Woman'.

27 May

→ All the Beatles flew off on their holidays. Paul and Jane went to Portugal where they stayed in Bruce Welch's villa in Albufera. Having had the melody in his head for some time under a working title of 'Scrambled Eggs', Paul began the lyrics to 'Yesterday' in the car on the way from the airport and completed them over the next two weeks.

Paul: "I fell out of bed. I had a piano by my bedside and I must have dreamed it because I tumbled out of bed and put my hands on the piano keys and I had a tune in my head. It was just all there, a complete thing. I couldn't believe it, it came too easy. In fact I didn't believe I'd written it. I thought maybe I'd heard it before, it was some other tune, and I went round for weeks playing the chords of the song for people, asking them, 'Is this like something? I think I've written it.' And people would say, 'No, it's not like anything else. But it's good...'."

4 June

→ The *Beatles For Sale 2* EP was released in the UK as Parlophone GEP 8938 (mono only). Side A: 'I'll Follow The Sun', 'Baby's In Black'; Side B: 'Words Of Love', 'I Don't Want To Spoil The Party'.

11 June

→ It was announced that The Beatles had been awarded the Members of the British Empire (MBE). Paul was interviewed by telephone by Ronald Burns for the BBC Radio *Late Night News Extra* which also included an interview with Brian Epstein.

187

Ringo: **"There's a proper medal as well as the letters, isn't there? I will keep it to wear when I'm old. It's the sort of thing you want to keep."**

→ John Lennon was always uneasy about accepting the award.

John: **"We had to do a lot of selling out then. Taking the MBE was a sell-out for me. You know, before you get an MBE the Palace writes to you to ask if you're going to accept it, because you're not supposed to reject it publicly and they sound you out first. I chucked the letter in with all the fan-mail, until Brian asked me if I had it. He and a few other people persuaded me that it was in our interests to take it, and it was hypocritical of me to accept it."**

13 June
→ Holders of MBE medals begin to return their awards in protest at the honour being given to The Beatles.

14 June
→ Abbey Road. Paul recorded 'Yesterday' entirely solo on his acoustic guitar. He followed the gentle ballad with the uptempo rocker, 'I'm Down' and finished the session with 'I've Just Seen A Face'.
→ The album *Beatles VI* was released in the US as Capitol T-2358 (mono) and ST-2358 (stereo). Side A: 'Kansas City'/ 'Hey-Hey-Hey-Hey', 'Eight Days A Week', 'You Like Me Too Much', 'Bad Boy', 'I Don't Want To Spoil The Party', 'Words Of Love'; Side B: 'What You're Doing', 'Yes It Is', 'Dizzy Miss Lizzy', 'Tell Me What You See', 'Every Little Thing'.

15 June
→ Abbey Road. John's 'It's Only Love' was recorded during an afternoon session.

16 June
→ The Beatles did more post-synchronisation work at Twickenham for *Help!* Later, at the Argyll Street office of NEMS, John did an interview and read 'The Fat Budgie' section from *A Spaniard In The Works* to promote his new book on the BBC Radio show *The World Of Books*. He was also interviewed by Tim Matthews for the BBC Home Service news magazine *Today*, during which he also read a story from the book called 'The National Health Cow'.

17 June
→ Abbey Road. Ringo recorded 'Act Naturally'. This was followed by the group recording 'Wait', which was held back to be used on the *Rubber Soul* album.

18 June
→ The Beatles were interviewed at the NEMS offices by the Italian-language section of the BBC World Service to coincide with their upcoming Italian dates.
→ Later, at the BBC's Lime Grove Studios, John appeared on BBC1's *Tonight* programme where he was interviewed by Kenneth Allsop and read two extracts from his book, 'The Wumberlog' and 'We Must Not Forget The General Erection'.

20 June
→ The Beatles' European tour opened in Paris. The Beatles arrived at Paris-Orly at 10 am and checked in to the George Cinq. Their reception was quiet by Beatles standards with only about 50 fans waiting outside the hotel. This pattern was repeated throughout the tour, as the group regularly played to less than capacity audiences.
→ In Paris, they played two concerts to 6,000 people each at the Palais des Sports.
→ The Beatles' set during the European tour consisted of: 'Twist And Shout', 'She's A Woman', 'I'm A Loser', 'Can't Buy Me Love', 'Baby's In Black', 'I Wanna Be Your Man', 'A Hard Day's Night', 'Everybody's Trying To Be My Baby', 'Rock And Roll Music', 'I Feel Fine', 'Ticket To Ride' and 'Long Tall Sally'.

22 June
→ Palais d'Hiver, Lyons (two shows).

Opposite: Filming *Help!*
on Salisbury Plain.
Below: John with *Help!*
film set hairdresser,
Betty Glasow.

23 June
→ The Beatles took the train to Milan.

24 June
→ Velodromo Vigorelli, Milan, a 22,000-seater open-air arena. Brian Epstein was not pleased at all the empty seats, particularly during the afternoon show when many of the fans were at school or work and only 7,000 people attended. The press suggested that a combination of high prices and a heat wave had kept the fans away.
→ John's book A *Spaniard In The Works* was published in the UK by Jonathan Cape at 10s 6d.

25 June
→ Palazzo dello Sport, Genoa, a 25,000-seated arena where, once again, there were many empty seats. The afternoon show attracted only 5,000 fans.

27 June
→ Two shows in Rome at the Teatro Adriano. While The Beatles were playing 'I Wanna Be Your Man,' which Ringo always sang, Paul, for some unknown reason was laughing so hard, he had to leave the stage. George was not amused and his displeasure was obvious. When Paul returned to the stage the microphone fell over and he continued laughing. This made John start laughing as well but George remained irritated by it all. At the end of the shows, Paul thanked the audience in Italian.

29 June
→ Two more shows at the Teatro Adriano, Rome, though neither was more than half full.

30 June
→ Palais des Expositions, Nice. The Beatles stayed at the Gresta Hotel.

1 July
→ John's *A Spaniard In The Works* was published in the USA.

2 July
→ Plaza de Toros de Las Ventas, Madrid. The Beatles were growing increasingly worried by the level of violence shown to fans by the police

and security in Italy and particularly in Spain.

3 July
→ Plaza de Toros Monumental, Barcelona. The Beatles were onstage at 10.30 that evening.

4 July
→ When the group arrived home at London at midday, 1,000 fans were waiting to greet them at Heathrow.

11 July
→ The album *Beatles VI* reached number one in the US album charts.

13 July
→ Paul accepted five Ivor Novello Awards, presented by David Frost, on behalf of John and himself at a luncheon at the Savoy. John refused to attend. He had been upset by the press comments about their receiving the MBE and did not want to put himself on show again. Paul was 40 minutes late because he had forgotten about the engagement. On receiving the award he quipped, 'Thanks. I hope nobody sends theirs back now.'

19 July
→ Ringo and Maureen bought 'Sunny Heights' in Weybridge for £37,000. They moved in just before Christmas.
→ 'Help!'/'I'm Down' was released in the US as Capitol 5476.

23 July
→ 'Help!'/'I'm Down' was released in the UK as Parlophone R 5305.

29 July
→ Some 10,000 fans gathered in Piccadilly Circus outside the London Pavilion on a humid summer evening for the royal premiere of *Help!* The Beatles arrived in a black Rolls-Royce and were presented to Princess Margaret and Lord Snowdon (who had delayed their summer holiday so they could attend the premiere).
→ BBC's *Top Of The Pops* showed a film clip from *Help!*

30 July
→ The Beatles spent the day rehearsing on stage at the Saville Theatre. They did two BBC interviews:

John: "When 'Help!' came out in '65, I was actually crying out for help. Most people think it's just a fast rock'n'roll song. Later, I knew I really was crying out for help. It was my fat Elvis period.... I was fat and depressed and I was crying out for help."

1965

group did not like the sound balance and continued rehearsals through the afternoon, watching playbacks until they were satisfied it was right. The final tape was made at 8:30 that evening. They performed 'I Feel Fine', 'I'm Down', and 'Act Naturally' during the first half, then 'Ticket To Ride', 'Yesterday' (Paul solo with string quartet accompaniment) and 'Help!' (during which John forgot some of the words).

Paul: "I had to sing 'Yesterday' live in front of all those people. It was pretty nerve-wracking but it was very exciting. I know I was nervous. We'd recorded 'Yesterday' but I'd never really had to perform it anywhere."

15 August

→ The Beatles played Shea Stadium. The police feared that fans would jam the tunnels in and out of Manhattan so the group was first escorted by limousine to the Manhattan East River Heliport and from there they flew to the World Fair site in Queens. There they transferred to a Wells Fargo armoured van. As usual, there was a full bill, and 55,600 fans sat through the King Curtis Band, Cannibal and The Headhunters, Brenda Holloway, and Sounds Incorporated before Ed Sullivan finally walked on stage to announce The Beatles: 'Now, ladies and gentlemen, honoured by their country, decorated by their Queen, and loved here in America, here are The Beatles!' The group did their standard 30-minute set of a dozen numbers then jumped straight back into the Wells Fargo van, $160,000 richer – amounting to $100 per second of their performance.

→ The usual set for this tour was: 'Twist And Shout', 'She's A Woman', 'I Feel Fine', 'Dizzy Miss Lizzy', 'Ticket To Ride', 'Everybody's Trying To Be My Baby', 'Can't Buy Me Love', 'Baby's In Black', 'I Wanna Be Your Man', 'A Hard Day's Night', 'Help!' and 'I'm Down'. Mick Jagger, Keith Richards and Andrew Loog Oldham were in the audience.

→ The concert was filmed by Brian Epstein's Subafilms organisation, and released as a documentary film called

---

one with Dibbs Mather for the British Information Service and the other with Lance Percival for his *Lance A Gogo* show on the BBC Light Programme.

1 August

→ The Beatles appeared on ABC TV's *Blackpool Night Out*. The Beatles closed the show, performing 'I Feel Fine', 'I'm Down', 'Act Naturally', 'Ticket To Ride', 'Yesterday' (Paul solo with string quartet accompaniment) and 'Help!'

6 August

→ The *Help!* album was released in the UK as Parlophone PMC 1255 (mono) and PCS 3071 (stereo). Side A: 'Help!', 'The Night Before', 'You've Got To Hide Your Love Away', 'I Need You', 'Another Girl', 'You're Going To Lose That Girl', 'Ticket To Ride'; Side B: 'Act Naturally', 'It's Only Love', 'You Like Me Too Much', 'Tell Me What You See', 'I've Just Seen A Face', 'Yesterday', 'Dizzy Miss Lizzy'.

8 August

→ *Help!* reached number one in the UK album charts.

9 August

→ Brian Epstein's new signing, The Silkie, recorded John's 'You've Got To Hide Your Love Away' under John's supervision. Paul played guitar and George the tambourine during the six-hour session.

11 August

→ The film *Help!* was premiered in New York, without any of The Beatles being present.

August 13

→ The Beatles arrived at JFK Airport to begin their third US tour. Their TWA flight touched down at 2:30 pm and was met by a huge battery of press, radio and TV reporters, but the police had the plane parked two miles from the main terminal so that thousands of waiting fans were unable to see them. The group went straight to the Warwick Hotel at 6th Ave and 54th Street where they gave an obligatory press conference to about 250 reporters. The Beatles had the whole 33rd floor to themselves, with

guards at all entrances to keep out unwanted visitors.

→ The album *Help!* was released in the US as Capitol MAS-2386 (mono) and SMAS-2386 (stereo). It contained fewer songs and included music from Ken Thorne's film score. Side A: 'The James Bond Theme' (The George Martin Orchestra), 'Help!', 'The Night Before', 'From Me To You Fantasy' (The George Martin Orchestra), 'You've Got To Hide Your Love Away', 'I Need You', 'In The Tyrol' (The George Martin Orchestra); Side B: 'Another Girl', 'Another Hard Day's Night' (The George Martin Orchestra), 'Ticket To Ride', 'The Bitter End'/'You Can't Do That' (The George Martin Orchestra), 'You're Going To Lose That Girl', 'The Chase' (The George Martin Orchestra).

14 August

→ New York police cleared the streets for a convoy of limousines to take The Beatles to rehearsals for *The Ed Sullivan Show* at CBS Studio 50 where they began work at 11 am. The

19 August

→ The Beatles played two sets to a total of 25,000 fans at the Sam Houston Coliseum. They were restrained performances in very hot weather with complete chaos backstage and no dressing room facilities. The group travelled to and from the show by armoured van.

20 August

→ The Beatles and entourage flew through the night from Texas, arriving in Chicago at three in the morning at Midway Airport. The police had heard of the trouble in Houston and had forbidden them to land at O'Hare because of the disruption it would cause. They put up at the O'Hare Sahara which had foolishly announced that The Beatles were to stay there, so the place was swarming with fans making so much noise that no-one was able to get any sleep. Nonetheless their two sets at the huge White Sox Park Stadium before a total of 50,000 fans went without a hitch.

21 August

→ In the afternoon The Beatles flew from Chicago to Minneapolis, Minnesota, for one show before 22,000 people at the Twin Cities Metropolitan Stadium. They stayed at the Leamington Motor Inn, which, like the hotel in Chicago, had announced that The Beatles were staying there.

22 August

→ The Beatles played two shows at the Memorial Coliseum, Portland.

23 August

→ The Beatles arrived in Los Angeles a few hours before dawn. They rented a house at 2850 Benedict Canyon, Beverly Hills, but in less than 10 hours the press and radio stations were giving out the supposedly secret address over the air. While The Beatles relaxed by the pool, the Beverly Hills police force had their work cut out keeping fans from invading the group's privacy.

24 August

→ The routine at Benedict Canyon consisted of breakfast at around

---

Opposite: John waves to some of the 56,000 fans attending the Beatles concert at Shea Stadium, New York, 15 August. Above: Alan Livingstone, president of Capitol Records, presents The Beatles with gold records at a special *Help!* press conference, Los Angeles, 29 August.

The Beatles At Shea Stadium the following year.

17 August

→ The Beatles flew to Toronto, Canada, in the Lockheed Electra hired by Brian Epstein for the tour. Years later, George was on a flight from New York to Los Angeles and met the pilot. He said,

"George, you don't remember me, I'm the pilot from the American Flyers Electra plane that you did the tours on. You'd never believe that plane! It was just full of bullet holes, the tail, the wings, everything – just full of bullet holes. Jealous fellows who would be waiting around, knowing that The Beatles were arriving at such-and-such a time. They'd all be there trying to shoot the plane!"

→ Maple Leaf Gardens, two shows

to an audience of 35,000 fans each. News had leaked that the group were staying at the King Edward Sheraton and dozens of fans had booked themselves in, causing a difficult security problem.

18 August

→ The Beatles flew in to Atlanta that morning and did just one concert, to 35,000 people at the Atlanta Stadium. The new baseball stadium had a very fine sound system which the group talked about for days after, since at most venues they could rarely hear themselves play. Their plane arrived at Houston airport at 2 am, having left Atlanta immediately after the gig. Local police had made no arrangements and fans swarmed onto the runway as the plane taxied in to the terminal. Fans began climbing over the plane before it had even stopped moving, some of them smoking cigarettes next to the plane's fuel tanks. The group and Brian Epstein were unable to leave the plane until a forklift truck arrived for them.

191

1965

2 pm, sunbathing and swimming during the afternoon, then dinner followed by a private screening of the latest films. The house had a magnificent view across the canyon and was the perfect place for The Beatles to unwind. Visiting guests included The Byrds, Joan Baez and Eleanor Bron.

28 August
→ Balboa Stadium, San Diego (to an audience of 20,000 fans).

29 August
→ In the afternoon there was a large press conference at the Capitol Tower at Hollywood and Vine, during which Alan Livingstone presented The Beatles with gold discs for *Help!*.
→ An armoured truck took them from there to the Hollywood Bowl for the first of two concerts. The show was watched by 18,000 fans.

30 August
→ The last night of a nine day stay in Beverly Hills. The Beatles' second concert at the Bowl was a success and (like its predecessor) was taped by Capitol Records for a possible future live record.

31 August
→ A total of 30,000 people attended two shows at the San Francisco Cow Palace where The Beatles performed their standard 12-number set. The show made news around the world because scores of fans fainted when loose seating allowed fans to push forward and rush the stage. The crowd got so out of hand at one point that the group had to leave the stage and wait in their backstage caravan until the situation had calmed down before returning to play.

1 September
→ The Beatles flew back to London from the US.

4 September
→ 'Help!' reached number one in the US charts.

12 September
→ *Help!* reached number one in the US album charts.

Meeting Elvis: 27 August

This evening, The Beatles met Elvis Presley at his home on Perugia Way in Bel Air next to the Country Club. The group arrived at 11 pm to find Elvis waiting on the doorstep. He took them through a huge circular lobby lit with his favourite red and blue lights into an enormous living room dominated by a giant colour television set with the sound turned off. Brian Epstein and Colonel Tom Parker stood together off to the side and watched the meeting. The atmosphere was stilted at first, with no-one saying anything until Elvis blurted out,

'If you damn guys are gonna sit here and stare at me all night I'm gonna go to bed.'

This broke the ice. Elvis produced guitars and he and The Beatles played along to rock records from Elvis' collection.

Paul played piano and guitar while Elvis played bass. They found they had things in common, discussing incidents with fans and problems of being on the road. George told Elvis how their plane caught fire while landing in Portland and Elvis remembered a similar episode when his aircraft engine failed in Atlanta. The Beatles were each given a complete set of Elvis albums, gun holsters with gold leather belts and a table lamp shaped like a wagon.

The visit lasted three hours and they left shortly after two in the morning. They were amazed to find that Elvis had 10 road managers, complete with their wives, living with him in the house, whereas The Beatles made do with two roadies for the four of them.

13 September
→ Maureen gave birth to Zak Starkey at Queen Charlotte's Hospital, Hammersmith, London.
→ 'Yesterday'/'Act Naturally' was released in The US as Capitol 5498. 'Yesterday' was not released as a single in the UK until 1976.

23 September
→ The charity Oxfam announced that, for the second year running, they would be printing a special Christmas card featuring a John Lennon cartoon – this time the drawing which accompanied 'The Fat Budgie' in his book, *A Spaniard In The Works*.

25 September
→ The Beatles cartoon series, *The Beatles*, made by King Features, began broadcasting in the US. The series featured genuine Beatles songs and cartoon characters with voices by Paul Frees (John and George) and Lance Percival (Paul and Ringo). The series was produced by Al Brodax who later produced the cartoon film *Yellow Submarine*. Due to pressure from The Beatles and NEMS, the series was not screened at the time in the UK.

1 October
→ The single 'Yesterday' reached number one in the US. One of the reasons proffered as to why it remained an album track in the UK is because The Beatles did not want their image as a rock'n'roll band damaged by the release of a solo ballad. The song did become the lead track on an EP, however.

12 October
→ Abbey Road. In the first session for the *Rubber Soul* album, John's 'Run For Your Life' was recorded in the afternoon, leading straight into 'Norwegian Wood', then still known as 'This Bird Has Flown'. John played acoustic guitar while George played sitar for the first time on a Beatles' recording; a cheap model he bought at Indiacraft.

John: "I was trying to write about an affair without letting my wife know I was writing about an affair."

13 October

→ Abbey Road. The recording of 'Drive My Car' was the first time that The Beatles had recorded past midnight – something which would soon become the norm.

16 October

→ Abbey Road. 'Day Tripper' was recorded during an afternoon and evening session, followed by work on George's 'If I Needed Someone'.

18 October

→ Abbey Road. 'If I Needed Someone' was completed while work started on 'In My Life'.

20 October

→ Abbey Road. Two extended sessions produced 'We Can Work It Out'.

21 October

→ Abbey Road. The Beatles were in the studio from 2:30 until after midnight working on 'Norwegian Wood' and 'Nowhere Man'.

22 October

→ Abbey Road. The Beatles continued work on 'Nowhere Man'.

24 October

→ Abbey Road. The Beatles began work at 2.30 pm, working on Paul's 'I'm Looking Through You'.

28 October

→ Abbey Road. Mixing session for 'We Can Work It Out'.

29 October

→ Abbey Road. A new vocal track was added to 'We Can Work It Out'.

1 – 2 November

→ The Beatles drove to Manchester to record *The Music Of Lennon And McCartney*, a special for Granada Television. John and Paul introduced the various acts which included Cilla Black, Peter & Gordon, Billy J. Kramer & The Dakotas and Peter Sellers. Paul mimed The Beatles version of 'Yesterday' and after 22 seconds the cameras cut away to Marianne Faithfull performing her version (Nearing full-term pregnancy, she was filmed from the neck up).

Opposite: The Beatles arrive in San Francisco, 31 August.
Above: MBE press conference, Saville Theatre, 26 October.

MBE day: October 26

The Beatles arrived at Buckingham Palace in John's black glass Rolls Royce in time for the 11 am honours ceremony in the Great Throne Room. At the investiture 189 people received awards, including six who were knighted. The Beatles were awarded the MBE, the lowest of the five divisions of the order, for service to their country. It ranks 120th of the 126 titles of precedence and is the most widely given honour.

Wearing dark suits and ties, they stood in a row while the Queen pinned their medals to the narrow lapels of their jackets.

'How long have you been together now?' she asked.

'Oh, for many years,' said Paul. '40 years,' said Ringo, to laughter.

'Are you the one that started it all?' the Queen asked Ringo.

He told her that the others started it. 'I'm the little one,' he said.

Paul later described the Queen as 'Lovely. Great! She was very friendly. She was just like a mum to us.'

Outside, 4,000 Beatles fans jostled with police who managed to hold them back, but could not prevent them climbing the gates and lamp-posts outside the palace.

Immediately afterwards there was a press conference arranged in the downstairs bar of the Saville Theatre for The Beatles to discuss their MBEs and give their reaction to the protests.

Above: The Beatles don smog masks at a press conference in Sheffield, 8 December.

The Beatles mimed to 'We Can Work It Out' and 'Day Tripper', their forthcoming single.

3 November

→ Abbey Road. An afternoon and an evening session recording 'Michelle'.

4 November

→ Abbey Road. An evening session recording Ringo's track, 'What Goes On'.

6 November

→ Abbey Road. A 7 pm until 3 am session working on 'I'm Looking Through You', but no-one was satisfied with the results.

8 November

→ Abbey Road. The group rehearsed George's 'Think For Yourself' and at about 3 am, they recorded *The Beatles Third Christmas Record*, a flexi-disc issued free to fan club members only.

10 November

→ Abbey Road. An evening session for 'The Word' and more work on 'I'm Looking Through You'.

11 November

→ Abbey Road. A 13-hour session, beginning at 6 pm and ending at 7 am, completing 'Wait', recording 'You Won't See Me' and 'Girl'. With the

finishing touches to 'I'm Looking Through You' added, *Rubber Soul* was finished.

15 November

→ The afternoon was spent sequencing songs for the new album with George Martin.

23 November

→ The Beatles filmed their own promotional film clips at Twickenham Film Studios. This way they would be able to appear on television in the US, Japan and the rest of the world instead of being restricted to just a few British TV shows. Film versions were made of

'We Can Work It Out', 'Day Tripper', 'Help!', 'Ticket To Ride' and 'I Feel Fine' which were distributed all over the world.

25 November
→ Harrods opened for three hours in the evening to enable The Beatles to do late-night Christmas shopping in private. Both Ringo and George purchased items of furniture, while John bought a giant slide for his son Julian to use in the garden.

29 November
→ The Beatles taped an interview with Brian Matthew at the BBC Aeolian Hall for use on the Christmas Day edition of BBC Light Programme's *Saturday Club*.

30 November
→ Brian Matthew interviewed George and John separately at NEMS Argyll Street office for the BBC Overseas Service.

1 December
→ The Beatles spent the day rehearsing at Mal and Neil's apartment for their upcoming British tour.
→ An art exhibition at the Nell Gwynne Club, London included some of John's drawings.

2 December
→ The Beatles drove to Berwick-on-Tweed. During the journey, one of George's Gretsch guitars fell off the back of the car and was smashed to pieces by following traffic.
→ BBC TV's *Top Of The Pops* premiered the new promo films for 'Day Tripper' and 'We Can Work It Out'.

3 December
→ 'Day Tripper'/'We Can Work It Out' was released in the UK as Parlophone R 5389. 'We Can Work It Out' was originally intended as the A-side of the single, but at John's insistence, both sides were given equal prominence in the press and on radio.
→ *Rubber Soul* was released in the UK as Parlophone PMC 1267 (mono) and PCS 3075 (stereo). Side A: 'Drive My Car', 'Norwegian Wood (This Bird Has Flown)', 'You Won't See Me', 'Nowhere Man', 'Think For Yourself', 'The Word',

'Michelle'; Side B: 'What Goes On', 'Girl', 'I'm Looking Through You', 'In My Life', 'Wait', 'If I Needed Someone', 'Run For Your Life'.
→ EMI made an initial pressing of 750,000 copies to cope with the expected demand.
→ The Beatles began their last UK tour in Glasgow, playing two sets at the Odeon Cinema. Also on the bill were their friends The Moody Blues. The Beatles' set consisted of: 'Dizzy Miss Lizzy', 'I Feel Fine', 'She's A Woman', 'If I Needed Someone', 'Ticket To Ride', 'Act Naturally', 'Nowhere Man', 'Baby's In Black', 'Help!', 'We Can Work It Out', 'Day Tripper' and 'I'm Down'.
→ Bad weather made Brian Epstein change their hotel from a small one just out of town to a grand hotel in the centre of Glasgow which posed a security problem.
→ The rest of the itinerary on the tour ran as follows: 4 December: City Hall, Newcastle-upon-Tyne; 5 December: Empire Theatre, Liverpool; 7 December: ABC Cinema, Ardwick, Manchester; 8 December: Gaumont Cinema, Sheffield; 9 December: Odeon Cinema, Birmingham; 10 December: Hammersmith Odeon, London; December 11: Finsbury Park Astoria, London; December 12: Cardiff Capitol Cinema.

5 December
→ All the Beatles friends and relatives attended the concert at the Empire which turned out to be the last time The Beatles played in their home town. During the second show, Paul joined support act The Koobas onstage to play drums on 'Dizzy Miss Lizzy'.
→ The double-A side single, 'We Can Work It Out'/'Day Tripper', reached number one in the UK charts. *Rubber Soul* reached number one in the UK album charts.

6 December
→ *Rubber Soul* was released in the US as Capitol T-2442 (mono) and ST-2442 (stereo). As usual it contained fewer tracks than the UK original: Side A: 'I've Just Seen A Face', 'Norwegian Wood (This Bird Has Flown)', 'You Won't See Me', 'Think For Yourself', 'The Word', 'Michelle'; Side B: 'It's Only

Love', 'Girl', 'I'm Looking Through You', 'In My Life', 'Wait', 'Run For Your Life'.
→ The single, 'Day Tripper'/'We Can Work It Out' was released in the US as Capitol 5555.
→ *The Beatles Million Sellers* EP was released in the UK as Parlophone GEP 8946. (mono only) Side A: 'She Loves You', 'I Want To Hold Your Hand'; Side B: 'Can't Buy Me Love', 'I Feel Fine'.

17 December
The Beatles Third Christmas Record flexi disc was sent to 65,000 members of The Beatles fan club.

23 December
→ Among Paul's Christmas gifts to the other Beatles were acetates of a special record called *Paul's Christmas Album* made in an edition of four copies only. On it Paul acted as a DJ playing his favourite tracks.

25 December
→ BBC Light Programme's *Saturday Club* broadcast clips from the pre-recorded interview on 29 November.
→ The pirate ship Radio Caroline broadcast a specially recorded Christmas message by the group who had always given their support to pirate stations.
→ BBC TV's *Top Of The Pops* Xmas edition showed film clips (taped on 23 November) of the group miming to 'I Feel Fine', 'Help!', 'Ticket To Ride' and 'Day Tripper'.

31 December
→ John's father, Freddie Lennon, released a single, 'That's My Life (My Love And My Home)' on Piccadilly Records, a subsidiary of Pye. This desperate piece of self-promotion unsurprisingly failed to sell and did little to reconcile Freddie with his estranged son.

> **George on the Finsbury Park Astoria: "This is one of the most incredible shows we've done. Not just because of the audience, but because they're Londoners. This is the funny thing. It's always been the other way round – fantastic in the North but just that little bit cool in London. It's incredible. It seems like the Beatlemania thing is happening all over again."**

Ticket To Ride

Words & Music by John Lennon
& Paul McCartney
© Copyright 1965 Northern Songs.

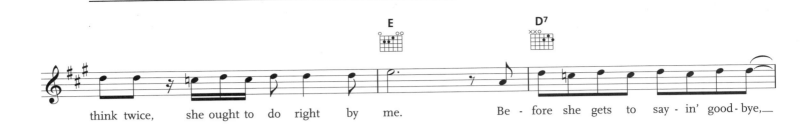

E

D⁷

think twice, she ought to do right by me. Be - fore she gets to say - in' good - bye,___

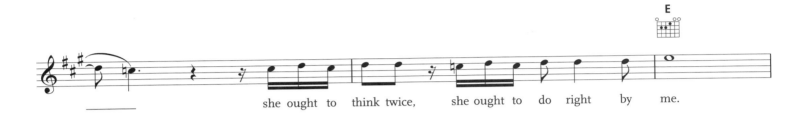

E

___ she ought to think twice, she ought to do right by me.

4.

A

Repeat to fade

3. I

4. She

My ba - by don't care, my ba - by don't

Verses 2 & 4:
She said that living with me
Was bringing her down, yeah!
For she would never be free
When I was around.

She's got a ticket to ride...

Yes It Is

Words & Music by John Lennon
& Paul McCartney
© Copyright 1965 Northern Songs.
All Rights Reserved.
International Copyright Secured.

♩. = 66

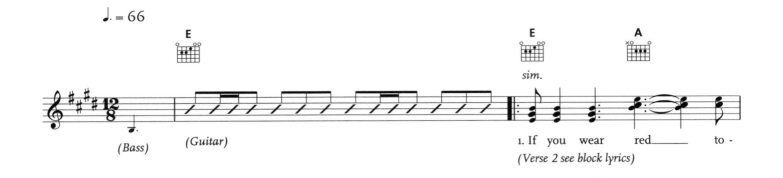

(Bass)   (Guitar)   *sim.*

1. If you wear red_____ to-
(Verse 2 see block lyrics)

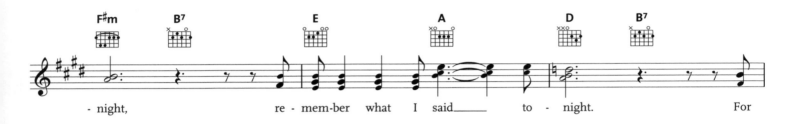

- night,   re - mem-ber   what   I   said_____   to - night.   For

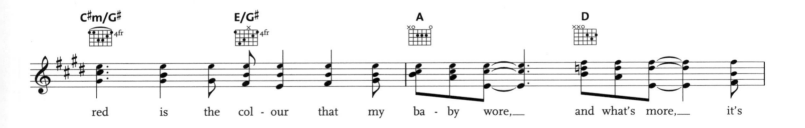

red   is   the   col - our   that   my   ba - by   wore,_____   and what's more,_____   it's

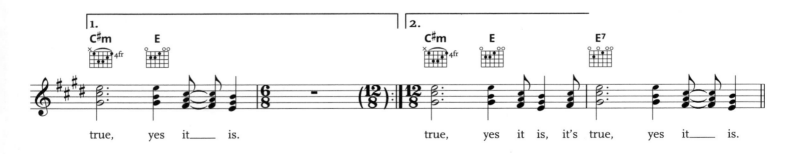

1.
true,   yes   it_____   is.

2.
true,   yes   it   is,   it's   true,   yes   it_____   is.

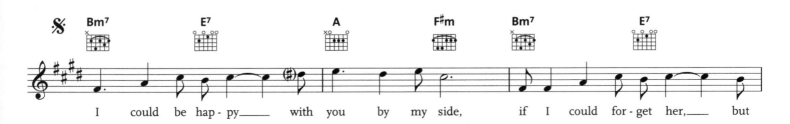

I   could   be   hap - py_____   with   you   by   my   side,   if   I   could   for - get   her,_____   but

it's my pride, yes it is, yes it is,____ oh yes it is, yeah.____
(Ah, ah, ah, ah.)

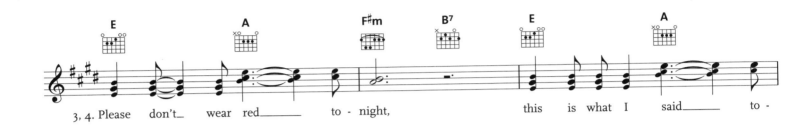

3, 4. Please don't_ wear red____ to-night, this is what I said____ to-

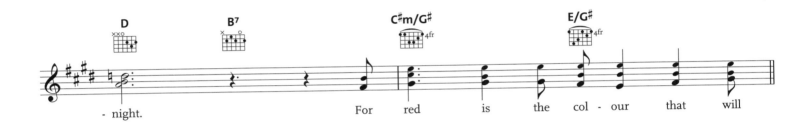

-night. For red is the col-our that will

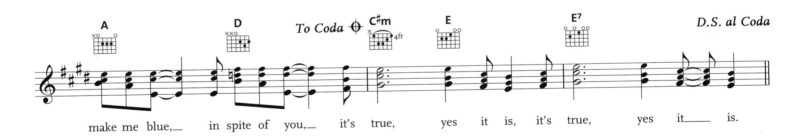

make me blue,_ in spite of you,_ it's true, yes it is, it's true, yes it___ is.

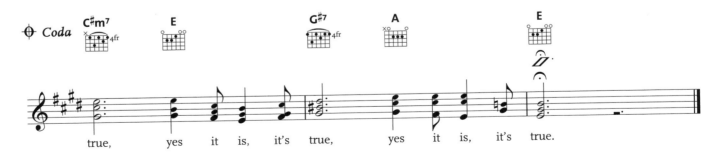

true, yes it is, it's true, yes it is, it's true.

Verse 2:
Scarlet were the clothes she wore,
Everybody knows I'm sure.
I would remember all the things we planned,
Understand, it's true,
Yes it is, it's true, yes it is.

Help!

Words & Music by John Lennon
& Paul McCartney
© Copyright 1965 Northern Songs.
All Rights Reserved.
International Copyright Secured.

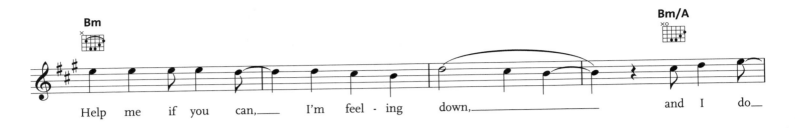

Help me if you can, I'm feel-ing down,_____ and I do__

__ ap-pre-ci-ate____ you be-ing 'round._____

Help me get___ my feet back on the ground,_____ won't you

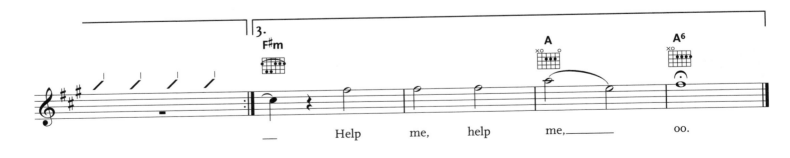

please, please__ help__ me.____

__ Help me, help me,_____ oo.

Verse 2:
And now my life has changed in oh so many ways,
My independence seems to vanish in the haze.
But every now and then I feel so insecure,
I know that I just need you like I've never done before.

I'm Down

Words & Music by John Lennon
& Paul McCartney
© Copyright 1965 Northern Songs.
All Rights Reserved.
International Copyright Secured.

1st time: N.C.

1. You tell lies, think-in' I can't see;___ you can't cry, 'cause you're

(Verses 2 & 3 see block lyrics)

1st time: N.C.

laugh-in' at me.__ I'm down,___   I'm real-ly down,___   down on the ground.__   I'm down,___

__   I'm down.___   I'm real-ly down.___   I'm down.___   How can you laugh,__ when you

To Coda

How can you laugh...

know I'm down,___   when you know I'm down,___   1.   2.   know I'm down,___

Wow!

(Guitar solo)

sim.

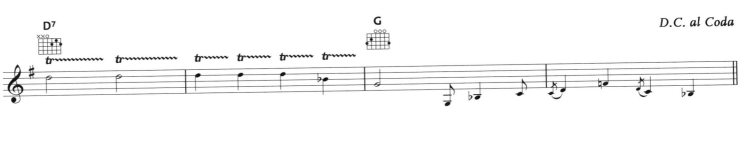

D.C. al Coda

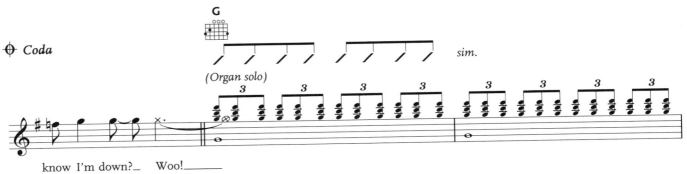

Coda

(Organ solo)

sim.

know I'm down?_ Woo!_____

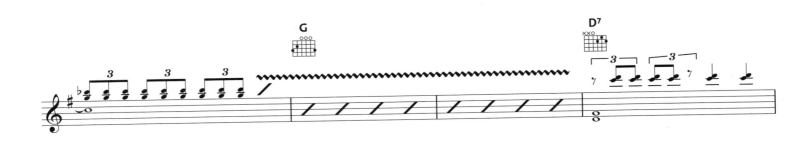

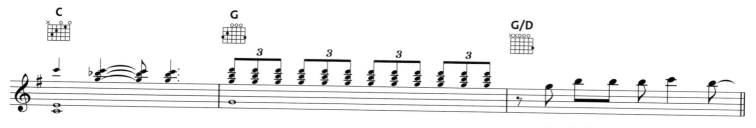

A - baby, you know I'm down,___

I'm real - ly down,___ I'm real - ly down,___
___ I guess I'm down.___ I'm down___ on the

I'm real - ly down.___ I'm real - ly down.___
ground. I'm___ down,___ ah, ba - by, I'm up - side___

Ah, ah, ah, ah. *Repeat to fade*
___ down. Oh yeah, yeah,___ yeah,_ yeah,___ yeah._ I'm down__

Verse 2:

Man buys ring, woman throws it away;
Same old thing happens every day.
I'm down, (I'm really down,)
I'm down, (down on the ground.)
I'm down. (I'm really down.)
How can you laugh when you know I'm down,
(How can you laugh)
When you know I'm down?

Verse 3:

We're all alone and there's nobody else;
She'll still moan, "Keep your hands to yourself!"
I'm down, (I'm really down,)
A-baby I'm down, (down on the ground.)
I'm down. (I'm really down.)
How can you laugh when you know I'm down,
(How can you laugh)
When you know I'm down? Woo!

You've Got To Hide Your Love Away

Words & Music by John Lennon
& Paul McCartney

1. Here I stand head in hand,___ turn my face to the wall.

(Verses 2, 3 & 4 see block lyrics)

If she's gone I can't go on,_____ feel-ing two foot small._____

Hey, you've__ got to hide your__ love a - way.

Hey, you've got to hide your__ love a - way.

Hey, you've got to hide your__ love a - way.

Hey, you've got to hide your__ love a -

- way.

(Alto Flutes duet)

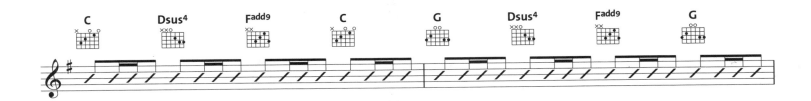

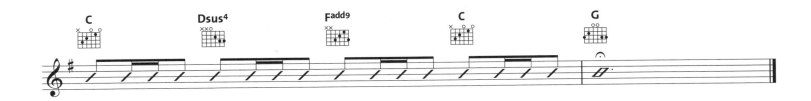

Verse 2:
Everywhere people stare,
Each and every day.
I can see them laugh at me,
And I hear them say...

Verse 3:
How can I even try,
I can never win,
Hearing them, seeing them
In the state I'm in?

Verse 4:
How could she say to me,
Love will find a way?
Gather round all you clowns,
Let me hear you say...

You're Going To Lose That Girl

Words & Music by John Lennon
& Paul McCartney
© Copyright 1965 Northern Songs.

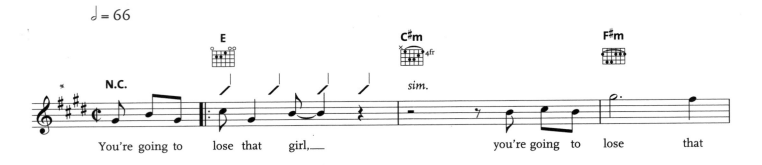

You're going to lose that girl,___ you're going to lose that

girl.___ 1, 3. If you don't take her out to-night,___ she's going to change her mind.___

(Verse 2 see block lyrics)

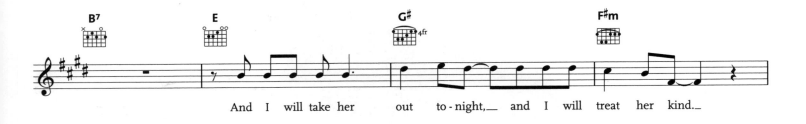

And I will take her out to-night,___ and I will treat her kind.___

You're going to lose that girl,___ you're going to lose that___

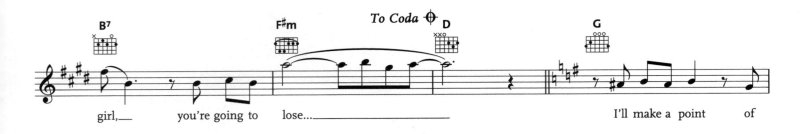

girl,___ you're going to lose...._____ I'll make a point of

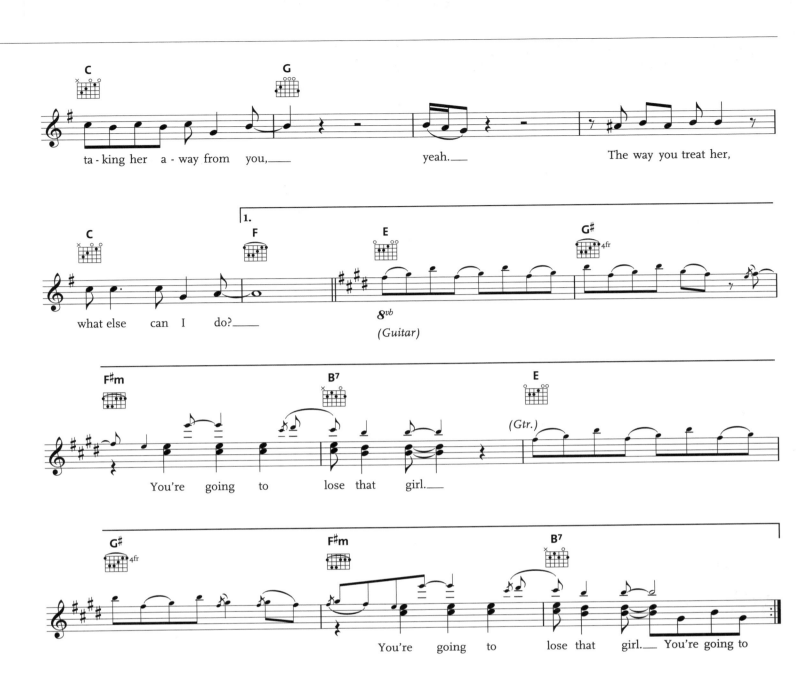

ta-king her a-way from you,___ yeah.___ The way you treat her,

what else can I do?___ *8vb* *(Guitar)*

You're going to lose that girl.___ *(Gtr.)*

You're going to lose that girl.___ You're going to

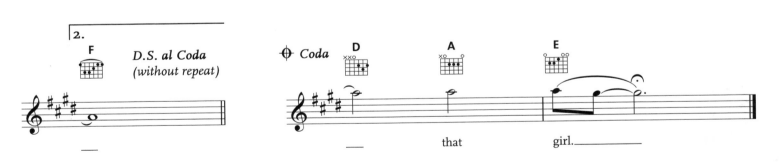

D.S. al Coda
(without repeat)

Coda

___ that girl.___

Verse 2:
If you don't treat her right my friend,
You're going to find her gone.
'Cause I will treat her right, and then
You'll be the lonely one.

You're going to lose that girl...

I've Just Seen A Face

Words & Music by John Lennon
& Paul McCartney

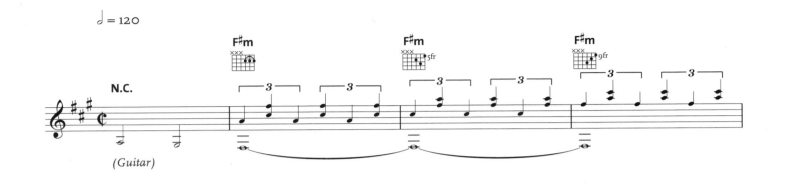

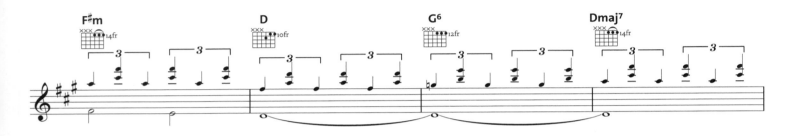

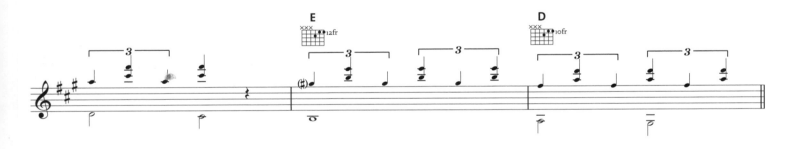

1. I've just seen a face,___ I can't for - get the time___ or place where we just

met; she's just the girl___ for me and I___ want all the world to see___ we've

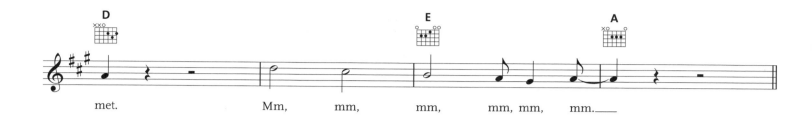

met.   Mm,   mm,   mm,   mm, mm,   mm.____

2. Had it been a - noth - er day, I might have looked__ the oth - er way, and
(Verses 3 & 5 see block lyrics)
(Verse 4: Instrumental for 12 bars)

I'd have nev - er been___ a - ware, but as___ it is, I'll dream__ of her__ to -

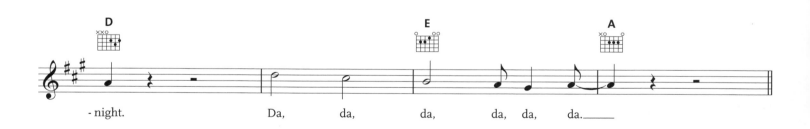

- night.   Da,   da,   da,   da, da,   da.____

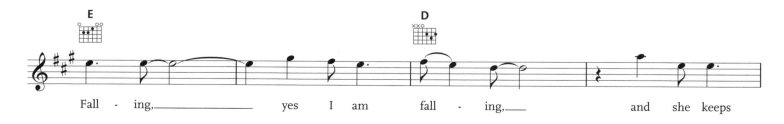

Fall - ing,_____ yes I am fall - ing,____ and she keeps

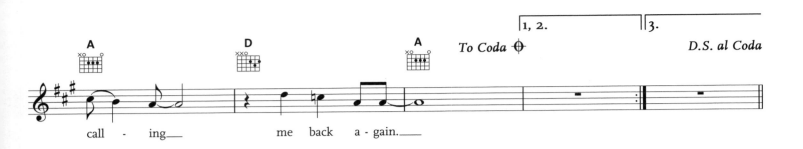

call - ing___ me back a - gain.___

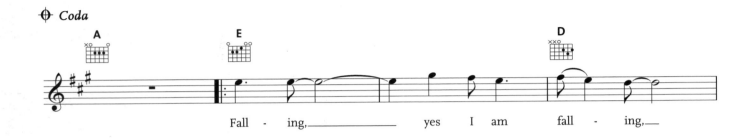

Fall - ing,___ yes I am fall - ing,___

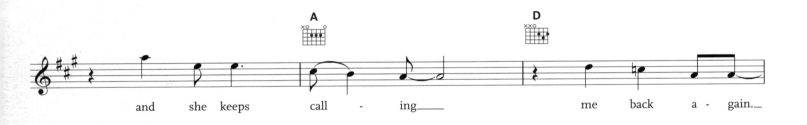

and she keeps call - ing___ me back a - gain.___

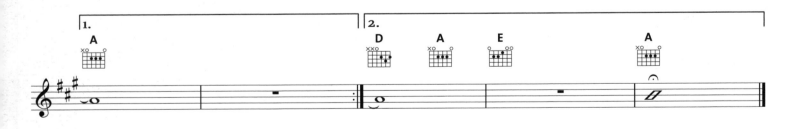

Verse 3:
I have never known the like of this,
I've been alone, and I have
Missed things and kept out of sight,
But other girls were never quite like this.
Da, da, da, da, da, da.

Verse 5:
I've just seen a face, I can't forget
The time or place where we just met;
She's just the girl for me,
And I want all the world to see we've met.
Mm, mm, mm, mm, mm, mm.

Yesterday

Words & Music by John Lennon
& Paul McCartney
© Copyright 1965 Northern Songs.
All Rights Reserved.
International Copyright Secured.

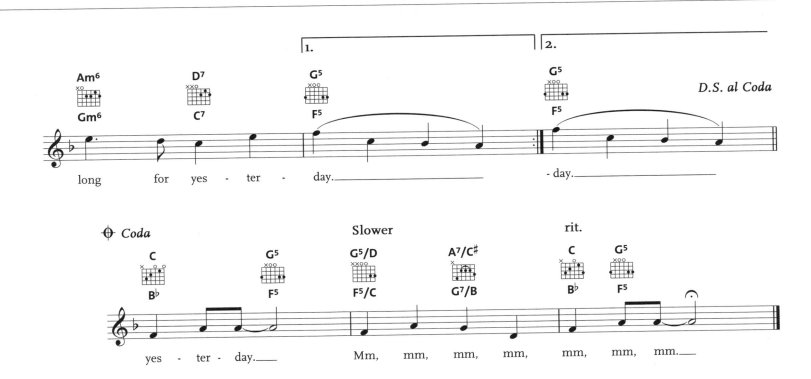

long   for   yes - ter - day._____   - day._____

D.S. al Coda

⊕ *Coda*   Slower   *rit.*

yes - ter - day.____   Mm,   mm,   mm,   mm,   mm,   mm,   mm.____

Verses 3 & 4:
Yesterday, love was such an easy game to play,
Now I need a place to hide away.
Oh, I believe in yesterday.

We Can Work It Out

Words & Music by John Lennon
& Paul McCartney

♩ = 104

1. Try to see it my way; do I have to keep_ on talk-ing till I can't go on?_

While you see it your way, run the risk of know-ing that our love may soon be gone._____

We can work it out,_ we can work it out._____ 2. Think of what you're say - ing;

(Verses 3 & 4 see block lyrics)

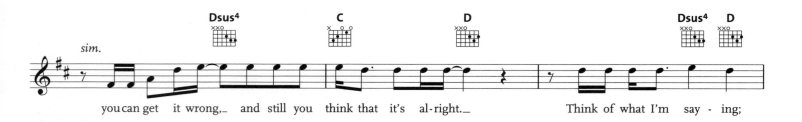

you can get it wrong,_ and still you think that it's al-right._ Think of what I'm say - ing;

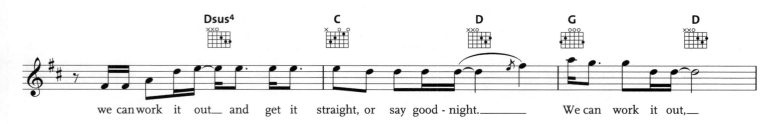

we can work it out_ and get it straight, or say good - night._____ We can work it out,_

we can work it out.____ Life is ve-ry short,__ and there's no time____

__ for fuss-ing and fight-ing, my friend.

I have al-ways thought____ that it's a crime,____

__ so I will ask you once a-gain.

- gain.

Verses 3 & 4:

Try to see it my way;
Only time will tell if I am right or I am wrong.
While you see it your way,
There's a chance that we may fall apart before too long.
We can work it out,
We can work it out.

Day Tripper

Words & Music by John Lennon
& Paul McCartney

(Guitar)

Ah,

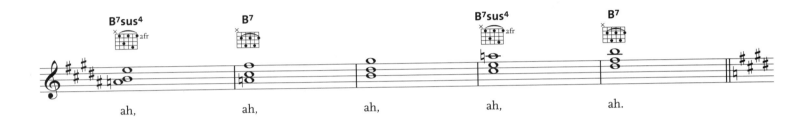

ah,   ah,   ah,   ah,   ah.

D.S. al Coda

(Guitar)

✛ *Coda*

(Guitar)

Play intro. under

Repeat to fade

Day   Trip - per,   Day   Trip - per,   yeah!

Verse 2:
She's a big teaser, she took me half the way there.
She's a big teaser, she took me half the way there, now.
She was a Day Tripper, one-way ticket, yeah!
It took me so long to find out, and I found out.

Verse 3:
Tried to please her, she only played one night stands.
Tried to please her, she only played one night stands, now.
She was a Day Tripper, Sunday driver, yeah!
It took me so long to find out, and I found out.

Drive My Car

Words & Music by John Lennon
& Paul McCartney

(Guitar)

1. Asked a girl what she want-ed to be,___
(Verses 2 & 3 see block lyrics)

she said, "Ba - by, can't you see?___ I wan-na be fa-mous, a star of the screen,___ but

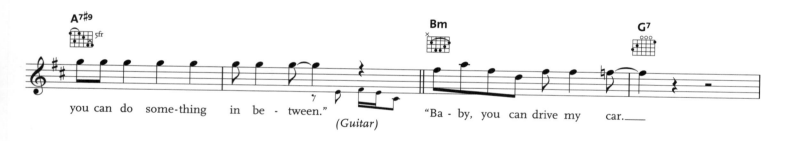

you can do some-thing in be - tween." (Guitar) "Ba - by, you can drive my car.___

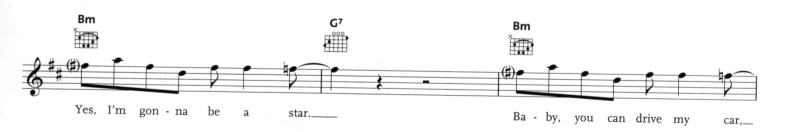

Yes, I'm gon - na be a star.___ Ba - by, you can drive my car,___

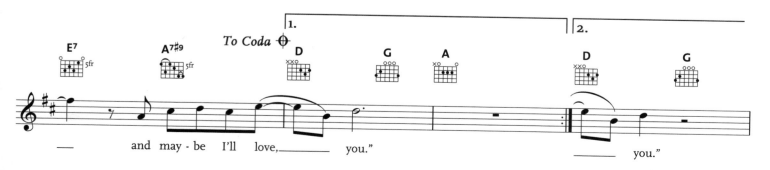

___ and may - be I'll love,___ you." ___ you."

Verse 2:

I told that girl that my prospects were good,
And she said, "Baby, it's understood,
Working for peanuts is all very fine,
But I can show you a better time."

"Baby, you can drive my car...

Verse 3:

I told that girl I could start right away,
And she said, "Listen babe, I've got something to say.
I got no car and it's breaking my heart,
But I've found a driver, and that's a start."

"Baby, you can drive my car...

Norwegian Wood (This Bird Has Flown)

Words & Music by John Lennon
& Paul McCartney
© Copyright 1965 Northern Songs.
All Rights Reserved.
International Copyright Secured.

♩ = 60

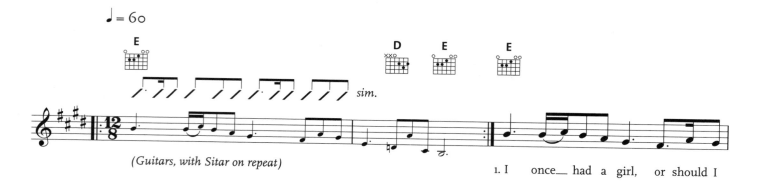

(Guitars, with Sitar on repeat)

1. I once__ had a girl, or should I

say, she once had me. She showed__ me her room, is-n't it good, Nor-weg ian Wood? She

asked me to stay and she told me to sit an - y - where. So

(Verse 2 see block lyrics)

I looked a-round and I not-iced there was-n't a chair. I sat on a rug, bid-ing my

To Coda ⊕

time, drink-ing her wine. We talked un - til two and then she said, "It's time for bed."

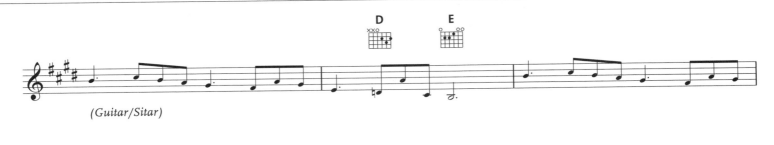

(Guitar/Sitar)

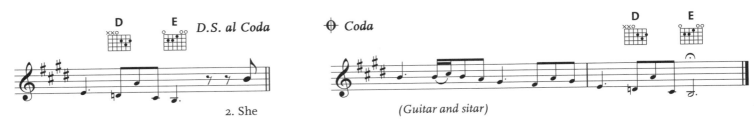

D.S. al Coda   ⊕ Coda

2. She

(Guitar and sitar)

Verse 2:
She told me she worked in the morning and started to laugh;
I told her I didn't and crawled off to sleep in the bath.
And when I awoke I was alone, this bird had flown.
So, I lit a fire, isn't it good, Norwegian Wood?

You Won't See Me

Words & Music by John Lennon
& Paul McCartney
© Copyright 1965 Northern Songs.
All Rights Reserved.
International Copyright Secured.

Verse 2:
I don't know why you should want to hide,
But I can't get through, my hands are tied.
I won't want to stay, I don't have much to say,
But I can turn away and you won't see me.
(You won't see me.)
You won't see me. (You won't see me.)

Nowhere Man

Words & Music by John Lennon
& Paul McCartney
© Copyright 1965 Northern Songs.
All Rights Reserved.
International Copyright Secured.

Ma -king   all____   his   no -where   plans___   for   no - bod - y.

Verse 3:

He's as blind as he can be,
Just sees what he wants to see.
Nowhere man, can you see me at all?

Refrain 2:

Nowhere man, don't worry,
Take your time, don't hurry.
Leave it all, till somebody else lends you a hand.

Verse 4:

Doesn't have a point of view,
Knows not where he's going to.
Isn't he a bit like you and me?

Refrain 3:

Nowhere man, please listen,
You don't know what you're missing.
Nowhere man, the world is at your command.

Michelle

Words & Music by John Lennon
& Paul McCartney

Verse 2:
Michelle, ma belle,
Sont les mots qui vont très bien ensemble,
Très bien ensemble.
I need to, I need to, I need to.
I need to make you see,
Oh, what you mean to me.
Until I do I'm hoping you will know what I mean.
I love you, I love you...

Verse 3:
I want you, I want you, I want you,
I think you know by now;
I'll get to you somehow.
Until I do I'm telling you so you'll understand.

Girl

1. Is there an-y-bod-y going to lis-ten to my sto-ry, all a-bout the girl who came to

(Verses 2 & 3 see block lyrics)

stay? She's the kind of girl you want so much it makes you sor-ry,

still you don't re-gret a sin-gle day. Ah, girl.____

oothss Girl, girl.____ 2. When I
(breathe in)

She's the kind of girl who puts you down when friends are there, you feel a

Verse 2:

When I think of all the times I tried so hard to leave her,
She will turn to me and start to cry.
And she promises the earth to me and I believe her,
After all this time I don't know why.
Ah, girl. Oothss. Girl, girl.

Verse 3:

Was she told when she was young that pain would lead to pleasure?
Did she understand it when they said,
That a man must break his back to earn his day of leisure?
Will she still believe it when he's dead?
Ah, girl. Oothss. Girl, girl.

I'm Looking Through You

Words & Music by John Lennon
& Paul McCartney
© Copyright 1965 Northern Songs.
All Rights Reserved.
International Copyright Secured.

1. I'm look-ing through you,__ where did you go?__
(Verse 2 see block lyrics)

__ I thought I knew you,__ what did I know?__

__ You don't__ look diff-'rent,__ but you have changed.__

__ I'm look-ing through you,__ you're not__ the same.__

__ *(Guitar)*

Why, tell me why__ did you__ not treat me right?__

Love has a nas - ty hab - it of dis - ap - pear - ing

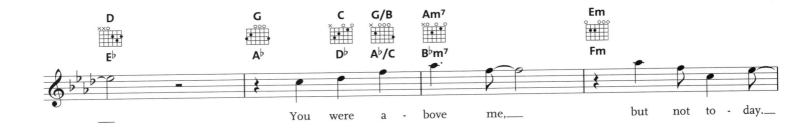

o - ver - night.   3. You're think - ing   of   me,__   the same old way.__
(Verse 4 see block lyrics)

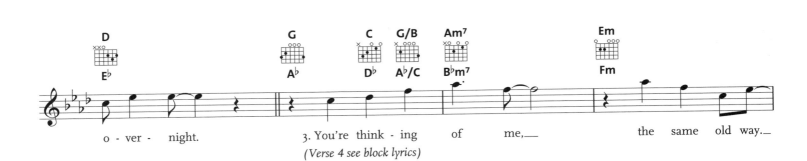

__   You were a - bove me,__   but not to - day.__

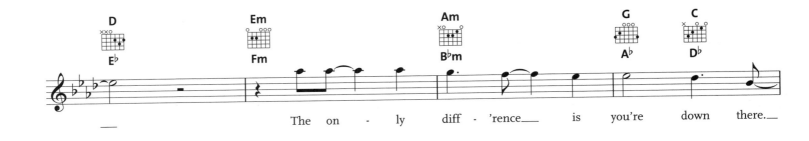

__   The on - ly diff - 'rence__ is you're down there.__

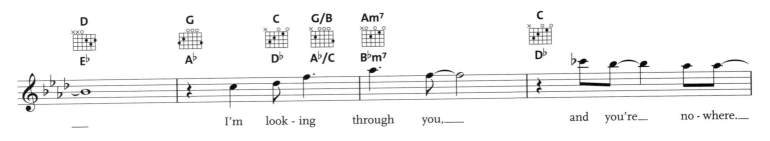

__   I'm look - ing through you,__   and you're__ no - where.__

To Coda ⊕

D.S. al Coda

(Guitar)

⊕ *Coda*

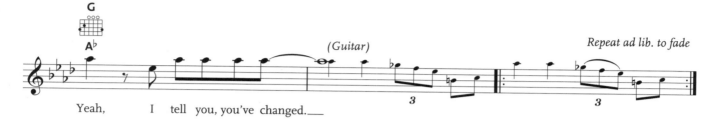

(Guitar)

Repeat ad lib. to fade

Yeah,   I   tell   you, you've changed.___

Verse 2:
Your lips are moving,
I cannot hear.
Your voice is soothing,
But the words aren't clear.
You don't sound different;
I've learnt the game.
I'm looking through you,
You're not the same.

Verse 4:
I'm looking through you,
Where did you go?
I thought I knew you,
What did I know?
You don't look different,
But you have changed.
I'm looking through you;
You're not the same,
Yeah, I tell you, you've changed.

In My Life

Words & Music by John Lennon
& Paul McCartney
© Copyright 1965 Northern Songs.
All Rights Reserved.
International Copyright Secured.

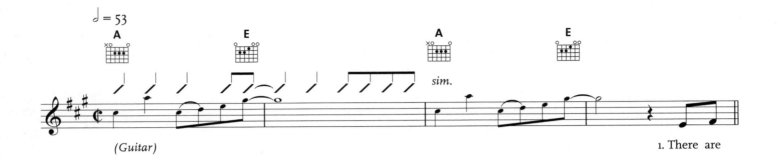

(Guitar)

1. There are

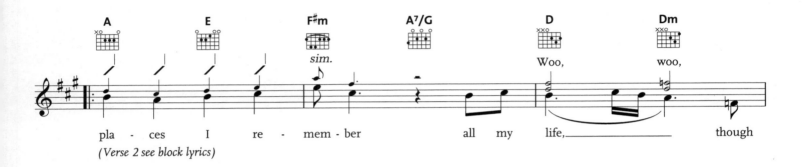

pla - ces I re - mem - ber all my life,_____ though

(Verse 2 see block lyrics)

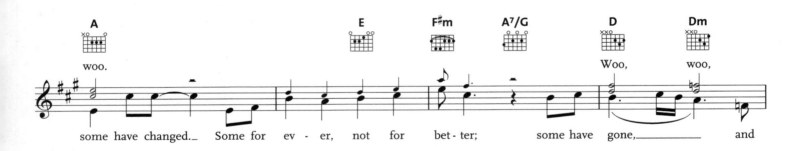

woo. some have changed._ Some for ev - er, not for bet - ter; some have gone,_____ and

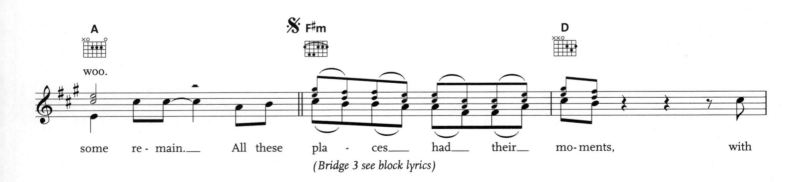

woo. some re - main._ All these pla - ces_ had_ their_ mo - ments, with

(Bridge 3 see block lyrics)

lov - ers and friends,_ I still can re - call._ Some are dead_ and_ some_ are_ liv - ing: in

Verse 2:
But of all these friends and lovers,
There is no one compares with you.
And these memories lose their meaning,
When I think of love as something new.

Though I know I'll never lose affection
For people and things that went before.
I know I'll often stop and think about them;
In my life, I'll love you more.

Bridge 3:
Though I know I'll never lose affection
For people and things that went before.
I know I'll often stop and think about them;
In my life, I'll love you more,
In my life, I'll love you more.

If I Needed Someone

Words & Music by George Harrison
© Copyright 1965 Harrisongs Limited.
All Rights Reserved.
International Copyright Secured.

__ like this._ But you see,_ now I'm_ too much in love.___

Carve your num - ber on_ my wall_ and may - be you_ will get_

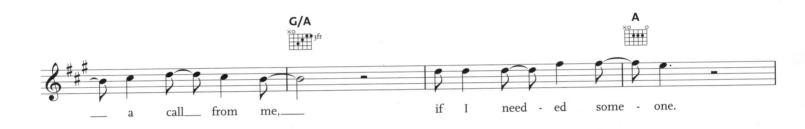

__ a call_ from me,_ if I need - ed some - one._

To Coda ⊕

Ah,____ ah,____

D.S. al Coda

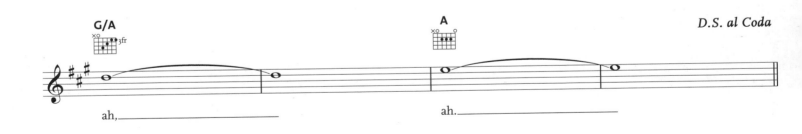

ah,____ ah.____

⊕ *Coda*

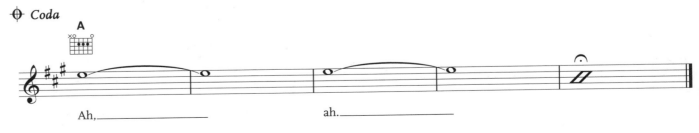

Ah,____ ah.____

1966

5 January

→ CTS Studios: The Beatles re-recorded and overdubbed sections of *The Beatles At Shea Stadium* soundtrack because the audience screaming and technical problems meant that the live sound was not up to exhibition standard. 'I Feel Fine' and 'Help!' were re-recorded from scratch.

8 January

→ *Rubber Soul* reached number one on the *Billboard* Hot 100 charts. The single 'We Can Work It Out' reached number one in the *Billboard* singles charts.

21 January

→ George married Patricia Anne Boyd at the Leatherhead and Esher Register Office, Surrey. Paul and Brian Epstein were the best men; John and Ringo were away on holiday and unable to attend.

→ That evening, the couple celebrated with a party at 'Kinfauns', George's American-style villa in Esher.

22 January

→ George and Patti gave a press conference before being driven to Heathrow to fly to Barbados for their honeymoon. 'How did you manage to keep it a secret?' a reported asked George. 'Simple,' he replied. 'We didn't tell anyone.'

February

→ John returns the advance he's been given by Jonathan Cape for his third book, effectively cancelling the project.

13 February

→ The Grammy Awards Committee in New York nominated The Beatles for ten awards – divided between six nominations for 'Yesterday', and a further four for 'Help!'

21 February

→ The single 'Nowhere Man'/'What Goes On' was released in the US as Capitol 5587.

28 February

→ The Cavern was closed by the Official Receiver with debts of £10,000. The Police had to break down barricades to evict fans who had holed up inside to resist the closure.

Above: George and Patti on their honeymoon in Barbados. Opposite: Robert Whitaker photo session, 25 March.

1 March

→ *The Beatles At Shea Stadium* was given its world premiere on BBC1 in black and white. It was originally filmed in colour, designed for the American market where it was shown in cinemas. Press advertisements for the show were designed by The Beatles' old friend from Hamburg, artist and musician Klaus Voormann.

4 March

The London *Evening Standard* published an interview with John Lennon by his friend Maureen Cleave. John: 'Christianity will go. It will vanish and shrink. I needn't argue about that. I'm right and I will be proved right. We're more popular than Jesus now. I don't know which will go first – rock 'n' roll or Christianity. Jesus was alright but his disciples were thick and ordinary. It's them twisting it that ruins it for me.' His words upset no-one in Britain but when they were reprinted in the US, Christian fundamentalists reacted with hate and outrage.

→ The EP *Yesterday* was released in the UK as Parlophone GEP 8952 (mono). Side A: 'Yesterday', 'Act Naturally'; Side B: 'You Like Me Too Much', 'It's Only Love'.

25 March

→ The Beatles did a photo session for Bob Whitaker at his studio at 1 The Vale, off the Kings Road, Chelsea. The Beatles posed in white coats, using sides of meat and broken dolls as props.

26 March

→ Drake's Drum, the racehorse that Paul bought for his father, won the Hylton Plate at the Aintree Racecourse in Liverpool, coming in at 20–1. Paul, his father and his brother Michael watched the race.

6 April

→ Abbey Road. An 8 pm until 1:15 am session recording 'Tomorrow Never Knows'.

John: "That's me in my Tibetan Book of the Dead period. I took one of Ringo's malapropisms as the title, to sort of take the edge off the heavy philosophical lyrics.

Often the backing I think of early on never comes off. With 'Tomorrow Never Knows' I'd imagined in my head that in the background you would hear thousands of monks chanting. That was impractical, of course, and we did something different. It was a bit of a drag, and I didn't really like it. I should have tried to get near my original idea, the monks singing; I realise now that was what it wanted."

Paul: "That was an LSD song. Probably the only one."

John: "The new album could include literally anything –

The 'Butcher Sleeve': 25 March

John: 'Bob was into Dali and making surreal pictures... it was inspired by our boredom and resentment at having to do another photo session and another Beatles thing. We were sick to death of it... That combination produced that cover.'

The so-called 'Butcher' sleeve was used for the Beatles next American album, *Yesterday... And Today* while the image was used in the UK in ads for the single 'Paperback Writer'. While at Whitaker's studio, The Beatles posed for a second, more conventional photo session for Nigel Dickson, working for *The Beatles Book* fan magazine. They also recorded an interview with Radio Caroline DJ Tom Lodge which was released as a flexi-disc called Sound Of The Stars given away free in a promotion by *Disc And Music Echo*, part-owned by Brian Epstein.

electronic music, jokes. One thing's for sure, it will be very different. We wanted to have the last record so that there was no space between the tracks – just continuous music throughout the whole LP. But EMI wouldn't wear it.

Paul and I are very keen on this electronic music. You make it clinking a couple of glasses together, or with bleeps from the radio, then you loop the tape so that it repeats the same noises at intervals. Some people build up whole symphonies from it. It would have been better than the background music we had for the last film."

7 April
Abbey Road. Paul's looped tapes were added to provide the unique sound on 'Tomorrow Never Knows'. The Beatles began work on 'Got To Get You Into My Life'.

John: "I think that was one of [Paul's] best songs, too, because the lyrics are good and I didn't write them."

8 April
→ Abbey Road. An afternoon and evening session resulted in the completion of a backing track for 'Got To Get You Into My Life.'

11 April
→ Abbey Road. More work was done on 'Got To Get You Into My Life' and then most of the afternoon and evening session was devoted to George's 'Love You To'.

13 April
→ Abbey Road. During the first session of the day they completed 'Love You To', then after a break for dinner, they recorded the backing tracks for 'Paperback Writer', finishing up at 2:30 am. A photographer from

George: "'Love You To' was one of the first tunes I wrote for sitar... this was the first song where I consciously tried to use sitar and tabla on the basic track. I overdubbed the guitars and vocal later."

the group's official fan magazine, *The Beatles Book*, was on hand to document the session.

14 April
→ Abbey Road. The afternoon was spent completing 'Paperback Writer' and in the evening, until 1:30 am, working on the future B-side 'Rain'.

16 April
→ Abbey Road. An afternoon and evening session during which they completed 'Rain'.

John: "I got home from the studio and I was stoned out of my mind on marijuana and, as I usually do, I listened to what I'd recorded that day. Somehow I got it on backwards and I sat there transfixed with the earphones on, with a big hash joint. I ran in the next day and said, 'I know what to do with it. I know… Listen to this!' So I made them all play it backwards. The fade is me actually singing backwards – 'Sharethsmnowthsmeaness'."

17 April
→ Abbey Road. The Beatles laid down the backing tracks for 'Dr. Robert'.

19 April
→ Abbey Road. 'Doctor Robert' was completed.

20 April
→ Abbey Road. A 12-hour session working on 'And Your Bird Can Sing' and George's 'Taxman'.

21 April
→ Abbey Road. 'Taxman' was finished, with Paul adding his distinctive guitar solo which was repeated on the song's fade out.

George: "I was pleased to have him play that bit on 'Taxman'. If you notice, he did like a little Indian bit on it for me."

22 April
→ Abbey Road. The Beatles worked on 'Taxman' and 'Tomorrow Never Knows'.

Last British concert: 1 May

The Beatles' last live appearance in the UK was at the *NME* Poll Winners concert at Empire Pool, Wembley. The bill also featured The Spencer Davis Group, Dave Dee, Dozy, Beaky, Mick & Tich, The Fortunes, Herman's Hermits, Roy Orbison, The Overlanders, The Alan Price Set, Cliff Richard, The Rolling Stones, The Seekers, The Shadows, The Small Faces, Sounds Incorporated, Dusty Springfield, Crispian St Peters, The Walker Brothers, The Who and The Yardbirds. The Beatles played a 15-minute set, for which they had staged a brief rehearsal the previous day, but Brian Epstein would not allow ABC TV to film it because they had not reached an agreement over the terms. The cameras were permitted to film them receiving their Poll Winners Awards.

Ringo: "My favourite piece of me is what I did on 'Rain'. I think I just played amazing. I was into the snare and hi-hat. I think it was the first time I used this trick of starting a break by hitting the hi-hat first instead of going directly to a drum off the hi-hat… I think it's the best out of all the records I've ever made. 'Rain' blows me away. It's out of left field. I know me and I know my playing, and then there's 'Rain'."

26 April
→ Abbey Road. The Beatles spent a 12-hour session working on 'And Your Bird Can Sing'.

27 April
→ Abbey Road. John's 'I'm Only Sleeping' was virtually finished when they called it a day at 3 am.

28 April
→ Abbey Road. The session was spent recording the eight-piece string section for 'Eleanor Rigby'.

Paul: "That started off with sitting down at the piano and getting the first line of the melody, and playing around with words. I think it was 'Miss Daisy Hawkins' originally, then it was her picking up the rice in a church after a wedding. That's how nearly all of our songs start with the first line just suggesting itself from books or newspapers.

At first I thought it was a young Miss Daisy Hawkins, a bit like 'Annabel Lee', but not so sexy, but then I saw I'd said she was picking up the rice in church, so she had to be a cleaner; she had missed the wedding, and she was suddenly lonely. In fact she had missed it all – she was the spinster type. Jane Asher was in a play in Bristol then, and I was walking round the streets waiting for her to finish. I didn't really like 'Daisy Hawkins' – I wanted a name that was more real, and I got the name from a shop called 'Rigby'."

Other sources suggest that the name Eleanor Rigby was taken from a tombstone in a Liverpool cemetery.

29 April
→ Abbey Road. The day was spent adding vocals to 'Eleanor Rigby' and 'I'm Only Sleeping'.

2 May
→ BBC Playhouse Theatre, London. The Beatles were interviewed by Brian Matthew for the 400th edition of *Saturday Club*.
→ Afterwards Paul and Ringo were interviewed separately for the BBC Overseas Service programme *Pop Profile*.

5 May
→ Abbey Road. George spent from 9:30 pm until 3 am recording the backwards guitar solo on 'I'm Only Sleeping'.

6 May
→ Abbey Road. The session was spent adding vocals to 'I'm Only Sleeping'.

9 May
→ Abbey Road. Paul and Ringo worked on 'For No One'.

Below and opposite:
The Beatles during
rehearsals for a live
appearance on BBC
TV's *Top Of The Pops*,
16 June.

14 May
→ *Melody Maker* reported that The Beatles had sold over 1,000,000 records in Denmark.

16 May
→ Abbey Road. Paul added his vocal to 'For No One'.

18 May
→ Abbey Road. A remake of 'Got To Get You Into My Life' was recorded, using Eddie Thornton, Ian Hamer and Les Condon on trumpets and Peter Coe and Alan Branscombe on tenor saxes.

May 19
→ Abbey Road. Beginning at 10 am, The Beatles taped promotional clips of 'Paperback Writer' and 'Rain' in both colour and black and white for television stations around the world. Director Michael Lindsay-Hogg had worked with them before at *Ready Steady Go!* and they were to use him again in the future.

→ The entourage had lunch at the Genevieve restaurant on Thayer Street, near EMI, and taped more film in the afternoon. That evening Alan Civil recorded his celebrated French horn solo on 'For No One'.

20 May
→ The day was also spent shooting promotional films for 'Paperback Writer' and 'Rain', this time on location at Chiswick House, west London.

26 May
→ Abbey Road. The backing track for 'Yellow Submarine' was recorded.

27 May
→ John made a guest appearance in D.A. Pennebaker's unreleased film documentary of Bob Dylan's UK tour *Eat The Document*. John, Dylan and his associate Bobby Neuwirth were filmed talking in the back of Dylan's limousine. Out-take footage revealed that both singers were suffering

Paul: "I wrote that in bed one night. As a kids' story. And then we thought it would be good for Ringo to do."

from the adverse effects of recent drug-taking, as filming was halted when Dylan needed to be sick.
→ Members of the Beatles spent time with Dylan in his Mayfair hotel suite and at various London nightclubs. They also attended his concerts at the Royal Albert Hall.

30 May
→ 'Paperback Writer'/'Rain' was released in the US as Capitol 5651.

31 May
→ Ringo allowed photographer Leslie Bryce to shoot an 'At Home' session at his house in Weybridge for *Beatles Monthly*.

1 June
→ Abbey Road. The sound effects were added to 'Yellow Submarine', assisted by Beatles roadies Mal and Neil and various other friends and associates.
→ That evening George saw Ravi Shankar play a recital at the Albert Hall.
→ In the US, an album of material by The Pete Best Group was released by Savage Records, under the cunning title, *Best Of The Beatles*.

2 June
→ Abbey Road. Most of the session was spent recording George's as-yet-untitled 'I Want To Tell You'.
→ BBC television's *Top Of The Pops* premiered The Beatles' promotional films of 'Paperback Writer' and 'Rain'.

3 June
→ Abbey Road. 'I Want To Tell You' was finished and 'Yellow Submarine' mixed in a session ending at 2:30 am.
→ The British popular press reacted with suitable outrage at the photographs of The Beatles covered with meat and dolls, which were used in the advertisements in the pop papers for the new single.

5 June
→ The promotional films for 'Paperback Writer' and 'Rain' were aired on CBS TV's *Ed Sullivan Show*.

6 June
→ Abbey Road. Most of the session was spent mixing various tracks. Paul added a vocal overdub to 'Eleanor Rigby'.

8 June
→ Abbey Road. Paul's 'Good Day Sunshine' recorded.

9 June
→ Abbey Road. 'Good Day Sunshine' completed.
→ The 'Paperback Writer' promo film was screened on BBC TV's Top Of The Pops.

10 June
→ 'Paperback Writer'/'Rain' was released in the UK as Parlophone R 5452.

14 June
→ Abbey Road. The Beatles began work on Paul's 'Here There And Everywhere'.

John: "This was a great one of his."

15 June
→ The day was spent rehearsing for their live appearance on Top Of The Pops to promote 'Paperback Writer'.
→ The album Yesterday... And Today was released in the US as Capitol T-2553 (mono) and ST-2553 (stereo). Side A: 'Drive My Car', 'I'm Only Sleeping', 'Nowhere Man', 'Dr Robert', 'Yesterday', 'Act Naturally'. Side B: 'And Your Bird Can Sing', 'If I Needed Someone', 'We Can Work It Out', 'What Goes On', 'Day Tripper'.

16 June
→ The Beatles went to the BOAC Air Terminal in Victoria to receive vaccinations against cholera in preparation for their forthcoming Far Eastern tour.
→ After this they travelled in John's black Rolls Royce to BBC Television Centre where they made their first live in-studio appearance on Top Of The Pops, which was also their last live television appearance playing music.
→ Afterwards, at Abbey Road, The Beatles worked until 3 am on 'Here There And Everywhere'.
→ The 'Butcher' sleeve on the Yesterday... And Today album was withdrawn in the US. A new bland sleeve was pasted on top of the withdrawn copies and all new pressings just had the new sleeve.

Collectors carefully peeled the replacement sleeves off and mint copies of the 'Butcher' sleeve are now sold at rare record auctions for huge sums of money.

17 June
→ Abbey Road. 'Here There And Everywhere' was completed and more work was done on 'Got To Get You Into My Life'.
→ Paul bought a 183-acre dairy farm in Machrihanish, Kintyre, Scotland.

20 June
→ Abbey Road. A short visit to the studio after tea for the mixing of 'Got To Get You Into My Life'.
→ The album Yesterday... And Today was re-released in the US with a new innocuous sleeve.

21 June
→ Abbey Road. The final song for Revolver, 'She Said She Said' was recorded in a single evening's session.

23 June
→ The Beatles took an 11 am flight to Munich where they were met by the press and a small number of fans, before a fleet of white Mercedes whisked them off to the Bayerischer Hof Hotel.

Paul: "It's 200 acres and a farmhouse as well. It was well worth the money as far as I'm concerned. But don't think I'm a big property tycoon. I only buy places I like."

24 June
→ Circus-Krone-Bau, with Cliff Bennett & The Rebel Rousers, The Rattles and Peter & Gordon. Two sets, at 5:15 and 9:00 pm, the second of which was filmed by German television station ZDF. Unusually, The Beatles staged an afternoon rehearsal to prepare for the TV performance.
→ Their set for the tour consisted of: 'Rock'n'Roll Music', 'She's A Woman', 'If I Needed Someone', 'Day Tripper', 'Baby's In Black', 'I Feel Fine', 'Yesterday', 'I Wanna Be Your Man', 'Nowhere Man', 'Paperback Writer' and 'I'm Down'.

25 June
→ Early in the morning, The Beatles arrived at Munich railway station in a fleet of Mercedes with motorcycle police guarding them. They boarded the Royal train, previously used by the Queen of England, to take them to Essen. They each had their own suite of rooms, and were on board in time for breakfast.
→ Grugahalle, Essen. The Beatles gave a press conference between their two shows and had a meal in their dressing room. They got back to their train, which travelled through the night to Hamburg, arriving at about 2 am.
→ The promotional film for 'Paperback Writer' was shown in the UK on the final edition of ABC TV's Thank Your Lucky Stars.

26 June
→ The Beatles train arrived in Hamburg at 6 am and they moved into the Schloss Hotel in Tremsbüttel, 30 miles away from Hamburg. They slept

until 1:30 pm then made a balcony appearance for the several hundred fans gathered outside. John visited Astrid Kirchherr, who gave him several letters written by Stuart Sutcliffe. The Beatles played two sets at Ernst Merck Halle with the usual press conference in between. Afterwards John and Paul went for a walk around the Reeperbahn after midnight, revisiting old haunts.

27 June

→ The Beatles left for Tokyo from Hamburg on the inaugural flight by Japanese Airlines over the North Pole. Unfortunately, a typhoon warning caused the plane to be grounded at Anchorage, Alaska, where they spent the night at the Westwood Hotel. That evening The Beatles visited the hotel's club, 'The Top Of The World' on the top floor and a local DJ gave them a quick tour of Anchorage.

28 June

→ The Beatles continued their flight to Tokyo. Ringo had recently bought himself one of the first portable cassette recorders, and took great delight in taping the conversations going on around him on the plane. Some of these tapes later turned up at auction 30 years later.

30 June

→ The Beatles arrived at Haneda airport, Tokyo at 3:40 am (having lost a day by crossing the International Dateline). They stayed at the Tokyo Hilton where they had their own floor, occupying the Presidential Suite. Hotel security was the tightest that The Beatles had yet endured, preventing them from making unplanned sightseeing trips around the Tokyo streets.

→ The Beatles played one concert at the Nippon Budokan Hall to 10,000 fans. There was considerable right-wing opposition – including death threats – to The Beatles playing the Budokan Hall (Martial Arts Hall), because the building was regarded as a national shrine to Japan's war dead, and it was therefore seen as sacrilegious for a rock'n'roll group to play there. Because of these threats, the Japanese lined the route from the airport and the perimeter of the hotel with 30,000 uniformed men. The Budokan went on to become one of the main rock venues in Tokyo.

1 July
→ Nippon Budokan Hall.
Japanese television filmed the first of today's two concerts.

2 July
→ Nippon Budokan Hall.
The final day of concerts. Fan hysteria was so great and the army security so tight that The Beatles were unable to leave their hotel. In order to buy some souvenirs, local tradesmen were brought to their suite. They purchased a brush painting set, which they used to collaborate on an elaborate abstract design, later presented to the president of the local branch of The Beatles Fan Club.

3 July
→ The Beatles flew to Hong Kong, where they rested in the VIP lounge while their plane refuelled, before continuing to Manila in the Philippines (then under the dictatorship of Ferdinand Marcos) where a crowd of 50,000 fans was waiting to greet them. The Filipinos, having noted the behaviour of the Japanese authorities, were not to be outdone. With typical heavy-handedness, military police burst into the plane and seized The Beatles, dragging them down the stairs and into protective custody.
→ Two army battalions in full combat gear met The Beatles and took them to navy headquarters before transferring them to a private yacht where a wealthy Filipino, Don Manolo Elizalde, showed them off to a party of rich friends. It was not until 4 am that Brian Epstein was able to regain control of the situation and The Beatles finally reached their suite at the Hotel Manila.

4 July
→ The Beatles were exhausted and slept late. Unfortunately, Imelda Marcos had organised a lunch party for 300 sons and daughters of top army officers and businessmen at the Malacanang Palace to introduce them

to The Beatles. The group were still asleep after the previous night's debacle when officials came looking for them. Brian Epstein claimed to know nothing of the invitation and refused to allow any further indignities to be perpetrated upon them. Naturally this was taken as a grave insult, with potentially dangerous repercussions. That afternoon they played the Rizal Memorial Football Stadium, before 30,000 fans, and again in the evening to 50,000 fans. The next day the hotel provided no room service. They found that their front man, Vic Lewis, had been questioned by high ranking military officials until dawn, and all military security had been withdrawn. The Beatles and their entourage had to run the gauntlet to get to their plane. They were spat at, insulted and jostled. At the airport Alf Bicknell was thrown to the floor and kicked by military security men and the escalator was turned off so that they had to struggle up with all their equipment. Mal Evans

George: "These gorillas, huge guys, no shirts, short sleeves, took us right off the plane. They confiscated our 'diplomatic bags'. They took all four of us, John, Paul, Ringo and me, without Brian or Neil or Mal. Then they removed us in a boat to Manila Bay surrounded by a ring of cops, guns everywhere... straight away we thought we were all busted because we thought they would find all the dope in our bags."

and Tony Barrow had to get off the plane again to sort out a passport and tax problem which officials suddenly invented before KLM flight 862 was finally allowed to leave Manila at 4:45 pm.

George summed up The Beatles' feelings succinctly: "The only way I'd ever return to the Philippines would be to drop an atom bomb on it."

6 July
→ Returning home, there was a refuelling stop in Bangkok after which The Beatles arrived in New Delhi, India, where they hoped to take a peaceful three day break. Unfortunately, 600 fans were already waiting at the airport when they landed and the Oberoi Hotel was soon under siege. They managed to sneak out the back way and do some shopping and sightseeing. They all bought Indian instruments from Rikhi Ram & Sons, on Connaught Circle.

George: "It turned out to be a good trip, except that when we went out of town, in old Fifties Cadillacs, and walked around the villages, I realised that the Nikon cameras given to us in Tokyo cost more than an Indian villager could earn in a lifetime."

8 July
→ The Beatles arrived back in London at 6 am. There was a short press conference when they landed and George and Ringo appeared on the morning edition of the BBC Home Service's radio show *Today*.

George: "We're going to have a couple of weeks to recuperate before we go and get beaten up by the Americans."

→ The EP *Nowhere Man* was released in the UK as Parlophone GEP 8952 (mono). Side A: 'Nowhere Man', 'Drive My Car'; Side B: 'Michelle', 'You Won't See Me'.

Above: A wearied-looking John and George at a press conference at New York's Warwick Hotel, 22 August. Significantly, it was Lennon and Harrison who pushed most for the Beatles to retire from touring.

12 July
→ The Beatles were awarded Ivor Novello Awards for 'We Can Work It Out' (top selling single of 1965), 'Yesterday' (most outstanding song of the year) and 'Help!' (second best selling single of 1965).

29 July
→ The American magazine *Datebook* published Maureen Cleave's interview with John in which his comment of 'We're bigger than Jesus now' was taken out of context. American Christian fundamentalists reacted with outrage. A DJ in Birmingham, Alabama, organised an immediate boycott of The Beatles' music, and broadcast his intention to conduct a 'Beatle-burning' bonfire of the group's records.

30 July
→ The album *Yesterday... And Today*

reached number one on the *Billboard Hot 100* charts where it stayed for five weeks.

31 July
→ Christian zealots in Birmingham, Alabama, were shown on BBC television news burning Beatles records just as the Nazis had burned books in the Thirties.

1 August
→ Paul recorded an interview for the BBC Light Programme's *David Frost At The Phonograph*.

5 August
→ 'Yellow Submarine'/'Eleanor Rigby' was released in the UK as Parlophone R 5493.
→ *Revolver* was released in the UK as Parlophone PMC 7009 (mono) and PCS 7009 (stereo). Side A: 'Taxman', 'Eleanor Rigby', 'I'm Only Sleeping',

'Love You To', 'Here There And Everywhere', 'Yellow Submarine', 'She Said She Said'; Side B: 'Good Day Sunshine', 'And Your Bird Can Sing', 'For No One', 'Doctor Robert', 'I Want To Tell You', 'Got To Get You Into My Life', 'Tomorrow Never Knows'.

6 August
→ Despite the fact he was still suffering from severe exhaustion after a recent bout of glandular fever, Brian Epstein flew to the US to try and sort out the problems caused by John's remarks about Jesus. There were fears that the entire American tour might have to be cancelled. By August 6 a total of 30 American radio stations had banned Beatles records.
→ John and Paul recorded an hour-long interview about songwriting for the BBC Light Programme at Paul's new house in Cavendish Avenue. It

was broadcast as *The Lennon And McCartney Songbook*.
→ Paul's interview with David Frost was broadcast on the BBC Light Programme's *David Frost At The Phonograph*.

8 August
→ Beatles records were banned by the South African Broadcasting Corporation after John's supposedly irreligious remarks offended the apartheid regime. The ban lasted five years, until after The Beatles broke up. After that Paul, George and Ringo's solo albums were allowed, but not John's, a ban which survived until well after his death.
→ 'Eleanor Rigby'/'Yellow Submarine' was released in the US as Capitol 5715. *Revolver* was released in the US as Capitol T-2576 (mono) and ST-2576 (stereo). As usual it had fewer tracks than the UK release. Side A: 'Taxman', 'Eleanor Rigby', 'Love You To', 'Here There And Everywhere', 'Yellow Submarine', 'She Said She Said'; Side B: 'Good Day Sunshine', 'For No One', 'Doctor Robert', 'I Want To Tell You', 'Got To Get You Into My Life', 'Tomorrow Never Knows'.

11 August
→ The Beatles flew to the US, landing first at Boston, then at Chicago, where they arrived at 4:18 pm.

12 August
→ International Amphitheater, Chicago.
→ The Beatles played two sets, each to 13,000 people. They played the same set on this US tour as on their German and Japanese tour: 'Rock'n'Roll Music', 'She's A Woman', 'If I Needed Someone', 'Day Tripper', 'Baby's In Black', 'I Feel Fine', 'Yesterday', 'I Wanna Be Your Man', 'Nowhere Man', 'Paperback Writer' and 'I'm Down' - sometimes substituting 'Long Tall Sally'.

13 August
→ Olympic Stadium, Detroit. (Two sets).
→ Station KLUE in Longview, Texas, getting on the bandwagon a bit late, organised a public burning of Beatles' records. The station manager said, 'We are inviting local teenagers to bring in their records and other symbols of the group's popularity to be burned at a public bonfire on Friday night, August 13.'
→ The Grand Dragon of the South Carolina Ku Klux Klan attached a Beatles record to the large wooden cross which he then set on fire as part of their ritual.
→ Spanish Radio was reported to have banned the airplay of Beatles records 'forever' because of John's 'blasphemous remark' and in Holland there were moves to ban The Beatles from playing in the country and to have their records banned from the airwaves.

George: 'They've got to buy them before they can burn them.'
→ Ringo was asked why neither 'Eleanor Rigby' nor 'Yellow Submarine' featured in the group's live repertoire. "Eleanor Rigby' is not suitable for the stage,' he replied, 'and would need to be re-arranged. I don't know how Paul would make up for the loss of the strings. 'Submarine' sounds like a good sing-along thing, so I'd like us to do it on stage sometime, perhaps in the autumn. But to be honest, we've kept the same list of titles we used last month in Germany and the Far East. We haven't had the chance to rehearse any new numbers since then.'
Revolver entered the UK charts at number one, and remained there for nine weeks.
→ After the second set in Detroit The Beatles left by bus for Cleveland, Ohio, arriving at 2 am.

14 August
→ Municipal Stadium, Cleveland, Ohio. Two sets to 20,000 fans. When 2,500 fans got into the arena area, the show was stopped midway through a performance of 'Day Tripper' and The Beatles retired backstage for about 20 minutes until order was restored. Radio station KLUE in Longview, Texas, was taken off the air the day after their Beatles records bonfire when a lightning bolt struck their transmission tower, destroying electronic equipment and knocking their news director unconscious.

John: "When they started burning our records... that was a real shock, the physical burning. I couldn't go away knowing I'd created another little piece of hate in the world... so I apologised."

John and Jesus: 11 August

The press and all three US television networks were waiting in Chicago and talked of nothing but John's remarks about Jesus. The Beatles had to do a live press conference from the 27th floor of the Astor Towers Hotel where they were staying. John was obviously very uncomfortable, being forced to apologise for something which the Americans had taken out of context.

John: 'Look, I wasn't saying The Beatles are better than God or Jesus. I said 'Beatles' because it's easy for me to talk about Beatles. I could have said 'TV' or 'the cinema', 'motorcars' or anything popular and I would have got away with it...

'I'm not anti-God, anti-Christ or anti-religion. I was not saying we are greater or better. I believe in God, but not as one thing, not as an old man in the sky. I believe that what people call God is something in all of us. I believe that what Jesus, Mohammed, Buddha and all the rest said was right. It's just the translations have gone wrong.

'I wasn't saying whatever they're saying I was saying. I'm sorry I said it, really. I never meant it to be a lousy anti-religious thing. From what I've read, or observed, Christianity just seems to me to be shrinking, to be losing contact.'

Reporter: 'A disc jockey in Birmingham, Alabama, who actually started most of the repercussions, has demanded an apology from you.'

John: 'He can have it, I apologise to him.'

15 August

→ DC Stadium, Washington, DC to 32,000 fans – and a handful of members of the Ku Klux Klan, who picketed the concert.

→ The Beatles flew into the capital that afternoon and travelled to Philadelphia by coach as soon as their one show was over.

→ The cash-in album *This Is Where It Started* by Tony Sheridan and The Beatles was released in the US.

16 August

→ Philadelphia Stadium, Philadelphia.

→ One evening show held before a crowd which filled little more than a third of the 60,000-seater stadium. The performance was staged amid the beginnings of an electric storm with almost continuous lightning. The rain did not start until just after their set had finished. They flew straight to Canada after the show.

17 August

→ Maple Leaf Gardens, Toronto, Canada.

At a press conference before the show, John aroused another controversy by expressing his support for American draft-dodgers who had fled over the border into Canada to escape being sent to Vietnam. The Beatles did two shows and stayed overnight before flying to Boston.

18 August

→ Suffolk Downs Racetrack, Boston. The bleachers were filled by 25,000 fans, while the stage was specially constructed in the middle of the racetrack.

19 August

→ Mid-South Coliseum, Memphis. An already tense atmosphere in the Deep South was heightened when a spokesman for the Memphis city authorities announced that 'The Beatles are not welcome in Memphis'. A local preacher, the Reverend Jimmy Stroad, organised a mass rally outside the stadium, to protest against the presence of the 'blasphemous' John Lennon within a municipal arena. Six Ku Klux Klansmen also picketed the

George: "Our performances over the last two years have deteriorated to such an extent that our 1966 stage shows are terrible compared to, say, the Cavern days or Hamburg. The audience can't hear it and we can't, which is why it's terrible. We used to play best in the old days when a larger proportion of our fans were boys. The more fame we got, the more girls came to see us, everybody making a noise so that nobody could hear us."

Opposite: The Beatles, with their ever-present aide Neil Aspinall (behind Paul), arrive in Boston, 18 August.

stadium in their costumes. A small number of fanatics threw rubbish on stage and exploded a firecracker. Outside, decoy cars were used to fool protestors, but The Beatles' coach was still surrounded by hordes of Christian demonstrators screaming abuse.

Paul: "They were zealots. It was horrible to see the hatred on their faces."

20 August

→ Crosley Field, Cincinnati. This show was postponed because of heavy rain and re-scheduled for the next day. The local promoter originally insisted that the show should go ahead, despite the danger of electrocution, but The Beatles refused to perform unless he could guarantee their safety.

21 August

→ Crosley Field, Cincinnati. A midday concert after which they flew 350 miles to St. Louis.

→ Busch Stadium, St. Louis, Missouri. The Beatles played at 8:30 pm during a heavy rain-storm to a very wet audience of 23,000 fans. The group were protected by a flimsy tarpaulin which dripped water on the amps. It was this gig which finally convinced Paul McCartney that The Beatles should stop live performances. The other Beatles had decided this long before.

22 August

→ The Beatles flew to New York, where John Lennon sparked further controversy at their Warwick Hotel press conference by speaking out against US participation in the Vietnam War.

23 August

→ Shea Stadium, New York. There were 44,000 fans at the show (compared with 55,000 the previous year), which earned the group $200,000. Once again, 'Day Tripper' prompted several thousand fans to try and invade the stage, although they were beaten back by security guards before they reached The Beatles. The group flew straight to Los Angeles after they left the stage.

→ Before the show, The Beatles took part in two backstage press conferences. The first was organised by the Official Fan Club, and featured an invited audience of 160 fans – who were later congratulated by the group on the intelligence of their questioning. A professional press conference immediately afterwards was less successful, having to be cut short when arguments arose between journalists over The Beatles' opposition to the Vietnam War.

24 August

→ The Beatles arrived in Los Angeles in the early hours of the morning and rested up at 7655 Carson Road, the private house in Beverly Hills that Brian Epstein had rented for them.

25 August

→ Seattle Coliseum, Seattle. The Beatles flew in that morning and stayed at the Edgewater Inn, where the expected press conference was held. Their flight back to Los Angeles from Seattle was delayed for five hours because one of the plane's wheels was discovered to be worn right down to the canvas and had to be replaced.

28 August

→ Dodger Stadium, Los Angeles. There were 45,000 fans for this show and only 102 security men. Dozens of fans were injured and 25 people detained during clashes between police and fans. The Beatles' limousine was besieged by fans and had to turn back. They eventually made their escape in an armoured van. Faced by continued press criticism of poor attendances at Beatles' shows, Brian Epstein issued a special statement: 'This tour compares phenomenally well with last year's. It's much better all round this year, from the point of view of increased interest and we are actually playing to bigger audiences. Here in Los Angeles, for example, 36,000 people saw The Beatles at the Hollywood Bowl. Today's concert at

Below: Los Angeles press conference, 28 August. Opposite: A paisley-patterned Ringo visits John on the set of *How I Won The War* in Almeria, Spain, 21 October.

Dodger Stadium is attracting 10,000 more. People have been saying things about diminishing popularity, but all one can go by is attendances, which are absolutely huge. By the time we leave, 400,000 thousand people will have seen this series of shows, and Sid Bernstein has already delivered his formal invitation to The Beatles to return to Shea Stadium for him in the summer of 1967.'

→ Before the show, John enlivened the customary press conference by repeating the 'blasphemous' remarks he had made about Jesus several months earlier – this time without apology.

29 August

→ Candlestick Park, San Francisco. This was the last time The Beatles performed before a paying audience, seen by 25,000 fans. The group's last number on stage was 'Long Tall Sally', one of their Hamburg show-stoppers. By this time all of them, even Paul who had held out the longest for a continuation of touring, knew that the concerts had to stop. With posterity in mind, he asked Beatles press officer Tony Barrow to tape the performance on his hand-held cassette recorder. George expressed his relief on the plane home: 'That's it. I'm no longer a Beatle,' he announced.

John: "On our last tour people kept bringing blind, crippled and deformed children into our dressing room and this boy's mother would say, 'Go on, kiss him, maybe you'll bring back his sight.' We're not cruel. We've seen enough tragedy in Merseyside, but when a mother shrieks, 'Just touch him and maybe he'll walk again', we want to run, cry, empty our pockets. We're going to remain normal if it kills us."

August 30-31

→ The Beatles flew from Los Angeles to London where they were greeted by several thousand screaming fans.

5 September

→ John flew to Hanover, Germany, to begin filming his part in *How I Won The War* with director Richard Lester on a NATO tank range in Celle, outside Hanover.

John: "There were many reasons for doing it: a) it was Dick Lester and he asked me; b) it was anti-war; and c) I didn't know what to do because The Beatles had stopped touring and I thought if I stopped and thought about it I was going to have a big bum trip for nine months so I tried to avoid the depression of the change of life by leaping into the movie. The thing I remember is that Dick Lester had more fun than I did."

6 September

→ John had his hair cut short for his role as Private Gripweed. The momentous event occurred in the breakfast room of the bar The Inn On The Heath in Celle. In addition to an army haircut, he wore small round National Health 'granny' glasses, which his use made fashionable.

10 September

→ *Revolver* reached number one on the *Billboard* Hot 100 charts, where it remained for six weeks.

14 September

→ George and Patti flew to Bombay, India, for George to take sitar lessons with Ravi Shankar and study yoga. They checked into the Taj Mahal, Bombay, under the names Mr. and Mrs. Sam Wells.

18 September

→ John and Neil Aspinall went to Spain where the filming for *How I Won The War* was due to continue the next day in Carboneras, Spain. John and Cynthia shared a villa in Almeria – owned by Sam Spiegal – with the actor Michael Crawford and his family.

19 September
→ Location filming began again. John had to get up at six each morning for his driver to take him to the film set in his black Rolls.
→ The press discovered that George and Patti were staying in India and George had to give a press conference at the Taj Mahal in which he explainedhe had come to India to study and get some peace and quiet.

28 September
→ Japanese artist Yoko Ono made her first public appearance in Britain, during a symposium on 'Destruction In Art'. She staged two 'concerts' at the Africa Centre in Covent Garden, London.

4 October
→ Ringo and Maureen flew to Almeria to spend a few days visiting John on the film set of *How I Won The War*.

17 October
→ The US record label Clarion became the latest company to recycle some of The Beatles' 1961 Hamburg recordings, on an album entitled *The Amazing Beatles And Other Great English Group Sounds*.

21 October
→ George did an interview with the BBC's correspondent in Bombay, Donald Milner, about his reasons for spending five weeks in India.
→ A charity Christmas card designed by John went on sale in the UK, with proceeds going to the Polio Research Fund.

26 October
→ When Ravi Shankar arrived at London Airport from India, George was there to meet him, dressed in Indian clothes. Ravi Shankar, European educated, was wearing a Western suit.

27 October
→ Penguin Books published *The Penguin John Lennon*, a double volume of John's two books.

4 November
→ NEMS finally vacated 13 Monmouth Street, Brian Epstein's first London office. Most of the operation had been in Argyll Street since 1964.

7 November
→ John celebrated his return from his film duties in Spain by indulging in a three-day orgy of LSD, during which he made several avant-garde recordings with the Mellotron that had recently been installed in his home studio at Kenwood.

9 November
→ John met Yoko Ono at the Indica Gallery, Mason's Yard, London. The day before the opening of her show, *Unfinished Paintings And Objects*, Yoko was introduced to John by the co-owner of the gallery, John Dunbar.

18 November
→ The single 'From Head To Toe'/ 'Night Time' by The Escorts, produced by Paul McCartney, was released in the UK as Columbia DB 8061.

19 November
→ Paul and Mal Evans flew back to London from Kenya where Paul had been on holiday.
During this plane trip, Paul first came up with the concept for the *Sgt. Pepper's Lonely Hearts Club Band* album.

Paul: "I thought, let's not be ourselves. Let's develop alter egos, so we're not having to project an image which we know. It would be much more free. What would really be interesting would be to actually take on the personas of this different band... So I had this idea of giving The Beatles alter egos simply to get a different approach. Then when John came up to the microphone or I did, it wouldn't be John or Paul singing, it would be the members of this band... so we'll be able to lose our identities."

24 November
→ Abbey Road. The Beatles reconvened to start work on a new album, beginning with John's 'Strawberry Fields Forever'.

John: "The awareness apparently trying to be expressed is – let's say in one way I was always hip. I was hip in kindergarten. I was different from the others. I was different all my life. The second verse goes, 'No one I think is in my tree.' Well I was too shy and self-doubting. Nobody seems to be as hip as me is what I was saying. Therefore, I must be crazy or a genius – 'I mean it must be high or low,' the next line. There was something wrong with me, I thought, because I seemed to see things other people didn't see. I thought I was crazy or an egomaniac for claiming to see things other people didn't see."

25 November
→ The Beatles' fourth Christmas record *Pantomime: Everywhere It's Christmas* was recorded in the demo studio in the basement of the New Oxford Street offices of Dick James, their music publisher.

27 November
→ John made a filmed appearance in Peter Cook and Dudley Moore's BBC television show *Not Only... But Also* in which he played a uniformed nightclub doorman. The filmed location for the club was the underground gentlemen's lavatory on Broadwick Street, near Berwick Street market, Soho. John was shown wearing his new 'granny' glasses.

28 November
→ Abbey Road. The Beatles recorded three more takes of 'Strawberry Fields Forever'.

29 November
→ Abbey Road. More work on 'Strawberry Fields Forever'.

6 December
→ Abbey Road. Work began on 'When I'm Sixty-Four'. The Beatles also taped Christmas greetings for the pirate stations Radio London and Radio Caroline.

8 December
→ Abbey Road. Paul added his vocal to 'When I'm Sixty-Four' in the afternoon and all four Beatles arrived for an evening session to continue work on 'Strawberry Fields Forever'.

9 December
→ Abbey Road. The Beatles continued to work on 'Strawberry Fields Forever'.

Opposite: John plays a doorman at 'the Ad Lav' nightclub, Broadwick Street, Soho, 27 November.

10 December

→ The album *A Collection of Beatles Oldies… But Goldies* was released in the UK as Parlophone PMC 7016 (mono) and PCS 7016 (stereo). Side A: 'She Loves You', 'From Me To You', 'We Can Work It Out', 'Help!', 'Michelle', 'Yesterday', 'I Feel Fine', 'Yellow Submarine'; Side B: 'Can't Buy Me Love', 'Bad Boy', 'Day Tripper', 'A Hard Day's Night', 'Ticket To Ride', 'Paperback Writer', 'Eleanor Rigby', 'I Want To Hold Your Hand'. The album marked the first UK release of the group's version of the Larry Williams rocker, 'Bad Boy'.

11 December

→ The BBC Home Service programme *The Lively Arts* broadcast an interview done with George in India in which he discussed philosophy and Indian music.

George: "Too many people have the wrong idea about India. Everyone immediately associates India with poverty, suffering and starvation, but there's much more than that. There's the spirit of the people, the beauty and the goodness. The people there have a tremendous spiritual strength which I don't think is found elsewhere. That's what I've been trying to learn about."

15 December

→ Abbey Road. The Beatles continued work on 'Strawberry Fields Forever'.

16 December

→ Members of The Beatles fan club were sent copies of The Beatles' fourth Christmas flexi disc called *Pantomime: Everywhere It's Christmas*. Side One: 'Song; Everywhere It's Christmas', 'Orowanyna', 'Corsican Choir And Small Choir', 'A Rare Cheese', 'Two Elderly Scotsmen', 'The Feast', 'The Loyal Toast'; Side Two: 'Podgy The Bear And Jasper', 'Count Balder And Butler', 'Felpin Mansions (Part Two)', 'The Count And The Pianist', 'Song; Please Don't Bring Your Banjo Back', 'Everywhere It's Christmas',

'Mal Evans', 'Reprise: Everywhere It's Christmas'.

Ringo: "We worked it out between us. Paul did most of the work on it. He thought up the 'Pantomime' title and the two song things."

Paul: "I drew the cover myself. There's a sort of funny pantomime horse in the design if you look closely. Well I can see one there if you can't."

18 December

→ Paul and Jane attended the premiere of *The Family Way* at the Warner Theatre, London which had an incidental soundtrack written by Paul and arranged by George Martin. John and Paul's friend Tara Browne was killed in a car crash, on his way to visit another friend of Paul's, David Vaughan. John later said that the tragedy inspired him to write the line 'He blew his mind out in a car' in 'A Day In The Life', although Paul has since challenged that theory.

19 December

→ The design team Binder, Edwards and Vaughan announced that Paul had agreed to make an experimental electronic tape for the 'Carnival Of Light' event to be held at the Roundhouse, Chalk Farm, in January.

20 December

→ Abbey Road. More vocals were added to 'When I'm Sixty-Four.' The Beatles recorded interviews with John Edwards for the ITN news programme *Reporting '66* when arriving for the evening's work at EMI Studios.

21 December

→ Abbey Road. Woodwind was added to 'When I'm Sixty-Four' and John added more vocals to 'Strawberry Fields Forever'.

John: "We don't often write entirely on our own – I mean, I did bits of 'Penny Lane' and Paul wrote some of 'Strawberry Fields'."

John: "I copped money for The Family Way, the film music that Paul wrote when I was out of the country filming How I Won The War. I said, 'You'd better keep that.' He said, 'Don't be soft.' It's the concept. We inspired each other so much in the early days. We write how we write now because of each other."

→ Paul played mellotron on the opening of 'Strawberry Fields' using the flute setting, while George and Paul played timpani and bongo drums.
→ The single 'Love In The Open Air'/ 'Theme From *The Family Way*' by The George Martin Orchestra and written by Paul McCartney was released in the UK as United Artists UP 1165.

29 December

→ Abbey Road. Working alone in the studio, Paul recorded a basic track to his 'Penny Lane'.

Paul: "'Penny Lane' is a bus roundabout in Liverpool and there is a barber's shop… There's a bank on the corner so we made up the bit about the banker in his motor car. It's part fact, part nostalgia for a place which is a great place – blue suburban skies as we remember it, and it's still there."

30 December

→ Abbey Road. The year ended with further work being done on 'When I'm Sixty-Four' and 'Penny Lane'.

Paperback Writer

Words & Music by John Lennon
& Paul McCartney
© Copyright 1966 Northern Songs.
All Rights Reserved.
International Copyright Secured.

(Wri - ter, wri - ter.)

Pap - er - back wri - ter._____

G7 (Guitar)

1. Dear___

G7

Sir or Mad-am, will you read my book, it took me years to write.__ Will you take a look? It's

(Verses 2, 3 & 4 see block lyrics)

based on a nov-el by a man named Lear and I need a job,__ so I want to be a pa-per-back

C   **G7**

1.

wri - ter, pap - er - back wri - ter._____ 2. It's the

2.

G7   N.C.

___ Pap - er - back wri - ter._____ (Guitar)

(Pap - er - back wri - ter, wri - ter.)

3. It's a

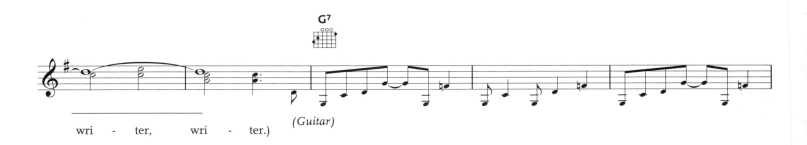

4. If you ___ Pap - er - back wri - ter.___
(Pap - er - back

wri - ter, wri - ter.) *(Guitar)*

Repeat to fade

Pap - er - back wri - ter.___
(Pap - er - back wri - ter.)___

Verse 2:
It's the dirty story of a dirty man,
And his clinging wife doesn't understand.
His son is working for the Daily Mail,
It's a steady job,
But he wants to be a paperback writer,
Paperback writer.

Verse 3:
It's a thousand pages give or take a few,
I'll be writing more in a week or two.
I can make it longer if you like the style,
I can change it 'round,
And I want to be a paperback writer,
Paperback writer.

Verse 4:
If you really like it you can have the rights,
It could make a million for you overnight.
If you must return it you can send it here,
But I need a break,
And I want to be a paperback writer,
Paperback writer.

Rain

Words & Music by John Lennon
& Paul McCartney

1. If the rain comes, they run and hide their heads; they might as well be dead, if the rain_____ comes,_____ if the rain_____ comes.

2. When the sun shines, they slip in-to the shade, and sip their lem-on-ade, when the sun_____ shines,_____

Backing Vox

When the sun shines down, when the sun shines down,_____

when the sun_____ shines.____

sun_____ shines.____

Rain,_____ I don't mind.__

Shine,_____

the weath-er's fine.__

3. I can show you that when it starts to
(Verse 4 see block lyrics)

rain, Ev-'ry-thing's the same; I can show you,_____

Backing Vox

When the rain comes down, when the rain comes down,_____

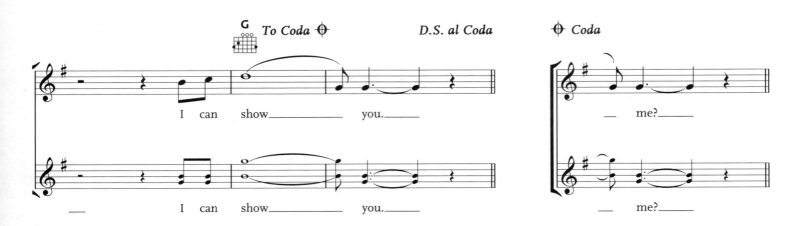

I can show_____ you._____

_____ I can show_____ you._____

_____ me?_____

_____ me?_____

(Guitar)

Fade to end, reverse vocal

sim.

Sdaeh rieht___ edih dna_____ nur yeht___ se-moc ni

Rain._____

-ar eht fi.

Niar._____

Rain._____

En - - ihs - nus._____

Verse 4:
Can you hear me,
That when it rains and shines,
(When it rains and shines)
It's just a state of mind?
(When it rains and shines)
Can you hear me,
Can you hear me?

Taxman

Words & Music by George Harrison
© Copyright 1966 Harrisongs Limited.
All Rights Reserved.
International Copyright Secured.

And you're___ work - ing___ for no one but___ me.___

Tax - man!___

Repeat to fade

8vb
(*Bass Guitar riff* + *Guitar solo*)

Verse 3:
Don't ask me what I want it for,
(A-ha, Mister Wilson!)
If you don't want to pay some more,
(A-ha, Mister Heath!)

'Cause I'm the taxman.
Yeah, I'm the taxman.

Verse 4:
Now, my advice
For those who die:
Declare the pennies
On your eyes.

'Cause I'm the taxman.
Yeah, I'm the taxman,
And you're working for no one but me.
(Taxman!)

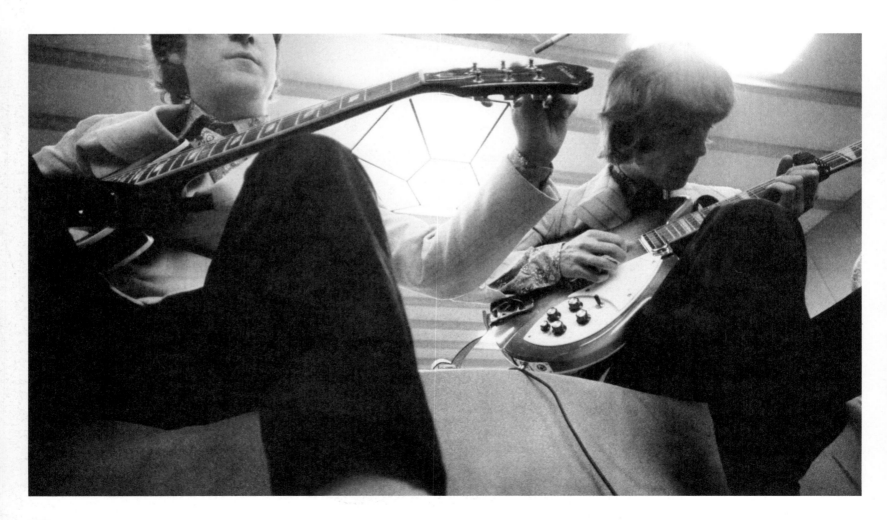

Eleanor Rigby

Words & Music by John Lennon
& Paul McCartney
© Copyright 1966 Northern Songs.
All Rights Reserved.
International Copyright Secured.

♩ = 138

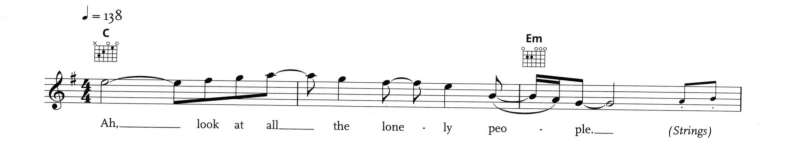

Ah,_____ look at all____ the lone - ly peo - ple.____ (Strings)

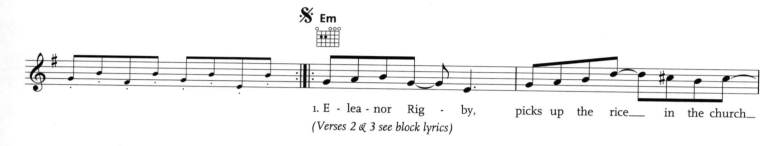

1. E - lea - nor Rig - by, picks up the rice___ in the church___
(Verses 2 & 3 see block lyrics)

___ where a wed - ding has been,___ lives in a dream._____ Waits at the win - dow,

wear - ing the face___ that she keeps___ in a jar___ by the door.___

To Coda ⊕

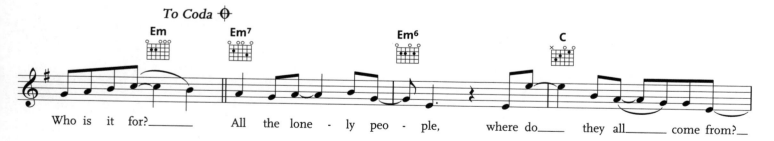

Who is it for?_____ All the lone - ly peo - ple, where do___ they all___ come from?___

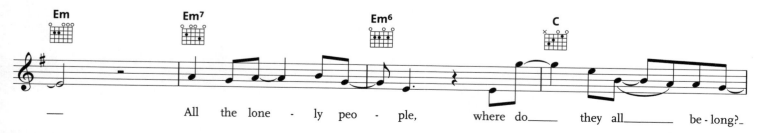

___ All the lone - ly peo - ple, where do___ they all___ be - long?_

Verse 2:
Father McKenzie, writing the words of a sermon that no one will hear,
No one comes near.
Look at him working, darning his socks in the night when there's nobody there,
What does he care?

All the lonely people...

Verse 3:
Eleanor Rigby, died in the church and was buried along with her name,
Nobody came.
Father McKenzie, wiping the dirt from his hands as he walks from the grave.
No one was saved.

All the lonely people...

I'm Only Sleeping

Words & Music by John Lennon
& Paul McCartney

(Original recording slightly flat)

1, 3. When I wake up ear-ly in the morn-ing; lift my head,_____
(Verse 2 see block lyrics)

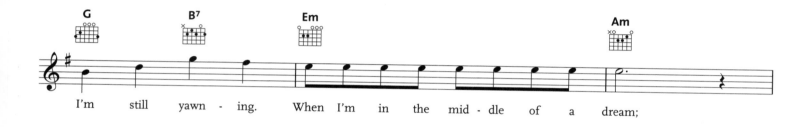

I'm still yawn-ing. When I'm in the mid-dle of a dream;

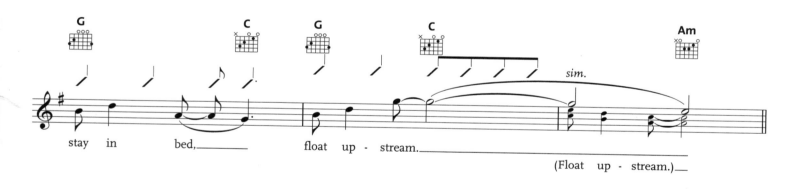

stay in bed,_____ float up - stream._____

(Float up - stream.)_____

Please don't wake__ me, no____ don't shake__ me, leave me where__ I am:__

Backing vox

Woo, woo, woo._____ Woo,_____ woo, woo, woo.__

I'm miles___ a - way, and af - ter all,___ I'm on - ly sleep - ing.___

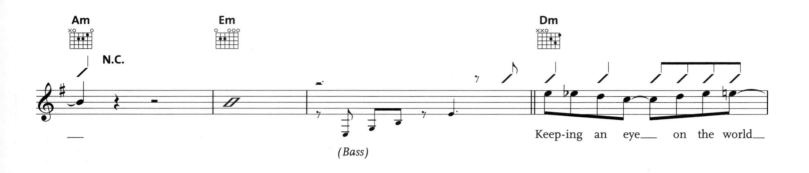

___ (Bass) Keep-ing an eye___ on the world___

D.C. al Coda   ⊕ *Coda*

___ go-ing by___ my win - dow. Ta-king my time.___ (Guitar) ___

Tempo Rubato

Fade to end

Verse 2:
Everybody seems to think I'm lazy;
I don't mind: I think they're crazy.
Running everywhere at such a speed,
Till they find there's no need.
(There's no need.)

Please don't spoil my day,
I'm miles away,
And after all, I'm only sleeping.

Here, There And Everywhere

Words & Music by John Lennon
& Paul McCartney

each one be - liev - ing that love___ nev - er dies,___ watch - ing her eyes___ and ho -

1. **2.**

- ping I'm al - ways there.___ I want her ___ I will be there and

ev - 'ry - where,___ here, there and ev - 'ry - where.___

Verse 2:
There, running my hands through her hair,
Both of us thinking how good it can be.
Someone is speaking, but she doesn't know he's there.

Yellow Submarine

Words & Music by John Lennon
& Paul McCartney
© Copyright 1966 Northern Songs.
All Rights Reserved.
International Copyright Secured.

friends_____ are all a - board, ma - ny more of them live next door. And the

3. Instrumental with sound effects

Chords 2nd time only

1.

band_____ be - gins to play... *(Brass band)*

2.

4. As we live_____ a life of ease, ev - 'ry one of us_____ has all we

need. Sky of blue_____ and sea of green, in our yel - low sub - mar -

D.S. al Coda   Coda

Fade to end

- ine.   yel - low sub - mar - ine.   We all live in a

yel - low sub - mar - ine,   yel - low sub - mar - ine,   yel - low sub - mar - ine.

We all live in a yel - low sub - mar - ine,   yel - low sub - mar - ine,   yel - low sub - mar - ine.

She Said She Said

Words & Music by John Lennon
& Paul McCartney
© Copyright 1966 Northern Songs.
All Rights Reserved.
International Copyright Secured.

Verse 2:

I said, "Who put all those things in your head?

Things that make me feel that I'm mad."

And you're making me feel like I've never been born.

Good Day Sunshine

Words & Music by John Lennon
& Paul McCartney
© Copyright 1966 Northern Songs.
All Rights Reserved.
International Copyright Secured.

Good - day sun - shine, good - day sun - shine,

good - day sun - shine. 1. I need to laugh, and when the

(Verses 2 & 3 see block lyrics)

sun is out,__ I've got some - thing I can laugh a - bout.__ I feel good,__

__ in a spec - ial way.__ I'm in love and it's a

sun - ny day. touch the ground.__ (Piano)

lov - ing me.___ She feels good;___ she knows she's look-ing fine.___

I'm so proud to know that she is mine.___ - shine.

Good - day___ sun - shine,___ good - day___ sun -

- shine,___ good - day___ sun - shine. Good - day___ sun -

Good - - day___ sun - shine.___

Repeat to fade

- shine,___ good - - day___ sun -

Verse 2:
We take a walk,
The sun is shining down.
Burns my feet as they touch the ground.
(Piano solo for 4 bars)

Verse 3:
And then we lie
Beneath a shady tree.
I love her and she's loving me.
She feels good;
She knows she's looking fine.
I'm so proud to know that she is mine.

And Your Bird Can Sing

Words & Music by John Lennon
& Paul McCartney
© Copyright 1966 Northern Songs.
All Rights Reserved.
International Copyright Secured.

(Guitars)

tell me that you've got ev - 'ry - thing you want, and your bird can sing, but you don't get me._

(Verses 2 & 3 see block lyrics)

You don't get me._____

When your prized_ pos - ses - sions start to weigh_ you down,_____

(Bridge 2 see block lyrics)

look in my_ di - rec - tion, I'll be 'round,___ I'll be 'round.___

(Guitars)

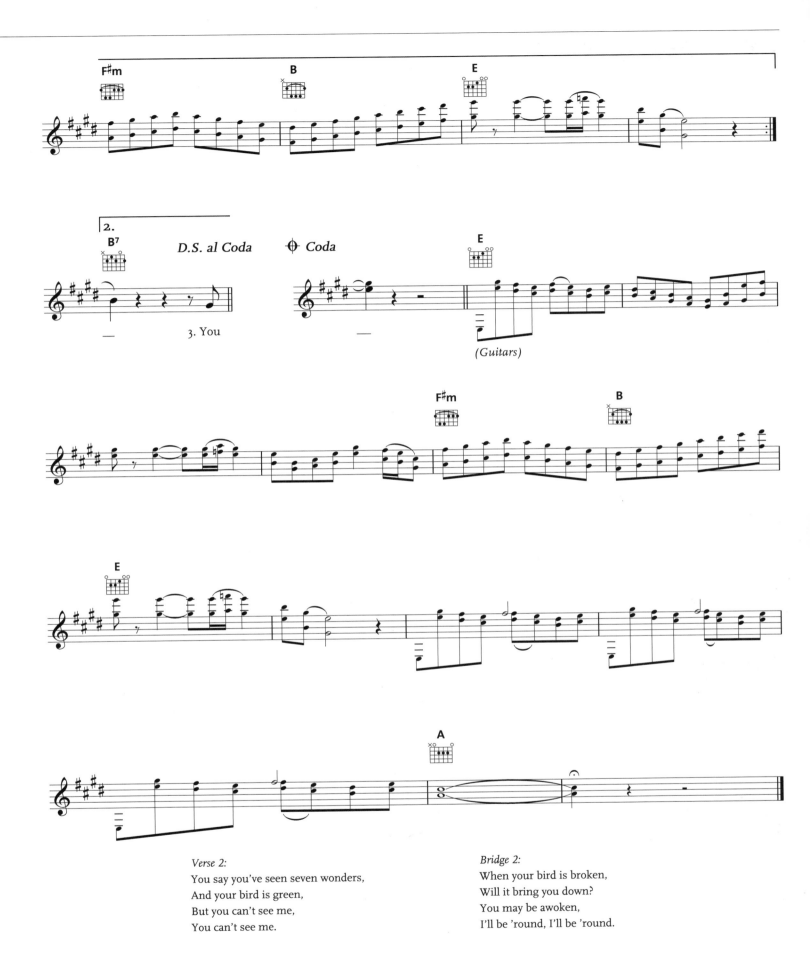

Verse 2:
You say you've seen seven wonders,
And your bird is green,
But you can't see me,
You can't see me.

Bridge 2:
When your bird is broken,
Will it bring you down?
You may be awoken,
I'll be 'round, I'll be 'round.

Verse 3:
You tell me that you've heard every sound there is,
And your bird can swing,
But you can't hear me,
You can't hear me.

For No One

Words & Music by John Lennon
& Paul McCartney
© Copyright 1966 Northern Songs.

♩ = 82

Capo on 2nd fret

1. Your day__ breaks, your mind aches, you find__ that all__ her words of
(Verse 2 see block lyrics)

kind - ness lin - ger on,__ when she no long - er needs__ you.__

— And in her eyes you see noth - ing,__ no sign of

love be - hind the tears__ cried for no__ one, a love that

should have last - ed years.__ 3. You want__ her,
(Verses 4 & 5 see block lyrics)

you need_ her, and yet__ you don't__ be - lieve her when she says her love_

Verse 2:
She wakes up, she makes up,
She takes her time and doesn't feel she has to hurry,
She no longer needs you.

Verse 4:
You stay home, she goes out,
She says that long ago she knew someone, but now he's gone,
She doesn't need him.

Verse 5:
Your day breaks, your mind aches,
There will be times when all the things she said will fill your head,
You won't forget her.

Got To Get You Into My Life

Words & Music by John Lennon
& Paul McCartney
© Copyright 1966 Northern Songs.
All Rights Reserved.
International Copyright Secured.

(Guitar)

Oo, got to get you in-to my life!_

(Horns)

I was a-lone,_____ I took a ride,_ I did-n't know what I would find_ there...

Fade to end, vocals ad lib.

(Trumpets)

(Sax)

Verse 2:
You didn't run, you didn't lie,
You knew I wanted just to hold you.
And had you gone you knew in time we'd meet again,
For I had told you.
Oo, you were meant to be near me,
Oo, and I want you to hear me,
Say we'll be together every day.

Verse 3:
What can I do, what can I be,
When I'm with you I want to stay there.
If I'm true I'll never leave,
And if I do I know the way there.
Oo, then I suddenly see you,
Oo, did I tell you I need you
Every single day of my life?

Tomorrow Never Knows

Words & Music by John Lennon
& Paul McCartney
© Copyright 1966 Northern Songs.
All Rights Reserved.
International Copyright Secured.

(Sitar)

(Bass Guitar riff)

(sim.)

1. Turn___ off your mind, re - lax and float down -

(Verses 2 & 3 see block lyrics)

- stream;   it   is   not   dy - ing,___   it   is   not

dy - ing.___   2. Lay___ ___

(Synth. solo, with effects,
over bass riff)

(Reverse Guitar solo)

4. That

love is all, and love___ is ev - 'ry - one; it is

(Verses 5, 6 & 7 see block lyrics)

know - ing,___ it is know - ing...___ 5. ...That

Of the be - gin - ning,___ of the be - gin - ning,___ of the be -

___ of the be - gin - ning.___

(Honky Tonk Piano)

Fade to end

Verse 2:
Lay down all thought,
Surrender to the void;
It is shining, it is shining.

Verse 3:
That you may see
The meaning of within;
It is being, it is being.

Verse 5:
...That ignorance and
Hate may mourn the dead;
It is believing, it is believing.

Verse 6:
But listen to the
Colour of your dreams;
It is not living, it is not living.

Verse 7:
Or play the game
'Existence' to the end,
Of the beginning, of the beginning.

Of the beginning...

1967

4 January

→ Abbey Road. *Sgt Pepper* sessions. Work continued on 'Penny Lane'.

5 January

→ Abbey Road. *Sgt Pepper* sessions. Paul's vocal track on 'Penny Lane' was followed by a free-form, 'Freak Out', The Beatles' only combined effort at producing 'a bit of random'. David Vaughan, of the design team Binder, Edwards and Vaughan, had asked Paul for some music for a sound and light rave to be held at the Roundhouse, Chalk Farm. Paul obliged, and at 13 minutes, 14 seconds, produced the longest Beatles track ever completed. There was no rhythm track, just heavily echoed bursts of percussion, shouts and random bits of piano and guitar. George refused to allow an edited version of it onto the *Anthology* series of CDs in 1996.

6 January

→ Abbey Road. *Sgt Pepper* sessions. More work on 'Penny Lane'. The album *The Family Way (Original Soundtrack Album)* with a score by The George Martin Orchestra, written by Paul McCartney, was released in the UK as Decca SKL 4847. Side One: 'Love In The Open Air' (cuts one to six); Side Two: 'Love In The Open Air' (cuts one to seven).

→ The Beatles' German friend, Hans-Walther Braun, appeared on the German TV programme *Damals In Hamburg*, and played an extract from a 1960 recording by the group which they had given him that year, featuring the earliest known rendition of Paul's song, 'I'll Follow The Sun'. Remarkably, this event passed unnoticed by Beatles fans outside Germany, and nothing more was heard of Braun's tape until similar material surfaced on bootleg albums in the mid-Eighties.

7 January

→ The *Daily Mail* newspaper published adjacent stories about the inquest into the death of John and Paul's friend, Tara Browne, and a report on the poor state of the roads in Blackburn, Lancashire, where 4,000 holes needed to be filled. Both themes found their way into the lyrics of 'A Day In The Life'.

9 January

→ Abbey Road. *Sgt Pepper* sessions. Wind instruments added to 'Penny Lane.'

10 January

→ Abbey Road. *Sgt Pepper* sessions. More work on 'Penny Lane'. American ABC TV broadcast the 1965 film of *The Beatles At Shea Stadium*.

11 January

→ Paul saw the BBC2 programme *Masterworks*, on which David Mason played piccolo trumpet on Bach's *Brandenburg Concerto No 2 In F Major* with the English Chamber Orchestra from Guildford Cathedral. Paul realised that this was the sound he wanted on 'Penny Lane'.

12 January

→ George Martin telephoned David Mason and booked him for a session on the 17th to play piccolo trumpet on 'Penny Lane'.

→ Abbey Road. *Sgt Pepper* sessions. More work on 'Penny Lane'.

17 January

→ Abbey Road. *Sgt Pepper* sessions. David Mason added his famous piccolo trumpet solo to 'Penny Lane'. Paul improvised the part by singing it to George Martin, who then wrote it out on score paper for Mason to play.

18 January

→ Paul was interviewed in London by Jo Durden-Smith for a Granada Television documentary on the London underground scene, of which Paul was part. The film, for the *Scene Special* programme, was subtitled *It's So Far Out, It's Straight Down* (whatever that meant) and was broadcast (in the North only) on 7 March.

19 January

→ Abbey Road. *Sgt Pepper* sessions. The basic track for 'A Day In The Life' was recorded with Mal Evans counting off the 24 empty bars in the middle and marking the end with an alarm clock.

20 January

→ Abbey Road. *Sgt Pepper* sessions. Vocal tracks added to 'A Day In The Life'.

Paul: "I got the idea of using trumpets in that pizzicato way on 'Penny Lane' from seeing a programme on television. I didn't know whether it would work, so I got the arranger for the session into the studio, played the tune on the piano and sang how I wanted the brass to sound. That's the way I always work with arrangers." The song was now complete.

Opposite: John on the set of the 'Strawberry Fields Forever' promo film, Sevenoaks, Kent, 30 January.

1967

John: "Well, it was a peak. Paul and I were definitely working together, especially on 'A Day In The Life' that was real... The way we wrote a lot of the time: you'd write the good bit, the part that was easy, like 'I read the news today', or whatever it was, then when you got stuck or whenever it got hard, instead of carrying on, you just drop it; then we would meet each other, and I would sing half, and he would be inspired to write the next bit and vice versa. He was a bit shy about it because I think he thought it's already a good song. Sometimes we wouldn't let each other interfere with a song either, because you tend to be a bit lax with someone else's stuff, you experiment a bit. So we were doing it in his room with the piano. He said 'Should we do this?' Yeah, let's do that. But *Pepper* was a peak all right."

25 January
→ Abbey Road. *Sgt Pepper* sessions. Paul supervised a new mix of 'Penny Lane' because he was not satisfied with the old one.
→ Brian Epstein signed a deal allowing *Sunday Times* newspaper journalist Hunter Davies to write an authorised biography of The Beatles, granting their co-operation in exchange for a percentage of the royalties.

27 January
→ The Beatles and Brian Epstein signed a new nine-year worldwide recording contract with EMI Records, updating their previous deal, which had expired the previous day.

30 January
→ EMI were desperate to release a new Beatles single, so Brian Epstein

asked George Martin for two tracks from the *Sgt Pepper* sessions. George reluctantly gave him 'Penny Lane' and 'Strawberry Fields Forever'.
→ The Beatles began filming the promotional films for 'Strawberry Fields Forever' and 'Penny Lane' at Knole Park, Sevenoaks in Kent where director Peter Goldmann filmed them next to a dead oak tree in the park.

31 January
→ Pirate station Radio London became the first station to play 'Penny Lane' on the air.
→ John bought an 1843 circus poster in an antique shop in Sevenoaks, near where they were filming. The poster provided him and Paul with almost the complete lyrics for 'Being For The Benefit Of Mister Kite', which they wrote together at Kenwood, where John had hung the poster on the wall of his den.
→ Filming was completed for the 'Strawberry Fields Forever' promo at Knole Park.

1 February
→ Abbey Road. *Sgt Pepper* sessions. The 'Sgt Pepper's Lonely Hearts Club Band' theme was recorded.

2 February
→ Abbey Road. *Sgt Pepper* sessions. Further work on 'Sgt Pepper's Lonely Hearts Club Band'.

3 February
→ Abbey Road. *Sgt Pepper* sessions. Work on 'A Day In The Life'. Ringo added his distinctive drum track, replacing the previous attempt.

5 February
→ Part of the horse-riding scene in the 'Penny Lane' promotional film was made at Angel Lane in Stratford, East London.

7 February
→ The Beatles returned to Knole Park, Sevenoaks, to shoot more horse-riding and the dining table scenes for the 'Penny Lane' promotional film.

8 February
→ Abbey Road. *Sgt Pepper* sessions. Work began on John's 'Good Morning,

Paul: "I had come to the conclusion that The Beatles were getting a little bit safe, and we were a little intimidated by the idea of making 'the new Beatles album'. It was quite a big thing: 'Wow, follow that!' So to relieve the pressure I got the idea, maybe from some friends or something I'd read, that we shouldn't record it as The Beatles. Mentally we should approach it as another group of people and totally give ourselves alter egos. So I came up with the idea of Sgt Pepper's Lonely Hearts Club Band and the song 'It Was Twenty Years Ago Today'."

Good Morning', which he had written the previous week (inspired by a TV commercial for Kellogg's breakfast cereal) and demoed in his home studio.

9 February
→ The Beatles recorded three takes of 'Fixing A Hole' at Regent Sound Studios, Tottenham Court Road, instead of at Abbey Road. It was their first time away from EMI's own studio facility.

10 February
→ Abbey Road. *Sgt Pepper* sessions. The famous orchestral chord on 'A Day In

Below: Filming
'Strawberry Fields' clip
at Sevenoaks. While in
Kent, on 31 January,
John purchased an
antique circus poster
which inspired the
lyrics for his *Sgt. Pepper*
song, 'Being For The
Benefit Of Mr. Kite'.

The Life' was recorded. To encourage the classical musicians to let down their hair, Paul ensured that they were kitted out in full evening dress, masks and false noses.

➔ Guests at the session included Mick Jagger and Marianne Faithfull, Keith Richards, Donovan, Mike Nesmith, Cynthia Lennon, Patti Harrison, clothes designers Simon Postuma and Marijke Koger of The Fool, and various friends.

Paul: "Once we'd written the main bit of the music, we thought, now look, there's a little gap there and we said 'oh, how about an orchestra? Yes, that'll be nice. And if we do have an orchestra, are we going to write them a pseudo-classical thing, which has been done better by people who know how to make it sound like that – or are we going to do it like we write songs?' Take a guess and use instinct. So we said, 'right, what we'll do to save all the arranging, we'll take the whole orchestra as one instrument.' And we just wrote it down like a cooking recipe: 24 bars; on the ninth bar, the orchestra will take off, and it will go from its lowest note to its highest note."

11 February
➔ BBC's *Juke Box Jury* showed part of the 'Penny Lane' promotional film.

13 February
➔ Abbey Road. Sgt Pepper sessions. George's 'Only A Northern Song' was begun. (While left off *Sgt. Pepper*, it was finally used for the *Yellow Submarine* soundtrack.)
➔ 'Penny Lane'/'Strawberry Fields Forever' was released in the USA as Capitol 5810.

14 February
➔ Abbey Road. *Sgt Pepper* sessions. More work on 'Only A Northern Song'.

1967

16 February

➜ Abbey Road. *Sgt Pepper* sessions. Work on 'Good Morning, Good Morning'.

➜ BBC Television's *Top Of The Pops* showed the 'Penny Lane' and 'Strawberry Fields Forever' promotional clips.

17 February

➜ Abbey Road. *Sgt Pepper* sessions. Work on 'Being For The Benefit Of Mister Kite.'

➜ 'Penny Lane'/'Strawberry Fields Forever' was released in the UK as Parlophone R5570.

20 February

➜ Abbey Road. *Sgt Pepper* sessions. Fairground sounds were added to 'Being For The Benefit Of Mister Kite'.

George Martin: "For The Benefit Of Mr Kite' was an attempt to create atmosphere. John wanted a circus fairground atmosphere and said he wanted to hear sawdust on the floor, so we had to try and provide that! I wanted a backwash, a general melange of sound, the kind you would hear at a fairground if you closed your eyes. To achieve this we found a load of old steam organ tapes which played things like 'Stars And Stripes Forever'. I chopped them up into foot-long sections and joined them together, sometimes back to front. The whole thing was to create a sound that was unmistakably a steam organ, but which had no particular tune at all."

21 February

➜ Abbey Road. *Sgt Pepper* sessions. 'Fixing A Hole' was completed.

22 February

➜ Abbey Road. *Sgt Pepper* sessions. The giant piano chord was added to 'A Day

In The Life'. Paul, John, Ringo and Mal Evans, seated at three pianos, all played E major. After overdubbing, the chord lasted for 53 seconds. The recording levels were turned up so high in the mix that the sound of Abbey Road's air conditioning system could be heard.

23 February
→ Abbey Road. *Sgt Pepper* sessions. Work began on 'Lovely Rita'.

24 February
→ Abbey Road. *Sgt Pepper* sessions. More work on 'Lovely Rita'.

26 February
→ Brian Epstein bought Rushlake Green Mansion in Sussex. It was always a great joke with Brian that in order to get to his country house he had to drive through the village of Black Boys.

27 February
→ A story in the *Daily Mail* newspaper about a missing teenager, headlined 'A-Level Girl Dumps Car And Vanishes', inspired Paul to begin writing 'She's Leaving Home'.

Paul: "That was enough to give us a storyline. I started to get the lyrics: she slips out and leaves a note and then the parents wake up... It was rather poignant. When I showed it to John, he added the Greek chorus, long sustained notes. (The lines) 'We gave her most of our lives, we gave her everything money could buy' may have been in the runaway story, it might have been a quote from the parents."

28 February
→ Abbey Road. *Sgt Pepper* sessions. The day was spent rehearsing 'Lucy In The Sky With Diamonds'. Three-year-old Julian had brought home a drawing from school showing a schoolmate and some diamond shaped stars in the sky. Julian's teacher had asked him what it was, and was told 'It's Lucy In The Sky With Diamonds'. The teacher then carefully wrote the title across the top of the drawing, which is where John found the title for his song.

"It's like modern poetry, but neither John nor I have read much. The last time I approached it I was thinking 'This is strange and far out', and I did not dig it all that much, except Dylan Thomas who I suddenly started getting, and I was quite pleased with myself because I got it, but I hadn't realised he was going to be saying exactly the same things.

It's just that we've at last stopped trying to be clever, and we just write what we like to write. If it comes out clever, OK. 'Love Me Do' was our greatest philosophical song. For it to be simple and true means that it's incredibly simple."

1 March
→ Abbey Road. *Sgt Pepper* sessions. Work on 'Lucy In The Sky With Diamonds'.

2 March
→ Abbey Road. *Sgt Pepper* sessions. Work on 'Lucy In The Sky With Diamonds'.

3 March
→ Abbey Road. *Sgt Pepper* sessions: four French horns were added to the 'Sgt. Pepper's Lonely Heart's Club Band' track. As usual, Paul hummed the melody, George Martin transcribed it and the session musicians played it. Afterwards they mixed 'Lucy In The Sky With Diamonds'.

6 March
→ Abbey Road. *Sgt Pepper* sessions. Sound effects of audience laughter and applause were added to the title track.

Paul: "So we had a nice title. We did the whole thing like an Alice In Wonderland idea, being in a boat on the river, slowly drifting downstream and those great Cellophane flowers towering over your head. Every so often it broke off and you saw Lucy in the sky, with diamonds all over the sky. This Lucy was God, the big figure, the white rabbit. You can just write a song with imagination on words and that's what we did."

7 March
→ Abbey Road. *Sgt Pepper* sessions. More work on 'Lovely Rita'.

9 March
→ Abbey Road. *Sgt Pepper* sessions. Work began on Paul's 'Getting Better', which had been inspired when he remembered how stand-in Beatles drummer Jimmy Nicol always used the expression 'It's getting better' whenever he was asked how things were going during his brief time on tour with The Beatles in 1964.

10 March
→ Abbey Road. *Sgt Pepper* sessions. More work on 'Getting Better.'

11 March
→ The Beatles won three Grammy Awards for their releases in 1966: 'Best Vocal Performance' for 'Eleanor Rigby'; 'Best Song' for 'Michelle'; and 'Best Cover Artwork' for Klaus Voormann's *Revolver* design.

The Pepper Sleeve: 30 March

Paul: 'I came up with the title and went to Robert with some drawings for the idea of the cover.

Robert Fraser: 'The whole concept of the cover was Paul McCartney's. He asked me if I knew anybody who could execute this idea. It was my suggestion to put it through Peter Blake and his wife [Jann Haworth] and Michael Cooper, as I knew they were the only people who would understand. It was built in Michael's studio in Flood Street and everybody came up with ideas – all The Beatles, all of us – it became a collaboration.'

Peter Blake: 'We had an original meeting with all four Beatles, Robert Fraser and Brian Epstein; most of the subsequent talking was done with Paul at his house and with John there sometimes.

Paul: 'The original idea was to be a presentation from the mayor and corporation, like a Northern thing. There'd be a floral clock and there'd be us, and then on a wall or something, we'd have photos of all

the band's heroes – they were going to be on a photo. So I said to everyone, 'Who are your favourites? Make a list.' Marlon Brando was one of the first choices, Brigitte Bardot, Monroe, James Dean – all obvious ones. Then George came up with a list of gurus, and all sorts of other things came in.'

The original 'heroes' list made by The Beatles before the *Sgt Pepper* sleeve was given to Robert Fraser and Peter Blake was as follows (sic throughout): Yoga's; Marquis de Sade; Hitler; Neitch; Lenny Bruce; Lord Buckley; Alistair Crowley; Dylan Thomas; James Joyce; Oscar Wilde; William Burroughs; Robert Peel; Stockhausen; Auldus Huxley; H.G. Wells; Izis Bon; Einstein; Carl Jung; Beardsley; Alfred Jarry; Tom Mix; Johnny Weissmuller; Magritte; Tyrone Power; Carl Marx; Richard Crompton; Tommy Hanley; Albert Stubbins; Fred Astaire. In addition, Paul's original sketch for the sleeve featured Brigitte Bardot six times larger than anyone else.

Paul: 'I took the idea of the floral clock, and the heroes and the presentation by a mayor to Robert and he and I went to Peter Blake and Peter developed it all from there. The lists were his idea, and all the cut-outs instead of using real people, and the floral clock got changed around; but basically it was the original theme.'

The list grew enormously, with Robert adding in his favourite LA painters, and Peter and Jann adding their favourites. The final line-up on the sleeve was: Stuart Sutcliffe; Aubrey Beardsley; five gurus; two anonymous women; drawings of three girls; Sonny Liston; George (in wax); John (in wax); Ringo (in wax); Paul (in wax); 'Cheeky' Max Miller; Sir Robert Peel; Aleister Crowley; Mae West; Lenny Bruce; Aldous Huxley; Dylan Thomas; Marlon Brando; Tom Mix; Terry Southern; Karlheinze Stockhausen; W.C. Fields; Dion; Tony Curtis; Oscar Wilde; Wallace Berman; C.G. Jung; Tyrone Power; Edgar Allan Poe;

Tommy Handley; Marilyn Monroe; Dr Livingstone (in wax); Larry Bell; Johnny Weismuller; Fred Astaire; William Burroughs; Stephen Crane; Issy Bonn; Merkin; Stan Laurel; George Bernard Shaw (in wax); Richard Lindner; Oliver Hardy; Albert Stubbins (footballer); Karl Marx; Huntz Hall (of The Bowery Boys); H.G. Wells; Einstein; Bobby Breen (singing prodigy); Marlene Deitrich; Simon Rodia (creator of Watts-Towers); Robert Allen Zimmerman (Bob Dylan); Lawrence of Arabia; Lewis Carroll; an American legionnaire; Diana Dors; and Shirley Temple.

Paul: 'Jesus and Hitler were on John's favourites list but they had to be taken off. John was that kind of guy but you couldn't very well have Hitler and so he had to go. Gandhi also had to go because the head of EMI, Sir Joe Lockwood, said that in India they wouldn't allow the record to be printed. There were a few people who just went by the wayside.'

13 March
→ Abbey Road. *Sgt Pepper* sessions. The brass section was added to 'Good Morning, Good Morning'.

15 March
→ Abbey Road. *Sgt Pepper* sessions. Work began on George's 'Within You, Without You' using four Indian musicians on tabla, dilruba, swordmandel and tamboura. The other Beatles did not play on this track but were present.

17 March
→ Abbey Road. *Sgt Pepper* sessions. The orchestral track for Paul's 'She's Leaving Home' was recorded. George Martin had been unavailable to orchestrate the song (he was producing a Cilla Black recording), so Paul used Mike Leander as an arranger instead, a move which upset Martin considerably. The Beatles themselves did not actually play on the finished track.

20 March

→ Abbey Road. *Sgt Pepper* sessions. John and Paul recorded the vocal track for 'She's Leaving Home'.

→ While at the studio, Brian Matthew interviewed John and Paul for the BBC Transcription Service programme *Top Of The Pops* (no relation to the TV show), and recorded acceptance speeches for three 1966 Ivor Novello Awards to be edited into the BBC Light Programme's *The Ivor Novello Awards For 1966* programme which John and Paul did not want to attend in person. During these interviews, the two Beatles hinted strongly that they would not be touring in the future.

21 March

→ Abbey Road. *Sgt Pepper* sessions. The piano solo was added to 'Lovely Rita' but vocals on 'Getting Better' were interrupted when John found himself on an accidental acid trip. John: 'I never took it [LSD] in the studio. Once I did, actually. I thought I was taking some uppers, and I was not in the state of handling it... I suddenly got so scared on the mike. I said, 'What is it? I feel ill.'

→ Because so many fans were gathered outside the studio, George Martin took John up onto the flat roof to get some air. When Paul and George realised what was happening they ran up the stairs after them. They knew that the studio roof had just a low parapet and were worried that John might try to fly. Paul and Mal Evans took John back to nearby Cavendish Avenue and Paul decided to keep him company on the trip – Paul's second.

Paul: "Me and John, we'd known each other for a long time. And we looked into each other's eyes, which is fairly mind-boggling. You dissolve into each other. And it was amazing. You would want to look away, but you wouldn't, and you could see yourself in the other person. It was a very freaky experience, and I was totally blown away."

22 March

→ Abbey Road. *Sgt Pepper* sessions. George continued work on 'Within You, Without You' while the others listened to playbacks.

23 March

→ Abbey Road. *Sgt Pepper* sessions. Further work on 'Getting Better'.

25 March

→ It was announced that The Beatles had won two Ivor Novello Awards for 1966.

28 March

→ Abbey Road. *Sgt Pepper* sessions. John taped his lead vocal for 'Good Morning, Good Morning'. The animal noises were added to it, and further work was done on 'Being For The Benefit Of Mister Kite'.

29 March

→ Abbey Road. *Sgt Pepper* sessions. Work began on 'With A Little Help From My Friends'.

→ The title of The Beatles' next album was announced as *Sgt. Pepper's Lonely Hearts Club Band*, a name which Paul and Mal Evans came up with on a plane flight, when Mal asked Paul what the 'P' on the paper packet with the in-flight meal meant.

30 March

→ Abbey Road. *Sgt Pepper* sessions. Further work was done on 'With A Little Help From My Friends'. During the afternoon, the iconic sleeve for *Sgt Pepper's Lonely Hearts Club Band* was shot at Michael Cooper's photographic studio at 4 Chelsea Manor Studios, Flood Street, off the King's Road, with a number of friends present.

1 April

→ Abbey Road. *Sgt Pepper* sessions. 'Sgt Pepper's Lonely Hearts Club Band (Reprise)' was recorded and mixed in one session.

3 April

→ Paul flew to Los Angeles with Mal Evans. Paul's American visa turned out to have expired but American customs and immigration at Los Angeles sorted it out in 30 minutes.

Paul: "I was just thinking nice words like Sergeant Pepper and Lonely Hearts Club, and they came together for no reason. But after you have written that down you start to think, 'There's this Sergeant Pepper who has taught a band to play, and got them going so that at least they found one number'. They're a bit of a brass band in a way, but also a rock band because they've got the San Francisco thing. We went into it just like that; just us doing a good show."

Opposite: Sgt Pepper album cover shoot, 30 March. Beatles assistant, Terry Doran stands next to Ringo with sleeve collage artist Peter Blake behind the drum.

A private Lear jet, hired from Frank Sinatra, then took them to San Francisco.

→ Abbey Road. *Sgt Pepper* sessions. George added his lead vocal to 'Within You, Without You'.

4 April

→ Paul and Mal Evans flew in to San Francisco. They stopped by the Fillmore Auditorium and found Jefferson Airplane rehearsing there. They returned to the band's house, where Paul jammed with them, and played them an acetate of *Sgt. Pepper* which he'd brought over from England. Paul smoked pot with them but declined the DMT he was offered, despite stories to the contrary still circulating in San Francisco.

Above: A smiling Paul returns to London from America with conga drum, 12 April. On the return flight he came up with the idea for the *Magical Mystery Tour* film.
Opposite: Paul meets the future Mrs. McCartney, New York photographer Linda Eastman, at the *Sgt. Pepper* press launch, 19 May.

5 April
→ Paul flew into Denver, Colorado, where Jane Asher was playing Shakespeare with the Bristol Old Vic company, to pay a surprise visit on her 21st birthday.
→ Paul filmed Jane walking among the trees in the park and it was then that he thought of the *Magical Mystery Tour* as an idea for a TV special.

8 April
→ In Chertsey, Surrey, John visited the workshops of coach builders J.P. Fallon Limited to discuss the possibility of having his Rolls-Royce repainted in a psychedelic pattern. They were happy to oblige and the car was driven to the workshop a few days later.

9 April
→ The Old Vic company flew out of Denver to continue their tour of America. In the afternoon, Paul and Mal went to see the Red Rocks Stadium, scene of a memorable Beatles concert three years before. Paul signed a lot of autographs and enjoyed himself. Bert Rosenthal then drove them to the airport. The Lear Jet was late in arriving but they were soon in Los Angeles and ensconced in the home of Derek Taylor.

10 April
→ In Los Angeles Paul visited The Beach Boys in the studio. Brian Wilson was producing the track 'Vegetables' released on The Beach Boys' *Smiley Smile* album. Paul is said to have had a hand in its production and played guitar on a version of the traditional 'On Top Of Old Smokey'.

12 April
→ Paul and Mal arrived at Heathrow airport. Paul told the press: 'The Beatles are definitely not splitting up. We have never even thought of splitting up. We want to go on recording together. The Beatles live!'

19 April
→ The Beatles' tax lawyers had suggested that they form an umbrella company controlling all their subsidiary interests. This company, later known as Apple, would have them under an exclusive contract. The Beatles themselves would become a legal partnership, sharing all their income, whether from group, live or solo work (except songwriting) and The Beatles & Co. was created to bind them together legally for 10 years on a goodwill share issue of £1 million.

20 April
→ Abbey Road. *Sgt. Pepper* sessions. Standing around a single microphone, The Beatles recorded several minutes of gibberish which was then overdubbed, reversed and edited to make the final run-out groove on the album. While recording this, Ringo felt faint. 'I think I'm going to fall over,' he said and toppled backwards, to be caught by the ever resourceful Mal Evans.
→ John also suggested that a high-pitched note, beyond the range of the human ear, be added especially for dogs and considerable time was spent with all The Beatles, several friends, and George Martin, seeing how high they could hear. All of them still had good hearing, due in part to the fact that stage foldback had not yet been introduced, so the volume at their concerts was low by modern standards. Also, mixing and playback was conducted at relatively low levels then compared to the practice in the Seventies and Eighties.

24 April
→ The single 'Love In The Open Air' by George Martin & His Orchestra, written by Paul McCartney, was released in the US as United Artists UA 50148.

25 April
→ Abbey Road. Work began on the 'Magical Mystery Tour' theme song. Despite the fact that *Sgt Pepper* was not yet released, The Beatles moved straight on to another project: Paul's idea for *Magical Mystery Tour* which Brian Epstein thought was a fine vehicle for all four Beatles.

John: "*Magical Mystery Tour* was something Paul had worked out with Mal and he showed me what his idea was and this is how it went, it went round like this, the story and how he had it all... the production and everything. Paul had a tendency to come along and say well he's written these 10 songs, let's record now. And I'd say, 'well, give us a few days and I'll knock a few off', or something like that."

26 April
→ Abbey Road. Further work on 'Magical Mystery Tour'.

27 April
→ Abbey Road. Vocals were added to 'Magical Mystery Tour'.

29 April
→ John Lennon and John Dunbar visited the 14 Hour Technicolor Dream event at north London's Alexandra Palace. Peter Whitehead's footage of the pair (with driver Terry Doran) wandering around the hall was released in the *Pink Floyd '66/'67* video & DVD.

3 May
→ Abbey Road. The trumpets were added to 'Magical Mystery Tour'.

4 May
→ Abbey Road. A mixing session for 'Magical Mystery Tour', which Paul and possibly some of the other Beatles attended.

9 May
→ Abbey Road. The Beatles recorded an instrumental jam which was possibly intended for the *Magical Mystery Tour* film, but was never completed or used.

11 May
→ 'Baby You're A Rich Man' session was held at Olympic Sound Studios in

Barnes, intended for the cartoon film *Yellow Submarine* but in fact was used on their next single. Mick Jagger was among the guests at the session.

12 May
→ Pirate station Radio London became the first station to play *Sgt Pepper's Lonely Hearts Club Band* in its entirety – before copies had even been pressed.
→ Abbey Road. 'All Together Now', for the *Yellow Submarine* film, was recorded and mixed in one session. The Beatles were committed to providing three exclusive new songs for the film.

15 May
→ Paul went to see Georgie Fame at the Bag O'Nails nightclub on Kingly Street, Soho. There he met Linda Eastman, who was there with Chas Chandler and The Animals. Afterwards they went on to the Speakeasy Club, on Margaret Street, where Procol Harum's 'A Whiter Shade Of Pale' was being played for the first time.

17 May
→ Abbey Road. Work began on 'You Know My Name, Look Up The Number', the lyrics to which John had found written on the front of the London

Paul: "She passed our table. I was near the edge and stood up just as she was passing, blocking her exit. And so I said, 'Oh, sorry. Hi. How are you? How're you doing?' I introduced myself, and said, 'We're going on to another club after this, would you like to join us?' That was my big pulling line! I'd never used it before, but it worked this time!"

Telephone Directory while visiting Paul at Cavendish Avenue. ('You know their name, look up the number'.)

18 May
→ Photo session in Hyde Park with Marvin Lichtner from *Time* magazine.
→ Paul and John sang backing vocals on The Rolling Stones' single 'We Love You' at Decca Studios. Allen Ginsberg attended the recording session and described them as 'two young princes in their finery'.

19 May
→ *Sgt Pepper's Lonely Hearts Club Band* was launched with a small press party held at Brian Epstein's house at 24 Chapel Street. Brian had only recently emerged from several weeks of seclusion at a private clinic called the Priory in Surrey, where he had been treated for his drug problems.
→ Linda Eastman was invited to the party as a press photographer and met Paul again.

George Martin: "Obviously Paul and John were the prime movers of *Sgt Pepper*, Paul

1967

probably more than John. But their inspiration, their creation of original ideas was absolutely paramount, it was fundamental to the whole thing. I was merely serving them in helping them to get those ideas down, so my role had become that of interpreter. In John's case, his ideas weren't all that concise so I had to try to realise what he wanted and how to effect it and I would do this either by means of an orchestra or sound effects or a combination of both. This role was an interesting one because it presented many challenges for me. I would come up to new problems every day because the songs themselves presented those problems. The songs in the early days were straightforward and you couldn't play around with them too much. Here we were building sound pictures.

It seemed obvious to us that peace, love and justice ought to happen. We were opening ourselves to millions of people's influences, things that arrived in the form of, say, 'A Day In The Life'."

20 May
→ DJs Kenny Everett and Pete Drummond officially previewed *Sgt Pepper's Lonely Hearts Club Band* on the BBC Light Programme show *Where It's At*. While most of the album's tracks were played in full, the final track was unable to be played because the Beeb's censors had banned 'A Day In The Life' on the grounds that it advocated the use of drugs. The show also featured pre-recorded interviews with John, Paul and Ringo about the album as well as Everett's zany sound effects added later.

Opposite: *Our World* press call, Studio One, Abbey Road, 24 June.

Paul: "Whereas we'd just been The Beatles and songwriters, I now started to sort of nudge with the avant-garde and said, 'Hell, we could do this'. The whole idea of taking on a new identity came out of all this. The idea that we didn't have to be The Beatles any more. We could be The Enlightened Beatles or we could be somebody altogether different – Sgt Pepper's Band'."

25 May
→ The Beatles started work on George's 'It's All Too Much' at De Lane Lea recording studios on Kingsway. John took delivery of his Rolls-Royce, now painted with psychedelic fairground patterns like a gypsy caravan. Rolls-Royce launched a formal objection.

28 May
→ All four Beatles attended a party at Brian Epstein's new country house near Heathfield in Surrey. John took the opportunity to convert former Beatles press officer Derek Taylor and his wife Joan to the delights of LSD.

31 May
→ Further work was done on 'It's All Too Much' at De Lane Lea.

1 June
→ An unstructured instrumental jam was recorded at De Lane Lea. *Sgt Pepper's Lonely Hearts Club Band* was released in the UK as Parlophone PMC 7027 (mono) and PCS 7027 (stereo). Side A: 'Sgt Pepper's Lonely Hearts Club Band', 'With A Little Help From My Friends', 'Lucy In The Sky With Diamonds', 'Getting Better', 'Fixing A Hole', 'She's Leaving Home', 'Being For The Benefit Of Mr Kite'; Side B: 'Within You Without You', 'When I'm Sixty Four', 'Lovely Rita', 'Good Morning, Good Morning', 'Sgt Pepper's Lonely Hearts Club Band (Reprise)', 'A Day In The Life'.

Paul: "We recorded *Sgt Pepper* to alter our egos, free ourselves and have a lot of fun."

John: "The people who have bought our records in the past must realise that we couldn't go on making the same type forever. We must change."

→ The amazing thing was that *Sgt Pepper* was recorded on an antique Studer J37 four-track machine. In 1981 it was auctioned by Jackson Music Ltd. for £500.

2 June
→ Work on 'It's All Too Much' at De Lane Lea.
→ *Yellow Submarine* film producer Al Brodax: 'The numbers they have been recording this month for the movie are brilliant – incredible! They are using sounds I have never heard, nor could ever have imagined before.'
→ *Sgt Pepper's Lonely Hearts Club Band* was released in the US as Capitol MAS 2653 (mono) and SMAS 2653 (stereo) with, for the first time on an American Beatles album, a corresponding track list to the UK release.
→ After the jailing the previous day of *International Times* founder John 'Hoppy' Hopkins on a charge of possessing cannabis, luminaries from the British underground met to discuss registering a protest. Barry Miles rang Paul to solicit his support, and Paul promised that the Beatles would finance an advertisement in *The Times* deploring the law on 'soft' drugs.

4 June
→ Paul and Jane, and George and Patti were in the audience at Brian Epstein's Saville Theatre to see the Jimi Hendrix Experience. Hendrix opened his set with the title track from *Sgt Pepper*.

Above and opposite: Ringo and Paul at the 'All You Need Is Love' session, 25 June, which was broadcast to a worldwide audience of millions via satellite.

We've got to prepare something.' John came back with 'All You Need Is Love' and Martin orchestrated it.

George Martin: "When it came to the end of their fade-away as the song closed, I asked them: 'How do you want to get out of it?' 'Write absolutely anything you like, George,' they said. 'Put together any tunes you fancy, and just play it out like that.' Martin came up with the 'Marseillaise', a Bach two-part invention, 'Greensleeves' and a short quote from 'In The Mood'."

17 June
→ *Life* magazine ran an interview with Paul McCartney in which he revealed that he had taken acid.

19 June
→ Abbey Road. Further work done on 'All You Need Is Love'.

21 June
→ Abbey Road. 'All You Need Is Love' was mixed.

23 June
→ Abbey Road. The orchestral track was added to 'All You Need Is Love'.

24 June
→ Abbey Road. The Beatles, the 13-man orchestra and their conductor did a full run-through for BBC cameramen in preparation for the following day's broadcast. More than 100 journalists and photographers were allowed into the studio for a late-morning photocall.

25 June
→ The Beatles performed 'All You Need Is Love' on the BBC *Our World* live worldwide TV link-up live from EMI's massive Studio One.
→ The studio was filled with potted flowers and The Beatles wore uniforms of green, pink and orange, similar to the *Sgt Pepper* cover. Waist long flowing scarves wafted from their necks but the medieval look was

Paul described it as among the greatest honours he ever had bestowed upon him, particularly as Jimi had only three days to rehearse the piece.

7 June
→ Abbey Road. Another take of 'You Know My Name, Look Up The Number' was made.
→ The animated *Yellow Submarine* film was announced to the press.

8 June
→ Abbey Road. Paul invited Brian Jones from The Rolling Stones to attend the recording session, thinking he might bring along a guitar and play some rhythm. Brian arrived with an alto saxophone, which used to be his instrument in his pre-Rolling Stones group, The Ramrods. He played a sax solo on 'You Know My Name, Look Up The Number' which remains one of Paul McCartney's

favourite Beatles' numbers.

9 June
→ Abbey Road. The backing track to 'You Know My Name, Look Up The Number' was mixed.

12 June
→ The album *The Family Way (Original Soundtrack Album)* by The George Martin Orchestra, written by Paul McCartney, was released in the USA as London MS 82007 with the same tracks as (but different sleeve to) the UK release.

14 June
→ The backing track for 'All You Need Is Love' was recorded at Olympic Studios, Barnes, for use on the first live worldwide satellite link-up which was expected to be seen by 200 million people. George Martin pleaded with them, 'You can't just go off the cuff.

marred slightly by the headphones they all wore, as well as the usual studio clutter of microphones, headphone leads, instruments and music stands.

→ Among the guests present were Keith Richards, Eric Clapton, Graham Nash and Gary Leeds. Keith Moon fooled around on the drums with Ringo during the long wait before transmission. Simon, Marijke and Joshi, from The Fool, wore the flowing patchwork patterns and headscarves they would shortly market through the Apple boutique. Mick Jagger sat on the floor with Marianne Faithfull, close by Paul's high stool, wearing a silk jacket with a pair of psychedelic eyes painted on it, surreptitiously smoking a very fat joint in front of the 200 million viewers, the day before he and Richards were to go to trial over drug possession.

→ 'All You Need Is Love!' streamers and balloons floated down from the ceiling and the audience all sang along. Placards with the message ALL YOU NEED IS LOVE written large in many languages were paraded before the cameras. The vocals, Paul's bass, Ringo's drums, George's solo and the orchestra were all mixed live on air. In the control room afterwards George Martin played back the tape. 'Another big hit!' said Paul.

26 June
→ Abbey Road. Ringo added the opening drum roll to 'All You Need Is Love' and the record was mixed, ready for instant release.

28 June
→ *The Family Way*, the film for which Paul had composed the soundtrack, was premiered in New York.

29 June
→ *The Beatles' Book Monthly* photographer, Leslie Bryce, photographed John at Kenwood, his mock-Tudor mansion in Weybridge, for an 'at home' session.

1 July
→ The BBC Light Programme show, *Where It's At* broadcast a pre-recorded interview with Paul talking about 'All You Need Is Love'.

Paul: "We had one message for the whole world – love. We need more love in the world. It's a period in history that needs love."

3 July
→ Vic Lewis of NEMS threw a private party for The Monkees at the Speakeasy. The guests included John and Cynthia, George and Patti, Paul and Jane, The Who, Eric Clapton, Manfred Mann, Lulu, Procol Harum, The Fool, Mickie Most, Vicki Wickham, Dusty Springfield, and Monkees Peter Tork, Mike Nesmith and Micky Dolenz (Davy Jones and Ringo were both away).

7 July
→ The single 'All You Need Is Love'/ 'Baby You're A Rich Man' was released in the UK as Parlophone R 5620. It was only decided 24 hours before the *Our World* show that 'All You Need Is Love' should be their next single, based on the demand that the world-wide viewing would cause.

Paul: "It does sound like we used to sound. But it's really next time round on the spiral. I'd sum it up as taking a look back with a new feeling."

→ 'Baby You're A Rich Man' was originally intended for the soundtrack of the full-length Beatles cartoon, *Yellow Submarine*. The song was originally called 'One Of The Beautiful People'.

17 July
→ 'All You Need Is Love'/'Baby You're A Rich Man' was released in the USA as Capitol 5964.

20 July
→ Paul and Jane attended a Chris Barber recording session at Chappell Recording Studios to see him record Paul's instrumental 'Catcall'.

Paul played piano, along with Brian Auger, and can be heard yelling in the chorus at the end.

→ John had long had the idea that The Beatles should all live together on an island with a recording studio/entertainment complex in the middle, surrounded by four separate villas. Beyond that would be housing for their friends and staff. Alex Mardas, a TV repairman whom John had dubbed 'Magic Alex', had friends in the Greek Military Junta, and arranged for The Beatles to island-seek there. Though the authorities had already banned both long hair and rock'n'roll, they felt that The Beatles visiting Greece might help prop up their tourist industry and undermine some of the bad press they had been getting for torturing dissidents.

→ Alex flew to Greece and came up with the object of John's dreams: the island of Leslo, about 80 acres surrounded by four habitable islands, one for each Beatle. The island was for sale for £90,000, including a small fishing village, four ideal beaches and 16 acres of olive groves.

→ George and Patti, Ringo and Neil Aspinall flew to Athens where they were met by Alex and his father, who was in the military police. They stayed at the Mardas house in suburban Athens until the remaining members of the party arrived.

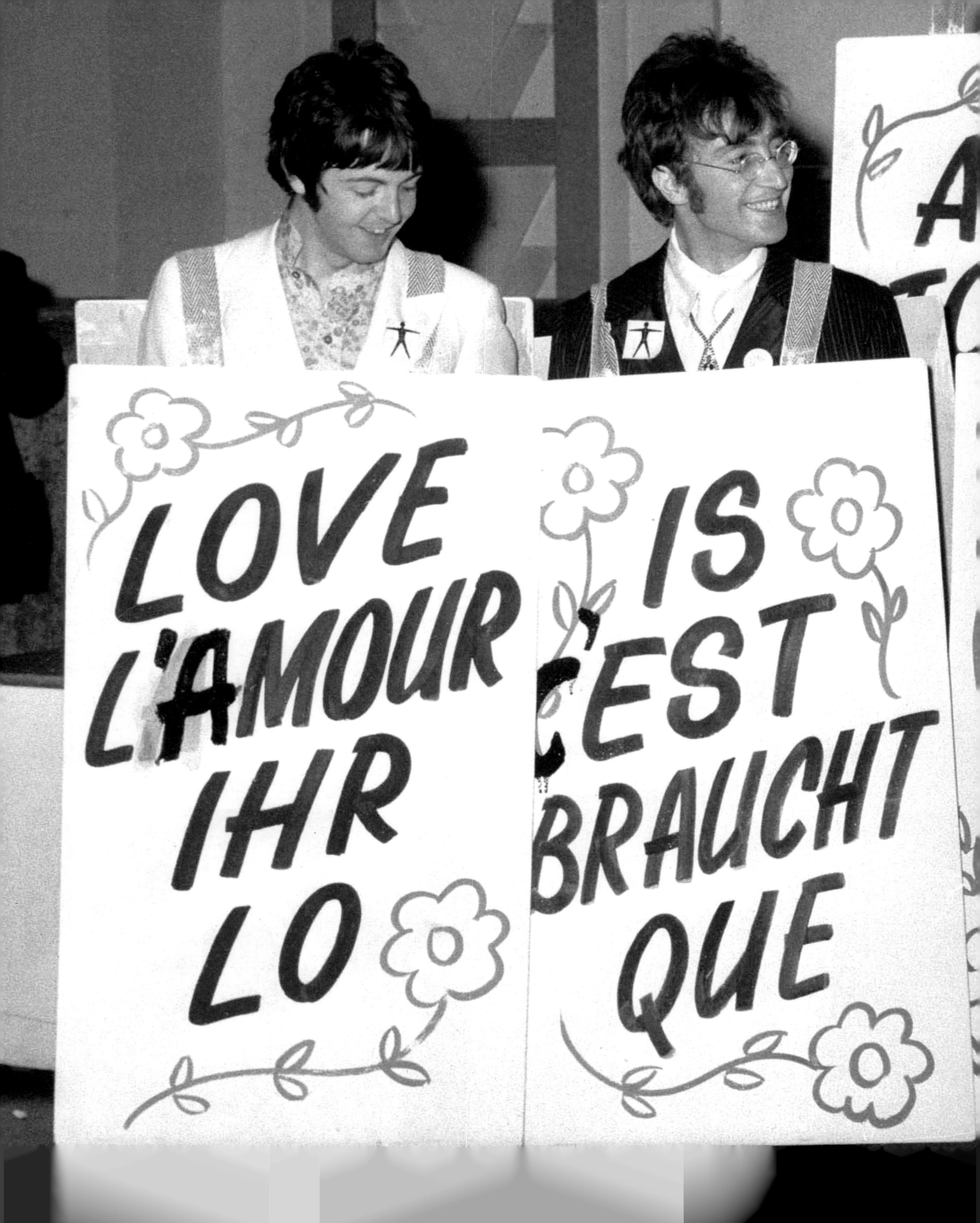
LOVE
L'AMOUR
IHR
LO
IS
C'EST
BRAUCHT
QUE

22 July

→ John and Cynthia with Julian, Paul and Jane, Patti's 16-year-old sister Paula, Mal Evans and Alistair Taylor from the NEMS office, who was in charge of buying the island, set off for Greece. Their hired yacht, the M.V. Arvi, was stuck near Crete in high winds and did not get to Athens until the 25th, so they all stayed in Athens.

23 July

→ In a convoy of a Mercedes and two huge American taxis, the party went out into the country. Paul, Jane and Neil's taxi caught fire in the extreme heat and when the others turned back to look for them they were found walking along the road, back towards the village where the party had eaten lunch.

→ Alex arranged a few sightseeing trips to prevent them from getting

Below: George and his sitar mentor, Ravi Shankar give a press conference, Los Angeles, 3 August. Opposite: Paul, George and John meet with the Maharishi Mahesh Yogi at the London Hilton, 24 August.

bored, but he also kept the Greek tourist authorities informed of their timetable so wherever they went there were crowds of people following. Alistair Taylor wrote, 'Once on a trip to a hill village, we came round a corner of the peaceful road only to find hundreds of photographers clicking away at us.'

24 July

→ The Oxford University drama company invited The Beatles to attend a performance of *Agamemnon* by Aeschylus, at the theatre at Delphi, but Alex had informed the tourist authorities who broadcast the fact they would be there on Athens Radio. They arrived in Delphi to an enormous crowd of fans and pushy journalists. They climbed back into their Mercedes and headed straight back to Athens.

26 July

→ Ringo and Neil Aspinall flew back to London from Athens. Maureen was pregnant and with the baby nearly due Ringo did not want to be away too long.

→ The others boarded their yacht. The first few days were spent swimming, sun-bathing, and taking LSD. Then they set off to inspect Leslo, where they were to build their commune. After a full day of exploring the island, planning where the recording studio would be located and who would live on which island, Alistair Taylor was instructed to fly straight back to London and make the arrangements to buy it.

→ Export controls meant that The Beatles had to buy special export dollars and then apply to the government for permission to spend them. Taylor eventually got the clearance but by then no-one was interested in the idea any more and he was told to sell the property dollars back to the government. In the meantime, their value had increased so The Beatles made £11,400 profit on the deal.

27 July

→ Music publishers KPM Music approached Northern Songs, claiming that copyright in the tune 'In The Mood' had been infringed by the incorporation of a few bars from the song in the fade-out of The Beatles' 'All You Need Is Love'. EMI ultimately had to pay settlement.

31 July

→ Ringo recorded a farewell message at the offices of pirate station Radio London, broadcast on their last day on the air before the government stamped them out and replaced them with their own anodyne version of pop radio.

1 August

→ George, Patti, 'Magic' Alex Mardas and Neil Aspinall flew from London to Los Angeles where they had rented a house on Blue Jay Way. That evening George called Derek Taylor and gave him directions to get to their house but Derek got lost in the LA fog. While he was waiting, George wrote a song with the street name as the title.

3 August

→ George, Alex and Neil went to Ravi Shankar's Music School where George and Ravi Shankar held a press conference to promote Shankar's Hollywood Bowl concert set for the following day. Patti and her sister Jenny, who flew down from San Francisco to join them, went sightseeing.

4 August

→ Polydor reissued their album of 1961 Hamburg recordings, *The Beatles' First*.

11 August

→ The Beatles were photographed by Richard Avedon at the penthouse photographic studio in Thompson House. Avedon used the images for a series of four psychedelic posters which appeared first in *Look* magazine before being published separately and adorning thousands of student bedrooms around the world.

13 August

→ EMI announced that the *Sgt. Pepper* album had now sold more than 500,000 copies in the UK alone.

16 August

→ The first press screening of *How I Won The War*, the film co-starring John Lennon, was held in London.

18 August
→ The single 'We Love You' by The Rolling Stones, with backing vocals by John Lennon and Paul McCartney, was released in the UK as Decca F 12654.

19 August
→ Maureen Starkey gave birth to a second son, Jason, at Queen Charlotte's Hospital, London.

22 August
→ The Beatles began work on 'Your Mother Should Know' at Chappell Recording Studios, London.

23 August
→ The Beatles finished work on 'Your Mother Should Know' at Chappell. Brian Epstein was on hand to watch part of the session, the last time he visited the group in the recording studio.

24 August
→ John and Cynthia, Paul and Jane, and George and Patti attended a lecture by the Maharishi Mahesh Yogi at the London Hilton on Park Lane. After the lecture they had a private audience with the Maharishi and arranged to attend his seminar which was to be held in Bangor that weekend.

The 'pot' ad: 24 July

The Times ran a full-page advertisement on 24 July headed, 'The law against marijuana is immoral in principle and unworkable in practice' which was signed by, among others, all four Beatles and Brian Epstein. The petition's arguments included the following: that the smoking of cannabis on private premises should no longer constitute an offence; cannabis should be taken off the dangerous drugs list and controlled, rather than prohibited; possession of cannabis should either be legally permitted or at most be considered a misdemeanour and that all persons now imprisoned for possession of cannabis or for allowing cannabis to be smoked on private premises should have their sentences commuted.

It was signed by 65 eminent names including Francis Crick, the co-discoverer of the DNA molecule and a Nobel laureate, novelist Graham Greene, and MPs Brian Walden and Tom Driberg, as well as future MP Jonathan Aitken, but the four MBEs caused the most press concern. Questions were asked in the House, and a chain of events set off, which did actually result in the liberalisation of the laws against pot in Britain. The £1,800 advertisement was paid for by The Beatles at the instigation of Paul McCartney, who had already publicly admitted his LSD use.

August 25
→ The Beatles, their wives and girlfriends, Mick Jagger and Marianne Faithfull took the train from Euston Station to Bangor to attend the Maharishi's teaching seminar. Cynthia Lennon got caught in the crush and a policeman refused to let her onto the train until it was too late as the train pulled away without her. Neil Aspinall drove her to Bangor.
→ For the four Beatles, it was the first time in five years that they had ever travelled anywhere without the protective cordon supplied by Brian, Neil or Mal.

John: "There's none of this sitting in the lotus position or standing on your head. You just do it as long as you like. (In a heavy accent) 'Twenty minutes a

day is prescribed for ze workers. Twenty minutes a morning and twenty minutes after verk. Makes you happy, intelligent and more energy'.

Even if you go into the meditation bit just curious or cynical, once you go into it, you see. We weren't so much sceptical because we'd been through that phase in the middle of all the Beatlemania like, so we came out of being sceptics a bit. But you've still got to have a questioning attitude to all that goes on. The only thing you can do is judge on your own experience and that's what this is about."

26 August
→ The Beatles informed the national press, who were besieging the Maharishi's meditation centre in Bangor, that they had renounced the use of hallucinogenic drugs. 2,000 fans gathered at Shea Stadium in New York a year on from The Beatles last concert there, to protest that the group had not played any concerts in the US during the summer of 1967.

27 August
→ Brian Epstein was found dead in his London house.
→ Jane Asher received the telephone call which brought The Beatles the news in Wales, and gave the receiver to Paul. Saddened, worried and confused, the group gave a brief press conference then departed for London.
→ On the afternoon of 25 August, Brian had driven down to his Sussex country home, dined with two companions then driven back to London late, evidently disappointed that expected houseguests had failed to arrive. He remained in his room throughout the following day and, on the Sunday morning, his housekeepers became concerned at his non-appearance. Eventually the door to

John: "I can't find words to pay tribute to him. It is just that he was lovable, and it is those lovable things we think about now."
Paul: "This is a great shock. I am deeply upset."
George: "He dedicated so much of his life to The Beatles. We liked and loved him. He was one of us."
Ringo: "We loved Brian. He was a generous man. We owe so much to him. We have come a long way with Brian along the same road."

Brian's bedroom was forced open by a doctor and Brian's assistant. His lifeless body was on the bed. At an inquest the cause of death was found to be accidental, resulting from 'incautious self-overdoses', with the drug Carbitol, taken to assist sleep, mentioned specifically.

John: "We were in Wales with the Maharishi. We had just gone down after seeing his lecture first night. We heard it then. I was stunned, we all were, I suppose, and the Maharishi, we went in to him. 'What, he's dead' and all that, and he was sort of saying 'Oh, forget it, be happy, like an idiot, like parents, smile, that's what the Maharishi said.' And we did.

I had that feeling that

anybody has when somebody close to them dies: there is a sort of little hysterical, sort of 'Hee, hee, I'm glad it's not me' or something in it, the funny feeling when somebody close to you dies. I don't know whether you've had it, but I've had a lot of people die around me and the other feeling is, 'What the fuck? What can I do?'

I knew we were in trouble then. I didn't really have any misconceptions about our ability to do anything other than play music and I was scared. I thought, 'We've fuckin' had it.'

I liked Brian and I had a very close relationship with him for years, because I'm not gonna have some stranger running things, that's all. I like to work with friends. I was the closest with Brian, as close as you can get to somebody who lives a sort of 'fag' life, and you don't really know what they're doin' on the side. But in the group I was closest to him and I did like him.

We had complete faith in him when he was runnin' us. To us, he was the expert. I mean originally he had a shop. Anybody who's got a shop must be all right. He went round smarmin' and charmin' everybody. He had hellish tempers and fits and lock-outs and y'know, he'd vanish for days. He'd come to a crisis every now and then and the whole business would fuckin' stop cause he'd go on sleepin' pills

Above: Mick Jagger, Marianne Faithfull and Paul, escorted by a jolly British bobby, walk through Euston Station to board the Bangor-bound train, 25 August.

for days on end and wouldn't wake up. Or he'd be missin', y'know, beaten up by some old docker down the Old Kent Road. But we weren't too aware of it. It was later on we started findin' out about those things. 'We'd never have made it without him and vice versa. Brian contributed as much as us in the early days, although we were the talent and he was the hustler. He wasn't strong enough to overbear us. Brian could never make us do what we didn't really want to do.

28 August

→ Brian's sudden death dominates the newspaper headlines in the UK and US. The Beatles confirmed that they intended to continue their study of meditation with the Maharishi.

→ 'We Love You' by The Rolling Stones (John Lennon and Paul McCartney on backing vocals) was released in the US as London 905.

29 August

→ The inquest into Brian Epstein's death was adjourned, although the coroner gave permission for the burial to go ahead at a Jewish cemetery in Liverpool.

→ Brian Epstein's funeral was a strictly family affair with none of his groups, not even The Beatles, in attendance.

30 August

→ Brian Epstein's brother Clive was elected as the new chairman of the family company, NEMS Enterprises, with Robert Stigwood as managing director.

31 August

→ The Beatles announced that they would continue to be managed by NEMS Enterprises until further notice, but that Clive Epstein would not be taking over his brother's role as their personal manager. 'No one could possibly replace Brian', Paul commented. An official statement issued to the press added: 'The Beatles would be willing to put money into NEMS if there was any question of a takeover from an outsider. The Beatles will not withdraw their shares from NEMS. Things will go on as before.'

→ EMI announced that worldwide sales of 'All You Need Is Love' had now topped three million.

1 September

→ The Beatles met at Paul's house to discuss their future. They decided to continue with the *Magical Mystery Tour* project and put everything else on hold. Before the other Beatles arrived, Paul held a separate meeting with publicist Tony Barrow, to discuss the special storybook which he wanted to accompany the *Magical Mystery Tour* album.

Tony Barrow: "Paul wanted me to surround the making of Magical Mystery Tour with a massive new publicity campaign, designed to keep The Beatles in the newspapers at home and abroad all through September. Without that, he thought, Epstein's death would look like the end of an era. In Paul's eyes, Magical Mystery Tour could be sold to the world as the beginning of a bright new era in The Beatles' history."

2 September

→ Before they began work in earnest on the *Magical Mystery Tour* project, the Beatles dispatched their aide Alistair Taylor to the seaside to check that coach companies still operated mystery tours. They did.

5 September

→ Abbey Road. *Magical Mystery Tour* sessions. Work began on 'I Am The Walrus.'

6 September

→ Abbey Road. *Magical Mystery Tour* sessions. Further work done on 'I Am The Walrus', including John's vocal. Paul recorded a demo version of 'The Fool On The Hill' and the basic tracks were recorded for George's 'Blue Jay Way'.

7 September

→ Abbey Road. *Magical Mystery Tour* sessions. Work on 'Blue Jay Way'.

8 September

→ Abbey Road. *Magical Mystery Tour* sessions. The instrumental 'Flying' was recorded. At this time the track was called 'Aerial Tour Instrumental', and featured a lengthy mellotron coda. This was meant for a flying sequence in the film in which The Beatles intended to have the coach actually fly, using special effects.

→ Westminster coroner Gavin Thurston recorded a verdict of 'accidental death' on Brian Epstein, ruling that The Beatles' manager had become confused about the quantity of sleeping tablets that he had taken in his final hours.

11 September

→ The coach for the *Magical Mystery Tour* was still being painted with its psychedelic livery and was delayed for two hours in leaving Allsop Place, where rock'n'roll package tours always started. The other three Beatles were picked up in Virginia Water, Surrey, near their homes. All 43 seats in the coach were filled with technicians, Beatles, Mal, Neil and even a few fan club secretaries. They drove to Teignmouth, Devon, stopping for lunch at the Pied Piper restaurant in Winchester en route. In Teignmouth the entire party stayed at The Royal Hotel where 400 local fans were waiting for them in the pouring rain. Paul gave a short press conference about the film.

Paul said, "Well, here's the segment, you write a little piece for that,' and I thought 'Bloody hell,' so I ran off and I wrote the dream sequence for the fat woman and all the things with the spaghetti. Then George and I were sort of grumbling about the fuckin' movie and we thought we'd better do it and we had the feeling that we owed it to the public to do these things."

12 September

→ The coach got stuck on a bridge on its way to Widecombe Fair, blocking the road, and had to back half a mile up the road to turn around. The AA redirected traffic. John was filmed losing his temper but the footage was not used. They abandoned plans to visit the fair and stopped at the Grand Hotel in Plymouth for lunch.

→ Paul gave a brief interview to Hugh Scully for the local BBC1 news magazine programme *Spotlight South West* and the group posed for a photo call on Plymouth Hoe.

→ The coach continued to Newquay,

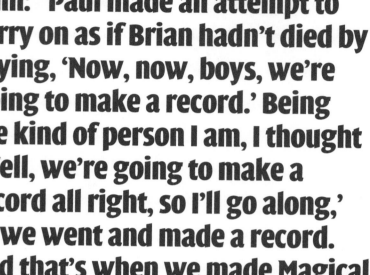

John: "Paul made an attempt to carry on as if Brian hadn't died by saying, 'Now, now, boys, we're going to make a record.' Being the kind of person I am, I thought 'Well, we're going to make a record all right, so I'll go along,' so we went and made a record. And that's when we made Magical Mystery Tour."

Cornwall, with several stops to film en route. In Newquay they stayed at the Atlantic Hotel, where they held a meeting with the film crew to discuss how they could bring the shooting back on schedule.

13 September

→ John directed a film sequence in which Scottish 'funny walks' specialist Nat Jackley chased bikini-clad girls around the Atlantic Hotel swimming pool. Simultaneously, Paul and Ringo directed a scene filmed on the beach at Newquay.

→ George was interviewed by Miranda Ward for the BBC's new Radio One programme *Scene And Heard*.

Paul: "We're not going to turn out records or films just for the sake of it. We don't want to have to talk unless we have something to say. We enjoy recording, but we want to go even further. I would like to come up with a completely new form of music, invent new sounds. But at the moment I'm thinking things out. There seems to be a pause in my life right now – a time for re-assessment."

14 September

→ Filming at various West Country locations.

→ Miranda Ward joined The Beatles' party and interviewed Ringo for *Scene And Heard*.

15 September

→ Filming in front of the Atlantic Hotel and various locations enroute back to London. The party stopped for lunch at a small fish and chip shop in Taunton (in Somerset) and also filmed there.

16 September

→ Abbey Road. *Magical Mystery Tour* sessions. Work continued on 'Your Mother Should Know'.

→ The Beatles decided to postpone their visit to India until all work on

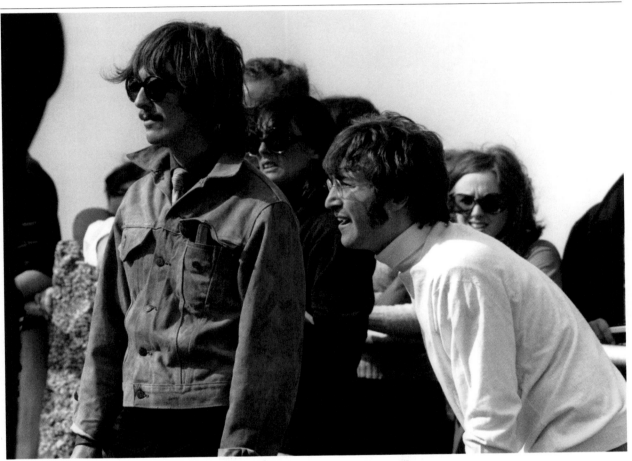

Opposite: The *Magical Mystery Tour* coach gets stuck on a Devon bridge, 12 September. Above: John and George on *MMT* location in Newquay, Cornwall, 13 September. The two Beatles weren't exactly sold on Paul's idea with Lennon later grumbling that he only did it because he felt the Beatles owed it to their fans.

Magical Mystery Tour was completed.

18 September
➜ The Beatles filmed at the Raymond Revue Bar in Soho with the Bonzo Dog Doo-Dah Band and stripper Jan Carson whose bare breasts were covered in the film with a superimposed CENSORED sign.

19 September
➜ The Beatles filmed at West Malling Air Station, Maidstone, Kent, when they found that film studios needed to be booked ahead of time.
➜ Steve Winwood's group Traffic were approached by Paul to film a special clip of them performing 'Here We Go Round The Mulberry Bush' for inclusion in *Magical Mystery Tour*.

20-24 September
➜ Filming at West Malling Air Station, Maidstone, Kent.

➜ The grand finale, with The Beatles trooping down the staircase singing 'Your Mother Should Know', was filmed on the last day with the aid of the 160 members of The Peggy Spencer Formation Dancing Team and two dozen Women's Royal Air Force cadets.

Paul: "That was the shot that used most of the budget."

25 September
➜ The Beatles had allowed two weeks for editing *Magical Mystery Tour*, but in the end it took 11. Editing began immediately and was done by Roy Benson in a rented Soho editing suite: Norman's Film Productions at the corner of Old Compton Street and Wardour Street. Paul was present throughout all 11 weeks, unless he was recording and the others appeared to a lesser degree.
➜ Abbey Road. *Magical Mystery Tour*

sessions. Work began on 'The Fool On The Hill'.

26 September
➜ Abbey Road. *Magical Mystery Tour* sessions. More work on 'The Fool On The Hill'.

27 September
➜ Abbey Road. *Magical Mystery Tour* sessions. The orchestra and the Mike Sammes Singers' parts were added to 'I Am The Walrus'. Paul added a new vocal to 'The Fool On The Hill'.

28 September
➜ Abbey Road. *Magical Mystery Tour* sessions. Work done on 'I Am The Walrus' and 'Flying'.

29 September
➜ John and George appeared on Rediffusion Television's *The Frost Programme*, discussing transcendental meditation with David Frost.

John: "Buddha was a groove, Jesus was all right.'

George: 'I believe in reincarnation. Life and death are still only relative to thought. I believe in rebirth. You keep coming back until you have got it straight. The ultimate thing is to manifest divinity, and become one with The Creator."

➜ Abbey Road. *Magical Mystery Tour* sessions. The sound effects were added to 'I Am The Walrus' including the radio fragment of Shakespeare's *King Lear*. Paul's 'Your Mother Should Know' was also finished.

1 October
➜ A further one-day shoot at West Malling.

2 October
➜ Abbey Road. Work began on The Beatles' next single, 'Hello, Goodbye'.

4 October
➜ John and George made a follow-up appearance on *The Frost Programme* continuing their discussion of transcendental meditation.

6 October

→ Abbey Road. *Magical Mystery Tour* sessions. 'Blue Jay Way' completed.

7 October

→ The Beatles turned down New York promoter Sid Bernstein's offer of $1 million for two concerts in the US.

11 October

→ Yoko's one-woman show, *Yoko Plus Me*, opened at the Lisson Gallery in London. The Me was anonymous benefactor John Lennon, who also underwrote the cost of the exhibition, which was subtitled 'Half A Wind' and featured objects which had been painted white and then sawn in half.

John: "She gave me her *Grapefruit* book and I used to read it and sometimes I'd get very annoyed by it; it would say things like 'Paint until you drop' or 'bleed' and then sometimes I'd be very enlightened by it and I went through all the changes that people go through with her work – sometimes I'd have it by the bed and I'd open it and it would say something nice and it would be alright and then it would say something heavy and I wouldn't like it.

There was all that and then she came to me to get some backing for a show and it was half a wind show. I gave her the money to back it and the show was, this was a place called Lisson Gallery, another one of those underground places. For this whole show everything was in half; there was half a bed, half a room, half of everything, all beautifully cut in half and painted white. And I said to her 'why don't you sell the other half in bottles?' having caught on by then what the game was

Above and opposite: Ringo, John and Paul, on location for *Magical Mystery Tour*. When premiered on Boxing Day in Britain, the film received a critical mauling and represented the Beatles first real career slip.

and she did that – this was still before we had the nuptials – and we still have the bottles from the show, it's my first. It was presented as Yoko Plus Me – that was our first public appearance. I didn't even go to see the show, I was too uptight."

12 October

→ George's 'It's All Too Much' was mixed at De Lane Lea Studios, where it was recorded.
→ Abbey Road. *Magical Mystery Tour* sessions. Mixing 'Blue Jay Way'

followed by John producing a recording of 'Shirley's Wild Accordion', a Lennon and McCartney composition played by Shirley Evans (accordion) and Reg Wale (percussion), for use in the film. While Evans appeared in the film, this particular recording was not used.

13 October

→ The single 'How I Won The War', by Musketeer Gripweed (John Lennon) and The Third Troop (Ken Thorne) was released in the UK as United Artists UP 1196. John's only contribution to the single was a few words of dialogue from the film soundtrack.

14 October

→ Miranda Ward's interview with Ringo was broadcast on Radio 1's *Scene And Heard*.

17 October

→ The Beatles, plus other guests including Cilla Black and Lulu, attended a memorial service for Brian Epstein held at 6 pm at the New London Synagogue, 33 Abbey Road, London.

18 October

→ This evening all four Beatles, plus their wives and girlfriends attended the première of Richard Lester's film *How I Won The War*, co-starring John Lennon, held at the London Pavilion. John and George both sported psychedelic jackets, while Paul and Ringo opted for normal evening suits. Also in attendance were celebrities like Jimi Hendrix, Keith Moon, David Hemmings and his actress wife Gayle Hunnicut, and singers Anita Harris, Cilla Black and 'Mama' Cass Elliot.

19 October

→ George and Paul flew to Sweden, via Copenhagen, to visit the Maharishi Mahesh Yogi at his Transcendental Meditation Academy in the coastal resort of Falsterbohus. They flew back to London the same day.
→ Abbey Road. *Magical Mystery Tour* sessions. Further work on 'Hello, Goodbye'.

20 October

→ Abbey Road. *Magical Mystery Tour* sessions. The flute passage was added

to 'The Fool On The Hill' and the viola to 'Hello, Goodbye'.

→ The single 'Catcall' by The Chris Barber Band, written by Paul McCartney, was released in the UK as Marmalade 598005.

24 October

→ *A Hard Day's Night* received its world television premiere, broadcast across the US by NBC-TV.

29 October

→ Paul and Mal Evans flew to Nice with cameraman Aubrey Dewar and engaged a taxi driver to wake them and take them to the mountains overlooking Nice before the break of dawn. Paul left home without his passport, but persuaded immigration authorities that as they knew who he was, he could travel without it.

→ Ringo filmed the getting-on-the-bus sequence for *Magical Mystery Tour* in Lavender Hill, south London.

30 October

→ Paul and Aubrey Dewar filmed the sunrise in the mountains behind Nice, for the 'Fool On The Hill' sequence in *Magical Mystery Tour*. They stayed on the mountain for most of the day, though mainly the dawn footage was eventually used.

→ Music publisher Dick James announced that Northern Songs had made £842,000 profit in the previous year.

2 November

→ Abbey Road. Paul added an extra bass line to 'Hello, Goodbye'.

3 November

→ George's 'Blue Jay Way' sequence was filmed at Ringo's house, 'Sunny Heights', in Weybridge, Surrey.

6 November

→ Abbey Road. Mixing session which The Beatles probably attended.

→ The group held a photo session in London, posing with a cut-out submarine as advance publicity for the *Yellow Submarine* film.

7 November

→ Abbey Road. Paul added a new vocal to 'Magical Mystery Tour'.

8 November

→ *How I Won The War* received its US premiere in New York.

10 November

→ Paul directed three separate versions of a promotional film for 'Hello, Goodbye' on stage at the Saville Theatre, Shaftesbury Avenue; each of them featuring Hawaiian dancing girls in grass skirts, and The Beatles wearing their 1963 collarless suits.

The Apple Boutique: 7 December

John: 'Clive Epstein or some other such business freak came up to us and said you've got to spend so much money, or the tax will take you. We were thinking of opening a chain of retail clothes shops or some barmy thing like that…and we were all thinking that if we are going to open a shop let's open something we're interested in, and we went through all these different ideas about this, that and the other. Paul had a nice idea about opening up white houses, where we would sell white china and things like that, everything white, because you can never get anything white, you know, which was pretty groovy, and it didn't end up with that, it ended up with Apple and all this junk and The Fool and all those stupid clothes and all that.'

12 November

→ The 'Hello, Goodbye' promotional films were edited, with Paul supervising operations.

17 November

→ The Beatles Limited changed its name to Apple Music Limited and Apple Music Limited became The Beatles Limited.

→ Neil Aspinall flew to New York to personally deliver copies of the 'Hello, Goodbye' promotional film to the producers of such television programmes as *The Ed Sullivan Show* and *The Hollywood Palace*.

21 November

→ The Musicians' Union closed shop prohibited miming, so The Beatles' promotional films for 'Hello, Goodbye' were not shown in Britain. An attempt was made to include the promo clip as a piece of footage being edited by The Beatles in the Soho cutting room, but it didn't work and was scrapped.

22 November

→ George worked on his solo *Wonderwall* film project at Abbey Road, with two flautists and a tabla player.

→ The film company Peacock Productions applied to the High Court for an injunction to prevent release of the *Yellow Submarine* movie, alleging that they had not been paid for their work on the project. The injunction was somewhat premature, as the film was still some months from completion.

23 November

→ George continued work on the *Wonderwall* soundtrack at Abbey Road.

→ ITV also banned The Beatles' 'Hello, Goodbye' promo film and a plan to screen one of the three films in colour on BBC2's *Late Night Line Up,* was also abandoned. Instead, *Top Of The Pops* played 'Hello, Goodbye' over a clip from *A Hard Day's Night*, much to The Beatles' annoyance.

24 November

→ The single 'Hello, Goodbye'/'I Am The Walrus' was released in the UK as Parlophone R 5655.

→ John and Paul attended a recording session by Apple Music's new signing, Grapefruit, held at the IBC Recording Studios on Portland Place. John gave them their name, coincidentally the name of Yoko Ono's book. Most of the group were former members of Tony Rivers & The Castaways, one of Brian Epstein's artists.

→ John also worked on a compilation of his home tapes at Abbey Road.

25 November

→ Radio 1's *Where It's At* programme transmitted an interview done with John Lennon by Kenny Everett and Chris Denning. The whole of the *Magical Mystery Tour* double EP was played, the only time 'I Am The Walrus' was broadcast by the BBC, which had unofficially banned it because the lyrics included the word 'knickers'. The song was also banned from the airwaves in the US.

John: "It always seems to happen now that people misinterpret what we write or say. We're happy with the words and I don't see how they can offend anyone. Do you think they're obscene?"

26 November

→ The 'Hello, Goodbye' promotional film was screened on *The Ed Sullivan Show* in the US, where there were no Musicians' Union restrictions on mimed performances.

27 November

→ 'Hello, Goodbye'/'I Am The Walrus' was released in the USA as Capitol 2056.

→ The album *Magical Mystery Tour* was released in the US as Capitol MAL 2835 (mono) and SMAL 2835 (stereo). Side A: 'Magical Mystery Tour', 'The Fool On The Hill', 'Flying', 'Blue Jay Way', 'Your Mother Should Know', 'I Am The Walrus'; Side B: 'Hello Goodbye', 'Strawberry Fields Forever', 'Penny Lane', 'Baby You're A Rich Man', 'All You Need Is Love'.

28 November

→ Abbey Road. The Beatles recorded *Christmas Time (Is Here Again),* their fifth Christmas record to be sent out to members of their fan club.

→ Afterwards John worked on sound effects tapes for his upcoming stage version of *The Lennon Play: In His Own Write.*

3 December

→ Ringo flew to Rome to begin work on his cameo role in the movie, *Candy,* directed by Christian Marquand and based on the Olympia Press novel by Terry Southern and Mason Hoffenberg. Ringo played Emmanuel, the Mexican gardener.

5 December

→ John and George represented The Beatles at a party to celebrate the impending opening of the Apple Boutique at 94 Baker Street, London.

7 December

→ Ringo's first day before the cameras in Rome filming *Candy*.
The Apple Boutique opened its doors to the public.

8 December

→ The EP *Magical Mystery Tour* was released in the UK as Parlophone MMT1 (mono) and SMMT1 (stereo). Side A: 'Magical Mystery Tour', 'Your Mother Should Know'; Side B: 'I Am The Walrus'; Side C: 'The Fool On The Hill', 'Flying'; Side D: 'Blue Jay Way'.

9-12 December

→ Ringo filmed scenes with Ewa Aulin, the former Miss Teen Sweden, who was playing the title role of *Candy*.

9 December

→ As usual, The Beatles were voted 'Top World Group' and 'Top British Vocal Group' in the readers' poll held by the *New Musical Express*.

13-14 December

→ Ringo filmed his *Candy* sex scene with Ewa Aulin.

15 December

→ The Beatles' fan club flexi-disc *Christmas Time (Is Here Again)* was released.
→ Ringo was filmed at a 'love-in'.

16 December

→ Ringo's last day of filming.

17 December

→ Ringo flew back to London from Rome, his role in the film *Candy* completed.
→ John and George acted as hosts at the *Magical Mystery Tour* preview party for the area secretaries of the Official Beatles Fan Club, at the Hanover Grand Film and Art Theatre, London. As well as an advance copy of *Magical Mystery Tour*, *The Beatles At Shea Stadium* film was shown.

Paul: "Film-making isn't as difficult as many people imagine. It's a matter of common sense more than anything. We'd never directed anything before and we didn't know about editing, but we're learning. Magical Mystery Tour was an experiment, and so far it's been successful."

Below: Maureen Starkey, Ringo, John, Paul and girlfriend Jane Asher at the fancy dress launch of *Magical Mystery Tour*, Royal Lancaster Hotel, 21 December.

19 December

→ Seven investment companies were registered and formed in London on behalf of The Beatles: Apricot Investments Ltd., Blackberry Investments Ltd., Cornflower Investments Ltd., Daffodil Investments Ltd., Edelweiss Investments Ltd., Foxglove Investments Ltd. and Greengage Investments Ltd.

21 December

→ A fancy dress party was held at the Royal Lancaster Hotel, London for the complete crew of *Magical Mystery Tour* including all the technical staff, plus relatives and a few friends. Robert Morley was Father Christmas. The Bonzo Dog Doo-Dah Band played. Paul and Jane arrived as a cockney pearly king and queen, Ringo as a Regency dandy, Maureen as an Indian squaw, George as a cavalier and John dressed as a teddy boy. John paid close personal attention to Patti during the party, until being reminded by fellow guest Lulu that he was supposed to be escorting his own wife for the evening.

25 December

→ Paul and Jane announced that they were engaged to be married.

26 December

→ *Magical Mystery Tour* was given its world television premiere in monochrome on BBC 1 at 8.35pm.

27 December

→ In order to answer and counter the adverse press criticism of *Magical Mystery Tour* Paul appeared live on Rediffusion's *The Frost Programme* where he discussed the film and wider issues with David Frost.

Strawberry Fields Forever

Words & Music by John Lennon
& Paul McCartney
© Copyright 1967 Northern Songs.
All Rights Reserved.
International Copyright Secured.

Begin fading

(Swarmandel)

*Repeat to fade,
with tape effects*

N.C.

Verse 3:
Always, no, sometimes think it's me,
But you know I know when it's a dream.
I think a 'No' I mean a 'Yes', but it's all wrong;
That is, I think I disagree.

Penny Lane

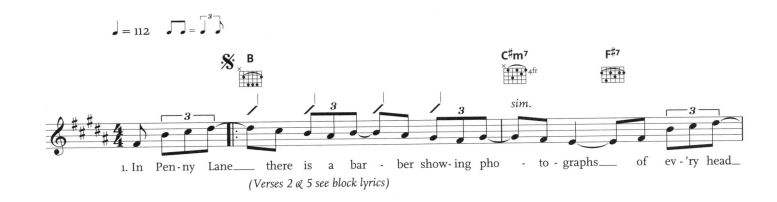

1. In Pen-ny Lane there is a bar-ber show-ing pho-to-graphs of ev-'ry head

(Verses 2 & 5 see block lyrics)

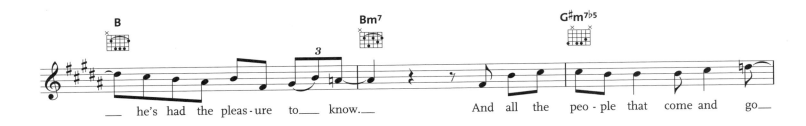

he's had the pleas-ure to know. And all the peo-ple that come and go

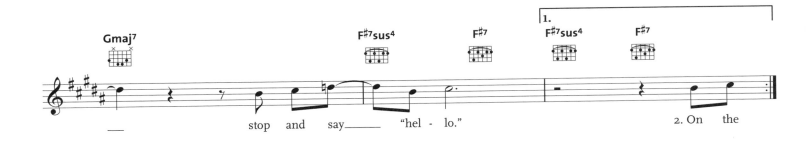

stop and say "hel-lo."

2. On the

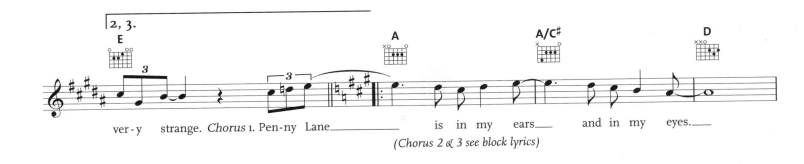

ver-y strange. *Chorus* 1. Pen-ny Lane is in my ears and in my eyes.

(Chorus 2 & 3 see block lyrics)

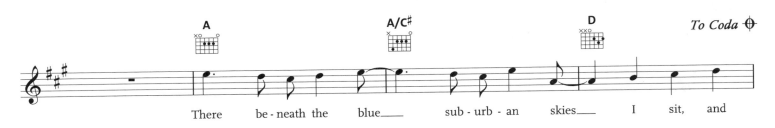

There be-neath the blue sub-urb-an skies I sit, and

mean-while back (3.) in Pen-ny Lane_____ there is a fire - man with an hour - glass,__ and in his pock -

(Verse 4 see block lyrics)

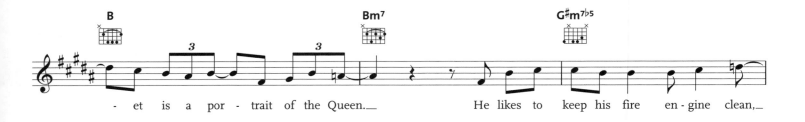

- et is a por - trait of the Queen.__ He likes to keep his fire en - gine clean,__

__ it's a clean__ mach-ine. *(Piccolo trumpet)*

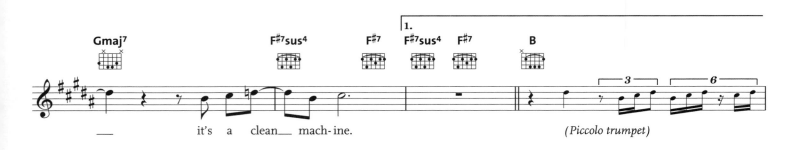

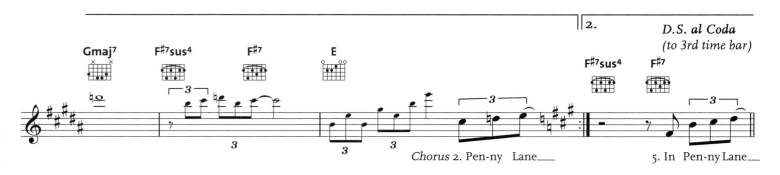

Chorus 2. Pen-ny Lane___ 5. In Pen-ny Lane___

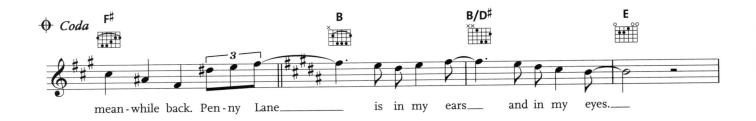

mean-while back. Pen-ny Lane_____ is in my ears___ and in my eyes.___

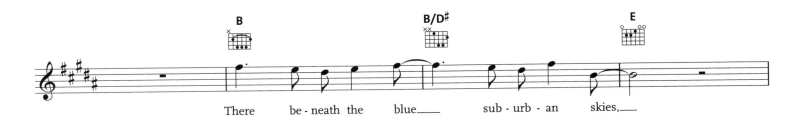

There be-neath the blue___ sub-urb-an skies,___

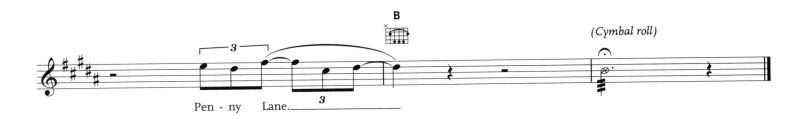

(Cymbal roll)

Pen-ny Lane._____

Verse 2:
On the corner is a banker with a motor car,
The little children laugh at him behind his back.
And the banker never wears a mac in the pouring rain, very strange.

Penny Lane is in my ears...

Chorus 2:
Penny Lane is in my ears and in my eyes,
Full of fish and finger pies in summer,
Meanwhile back...

Verse 4:
...behind the shelter in the middle of the roundabout,
A pretty nurse is selling poppies from a tray.
And though she feels as if she's in a play,
She is anyway.

Verse 5:
In Penny Lane the barber shaves another customer,
We see the banker sitting waiting for a trim.
And the fireman rushes in from the pouring rain, very strange.

Chorus 3:
Penny Lane is in my ears and in my eyes.
There beneath the blue suburban skies I sit,
And meanwhile back.
Penny Lane is in my ears...

Sgt. Pepper's Lonely Hearts Club Band

Words & Music by John Lennon
& Paul McCartney

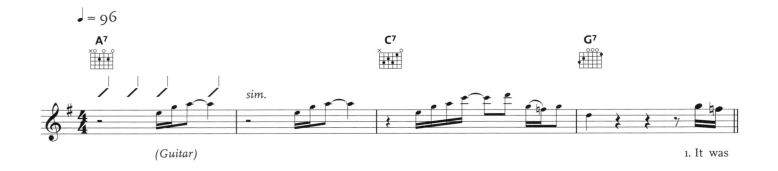

(Guitar)

1. It was

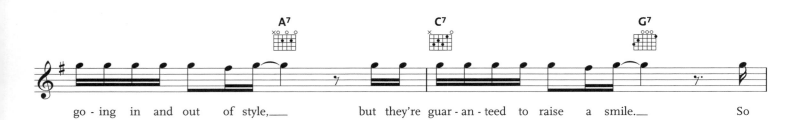

twen-ty years a-go to-day,_____ that Ser-geant Pep-per taught the band to play.___ They've been

(Verse 2 see block lyrics)

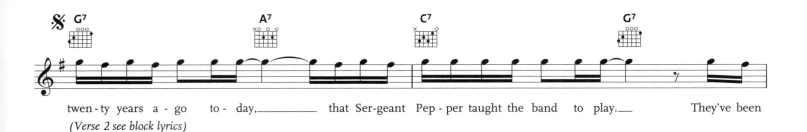

go-ing in and out of style,___ but they're guar-an-teed to raise a smile.___ So

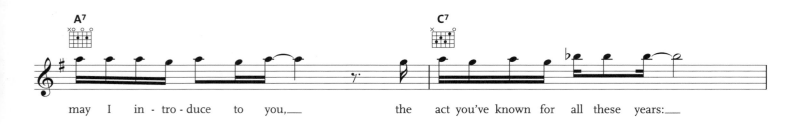

may I in-tro-duce to you,___ the act you've known for all these years:___

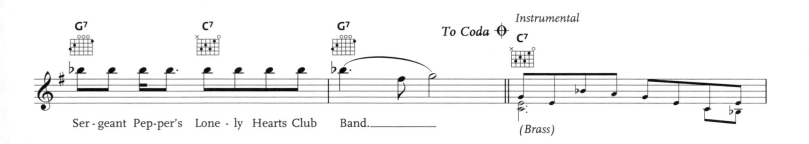

Ser-geant Pep-per's Lone-ly Hearts Club Band._____

(Brass)

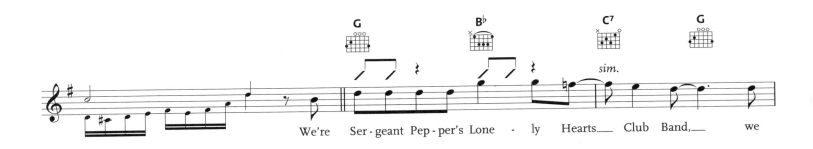

We're Ser - geant Pep - per's Lone - ly Hearts_ Club Band,_ we

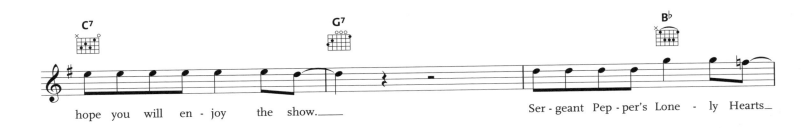

hope you will en - joy the show._ Ser - geant Pep - per's Lone - ly Hearts_

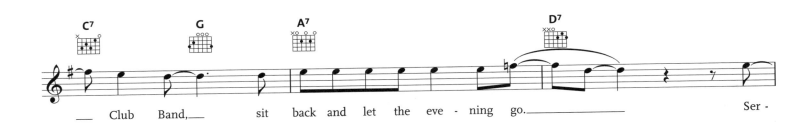

_ Club Band,_ sit back and let the eve - ning go._ Ser -

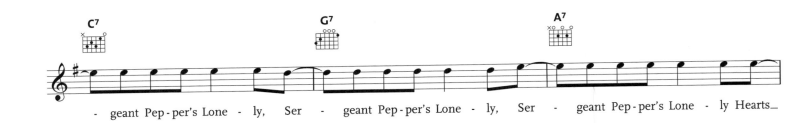

- geant Pep - per's Lone - ly, Ser - geant Pep - per's Lone - ly, Ser - geant Pep - per's Lone - ly Hearts_

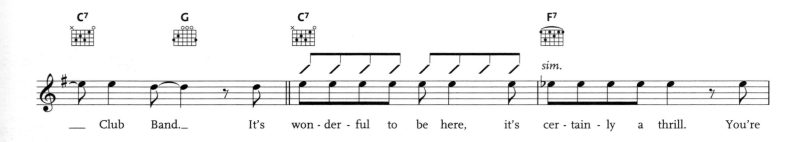

___ Club   Band.___   It's   won - der - ful   to   be   here,   it's   cer - tain - ly   a   thrill.   You're

such   a   love - ly   au - di - ence, we'd   like   to   take   you home with   us,   we'd   love   to   take   you home.   2. I   don't

✛ *Coda*

(Bass)

[Segue to 'With A Little Help From My Friends']

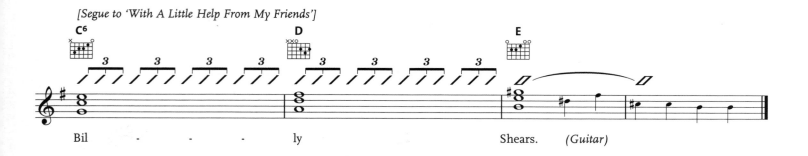

Bil   -   -   -   ly   Shears.   *(Guitar)*

Verse 2:

I don't really want to stop the show,
But I thought you might like to know,
That the singer's going to sing a song,
And he wants you all to sing along.
So let me introduce to you:
The one and only Billy Shears,
And Sergeant Pepper's Lonely Hearts Club Band.
Billy Shears.

With A Little Help From My Friends

Words & Music by John Lennon
& Paul McCartney

♩ = 112

Segue from 'Sgt. Pepper's Lonely Hearts Club Band'

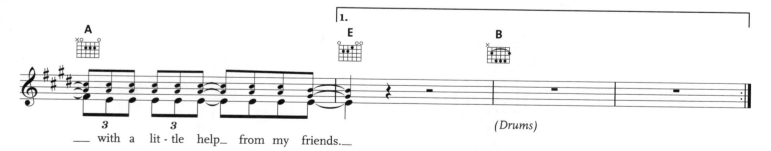

1. What would you think___ if I sang___ out of tune,___ would you stand___ up and walk___ out on me?___
(Verses 2 & 3 see block lyrics)

___ Lend me your ears___ and I'll sing___ you a song,___ and I'll try___

___ not to sing___ out of key.___ Oh,___ I get by___ with a lit-tle help___ from my friends.___

___ Mm,___ I get high___ with a lit-tle help___ from my friends.___ Mm,___ gon-na try___

1.
___ with a lit-tle help___ from my friends.___   *(Drums)*

2, 3.
___ *(Do you need___ an - y - bod - y?)*   { I need some-bod - y to love.___
{ I just need some-one to love.___

334

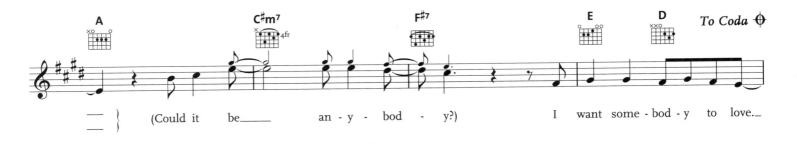

(Could it be___ an-y-bod-y?) I want some-bod-y to love.___

D.C. al Coda
(to 3rd time bar)

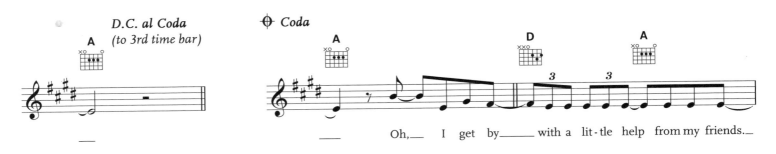

___ Oh,___ I get by___ with a lit-tle help from my friends.___

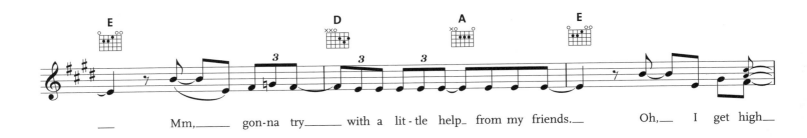

___ Mm,___ gon-na try___ with a lit-tle help_ from my friends.___ Oh,___ I get high___

___ with a lit-tle help_ from my friends.___ Yes,___ I get by___ with a lit-tle help_ from my friends,___

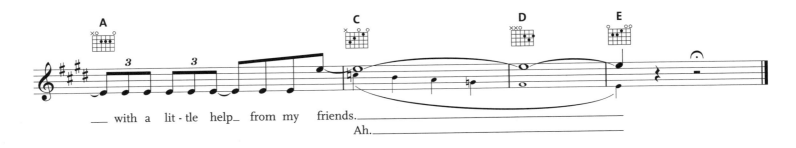

___ with a lit-tle help_ from my friends.___
Ah.___

Verse 2:

What do I do when my love is away?

(Does it worry you to be alone?)

How do I feel by the end of the day?

(Are you sad because you're on your own?)

No, I get by with a little help from my friends.

Mm, get high with a little help from my friends.

Mm, gonna try with a little help from my friends.

Verse 3:

(Would you believe in a love at first sight?)

Yes, I'm certain that it happens all the time.

(What do you see when you turn out the light?)

I can't tell you, but I know it's mine.

Oh, I get by with a little help from my friends.

Mm, get high with a little help from my friends.

Oh, I'm gonna try with a little help from my friends.

Lucy In The Sky With Diamonds

Words & Music by John Lennon
& Paul McCartney

Look for the girl with the sun in her eyes, and she's gone.

Lu-cy in the sky___ with dia - monds, Lu-cy in the sky___ with dia - monds,

1. **2.** *D.S. al Coda* ✛ *Coda*

Lu-cy in the sky___ with dia - monds, ah. ah.

Slower ♩ = 96

Lu-cy in the sky___ with dia - monds, Lu-cy in the sky___ with

Repeat to fade

dia - monds, Lu-cy in the sky___ with dia - monds, ah.___

Verse 2:
Follow her down to a bridge by a fountain,
Where rocking horse people eat marshmallow pies.
Everyone smiles as you drift past the flowers
That grow so incredibly high.

Newspaper taxis appear on the shore,
Waiting to take you away.
Climb in the back with your head in the clouds,
And you're gone.

Lucy in the sky with diamonds...

Verse 3:
Picture yourself on a train in a station,
With plasticine porters with looking-glass ties.
Suddenly someone is there at the turnstile,
The girl with kaleidoscope eyes.

Lucy in the sky with diamonds...

Fixing A Hole

Words & Music by John Lennon
& Paul McCartney

1. I'm
fix-ing a hole___ where the rain___ gets_ in___ and stops my mind_ from won-

(Verse 2 see block lyrics)

1.
- der-ing___ where it will___ go.___ *(Guitar)* 2. I'm

2.
(Guitar) Bridge 1. And it real-ly does-n't mat-ter if I'm wrong,___

(Bridge 2 see block lyrics)

___ I'm right where I be-long,___ I'm right where I be-long.___

See the peo-ple stand-ing there who dis-a-gree_ and nev-er win,_ and won-der why they don't get in my_

door.. 3. I'm paint-ing the room in a col - our-ful way, and when my mind_ is wan-

- der - ing, there I will_ go._____ (Guitar)

Oo,_____ oh, ah._

Hey, hey, ey - ey.

(Guitar solo)

Bridge 2. And it

_ go._

(Guitar)

I'm fix - ing a hole_ where the rain_ gets in_ and

339

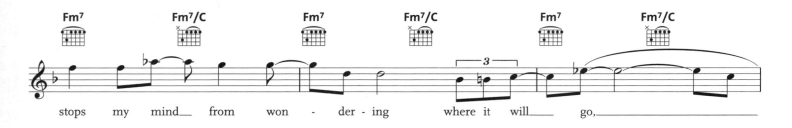

stops   my   mind__   from   won   -   der - ing   where   it   will__   go,_____

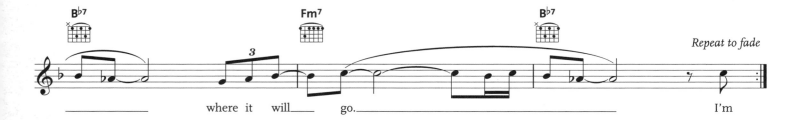

_____   where   it   will__   go.   *Repeat to fade*   I'm

Verse 2:

I'm filling the cracks that ran through the door
And kept my mind from wondering where it will go.

Bridge 2:

And it really doesn't matter if I'm wrong,
I'm right where I belong, I'm right where I belong.
Silly people run around, they worry me and never ask me
Why they don't get past my door.
I'm taking the time for a number of things
That weren't important yesterday, and I still go.

I'm fixing a hole...

She's Leaving Home

Words & Music by John Lennon
& Paul McCartney

(Harp)

1. Wednes - day morn - ing at five o' - clock as the day be - gins.____

(Verse 2 see block lyrics)

Si - lent - ly clo - sing her bed - room door,____

leav - ing the note that she hoped would say more. She goes down - stairs to the

(Verse 3 see block lyrics)

kitch - en, clutch - ing her hand - ker - chief.____

Qui - et - ly turn - ing the back - door key,____ step - ping out - side she is

She____

free.   (We gave her most of our____

Verse 2:
Father snores as his wife gets into her dressing gown.
Picks up the letter that's lying there,
Standing alone at the top of the stairs.
She breaks down and cries to her husband,
"Daddy, our baby's gone.
Why would she treat us so thoughtlessly?
How could she do this to me?"
She (We never thought of ourselves),
Is leaving (Never a thought for ourselves),
Home (We struggled hard all our lives to get by),
She's leaving home after living alone for so many years,
(Bye-bye).

Verse 3:
Friday morning at nine o'clock, she is far away.
Waiting to keep the appointment she made,
Meeting a man from the motor trade.
She (What did we do that was wrong?),
Is having (We didn't know it was wrong),
Fun (Fun is the one thing that money can't buy),
Something inside that was always denied for so many years,
(Bye-bye.)
She's leaving home (Bye-bye).

Being For The Benefit Of Mr. Kite

Words & Music by John Lennon
& Paul McCartney

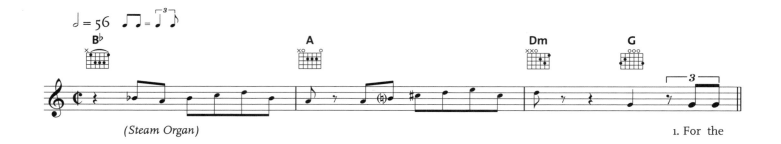

(Steam Organ)

1. For the

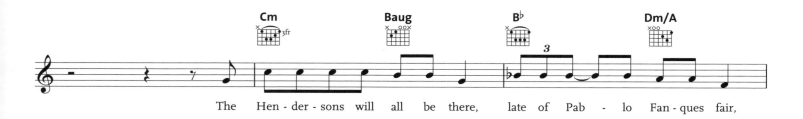

ben - e - fit___ of Mis - ter Kite there will be a show to - night on tram - po - line.___

(Verses 2 & 3 see block lyrics)

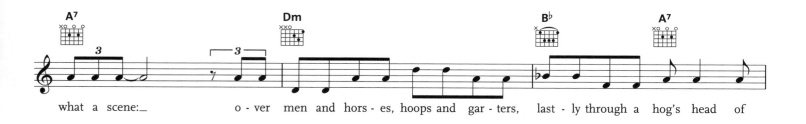

The Hen - der - sons will all be there, late of Pab - lo Fan - ques fair,

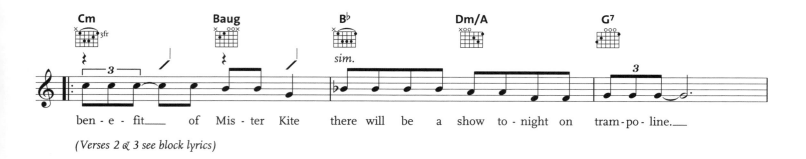

what a scene:___ o - ver men and hors - es, hoops and gar - ters, last - ly through a hog's head of

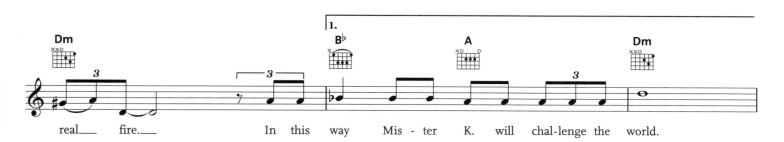

real___ fire.___ In this way Mis - ter K. will chal - lenge the world.

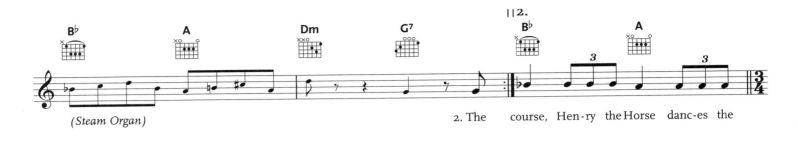

(Steam Organ)

2. The   course, Hen-ry the Horse danc-es the

Faster   ♩ = 168   ♩ = ♩.

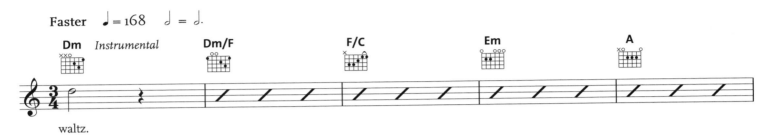

Instrumental

waltz.

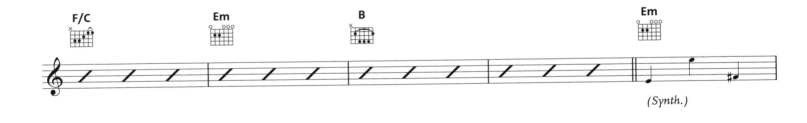

(Synth.)

Tempo 1   ♩ = 56

3. The

night   Mis - ter   Kite   is   top -ping the   bill.

(Steam Organ)

Instrumental with tape/synth. effects

Verse 2:
The celebrated Mister K. performs his feat on Saturday at Bishopsgate.
The Hendersons will dance and sing as Mister Kite flies through the ring; don't be late.
Messrs K. and H. assure the public their production will be second to none.
And of course, Henry the Horse dances the waltz.

Verse 3:
The band begins at ten to six, when Mister K. performs his tricks without a sound.
And Mister H. will demonstrate ten summersets he'll undertake on solid ground.
Having been some days in preparation, a splendid time is guaranteed for all.
And tonight Mister Kite is topping the bill.

When I'm Sixty-Four

Words & Music by John Lennon
& Paul McCartney

you'll be old - er too._____ Ah,_____ and if you
(Ah.)_____

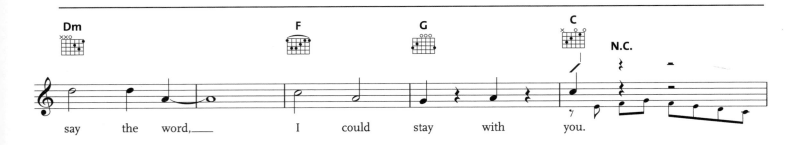

say the word,___ I could stay with you.

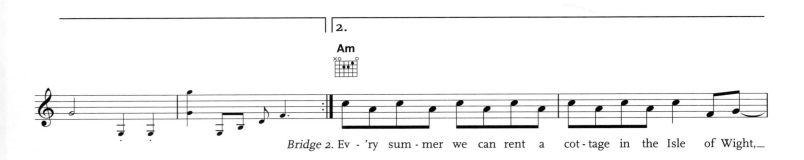

2.

Bridge 2. Ev - 'ry sum - mer we can rent a cot - tage in the Isle of Wight,___

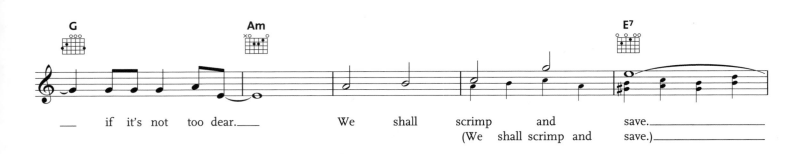

___ if it's not too dear.___ We shall scrimp and save._____
(We shall scrimp and save.)_____

___ Ah,_____ grand - chil - dren on your knee,___

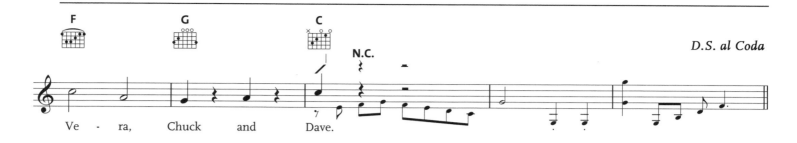

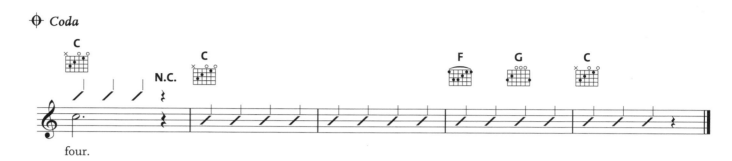

Ve - ra, Chuck and Dave.

D.S. al Coda

Coda

four.

Verse 2:

I could be handy mending a fuse,
When your lights have gone.
You can knit a sweater by the fireside,
Sunday mornings, go for a ride.
Doing the garden, digging the weeds,
Who could ask for more?
Will you still need me, will you still feed me,
When I'm sixty four?

Verse 3:

Send me a postcard, drop me a line,
Stating point of view.
Indicate precisely what you mean to say,
Yours sincerely wasting away.
Give me your answer, fill in a form,
Mine for evermore;
Will you still need me, will you still feed me,
When I'm sixty four?

A Day In The Life

Words & Music by John Lennon
& Paul McCartney
© Copyright 1967 Northern Songs.
All Rights Reserved.
International Copyright Secured.

fell out of bed, dragged a comb a-cross my head.

Dsus² **E** **B⁷sus⁴**

Found my way down-stairs and drank a cup, and

E **B⁷sus⁴** **B⁷** **E**

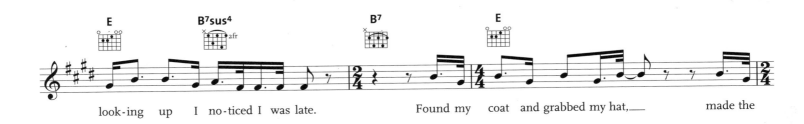

look-ing up I no-ticed I was late. Found my coat and grabbed my hat,__ made the

Dsus² **E** **B⁷sus⁴**

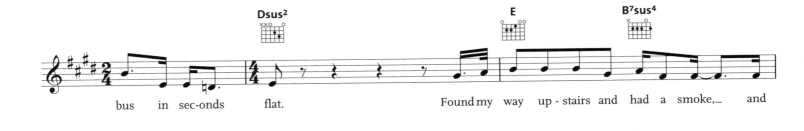

bus in sec-onds flat. Found my way up-stairs and had a smoke,__ and

E **B⁷sus⁴** **C** **G** **D**

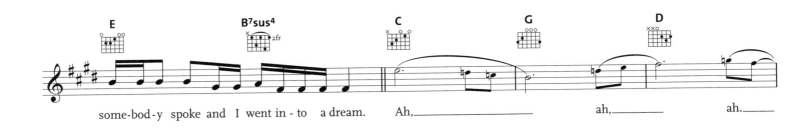

some-bod-y spoke and I went in-to a dream. Ah,_____ ah,____ ah.__

A **E** **C** **G**

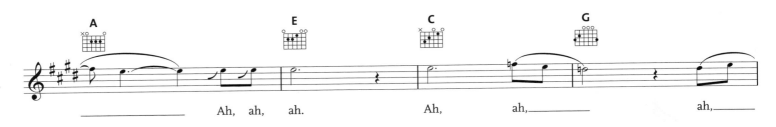

_____ Ah, ah, ah. Ah, ah,____ ah,____

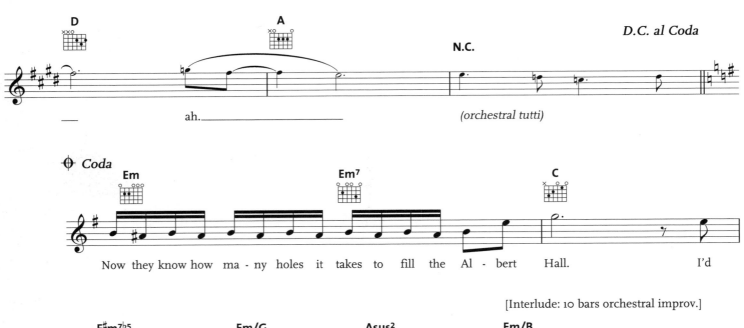

D.C. al Coda

ah._____

(orchestral tutti)

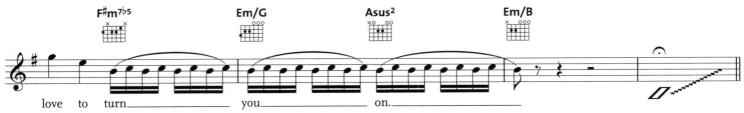

Coda

Now they know how ma - ny holes it takes to fill the Al - bert Hall. I'd

[Interlude: 10 bars orchestral improv.]

love to turn_____ you_____ on._____

(laughing) Tape loop effects ad lib. Repeat to fade

I nev - er could be a - ny oth - er way,

Verse 2:
He blew his mind out in a car,
He didn't notice that the lights had changed.
A crowd of people stood and stared,
They'd seen his face before.
Nobody was really sure if he was from the House of Lords.

Verse 3:
I saw a film today, oh boy,
The English army had just won the war.
A crowd of people turned away,
But I just had to look, having read the book.
I'd love to turn you on.

Verse 4:
I read the news today, oh boy,
Four thousand holes in Blackburn, Lancashire.
And though the holes were rather small,
They had to count them all.
Now they know how many holes it takes to fill the Albert Hall.
I'd love to turn you on.

All You Need Is Love

Words & Music by John Lennon
& Paul McCartney
© Copyright 1967 Northern Songs.
All Rights Reserved.
International Copyright Secured.

(Horns)

Love, love, love. Love, love, love.

Love, love, love. (Strings)

1. There's noth-ing you can do that can't be done,_____ noth-ing you can sing that can't be

(Verses 2 & 3 see block lyrics)

sung, noth-ing you can say, but you can learn how to play the game; it's

ea - sy. All you need is love,_____

all you need is love._____ All you need is love,_____ love,_____

love is all___ you need. Love, love, love. Love, love,

love. Love, love, love.

2. *D.S. al Coda* ⊕ *Coda*

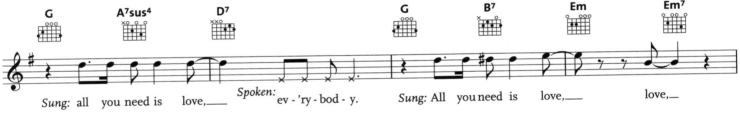

All you need is love,___ *Spoken:* all to-geth-er now,___

Sung: all you need is love,___ *Spoken:* ev-'ry-bod-y. *Sung:* All you need is love,___ love,___

love is all___ you need. Love is all you need,

(love is all you need)

love is

Fade ad lib.

Verse 2:
Nothing you can make that can't be made,
No one you can save that can't be saved,
Nothing you can do, but you can learn how to be you in time; it's easy.

Verse 3:
There's nothing you can know that isn't known,
Nothing you can see that isn't shown,
There's nowhere you can be that isn't where you're meant to be; it's easy.

Hello, Goodbye

Words & Music by John Lennon
& Paul McCartney

♩ = 100

1. You say "yes",— I say "no",— you say "stop"— and I say "go,— go, go."—

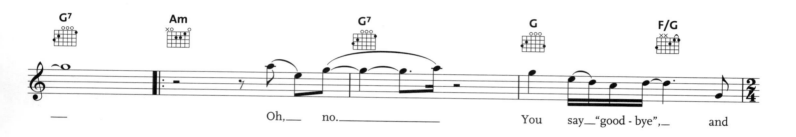

— Oh,— no.— You say— "good - bye",— and

I say "hel - lo,— hel - lo,— hel - lo",— I don't— know

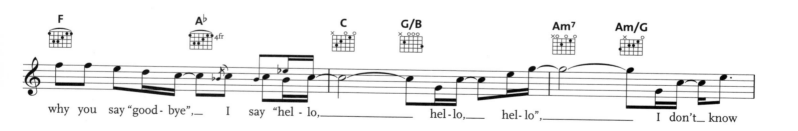

why you say "good - bye",— I say "hel - lo,— hel - lo,— hel - lo",— I don't— know

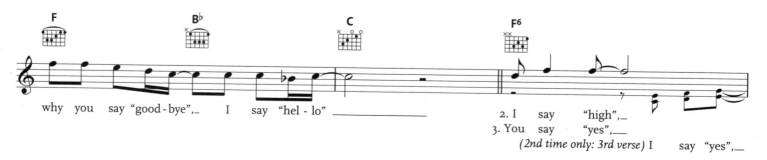

why you say "good - bye",— I say "hel - lo" _____ 2. I say "high",—
3. You say "yes",—
(2nd time only: 3rd verse) I say "yes",—

"Hel-lo,___ hel-lo",_____ I don't___ know why you say "good-bye",___ I say "hel-lo".__

Oo,_____ oh,___ oo,_____ oh._____ Hel - lo._____

He - la,_____ he_____ ba, hel - lo - a, cha, cha.

Repeat to fade

I Am The Walrus

Words & Music by John Lennon
& Paul McCartney

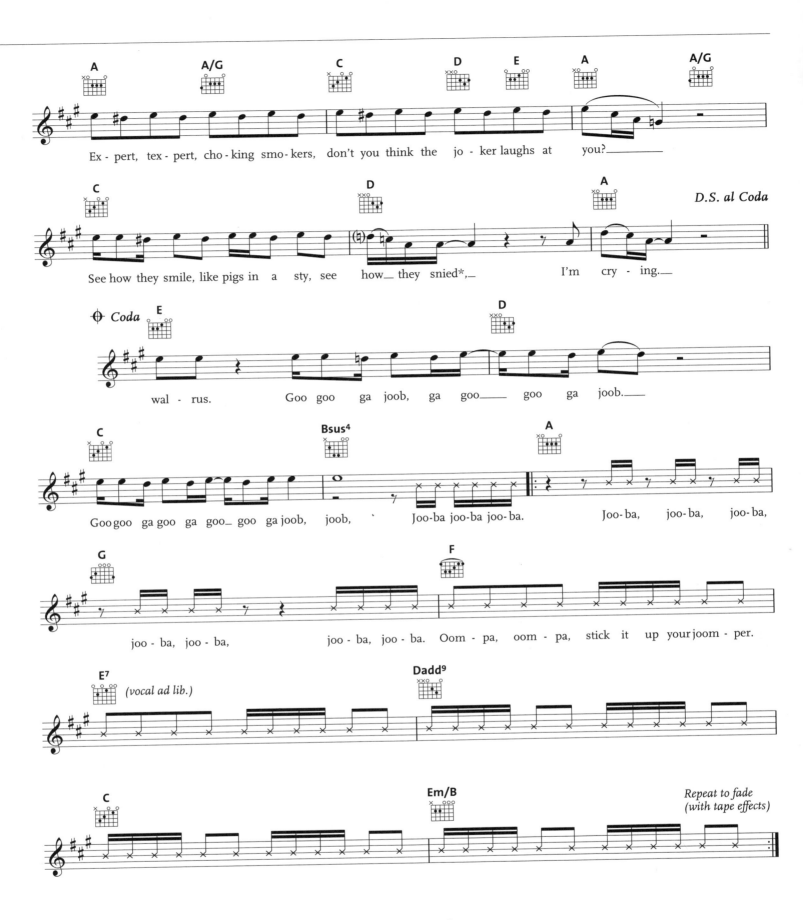

Verse 2:
Yellow matter custard dripping from a dead dog's eye.
Crabalocker fishwife, pornographic priestess,
Boy, you been a naughty girl, you let your knickers down.

I am the eggman...

Verse 3:
Semolina pilchard climbing up the Eiffel Tower.
Elementary penguin, singing Hare Krishna,
Man, you should have seen them kicking Edgar Allan Poe.

I am the eggman...

* Lennon's spelling

361

Magical Mystery Tour

Words & Music by John Lennon
& Paul McCartney
© Copyright 1967 Northern Songs.
All Rights Reserved.
International Copyright Secured.

(Brass)

(Spoken) Roll up! Roll up!

For the magical mystery tour, step right this way!

Roll up,_____

(Slower tempo at D.S., gradually getting faster)

roll up__ for the mys - ter - y tour.__

Roll up,_____

roll up__ for the mys - ter - y tour.__

sim.

Roll up,_____

(And that's an in - vi - ta - tion.)

roll up__ for the mys - ter - y tour.__

Roll up,_____

(To make a res - er - va - tion.)

To Coda ⊕

roll up__ for the mys - ter - y tour.__

The mag - i - cal mys - ter - y tour__ is

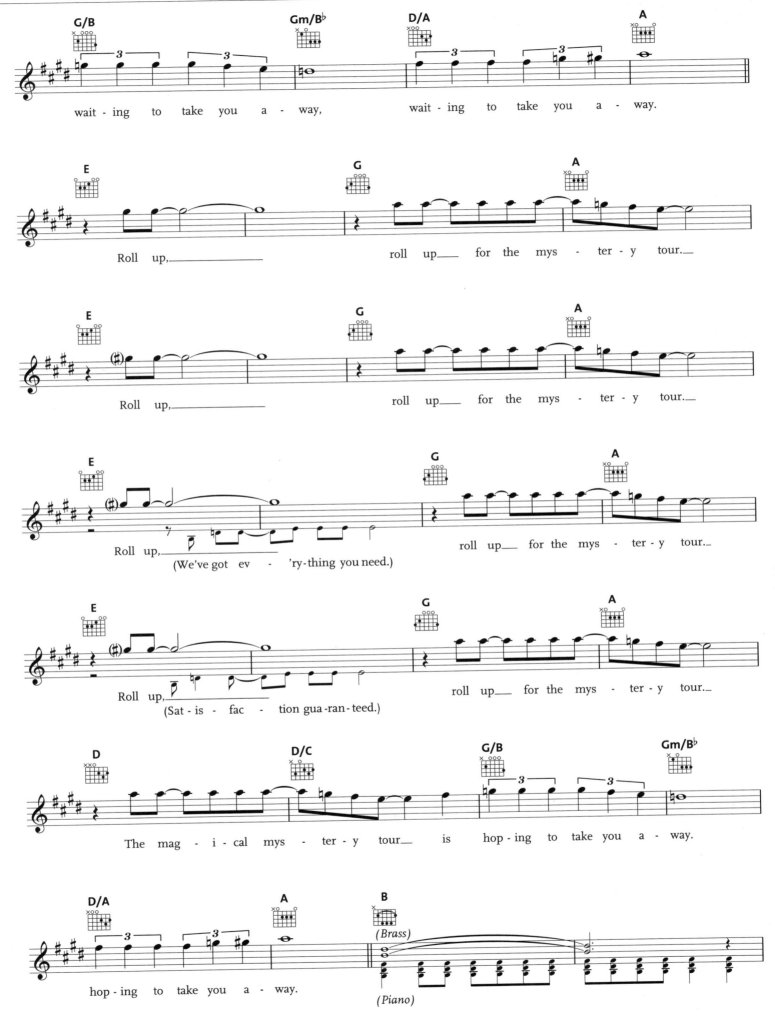

waiting to take you away, waiting to take you away.

Roll up,_____ roll up__ for the mystery tour.__

Roll up,_____ roll up__ for the mystery tour.__

Roll up,_____ roll up__ for the mystery tour.__
(We've got ev - 'ry-thing you need.)

Roll up,_____ roll up__ for the mystery tour.__
(Sat - is - fac - tion gua-ran-teed.)

The mag - i - cal mys - ter - y tour__ is hop - ing to take you a - way.

hop - ing to take you a - way.
(Brass)
(Piano)

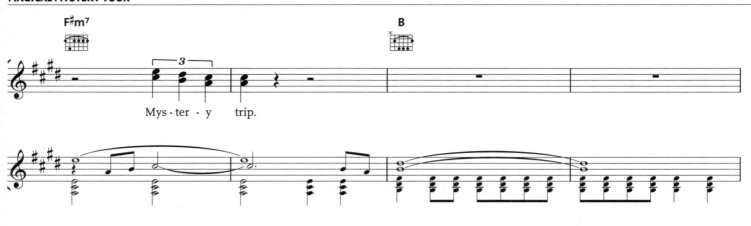

Mys - ter - y   trip.

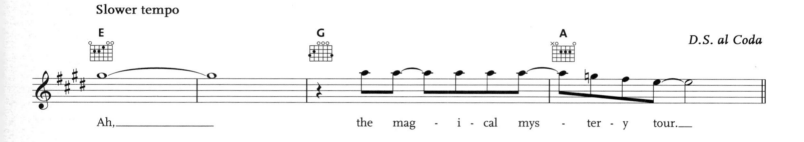

Slower tempo

D.S. al Coda

Ah,_____   the   mag - i - cal   mys - ter - y   tour.__

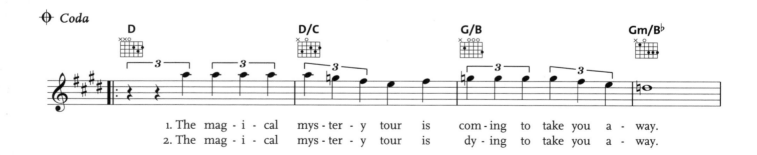

Coda

1. The mag - i - cal   mys - ter - y   tour   is   com - ing   to   take   you   a - way.
2. The mag - i - cal   mys - ter - y   tour   is   dy - ing   to   take   you   a - way.

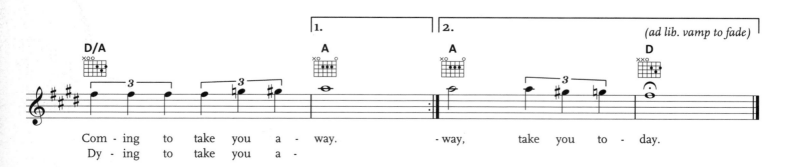

1.   **2.**   *(ad lib. vamp to fade)*

Com - ing   to   take   you   a - way.   - way,   take   you   to - day.
Dy - ing   to   take   you   a -

The Fool On The Hill

Words & Music by John Lennon
& Paul McCartney
© Copyright 1967 Northern Songs.
All Rights Reserved.
International Copyright Secured.

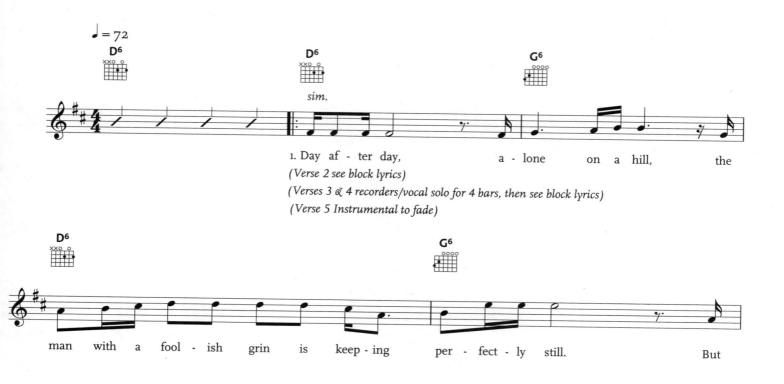

1. Day af - ter day, a - lone on a hill, the
(Verse 2 see block lyrics)
(Verses 3 & 4 recorders/vocal solo for 4 bars, then see block lyrics)
(Verse 5 Instrumental to fade)

man with a fool - ish grin is keep - ing per - fect - ly still. But

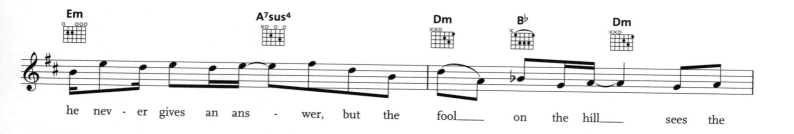

no - bod - y wants to know__ him,___ they can see that he's just a fool._____ And

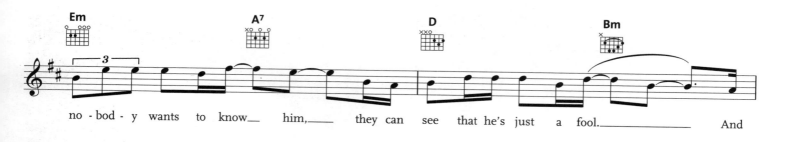

he nev - er gives an ans - wer, but the fool__ on the hill__ sees the

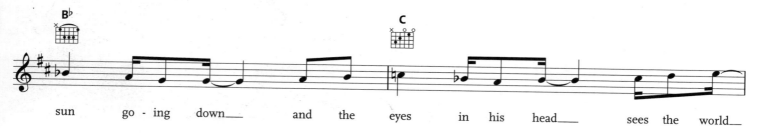

sun go - ing down__ and the eyes in his head__ sees the world__

spin-ning round.＿ *(Flutes)*

Repeat to instrumental and fade

Verse 2:
Well on the way, head in a cloud,
The man with a thousand voices talking perfectly loud.
But nobody ever hears him,
Or the sound he appears to make.
And he never seems to notice,
But the fool on the hill sees the sun going down,
And the eyes in his head see the world spinning round.

Verse 3:
(Recorders/vocal solo for 4 bars)

And nobody seems to like him,
They can tell what he wants to do.
And he never shows his feelings,
But the fool on the hill sees the sun going down,
And the eyes in his head see the world spinning round.

Verse 4:
(Recorders/vocal solo for 4 bars)

He never listens to them,
He knows that they're the fools.
They don't like him;
The fool on the hill sees the sun going down,
And the eyes in his head see the world spinning round.

Verse 5:
(Recorders/vocal solo for 4 bars, then repeat
to instrumental & fade)

Your Mother Should Know

Words & Music by John Lennon
& Paul McCartney
© Copyright 1967 Northern Songs.
All Rights Reserved.
International Copyright Secured.

Ooh_____

1, 2. Let's all get up and dance
(Verses 3 & 4 see block lyrics)

____ to a song_____ that was a hit be - fore_____ your

moth - er was born._____ Though she was born_____ a long,_____ long time a - go,_____

Your mo - ther should

Ah_____

To Codas

____ your moth - er should know,_____

Your moth - er should know._____

1. Sing it a - gain._____

2. (Organ)

Verse 3:
Lift up your hearts and sing me a song,
That was a hit before your mother was born.
Though she was born a long, long time ago,
Your mother should know,
Your mother should know.
Your mother should know,
Your mother should know.

Verse 4:
Da da da da da da da da da da da da,
Da da da da da da da da,
Though she was born a long, long time ago,
Your mother should know,
Your mother should know.
Your mother should know,
Your mother should know. *etc.*

1968

5 January

→ John got together with his father Freddie once more, this time at Kenwood, John's house in Weybridge. Freddie had been washing dishes in a nearby hotel. John told the *Daily Mirror* that he had ended his feud with his father:

"From now on I hope we'll be in close contact all the time."

→ George continued work on the soundtrack to *Wonderwall* at Abbey Road.

→ *Magical Mystery Tour* was repeated on BBC2, this time as it was originally intended to be seen, in colour.

6 January

→ The *Daily Telegraph* reported that Brian Epstein had left £486,032 (£266,032 net) and that his mother was to control the estate.

7 January

→ George flew from London to Bombay, to continue recording the *Wonderwall* film soundtrack using local Indian musicians.

9 January

→ George began work at EMI's Bombay recording studios.

11 January

→ George recorded the backing track for 'The Inner Light' at EMI Bombay.

12 January

→ The Beatles Film Productions Limited changed its name to Apple Film Limited and Apple Music Limited changed its name to Apple Corps Limited.

→ George completed the recordings needed for *Wonderwall* and began recording ragas and other traditional pieces of music for possible use on Beatles records. He returned to London on 18 January.

19 January

→ The single 'Dear Delilah' by Grapefruit (managed by Apple) was released in the UK.

22 January

→ Apple Corps opened offices at 95 Wigmore St, London.

Above: Paul gives the thumbs-up to *Yellow Submarine*, Twickenham, 25 January. Opposite: Paul, Jane Asher, Maureen & Ringo prepare to fly to India, 19 February. The Starkey's returned home after just 10 days with Ringo saying the Maharishi's retreat reminded him of a Butlin's holiday camp.

25 January

→ Twickenham Film Studio. The Beatles filmed their cameo appearance at the end of the animated cartoon *Yellow Submarine*.

27 January

→ John was interviewed by Kenny Everett at home for BBC Radio 1's *The Kenny Everett Show*.

30 January

→ George completed work on the soundtrack for the film *Wonderwall* at Abbey Road.

1 February

→ Ringo attended rehearsals for his live appearance on Cilla Black's new television show *Cilla* with its theme tune, 'Step Inside Love', written by Paul.

2 February

→ Ringo attended a second day of rehearsals for *Cilla*.

3 February

→ Abbey Road. Work began on 'Lady Madonna'.

4 February

→ Abbey Road. Work began on 'Across The Universe'. Two fans, Lizzie Bravo (from Brazil) and Gayleen Pease, who were waiting outside, were brought into the studio to provide the high falsetto harmonies needed.

5 February

→ Ringo attended camera rehearsals for his appearance on *Cilla*.

→ Paul appeared at a press conference held at the Royal Garden Hotel, London to publicise the Leicester Arts Community Festival.

6 February

→ Ringo appeared live on BBC Television's *Cilla*, taking part in sketches, singing and even tap dancing.

→ Abbey Road. The other three Beatles worked on 'The Inner Light' and completed 'Lady Madonna' (taking a break to watch Ringo's appearance on *Cilla*). 'Lady Madonna' featured the saxophone talents of Ronnie Scott, Harry Klein, Bill Povey and Bill Jackman. Paul played piano, and the comb and paper routine was achieved by John, Paul and George singing through cupped hands.

8 February

→ Abbey Road. 'The Inner Light' was completed and most of the session was spent working on 'Across The Universe'. John remained unsatisfied with the results. Spike Milligan, who watched the session as George Martin's guest, asked if he could use 'Across The Universe' on a wildlife charity record he was organising and The Beatles agreed.

9 February

→ The *New Musical Express* carried the first of a series of ads, carrying the one-word message 'Apple'.

11 February

→ Abbey Road. While Tony Bramwell, head of Apple Films, was present at the studio to shoot a promo clip for 'Lady Madonna', The Beatles decided to take advantage of the situation by recording a new song, 'Hey Bulldog'.

→ Yoko Ono attended a Beatles session for the first time as John's guest, and demanded to know why all The Beatles' songs used exactly the same rhythm, and why they didn't

1968

attempt something more adventurous.

14 February
→ Mal Evans collected luggage belonging to George and Patti, her sister Jenny, John and Cynthia, and took Qantas flight 754 to Delhi paying £195.19.6d. in excess baggage charges. He went early in order to organise transport for John and George when they arrived to begin their much delayed study of transcendental meditation with Maharishi Mahesh Yogi.

15-16 February
→ George, Patti, John and Cynthia flew from London Airport to Delhi on the overnight flight arriving at 8:15 am. Mal met them at the airport with Mia Farrow, who had already decided that she was part of The Beatles' entourage. Mal had organised three cars for the 150-mile drive from Delhi to Rishikesh.

18 February
→ Paul was interviewed by the London *Evening Standard* newspaper.

19 February
→ Paul and Jane, and Ringo and Maureen flew from London Airport to India.

20 February
→ Paul, Jane, Ringo and Maureen arrived in Delhi, attracting much more press attention as the media were now alterted to what was going on. A film crew was on hand as they stepped from the plane after the exhausting 20-hour flight.

23 February
→ The *Daily Express* newspaper in London published colour photographs of each of The Beatles, taken by Richard Avedon, and offered readers the chance to buy enlargements of the set, plus a special Beatles poster.

Below: George's 25th birthday party, 25 February, at the Maharishi's ashram. The meditation trip was to end in bad vibes after the Holy Man was suspected of having earthly desires towards a female meditator. Opposite: Paul and John arrive in New York to launch Apple, 11 May.

1 March
→ Ringo and Maureen left Rishikesh much earlier than anticipated. They were unhappy away from their children and did not like the food. Ringo told the press it was like a Butlin's holiday camp.

8 March
→ The single 'And The Sun Will Shine' by Paul Jones, featuring Paul on drums, was released in the UK as Columbia DB 8379.

9 March
→ *Sgt Pepper's Lonely Hearts Club Band* won four Grammy awards at the annual ceremony in Los Angeles: Best Album of the Year, Best Contemporary Album, Best Engineered Record (later presented to Geoff Emerick by Ringo at Abbey Road) and Best Album Cover.

13 March
→ Ringo gave an interview to the *New Musical Express* to explain why he had returned from India before the rest of The Beatles.

14 March
→ Tony Bramwell's promotional film for 'Lady Madonna' (which actually showed them recording 'Hey Bulldog') was shown on BBC TV's *Top Of The Pops*.

15 March
→ The single 'Lady Madonna'/'Inner Light' was released in the UK as Parlophone R 5675.
→ The promotional film for 'Lady Madonna' was shown on BBC Television's *All Systems Freeman* presented by Alan Freeman.

18 March
→ 'Lady Madonna'/'The Inner Light' was released in the USA as Capitol 2138.

26-27 March
→ Paul, Jane and Neil Aspinall flew back to England overnight from Rishikesh, leaving behind George and Patti, John and Cynthia and John's friend 'Magic' Alex who had come out to join them.

2 April
→ A new Beatles music publishing

company, Python Music Limited, was formed.

8 April
→ Paul directed a promotional film for 'Elevator', the next single by Grapefruit.
→ Derek Taylor began work as The Beatles' and Apple's press officer, having been persuaded by The Beatles to return to Britain from Los Angeles.

12 April
→ John and Cynthia, George and Patti and 'Magic' Alex left in a hurry from Rishikesh, India, after 'Magic' Alex convinced John and George that the Maharishi was using his position to gain sexual favours from at least one of the female meditators. The Maharishi had never claimed to be celibate, and since he was not given a chance to explain or deny the charge, the reasons for their departure remain unclear. Alex Mardas certainly did not want to relinquish his claim to be John's 'guru' and it would appear that he engineered the whole thing. At Delhi Airport, John wrote 'Sexy Sadie', at that time called 'Maharishi'.
→ While John and Cynthia returned to London, George and Patti flew to Madras to visit Ravi Shankar. During the flight back to London, John informed Cynthia of the extent of his marital infidelities during the Beatlemania years.

16 April
→ Apple Publicity Limited was formed.

19 April
→ Apple Music published an advertisement in the *New Musical Express*, showing Alistair Taylor as a one-man-band busker, soliciting tapes from unknown artists.

Apple's advert: "This man has talent. One day he sang his songs to a tape recorder (borrowed from the man next door). In his neatest handwriting he wrote an explanatory note (giving his name and address) and, remembering to enclose a picture of himself, sent the tape, letter and photograph to Apple Music, 94 Baker Street, London W1. If you were thinking of doing the same thing yourself – do it now! This man now owns a Bentley!"

→ Apple was promptly inundated and only a tiny percentage of tapes were actually played.

21 April
→ George and Patti returned to London from India.

25 April
→ George spoke to newspaper reporters in London about his experiences in India.

5 May
→ Twiggy saw Mary Hopkin on the television talent show *Opportunity Knocks* and telephoned Paul to suggest she would be a good singer for Apple to sign.

11 May
→ John and Paul, accompanied by 'Magic' Alex, Neil Aspinall, Mal Evans, Ron Kass and Derek Taylor, flew to New York to launch Apple in the US.

13 May
→ John and Paul conducted interviews with the *New York Times* and

India: 20th February

The Academy of Transcendental Meditation was built 150 feet above the Ganges surrounded on three sides by jungle-covered mountains. The students lived in six stone cottages. Each room had twin beds and modern bathroom facilities though the water supply sometimes broke down.

Breakfast from 7 until 11 am was followed by meditation practice, with no rules or timetable. Lunch and dinner both consisted of soup followed by a vegetarian main dish; John and George were already vegetarians so the diet was nothing strange, but Ringo found the spices too hot for his taste so Mal assembled a stock of eggs so that he could cook for him.

While in India, The Beatles were on a TM teachers' course: there were 90-minute lectures at 3:30 and 8:30 pm with questions and answers, and progressively longer meditation sessions but they were three weeks behind the other students so the Maharishi gave them extra tuition in the afternoons. These took place in the open air, sometimes on his flat sun roof. If it was a cool day, they would go to his bungalow and sit on cushions.

Below: Lennon and McCartney promote Apple Corp. Ltd as a "kind of Western capitalism" in New York, 14 May. The Beatles' naïve charitable enterprise attracted freeloaders by the dozen.

other newspapers all day from a suite at the St. Regis Hotel.

14 May

→ John and Paul gave a press conference at the Americana Hotel on Central Park West.

→ At the Americana press conference Paul met up once again with Linda Eastman, who wrote her telephone number on an unused cheque and gave it to him.

→ The Beatles taped an interview with Mitchell Krause for WNDT, the non-commercial Channel 13's programme *Newsfront*.

→ That evening they appeared on NBC's *The Tonight Show*.

15 May

→ Accompanied by Linda, Nat Weiss drove John, Paul and 'Magic' Alex to the airport for their overnight flight back to London.

→ George, Patti, Ringo and Maureen flew to Cannes, in the south of France to attend the premiere of *Wonderwall* at the Cannes Film Festival.

John: "The aim of the company isn't a stack of gold teeth in the bank. We've done that bit. It's more of a trick to see if we can't get artistic freedom within a business structure; to see if we can create things and sell them without charging three times our cost."

16 May

→ Apple Management Limited was incorporated.

17 May

→ The album *McGough & McGear* by Roger McGough and Mike McGear, produced by Paul McCartney, was released in the UK as Parlophone PCS 7047.

→ The world premiere of *Wonderwall* was given at the Cannes Film Festival with George, Patti, Ringo and Maureen in attendance.

19 May

→ With Cynthia taking a short holiday in Greece, John called Yoko Ono and invited her over to Kenwood. They made a random sound tape, which was later issued as *Two Virgins* with the notorious sleeve showing them both naked. When Cynthia returned, she found Yoko ensconced in the bedroom, wearing Cynthia's dressing gown.

22 May

→ George and John, accompanied by Patti and Yoko, attended the press launch and press conference for Apple's second boutique, Apple Tailoring (Civil and Theatrical) housed at 161 New King's Road, London and run by designer John Crittle.

George: "We bought a few things from him, and the next thing I knew, we owned the place!"

23 May

→ Paul and Ringo were interviewed at Abbey Road for Tony Palmer's BBC Television *Omnibus* documentary on pop music called *All My Loving*.

26 May

→ Paul directed a promotional film for Grapefruit's new single, 'Elevator', at the Albert Memorial in Hyde Park, London.

→ Towards the end of May, The Beatles gathered at George's bungalow 'Kinfauns' in Esher, to record a demo tape of songs on Harrison's four-track tape machine, from which they would choose what to put on their next album. Most of

John and Yoko: 19 May

John: 'I'd never known love like this before, and it hit me so hard that I had to halt my marriage to Cyn... When we got back from India we were talking to each other on the phone. I called her over, it was the middle of the night and Cyn was away, and I thought 'Well now's the time if I'm gonna get to know her anymore'. She came to the house and I didn't know what to do; so we went upstairs to my studio and I played her all the tapes that I'd made, all this far out stuff, some comedy stuff, and some electronic music. She was suitably impressed and then she said well let's make one ourselves so we made *Two Virgins*. It was midnight when we started *Two Virgins*, and it was dawn when we finished, and then we made love at dawn. It was very beautiful.'

the songs had been written during their visit to India earlier in the year. They first recorded John's songs: 'Cry Baby Cry', 'Child Of Nature', 'The Continuing Story Of Bungalow Bill', 'I'm So Tired', 'Yer Blues', 'Everybody's Got Something To Hide Except Me And My Monkey', 'What's The New Mary Jane' and 'Revolution'. Then came George's new compositions: 'While My Guitar Gently Weeps', 'Circles', 'Sour Milk Sea', 'Not Guilty' and 'Piggies'. They returned to John's notebook for 'Julia', then came Paul's songs: 'Blackbird', 'Rocky Racoon', 'Back In The USSR', 'Honey Pie', 'Mother Nature's Son', 'Ob-La-Di, Ob-La-Da' and 'Junk'. They finished with two more of John's: 'Dear Prudence' and 'Sexy Sadie'.

George: "There's about 35 songs we've got already, and a few of them are mine. God knows which one will be the next single. I suppose we've got a vague overall conception of the kind of album we want to do, but it takes time to work out. We could do a double album, I suppose – or maybe a triple album. There's enough stuff there."

30 May
→ Abbey Road. Work began on what was to become the double album *The Beatles*, colloquially known as 'The White Album'. The first song worked on was John's 'Revolution 1'.

31 May
→ Abbey Road. *The Beatles* sessions. Work continued on 'Revolution 1' and the last six minutes was removed to form the basis of the chaotic 'Revolution 9'. Yoko spoke on the track, her first appearance on a Beatles recording.

4 June
→ Abbey Road. *The Beatles* sessions. Further work on 'Revolution 1'.
→ Paul began seeing American scriptwriter, Francie Schwartz.

5 June
→ Abbey Road. *The Beatles* sessions. Recording began on Ringo's 'Don't Pass Me By', his first full composition used on a Beatles record.

6 June
→ Abbey Road. *The Beatles* sessions. Further work on 'Don't Pass Me By'.
→ Kenny Everett visited the studio to record an interview for his BBC Radio 1 programme *The Kenny Everett Show*.
→ John and Victor Spinetti were filmed for the BBC2 arts programme *Release* discussing *The John Lennon Play: In His Own Write*, directed by Victor Spinetti, which was due to open in London on the 18th.
→ Around this time, Cynthia returned from a brief holiday abroad, to be informed by Magic Alex that John

intended to divorce her, and that he wanted her and their son Julian to move out of Kenwood.

7 June
→ George, Patti, Ringo, Maureen and Mal Evans flew to California to enable George to film a guest appearance in Ravi Shankar's film *Raga*.

10 June
→ Abbey Road. *The Beatles* sessions. John worked on 'Revolution 9', adding more sound effects.

11 June
→ Abbey Road. *The Beatles* sessions. John did further work on 'Revolution 9', while Paul, in a separate studio, recorded and mixed 'Blackbird', without the aid of the other Beatles.
→ Tony Bramwell from Apple Films shot a colour promotional film of Paul with new Apple signing, Mary Hopkin.
→ In California, George and Ravi Shankar were filmed playing sitars together on the coast-cliffs in Big Sur and taking part in a 'teach-in'.

15 June
→ John and Yoko held their first public event by planting acorns for peace at Coventry Cathedral. Their intended site had to be altered because Canon Verney refused to allow an unmarried couple to bury anything in consecrated ground. The original acorns were soon stolen by Lennon fans, and the replacements sent by John and Yoko had to be placed under 24-hour guard.

16 June
→ Intertel TV Studios, Wembley. David Frost interviewed Paul before a live audience for an all-British Frost programme taped for transmission in America. The programme was called *David Frost Presents... Frankie Howerd*, and on it, Howerd interviewed Paul about Apple, then Paul introduced Mary Hopkin who sang two songs.

18 June
→ The National Theatre production of *The John Lennon Play: In His Own Write*, directed by Victor Spinetti, opened at the Old Vic Theatre, London. John and Yoko's arrival together at the theatre

1968

was seized upon by the press, several of whom called out to John, 'Where's your wife, Mr Lennon?'

20 June
→ Paul, Tony Bramwell and his old school friend Ivan Vaughan flew to Los Angeles where Paul was due to address the Capitol Records sales conference (Capitol were the American distributors of Apple records). He contacted Linda Eastman who flew out from New York the next day to join him.
→ Abbey Road. *The Beatles* sessions. John and Yoko utilised three studios to continue the assembly of tape loops for 'Revolution 9'. One was made from a Royal Academy of Music examination tape in which an anonymous man, asking question number nine, had his voice turned into an endless loop which John and Yoko faded in and out at will.

21 June
→ Abbey Road. *The Beatles* sessions. 'Revolution 1' was finished with the addition of the horn section and guitar solo.
→ In Los Angeles, Paul addressed a Capitol Records sales conference and announced that in future all Beatles records would appear on the Apple label, although the group technically was still on EMI/Capitol.

22 June
→ John and Victor Spinetti appeared on the BBC2 arts programme *Release*, discussing the *In His Own Write* play.
→ Apple paid half a million pounds for a new headquarters building at 3 Savile Row, the former home of Nelson's Lady Hamilton.

24 June
→ Abbey Road. George began work as a producer, recording 'Sour Milk Sea' with new Apple signing, Jackie Lomax, an old friend from Liverpool.
→ *The Beatles* sessions. John and Yoko worked on the stereo mix of 'Revolution 9'.

25 June
→ Abbey Road. George continued work with Jackie Lomax on 'Sour Milk Sea'.
→ *The Beatles* sessions: John and Yoko cut one minute from 'Revolution 9',

though it was to remain the public's least favourite 'Beatles' track.

26-27 June
→ Abbey Road. *The Beatles* sessions: work on John's 'Everybody's Got Something To Hide Except Me And My Monkey'.

28 June
→ Abbey Road. *The Beatles* sessions. Recording began on 'Good Night', John's lullaby for five-year-old Julian. John sang it through in the studio several times so that Ringo would get the phrasing but declined to record it himself, thinking it too 'soft' for his hard image. Unfortunately no recording of John's acoustic version was made.

30 June
→ Paul recorded The Black Dyke Mills Band in Saltaire, near Bradford, playing one of his own compositions, 'Thingumybob' (which he wrote as the theme tune for a London Weekend Television comedy series of the same name) and 'Yellow Submarine' as a B-side.
→ While in Saltaire he was interviewed by Tony Cliff for the local BBC television programme *Look North*.

1 July
→ Abbey Road. *The Beatles* sessions. John added his lead vocal to 'Everybody's Got Something To Hide Except Me And My Monkey'. Before the session, John and Yoko arrived dressed in white at the opening of John's first full art exhibition, *You Are Here*, at the Robert Fraser Gallery, London, which consisted mostly of charity collecting boxes. The exhibition was subtitled: 'To Yoko from John Lennon'. John marked the opening by releasing 365 helium-filled balloons over London. Each balloon was launched with a postcard attached, and a message asking the finder to return them to Apple. John was discouraged to learn that a high percentage of finders chose to decorate their cards with racist comments about Yoko.

2 July
→ Abbey Road. *The Beatles* sessions.

John: "I declare these balloons high."

Opposite: Paul, Ringo and George with cartoon stand-in John at the *Yellow Submarine* press screening, 8 July. Below: John & Yoko, 'You Are Here' exhibition, 1 July.

Ringo recorded more vocals for 'Good Night'.

3-5 July
→ Abbey Road. *The Beatles* sessions. Work on 'Ob-La-Di, Ob-La-Da'.

8 July
→ Abbey Road. *The Beatles* sessions. Paul did not like the results so far on 'Ob-La-Di, Ob-La-Da' and started afresh to the disgruntlement of John and George, who had already made their lack of enthusiasm for the song clear.
→ Rehearsals began for 'Revolution', intended by John as an A-side for The Beatles next single (but ultimately used as the B-side).
→ Paul, George and Ringo attend a press screening of *Yellow Submarine* at the Bowater House Cinema in Knightsbridge. This was the first time any of The Beatles had seen the animated movie.

10 July
→ Abbey Road. *The Beatles* sessions. More work on John's 'Revolution'. Both Yoko Ono and Francie Schwartz attended the session.

11 July
→ Abbey Road. *The Beatles* sessions. Piano and bass were added to 'Revolution' and horns added to 'Ob-La-Di, Ob-La-Da'.

12 July
→ Abbey Road. *The Beatles* sessions: 'Don't Pass Me By' was virtually completed and from midnight on, a new bass and guitar part was added to 'Revolution'.

15 July
→ Abbey Road. *The Beatles* sessions. Paul added a new vocal to 'Ob-La-Di, Ob-La-Da' and John remixed 'Revolution'. After this they rehearsed 'Cry Baby Cry'.

16 July
→ Abbey Road. *The Beatles* sessions. More work done on 'Cry Baby Cry'.
→ Balance engineer Geoff Emerick finally quit working with The Beatles. He could no longer tolerate the swearing and ill-mannered attitude

shown towards the engineers (particularly from John) and the tense atmosphere in the studio.

17 July
→ The world premiere of the animated *Yellow Submarine* film washeld at the London Pavilion in Piccadilly Circus. Fans as usual brought traffic to a standstill and blocked the streets. Ringo and Maureen, John and Yoko and George and Patti werepresent but Paul attended alone.
→ Afterwards they attended the celebration party at the Royal Lancaster Hotel, where the discotheque had been renamed Yellow Submarine for the occasion (and was to remain so for several years after).

18 July
→ Abbey Road. *The Beatles* sessions. More work on 'Cry Baby Cry' and rehearsals for 'Helter Skelter', including the taping of a legendary

27-minute rendition of the latter song.

19 July
→ Abbey Road. *The Beatles* sessions. Work began on 'Sexy Sadie'.

20 July
→ Jane Asher, appearing on Simon Dee's BBC television show *Dee Time*, said that her engagement to Paul was off – but that it was not she that had broken it. She told Dee that they had been engaged for seven months, after knowing each other for five years.

22 July
→ Abbey Road. *The Beatles* sessions. 'Don't Pass Me By' was completed, along with a new version of 'Good Night', recorded with the orchestra and Mike Sammes Singers.

23 July
→ Abbey Road. *The Beatles* sessions. 'Everybody's Got Something To Hide Except Me And My Monkey' was completed.

Above: John and Paul each bring an apple to the *Yellow Submarine* film premiere, London Pavilion, 17 July.

24 July
→ Abbey Road. *The Beatles* sessions. More work on 'Sexy Sadie'.

25 July
→ Abbey Road. *The Beatles* sessions. Work began on George's 'While My Guitar Gently Weeps'.

28 July
→ The Beatles spent almost the entire day in and around London on various promotional photographic assignments, as part of what came to be known as their 'Mad Day Out'. Photos were taken in Hyde Park, in London's Docklands, and in the garden of Paul's St. John's Wood home.

29 July
→ Abbey Road. Work began on 'Hey Jude', destined to become the next single.

30 July
→ Abbey Road. More work in preparing 'Hey Jude' for final recording which was to take place in

an independent studio.

→ The Beatles were filmed at work by James Archibald for a documentary film intended for cinematic exhibition called *Music*.

→ The Beatles decided to close down the Apple Boutique from tomorrow, giving away all the stock, having taken their choice of items off the shelves. Apple gave the other boutique at 161 King's Road to the store manager.

31 July

→ Trident Studios, Soho. The backing track for 'Hey Jude' was laid down.

August

→ John and Yoko collaborated on their first film projects, *Film No. 5 (Smile)* (a slow-motion record of John doing just that) and *Two Virgins* (in which the couple's faces merged into one).

1 August

→ Trident Studios, Soho. The orchestra, bass and lead vocals were added to 'Hey Jude' using Trident's eight-track facility (EMI still used four-track). There were fierce arguments between John and Paul about who was to get the A-side of the new single, their first on the Apple label, but Paul eventually won and 'Hey Jude' became the first Apple release and the biggest selling Beatles single of all time.

2 August

→ Trident Studios. 'Hey Jude' was completed with overdubs and mixed.

→ The London Weekend Television series *Thingumybob*, starring Stanley Holloway and with Paul's title tune, began transmission.

4 August

→ The *Yellow Submarine* film went on general release across the UK.

6 August

→ Trident Studios. 'Hey Jude' was mixed from stereo to mono.

→ John, Yoko, Patti Harrison and fashion editor Suzy Menkes attended a fashion show at the Revolution club. John was interviewed by Matthew Robinson for that evening's edition of the BBC Radio programme *Late Night Extra*.

Paul: "We decided to close down the shop last Saturday – not because it wasn't making any money, but because we thought the retail business wasn't our particular scene. We want to be free to devote more time to recording and films. So we went along, chose all the stuff we wanted – I got a smashing overcoat – and then told our friends. Now everything that is left is for the public."

7 August

→ Abbey Road. *The Beatles* sessions. Work continued on George's 'Not Guilty'.

→ The session didn't end until 5:30 am, after which Paul went with Francie Schwartz to the now empty Apple Boutique and painted the names of The Beatles' new single on the whitewashed windows. When local Jewish traders misunderstood the title 'Hey Jude' and complained, Paul said he was sorry if he offended them, it was nothing to do with Jews and told the *Evening Standard*:

"We thought we'd paint the windows for a gas. What would you do if your shop had just closed?"

8 August

→ Abbey Road. *The Beatles* sessions. George's 'Not Guilty' reached take 101. It was not included on the final album.

9 August

→ Abbey Road. *The Beatles* sessions. More work on 'Not Guilty'.

→ After the session, Paul recorded 'Mother Nature's Son' which the other Beatles did not play on.

10 August

→ Paul gave a controversial interview to Alan Smith of *the New Musical Express*. He admitted: 'The truth about me is that I'm pleasantly insincere.'

Paul: "Starvation in India doesn't worry me one bit, not one iota. It doesn't, man. And it doesn't worry you, if you're honest. You just pose. You've only seen the Oxfam ads. You can't pretend to me that an Oxfam ad can reach down into the depths of your soul and actually make you feel for those people – more, for instance, than you feel about getting a new car."

11 August

→ Apple Records was officially launched with 'National Apple Week'. The press received a special pack,

labelled 'Our First Four', containing copies of 'Hey Jude' by The Beatles, 'Sour Milk Sea' by Jackie Lomax, 'Thingumybob' by The Black Dyke Mills Band and Mary Hopkin's 'Those Were The Days.' 'Hey Jude' became the biggest selling Beatles single ever, selling six million copies in four months (ultimately eight million worldwide). In addition, Mary Hopkin's 'Those Were The Days' sold four million copies worldwide in four months, getting Apple Records off to a good start.

12 August
➔ Abbey Road. *The Beatles* sessions: George's vocal on 'Not Guilty' was

Below: Recording the 'White Album' at Abbey Road and (opposite) Trident Studios.

taped in the control booth, with the microphone plugged straight into the board.

13 August
➔ Abbey Road. *The Beatles* sessions. 'Sexy Sadie' was remade and 'Yer Blues' begun. The group crowded into a small tape room off the main studio to try and re-create the cramped Cavern feeling for 'Yer Blues' and were very pleased with the acoustics in there.

14 August
➔ Abbey Road. *The Beatles* sessions. 'Yer Blues' was virtually finished, then, after Paul and Ringo left, John and George recorded 'What's The New Mary Jane', one of John's 'experimental', Yoko-influenced numbers.

15 August
➔ Abbey Road. *The Beatles* sessions. Paul's 'Rocky Raccoon' recorded.

16 August
➔ Abbey Road. *The Beatles* sessions. A new version of George's 'While My Guitar Gently Weeps'.

20 August
➔ Abbey Road. *The Beatles* sessions continued in George's absence (he was taking a short holiday). 'Yer Blues' was finished off.
➔ Paul added the brass overdubs to 'Mother Nature's Son'. After this he recorded the short 'Wild Honey Pie' and 'Etcetera' (for use as a demo by Marianne Faithfull – she declined to record it). The tension in the studio between the members of the group was reported as being very bad at this point.

21 August
➔ Abbey Road. *The Beatles* sessions. John added a new lead vocal to 'Sexy Sadie.'

22 August
➔ Abbey Road. *The Beatles* sessions. 'Back In The USSR' was recorded (minus Ringo) with Paul playing drums.
➔ The bad feelings between the group reached crisis point and Ringo announced he was quitting. He left to

John: "That was me, George and Yoko, out of our heads on the floor at EMI."

consider his future. The actual incident that caused him to storm out was a fluffed tom-tom fill. Ringo flew to the Mediterranean to spend a fortnight on Peter Sellers' yacht. It was there, after refusing to eat the squid served to him, that Ringo wrote 'Octopus's Garden'.
➔ Cynthia filed for divorce, citing John's adultery with Yoko. John did not contest the order.

23 August
➔ Abbey Road. The Beatles sessions. 'Back In The USSR' was completed.

24 August
➔ John and Yoko appeared live, talking about art and happenings on David Frost's London Weekend Television programme *Frost On Saturday*, broadcast from Wembley.

26 August
➔ 'Hey Jude'/'Revolution' was released in the US as Apple (Capitol) 2276.
➔ 'Thingumybob'/'Yellow Submarine' by The Black Dyke Mills Band, written and produced by Paul McCartney, was released in the US as Apple 1800.
➔ 'Those Were The Days'/'Turn! Turn! Turn! (To Everything There Is A Season)' by Mary Hopkin, produced by Paul McCartney, was released in the US as Apple 1801.
➔ 'Sour Milk Sea'/'The Eagle Laughs At You' by Jackie Lomax, written and produced by George Harrison, was released in the US as Apple 1802.

28 August
➔ Trident Studios, Soho. *The Beatles* sessions. The Beatles, still minus Ringo, began work on 'Dear Prudence'.

29 August

→ Trident Studios, Soho. *The Beatles* sessions. Overdubs were added to 'Dear Prudence'.

30 August

→ Trident Studios, Soho: *The Beatles* sessions. The completed 'Dear Prudence' was mixed.

→ 'Hey Jude'/'Revolution' was released in the UK as Apple (Parlophone) R 5722.

→ 'Those Were The Days'/'Turn! Turn! Turn! (To Everything There Is A Season)' by Mary Hopkin, produced by Paul McCartney was released in the UK as Apple 2.

→ 'Sour Milk Sea'/'The Eagle Laughs At You' by Jackie Lomax, written and produced by George Harrison, was released in the UK as Apple 3.

Neil Aspinall married Susan Ornstein at Chelsea Register Office. The Beatles gave them a house as a wedding present but Paul was the only member of the group to attend the ceremony.

3 September

→ Abbey Road. *The Beatles* sessions. Having decided to remain in the group, Ringo returned to the studio to find his drum kit smothered in flowers. In fact he did not record that day; the time was spent 'liberating' EMI's new eight-track machine which was still being 'evaluated' by EMI technical experts.

4 September

→ Twickenham Film Studios. Promotional films, directed by Michael Lindsay-Hogg, were made for both 'Hey Jude' and 'Revolution'. While at the film studios, David Frost taped an introduction to the clips to use on his *Frost On Sunday* programme, giving the viewers the illusion that The Beatles were playing live on his show and fooling the Musicians' Union into believing that no miming was involved. On the promotional films, an orchestra was present and The Beatles had their instruments, but it was only the lead vocals that were actually live – and even they were taped on top of the existing vocals on the track, to guard against mistakes.

5 September

→ Abbey Road. *The Beatles* sessions.

Ringo: "I felt tired and discouraged... took a week's holiday, and when I came back to work everything was all right again.' However, he added, 'Paul is the greatest bass guitar player in the world. But he is also very determined; he goes on and on to see if he can get his own way. While that may be a virtue, it did mean that musical disagreements inevitably arose from time to time."

More work was done on George's 'While My Guitar Gently Weeps'. John played the original lead guitar part on the song.

6 September

→ Thames Television filmed Paul and Mary Hopkin at the Apple offices, 3 Savile Row, for their new children's series, *Magpie*.

→ Abbey Road. *The Beatles* sessions. Eric Clapton added his prized solo to George's 'While My Guitar Gentle Weeps', wiping out John's less proficient effort of the previous day, with Ringo on percussion and Paul playing fuzz bass and doing vocal harmonies as George recorded his lead vocal.

→ 'Thingumybob'/'Yellow Submarine' by The Black Dyke Mills Band, produced by Paul McCartney was released in the UK as Apple 4.

8 September

→ The film clip of 'Hey Jude' was given its premiere performance on London Weekend Television's *Frost On Sunday*.

9 September

→ Abbey Road. *The Beatles* sessions. A new version of 'Helter Skelter' was recorded.

10 September

→ Abbey Road. *The Beatles* sessions. Overdubs added to 'Helter Skelter'.

11 September

→ Abbey Road. *The Beatles* sessions. Work began on 'Glass Onion'.

12 September

→ Abbey Road. *The Beatles* sessions. More work on 'Glass Onion'.

13 September

→ Abbey Road. *The Beatles* sessions. Drums and piano for 'Glass Onion'.

15 September

→ Around this date, John and Yoko photographed themselves in the nude, from the front and rear, intending to use the shots as cover art for their first collaborative album.

16 September

→ Abbey Road. *The Beatles* sessions.

Recording began on 'I Will' and overdubs were added to 'Glass Onion'.

17 September
→ Abbey Road. *The Beatles* sessions. 'I Will' was completed.

18 September
→ Abbey Road. *The Beatles* sessions. Paul arrived at the session early and had already mapped out 'Birthday' before the others arrived. By mid-evening most of it was finished. All of The Beatles, plus Yoko, Patti, acting producer Chris Thomas and others, walked round the corner to Paul's house to see *The Girl Can't Help It*, starring Jayne Mansfield, featuring Little Richard, Fats Domino, The Platters, Gene Vincent and Eddie Cochran which was screened on BBC2 at 9:05 pm. Afterwards they returned to the studio and by 5 am they had finished and mixed the song.
→ George was interviewed by Alan Smith for BBC Radio 1's *Scene And Heard*.
→ John was interviewed by Jonathan Cott for *Rolling Stone* magazine.

19 September
→ Abbey Road. *The Beatles* sessions. George's 'Piggies' was recorded, with producer Chris Thomas on harpsichord.
→ The promotional film for 'Revolution' is screened for the first time in the UK on BBC TV's *Top Of The Pops*.

20 September
→ Abbey Road. *The Beatles* sessions. 'Piggies' was completed.

22 September
→ Apple announced that The Beatles' next album would be a 24-song, two-record set.

23 September
→ Abbey Road. *The Beatles* sessions. Work began on John's 'Happiness Is A Warm Gun', which he had written with uncredited assistance from Apple press officer Derek Taylor.

24 September
→ Abbey Road. *The Beatles* sessions. More work was done on the rhythm track for 'Happiness Is A Warm Gun'.

25 September
→ Abbey Road. *The Beatles* sessions. Recording of 'Happiness Is A Warm Gun' was completed.

26 September
→ Abbey Road. *The Beatles* sessions. 'Happiness Is A Warm Gun' was mixed and John spent most of the session making a sound effects tape for 'Glass Onion' which went unused until heard on *Anthology 3* in 1996.

1 October
→ Trident Studios, Soho. *The Beatles* sessions. 'Honey Pie' was virtually completed.

2 October
→ Trident Studios, Soho. *The Beatles* sessions. Paul added lead vocal and guitar to 'Honey Pie'.
→ George joined a Cream recording session to add backing vocals and rhythm guitar to 'Badge', a song he had written with guitarist Eric Clapton.

3 October
→ Trident Studios, Soho. *The Beatles* sessions. George's 'Savoy Truffle' was begun. The song was inspired by the contents of a box of Mackintosh's Good News chocolates – Eric Clapton's favourite.

4 October
→ Trident Studios, Soho. *The Beatles* sessions: Paul and a 14-piece orchestra recorded 'Martha My Dear' and added the finishing touches to 'Honey Pie'.

5 October
→ Trident Studios, Soho. *The Beatles* sessions. George added lead vocal and Paul, the bass and drums to 'Savoy Truffle'.

7 October
→ Abbey Road. *The Beatles* sessions. A long session, from 2:30 pm until 7 the next morning, was spent on perfecting the rhythm track for George's 'Long Long Long'. John was not present.

8 October
→ Abbey Road. *The Beatles* sessions. Another long session, 4 pm until 8 am the following morning, during which

Opposite: John and Yoko unsafe from the long arm of the law at Marylebone Magistrates' Court, 19 October.

John's 'I'm So Tired' and 'The Continuing Story Of Bungalow Bill' were both recorded and finished, and more work was done on George's 'Long Long Long'. Yoko Ono made a cameo vocal appearance on 'The Continuing Story Of Bungalow Bill'.

9 October
→ Abbey Road. *The Beatles* sessions. Final work was done on 'The Continuing Story Of Bungalow Bill' and 'Long Long Long'. While this was going on, Paul quickly recorded 'Why Don't We Do It In The Road' in the next door studio. Once again, John was absent.
→ The *David Frost Show* on US TV broadcast a clip of Paul introducing Mary Hopkin to the American audience.

10 October
→ Abbey Road. *The Beatles* sessions. 'Piggies' and 'Glass Onion' were completed. Paul again slipped away, this time with Ringo, and the two of them completed 'Why Don't We Do It In The Road'.
→ George Harrison formed a new music publishing company, Singsong Limited.

11 October
→ Abbey Road. *The Beatles* sessions. Six saxophones were added to 'Savoy Truffle'.
→ The single 'I'm The Urban

John busted: 18 October

The Drugs Squad raided John and Yoko who were living in a flat at 34 Montagu Square, London, on loan to them from Ringo. John had earlier received a tip-off from a member of the press that the police were planning to raid his home, and had 'springcleaned' the flat to make sure that it was clear of drugs.

The police conveniently found 219 grains of cannabis resin and took the couple to Paddington Green police station where they also charged them with obstructing the police in execution of a search warrant.

John: 'So all of a sudden like, there was this knock on the door and a woman's voice outside and I look around and there is a policeman standing in the window wanting to be let in. We'd been in bed and our lower regions were uncovered like. Yoko ran into the bathroom to get dressed with her head poking out so they wouldn't think she was hiding anything. And then I said 'Ring the lawyer, quick', but she went and rang Apple, I'll never know why. So then they got us for obstruction which was ridiculous because we only wanted to get our clothes on.'

Spaceman' by The Bonzo Dog Doo-Dah Band, produced by Paul McCartney as Apollo C. Vermouth, was released in the UK as Liberty LBF 15144.

12 October
→ Abbey Road. *The Beatles* sessions. The whole evening was spent mixing various tracks.

13 October
→ Abbey Road. *The Beatles* sessions. John recorded and mixed his ballad, 'Julia'.

14 October
→ Abbey Road. *The Beatles* sessions. Overdubs were added to 'Savoy Truffle' and the rest of the session was spent mixing the tracks for the now completed double album.
→ No longer needed for the final mixing and sequencing of the album, Ringo went on holiday to Sardinia with his family.

15 October
→ Abbey Road. *The Beatles* sessions. Mono and stereo mixing sessions.

16 October
→ Abbey Road. *The Beatles* sessions. Paul, John and George Martin held a 24 hour session, beginning at 5 pm and ending at 5 pm the following day, choosing the songs and working out the sequencing of the four sides of the double album. They were up against a tight deadline, and every studio and listening room at Abbey Road was used for this marathon task: studios one, two and three as well as listening rooms 41 and 42. In the end 30 songs were presented to the public as *The Beatles* (and, as usual, the two sides of their new single were not included).
→ George was not involved in the final selection and sequencing because he flew to Los Angeles that day to continue working with Jackie Lomax on his forthcoming Apple album.

19 October
→ John and Yoko appeared at Marylebone Magistrates' Court. They were remanded on bail and their case was adjourned until 28 November.

20 October

→ George produced a session for Apple artist Jackie Lomax in Los Angeles.

25 October

→ The single 'Quelli Erand Giorni'/ 'Turn! Turn! Turn! (To Everything There Is A Season)' by Mary Hopkin and produced by Paul McCartney was released in Italy as Apple 2.

→ John and Yoko announced that Yoko was pregnant and they were expecting a baby in February 1969.

28 October

→ Cynthia Lennon's divorce petition was officially listed.

31 October

→ Linda Eastman moved to London to

live with Paul, bringing her daughter Heather with her and enrolling her in a local private school.

November

→ George spent nearly seven weeks in Los Angeles recording six more tracks with Jackie Lomax for the album *Is This What You Want?* at Sound Recorders Studio, using the best Los Angeles session men including Hal Blaine on drums, Larry Knechtel on keyboards and Joe Osborn on bass.

1 November

→ The album *Wonderwall Music* by George Harrison & Band/Indian Orchestra, written and produced by George Harrison, was released in the UK by Apple as APCOR 1 (mono) and SAPCOR 1 (stereo). Side One: 'Microbes', 'Red Lady', 'Medley', 'Tabla and Pakavaj', 'In The Park', 'Medley', 'Greasy Legs', 'Ski-ing and Gat Kirwani', 'Dream Scene'; Side Two: 'Party Seacombe', 'Medley', 'Love Scene', 'Crying', 'Cowboy Museum', 'Fantasy Sequins', 'Glass Box', 'On The Bed', 'Wonderwall To Be Here', 'Singing Om'.

3 November

→ George recorded his synthesiser 'composition', 'No Time Or Space', with the assistance of Moog maestro Bernie Krause in California.

4 November

→ Yoko Ono was admitted to Queen Charlotte's Hospital in London, after doctors feared that the stress of her recent arrest, and the press backlash which had been affecting the Lennons, might endanger her unborn child. John remained by her bedside, and over the next fortnight the couple made a series of *verite* recordings in the hospital.

7 November

→ John penned a cartoon strip entitled 'A Short Essay On Macrobiotics' for the health magazine *Harmony*.

8 November

→ Cynthia was granted a decree nisi in the London Divorce Court because of John's admitted adultery with Yoko. She retained custody of Julian.

→ It was reported that George's five-year songwriting contract with Northern Songs Limited had expired in March and had not been renewed.

→ John and Yoko financed newspaper advertisements for the Peace Ship, a radio station run by Ronan O'Rahilly, intended to end the conflict in the Middle East.

11 November

→ The album *Unfinished Music No.1 – Two Virgins* by John Lennon and Yoko Ono and written and produced by John and Yoko was released in the US as Apple T 5001. Side One: 'Two Virgins No.1', 'Together', 'Two Virgins (numbers 2 to 6)'. Side Two: 'Two Virgins', 'Hushabye Hushabye', 'Two Virgins (numbers 7 to 10) '.

→ The photograph of the two of them in the nude on the sleeve caused offence in some quarters, and EMI refused to distribute it. Track Records did the job instead. In the US, Capitol also refused to have anything to do with it, for fear that the Bible Belt would react with their customary prurience. A small label called Tetragrammaton, mostly known for spoken word records, took up the challenge but even they felt obliged to put the record into a brown paper sleeve, with a cut-away allowing John and Yoko's faces to peer through.

John: "Originally, I was going to record Yoko, and I thought the best picture of her for an album would be naked. So after that, when we got together, it just seemed natural for us both to be naked. Of course, I've never seen my prick out on an album before."

13 November

→ The *Yellow Submarine* movie was belatedly premiered in the US. Despite staying only a few hundred yards from the Hollywood cinema which hosted the event, George declined to attend. 'I've already seen it twice', he explained.

15 November

→ While in Los Angeles, George made

Opposite: Cynthia
Lennon at the London
Divorce Court,
8 November.
Above: Paul, George
and John at a private
reception at the Royal
Lancaster Hotel to
launch Apple Records
for American excutives.
The photo was taken
by the label's promo
man, Tony Bramwell.

a short, unannounced appearance on the CBS TV show *The Smothers Brothers' Comedy Hour* before a live audience in Hollywood. It was broadcast two nights later.

19 November
→ Ringo, Maureen and their children moved from 'Sunny Heights' in Weybridge to a new home, 'Brookfields' near Elstead.

20 November
→ Paul was interviewed at his home in Cavendish Avenue, St John's Wood, by Tony MacArthur for a two-hour Radio Luxembourg special on *The Beatles*.

21 November
→ Yoko suffered a miscarriage of her baby at Queen Charlotte's Hospital, London, caused almost certainly by the stress of being arrested. John stayed at

her side, sleeping overnight in a spare hospital bed. When the bed was needed for a patient, John slept on the floor (a picture was used on the cover of their next album collaboration, *Life With the Lions*)
→ The unborn child was named John Ono Lennon II, and was buried by the couple in a secret location.

22 November
→ *The Beatles* (a.k.a. 'The White Album') was released in the UK as Apple (Parlophone) PMC 7067-7068 (mono) and PCS 70677068 (stereo). Side One: 'Back In The USSR', 'Dear Prudence', 'Glass Onion', 'Ob-La-Di, Ob-La-Da', 'Wild Honey Pie', 'The Continuing Story Of Bungalow Bill', 'While My Guitar Gently Weeps', 'Happiness Is A Warm Gun'; Side Two: 'Martha My Dear', 'I'm So Tired', 'Blackbird', 'Piggies', 'Rocky Raccoon', 'Don't Pass Me By', 'Why Don't We Do

It In The Road', 'I Will', 'Julia'; Side Three: 'Birthday', 'Yer Blues', 'Mother Nature's Son', 'Everybody's Got Something To Hide Except Me And My Monkey', 'Sexy Sadie', 'Helter Skelter', 'Long Long Long'; Side Four: 'Revolution 1', 'Honey Pie', 'Savoy Truffle', 'Cry Baby Cry', 'Revolution 9', 'Good Night'.
→ Robert Fraser proposed that, since Peter Blake had art directed *Sgt Pepper*, Richard Hamilton, another leading figure in British Pop Art, should do the next. He was asked to meet The Beatles at the Apple office in Savile Row, and after being kept waiting for an hour or more he was ushered in. By then Hamilton was having second thoughts about getting involved with the pop music business and asked Paul, 'Why don't you do it yourself? You don't need me. I'm the wrong sort of artist for you.' He said that as *Sgt Pepper* was so over the top, he would be inclined to do a very prissy thing, almost like a limited edition, and went on to propose a plain white album. He also suggested that they number each copy, a joke numbered edition of something like five million copies. Paul thought this was an amusing idea and agreed.

Richard Hamilton: "Then I began to feel a bit guilty at putting their double album under plain wrappers; I suggested it could be jazzed up with a large edition print, an insert that would be even more glamorous than a normal sleeve.

That's why the album ended up the way it did. Most people, among them Yoko, think it was Yoko's idea. I've no doubt that she would have been very supportive – from what I knew of her work and Fluxus background, the approach would have been right up her street. It was at the time when Yoko was really moving into the Beatle business and putting her

1968

oar in strongly. But my contact with the project was only through Paul – even EMI was held off."

23 November

→ In the wake of the controversy aroused by John and Yoko's nude album sleeve, the press were quick to seize upon a tiny nude photograph of Paul, which formed part of the collage on the poster accompanying *The Beatles*. Apple press officer Derek Taylor retorted: 'All this work, all these tracks, all this talent – and all their dirty little minds focus on is one tiny picture.'

25 November

→ *The Beatles* was released in the US as Apple (Capitol) SWBO 101 (stereo only).

27 November

→ Invited to contribute an original piece of writing to *Aspen* magazine, John filled out a nonsensical version of 'My Diary', repeating the same banal information for each day's entry.

28 November

→ Dressed soberly in a dark suit, John pleaded guilty to the charge of unauthorised possession of cannabis resin at Marylebone Magistrates' Court. In an effort to gain sympathy for the couple, John's solicitor told the court that after the raid, Yoko had lost her baby and that this had been a terrible blow to them. John was fined £150 and ordered to pay costs of 20 guineas. He and Yoko were found not guilty on the charge of obstructing the police in execution of a search warrant. In court it was reported that while being questioned after the raid, in an effort to protect Yoko, whom he feared might be deported because she was not a British citizen, John asked,

"Can I just ask a question? As this stuff is all mine, will it be me only who is involved?"

This drug conviction was to haunt John throughout the Seventies and was used by the Nixon administration in repeated attempts to deny him a Green Card for residence in the US.

Paul: "Richard and I worked together on the collage for The Beatles' White Album. Richard and I sat down all week while he did the collage from childhood photos of us all. The thing that impressed me at the end of the week was that after he'd filled the whole board with pictures and got his composition right, his final move was to take pieces of white paper and place them strategically to give space through the whole thing so that it wasn't just crammed with pictures. It was beautiful and I remember being very impressed with the way he put this negative space on – it was the first time that I'd ever seen that idea."

29 November

→ The album *Unfinished Music No.1 – Two Virgins* by John Lennon and Yoko Ono and written and produced by John and Yoko was released in the UK as Apple APCOR 2 (mono) and SAPCOR 2 (stereo).

December

→ During December and January, John and Yoko made the film *Rape* for Austrian television. A camera team hounded a young woman until she was near to a breakdown.

John: "We are showing how all of us are exposed and under pressure in our contemporary world... what is happening to this girl on the screen is happening in Biafra, Vietnam, everywhere."

→ December also saw a continued media backlash against John and Yoko, inspired by the controversial *Two Virgins* album sleeve. John's new songs reflected his darkening mood: they included 'A Case Of The Blues', 'Everybody Had A Hard Year', and 'Oh My Love', the initial draft of which was a love song to the child that the couple had lost.

→ Also during this period, John and Yoko sank into the morass of heroin addiction, a burden which left its mark on John's demeanour and enthusiasm for The Beatles over the next two months.

2 December

→ The album *Wonderwall Music* by George Harrison & Band/Indian Orchestra, written and produced by George Harrison, was released in the US as Apple ST 3350.

4 December

→ George circulated a memo to the staff of Apple warning them that he had invited a group of Californian Hell's Angels over to stay at 3 Savile Row:

'Hell's Angels will be in London within the next week, on the way to straighten out Czechoslovakia. There will be 12 in number complete with black leather jackets and motor cycles. They will undoubtedly arrive at Apple and I have heard they may try to make full use of Apple's facilities. They may look as though they are going to do you in but are very straight and do good things, so don't fear them or uptight them. Try to assist them without neglecting your Apple business and without letting them take control of Savile Row.'

6 December

→ The readers of the *New Musical Express* gave The Beatles their customary victories in the 'Best British Group' and 'Best World Group' categories of the annual poll. 'Hey Jude' was voted 'Best Single Of 1968'.

→ The album *James Taylor* by James Taylor, featuring Paul McCartney on bass guitar ('Carolina On My Mind') was released in the UK as Apple SAPCOR 3.

10 December

→ 'Kenwood', John and Cynthia's

Opposite: Yoko, five-year-old Julian Lennon and John at the Rolling Stones' *Rock And Roll Circus*, 10 December.

house on the St. George's Hill Estate in Weybridge, was put up for sale.

→ John and Yoko attended rehearsals at Wembley Studios for the next day's filming of The Rolling Stones' extravaganza: *Rock And Roll Circus*. John sang 'Yer Blues', and also took part in a jam session on some Fifties rock'n'roll standards with Taj Mahal's guitarist, Jesse Ed Davis.

11 December

→ John and Yoko, with John's son, Julian, spent the day and most of the night at Wembley Studios filming the all-star jam session: The Rolling Stones' *Rock And Roll Circus*. John led a band that called themselves The Dirty Macs which included Yoko, Eric Clapton, Keith Richards (on bass) and Mitch Mitchell (drums), performing 'Yer Blues' and a free-form jam (dubbed 'Her Blues') that featured Yoko's unusual vocals and guest

violinist Ivry Gitlis.

→ In the event, Mick Jagger thought the Stones were outperformed by The Who and the project was shelved until 1996 when it was released on video. Around midnight John and Yoko drove back to central London to appear live on BBC Radio's *Night Ride* where they talked to DJ John Peel about their *Two Virgins* album and played a few minutes of *The Beatles* album.

17 December

→ *Candy*, with Ringo in a starring role, was premiered in New York.

18 December

→ The single 'I'm The Urban Spaceman' by The Bonzo Dog Doo-Dah Band (Paul as Apollo C. Vermouth) and produced by Paul McCartney was released in the US as Imperial 66345.

→ John and Yoko appeared onstage in a large white bag as part of a Christmas happening, the Underground Christmas Party, at the Royal Albert Hall. The bag, they explained, was a vehicle to ensure 'total communication'. During their brief appearance, a protestor ran to the edge of the stage, holding a banner complaining about the British government's involvement in the civil war afflicting Nigeria. 'Do you care, John Lennon, do you care?' the demonstrator shouted to the figures in the bag.

20 December

→ The fan club flexi-disc, *The Beatles' 1968 Christmas Record*, was released. It included John reciting a satirical poem, 'Jock And Yono', which contained a thinly veiled attack on the other members of The Beatles.

23 December

→ Apple's first Christmas party was held at 3 Savile Row, which featured what its suppliers assured everyone was the Largest Turkey in the World, Hell's Angels, and members of a visiting Californian hippie commune. John and Yoko, who had hardly been seen at Apple since it opened its new headquarters, dressed up as Father and Mother Christmas and handed out presents to all the children attending.

Lady Madonna

Words & Music by John Lennon
& Paul McCartney

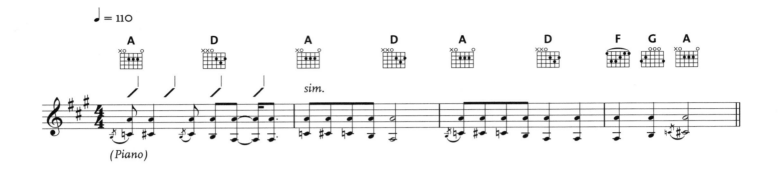

(Piano)

La - dy Mad - on - na,_____ chil - dren at your feet, won - der how you man - age to make_

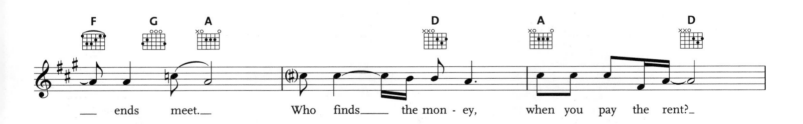

_ ends meet._ Who finds_____ the mon - ey, when you pay the rent?_

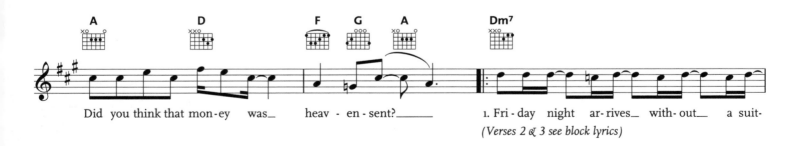

Did you think that mon - ey was_ heav - en - sent?_____ 1. Fri - day night ar - rives_ with - out_ a suit-
(Verses 2 & 3 see block lyrics)

- case, Sun - day morn - ing creep - ing like a nun._____

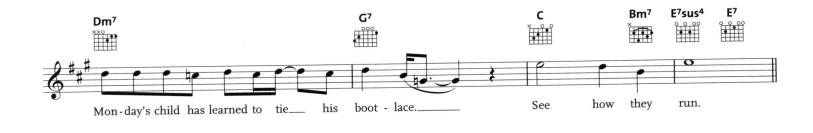

Mon-day's child has learned to tie___ his boot-lace.___ See how they run.

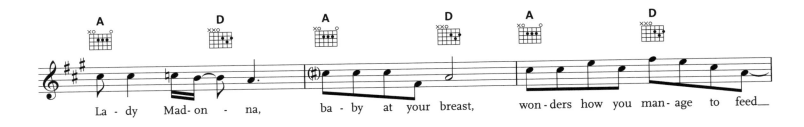

La-dy Mad-on-na, ba-by at your breast, won-ders how you man-age to feed___

1, 2.

___ the rest.___ (Guitar/Sax)

3.

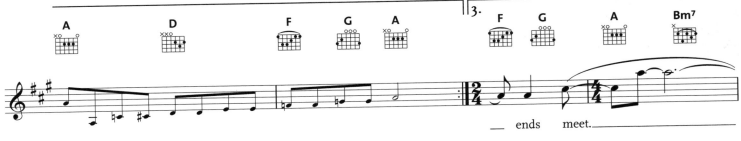

___ ends meet.___

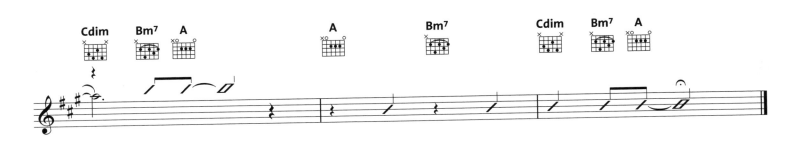

Verse 2:
Instrumental ad lib. (for 6 bars)

See how they run.

Lady Madonna, lying on the bed,
Listen to the music playing in your head.

Verse 3:
Tuesday afternoon is never ending,
Wednesday morning papers didn't come.
Thursday night, your stockings needed mending.
See how they run.

Lady Madonna, children at your feet,
Wonder how you manage to make ends meet.

Hey Jude

Words & Music by John Lennon & Paul McCartney

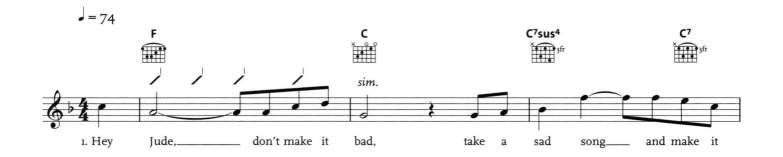

1. Hey Jude,_____ don't make it bad, take a sad song___ and make it

bet - ter._____ Re - mem - ber to let her in - to your heart, then you can start_

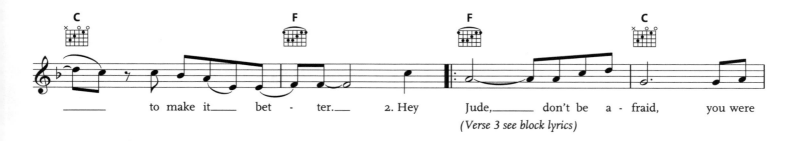

_____ to make it___ bet - ter.___ 2. Hey Jude,_____ don't be a - fraid, you were

(Verse 3 see block lyrics)

made to_____ go out and get her.___ The min - ute you let her un - der your

skin, then you be - gin_____ to make it___ bet - ter.___

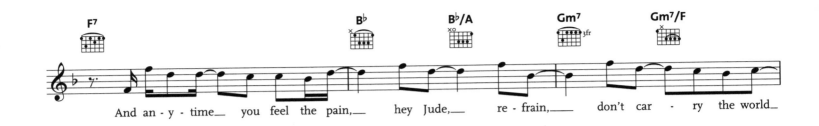

And an - y - time___ you feel the pain,___ hey Jude,___ re - frain,___ don't car - ry the world

___ up - on___ your shoul - ders.___ For well, you know that it's a fool___

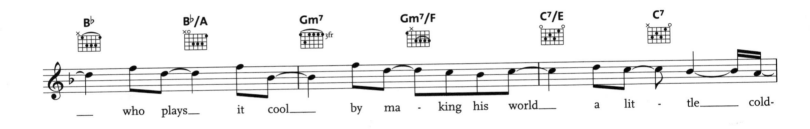

___ who plays___ it cool___ by ma - king his world___ a lit - tle___ cold-

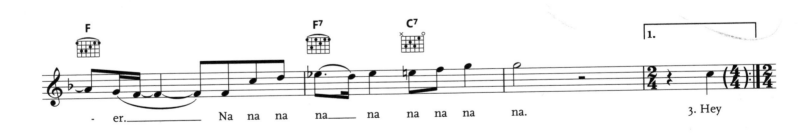

- er.___ Na na na na___ na na na na na.   3. Hey

4. Hey___ Jude,___ don't make it bad,   take a sad song___ and make it

397

bet - ter._____ Re - mem-ber to let her un - der your skin, then you'll be - gin__

— to make it bet - ter, bet - ter, bet - ter, bet - ter, bet - ter, bet - ter, oh!

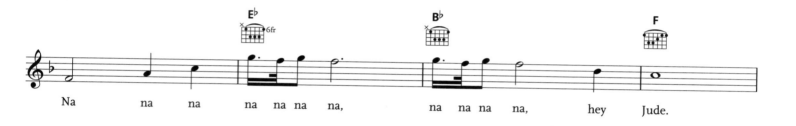

Na na na na na na na, na na na na, hey Jude.

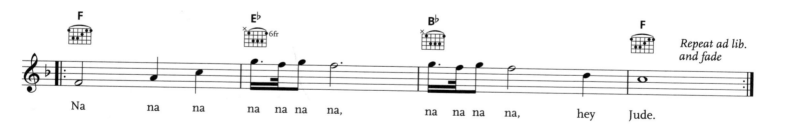

*Repeat ad lib.
and fade*

Na na na na na na na, na na na na, hey Jude.

Verse 3:
Hey Jude, don't let me down,
You have found her, now go and get her.
Remember to let her into your heart,
Then you can start to make it better.

So let it out and let it in,
Hey Jude, begin,
You're waiting for someone to perform with.
And don't you know that it's just you,
Hey Jude, you'll do,
The movement you need is on your shoulder.
Na na na na na na na na na.

Revolution

Words & Music by John Lennon
& Paul McCartney
© Copyright 1968 Northern Songs.
All Rights Reserved.
International Copyright Secured.

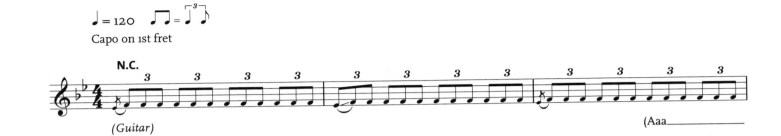

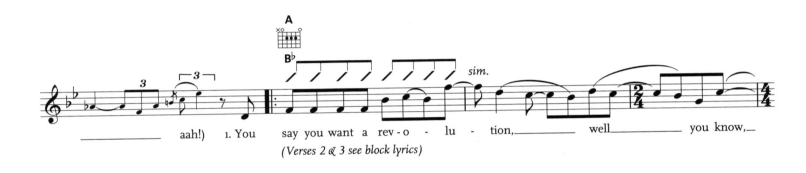

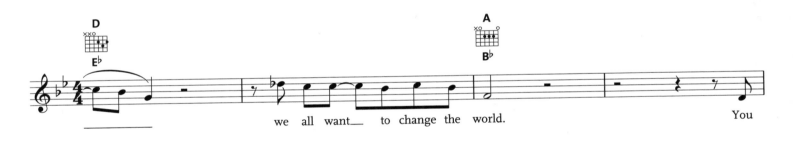

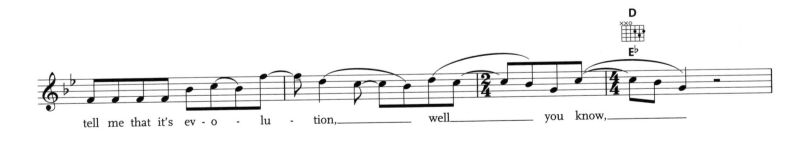

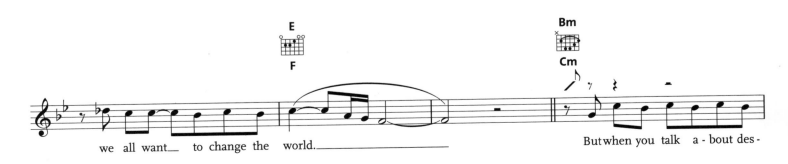

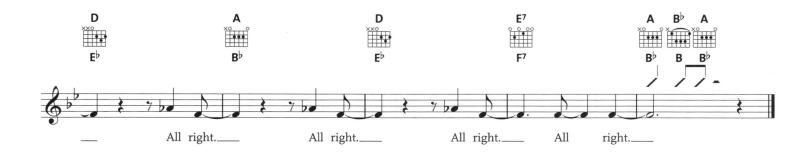

_ All right.___ All right.___ All right.___ All right.___

Verse 2:
You say you got a real solution,
Well you know,
We'd all love to see the plan.
You ask me for a contribution,
Well you know,
We're all doing what we can.
But if you want money for people with minds that hate,
All I can tell you is brother, you'll have to wait.

Don't you know it's gonna be all right,
All right, all right?

Verse 3:
You say you'll change the constitution,
Well you know,
We all want to change your head.
You tell me it's the institution,
Well you know,
You'd better free your mind instead.
But if you go carrying pictures of Chairman Mao,
You ain't gonna make it with anyone, anyhow.

Don't you know it's gonna be alright,
All right, all right?

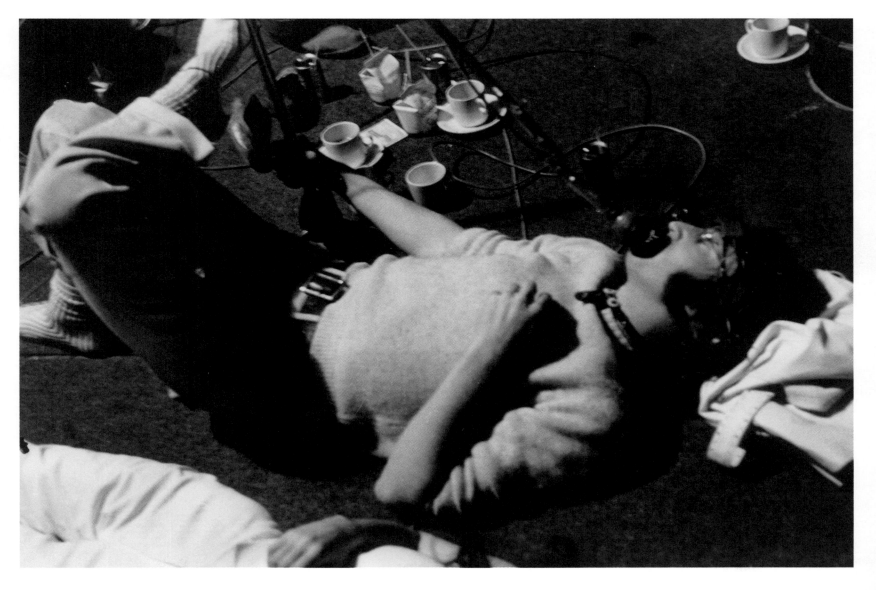

Back In The USSR

Words & Music by John Lennon
& Paul McCartney
© Copyright 1968 Northern Songs.
All Rights Reserved.
International Copyright Secured.

(Guitar)

1. Oh, flew in from Mi - a - mi Beach B. O. A. C.;___ did -

(Verses 2 & 4 see block lyrics)

- n't get to bed last night.___ On___ the way the pa - per bag was

on my knee;___ man,___ I had a dread - ful flight.___ I'm back in the U. S. S. R.___

— (On 𝄋 only) Hey! You don't___ know how luck - y you are,___ boy,___

1.

back in the U. S. S. R.___

2.

back in the U. S.,

back   in the U. S.,   back   in the U. S. S. R.___   Well, the

U - kraine girls real - ly knock me out,___ they leave___ the___ West be - hind.___   And

Mos - cow girls make me sing and shout,___ that Geor-gia's al - ways on my mi - mi -

-mi - mi - mi - mi - mi - mi - mind.___

(Guitar solo)

I'm back in the U. S. S. R.___

You don't__ know how luck - y you are,_____ boy,___

Verse 2:
Been away so long, I hardly knew the place;
Gee, it's good to be back home.
Leave it till tomorrow to unpack my case;
Honey, disconnect the phone.

I'm back in the U.S.S.R.,...

Verse 4:
Show me round your snow-peaked mountains way down South;
Take me to your daddy's farm.
Let me hear your balalaikas ringing out;
Come and keep your comrade warm.

I'm back in the U.S.S.R.,...

Glass Onion

Words & Music by John Lennon
& Paul McCartney
© Copyright 1968 Northern Songs.
All Rights Reserved.
International Copyright Secured.

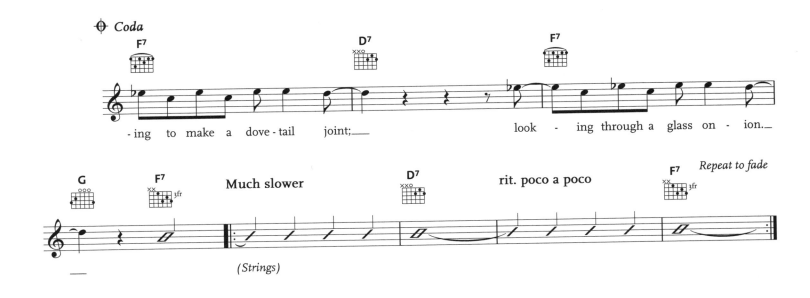

✛ *Coda*

F⁷   D⁷   F⁷

-ing   to   make   a   dove - tail   joint;___   look - ing   through   a   glass   on - ion.___

G   F⁷   **Much slower**   D⁷   *rit. poco a poco*   F⁷   *Repeat to fade*

___   *(Strings)*

Verse 2:
I told you 'bout the Walrus and me, man,
You know that we're as close as can be, man.
Well, here's another clue for you all:
The Walrus was Paul,
Standing on a cast iron shore, yeah.
Lady Madonna tryin' to make ends meet, yeah,
Looking through a glass onion.

Verse 3:
I told you 'bout the Fool on the Hill,
I tell you, man, he living there still.
Well, here's another place you can be,
Listen to me,
Fixing a hole in the ocean,
Trying to make a dovetail joint;
Looking through a glass onion.

Ob-La-Di, Ob-La-Da

Words & Music by John Lennon
& Paul McCartney

♩ = 114

1. Des - mond has a bar - row in the

mar - ket place,___ Mol - ly is the sing - er in a band; Des -

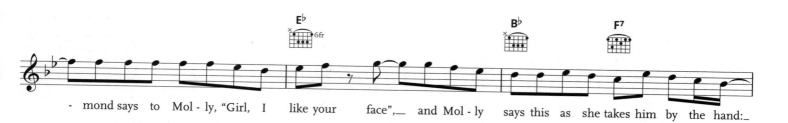

- mond says to Mol - ly, "Girl, I like your face",___ and Mol - ly says this as she takes him by the hand:___

___ Ob - la - di,___ ob - la - da,___ life goes on,___ bra, la -

- la, how the life goes on.___ Ob - la - di,___ ob - la - da,___ life goes on,___

bra, la - la, how the life goes on. ___

2. Des - mond takes a trol - ley to the jew-el-er's store, ___ buys ___ a twen - ty car - at gold - en
(Verses 3 & 4 see block lyrics)

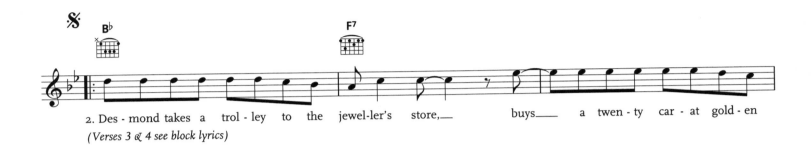

ring. Takes ___ it back to Mol - ly wait - ing at the door, ___ and as he

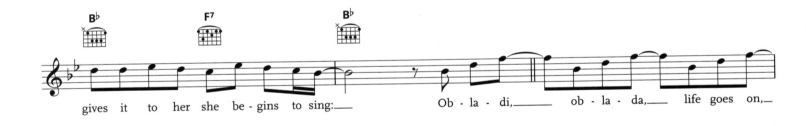

gives it to her she be - gins to sing: ___ Ob - la - di, ___ ob - la - da, ___ life goes on, ___

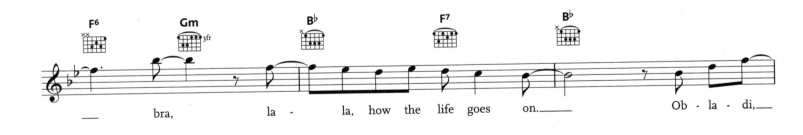

___ bra, la - la, how the life goes on. ___ Ob - la - di,

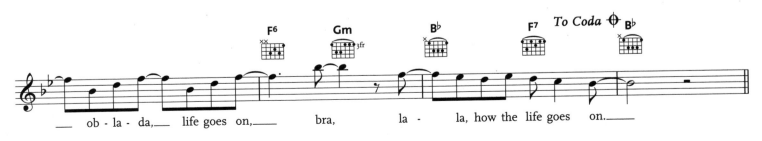

___ ob - la - da, ___ life goes on, ___ bra, la - la, how the life goes on. ___

In a coup-le of years they have built a home,— sweet home.——
(Horns)

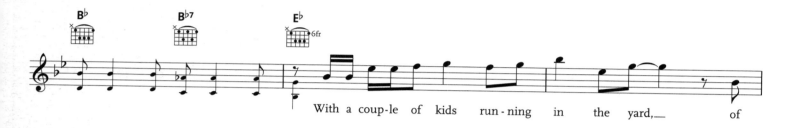

With a coup-le of kids run - ning in the yard,— of

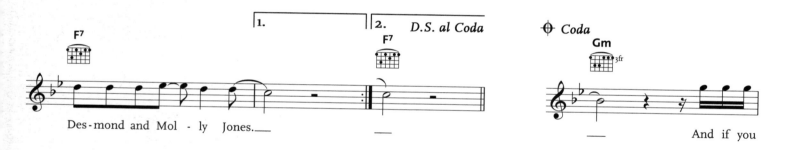

1. **2.** *D.S. al Coda* ⊕ *Coda*

Des-mond and Mol - ly Jones.—— —— — And if you

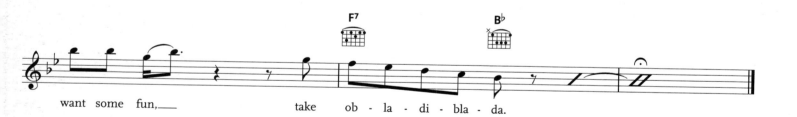

want some fun,— take ob - la - di - bla - da.

Verse 3:
Happy ever after in the market place,
Desmond lets the children lend a hand.
Molly stays at home and does her pretty face,
And in the evening she still sings it with the band:

Ob-la-di, ob-la-da, life goes on, bra,
La-la, how the life goes on.
Ob-la-di, ob-la-da, life goes on, bra,
La-la, how the life goes on.

In a couple of years...

Verse 4:
Happy ever after in the market place,
Molly lets the children lend a hand.
Desmond stays at home and does his pretty face,
And in the evening she's a singer with the band...

Ob-la-di, ob-la-da, life goes on, bra,
La-la, how the life goes on.
Ob-la-di, ob-la-da, life goes on, bra,
La-la, how the life goes on.
And if you want some fun,
Take ob-la-di-bla-da.

While My Guitar Gently Weeps

Words & Music by George Harrison
© Copyright 1968 Harrisongs Limited.

Verse 2:
I look at the world and I notice it's turning,
While my guitar gently weeps.
With every mistake, we must surely be learning,
While my guitar gently weeps.

Bridge 2:
I don't know how you were diverted,
You were perverted too.
I don't know how you were inverted,
No one alerted you.

Happiness Is A Warm Gun

Words & Music by John Lennon
& Paul McCartney
© Copyright 1968 Northern Songs.
All Rights Reserved.
International Copyright Secured.

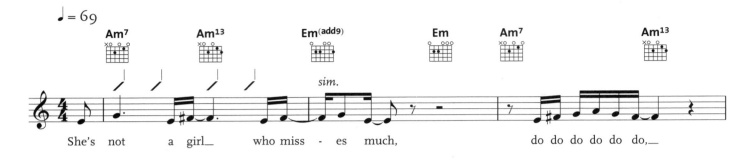

She's not a girl__ who miss - es much, do do do do do do,__

oh__ yeah. She's well ac - quain - ted with the touch of the vel - vet hand,__

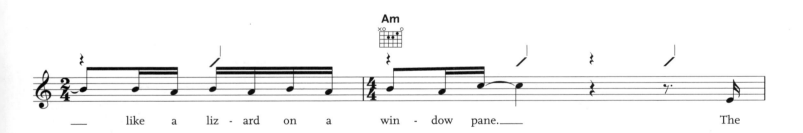

__ like a liz - ard on a win - dow pane.__ The

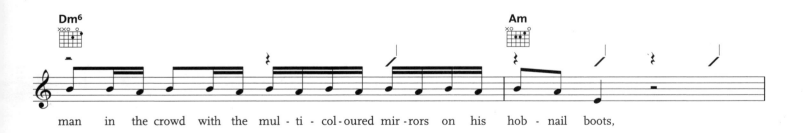

man in the crowd with the mul - ti - col - oured mir - rors on his hob - nail boots,

ly - ing with his eyes, while his hands are bu - sy work - ing o - ver - time.__

A soap im-press-ion of his wife which he ate and do-na-ted to the Natio-nal Trust.

(Guitar)

I need a fix, 'cause I'm going down,

down to the bits that I left up - town. I need a fix, 'cause I'm going down.

Moth-er Su-per-ior jump the gun, Moth-er Su-per-ior jump the gun.

Mother Su-per-ior jump the gun, Mother Su-per-ior jump the gun.

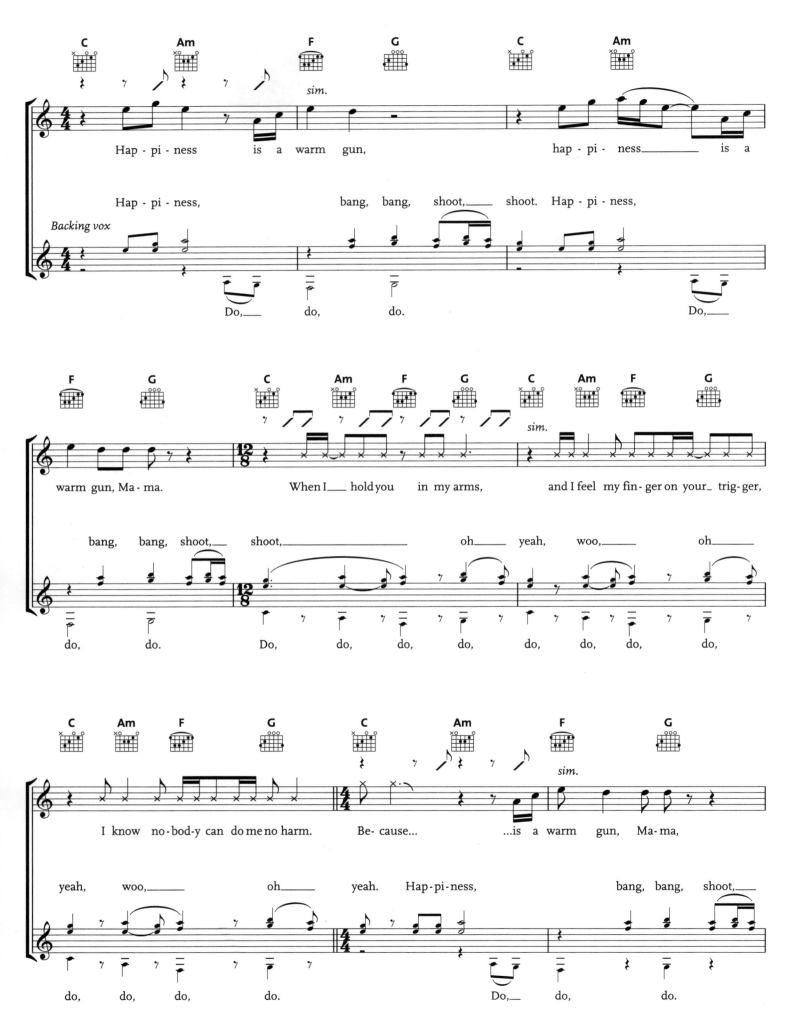

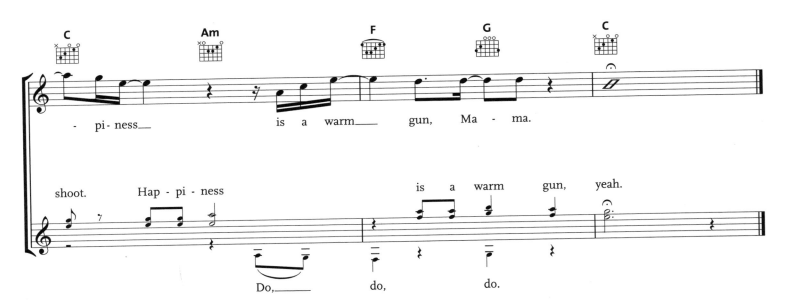

I'm So Tired

1. I'm so_____ tired, I have-n't slept a wink;_ I'm_ so_____ tired,_

(Verse 2 see block lyrics)

my mind is on_ the blink._ I won-der, should I get up_ and fix my-self a drink? No, no, no._

_____ 2. I'm won-der, should I call_ you, but I know what you would do._

You'd say, I'm put-ting you on,_ but it's no joke; it's do-ing me harm._ You know I

can't sleep, I can't stop my brain;_ you know it's three weeks, I'm go-ing in-sane._ You know I'd

Verse 2:
I'm so tired, I don't know what to do;
I'm so tired, my mind is set on you.
I wonder, should I call you,
But I know what you would do.

Blackbird

Words & Music by John Lennon
& Paul McCartney
© Copyright 1968 Northern Songs.

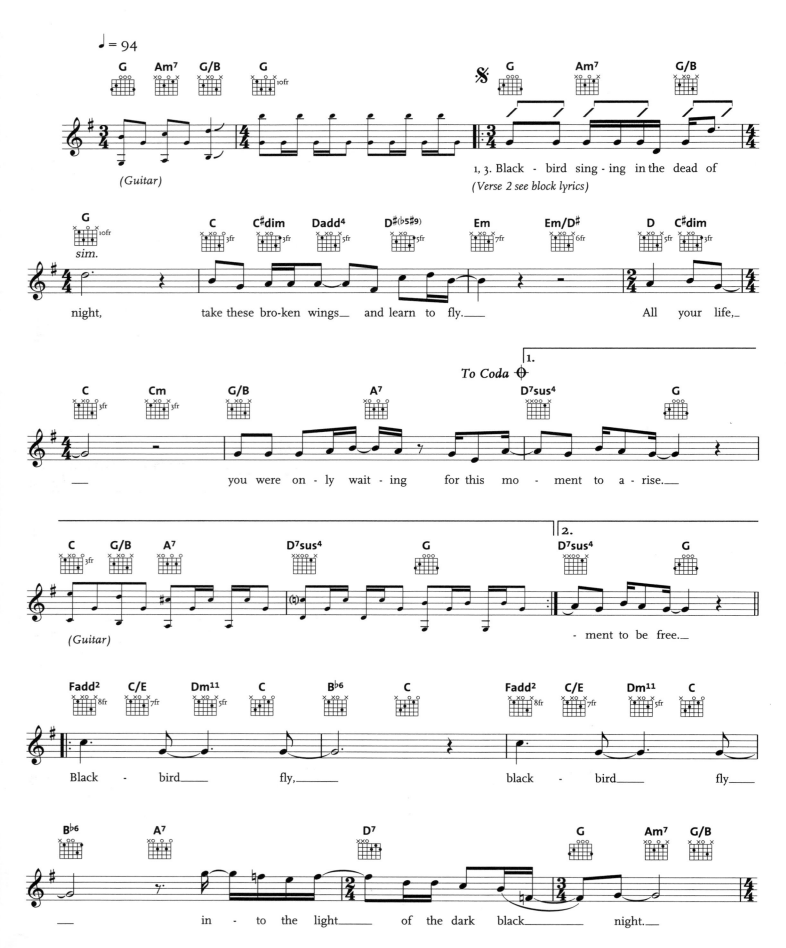

1, 3. Black - bird sing - ing in the dead of
(Verse 2 see block lyrics)

night, take these bro-ken wings and learn to fly. All your life,

you were on - ly wait - ing for this mo - ment to a - rise.

- ment to be free.

Black - bird fly, black - bird fly

in - to the light of the dark black night.

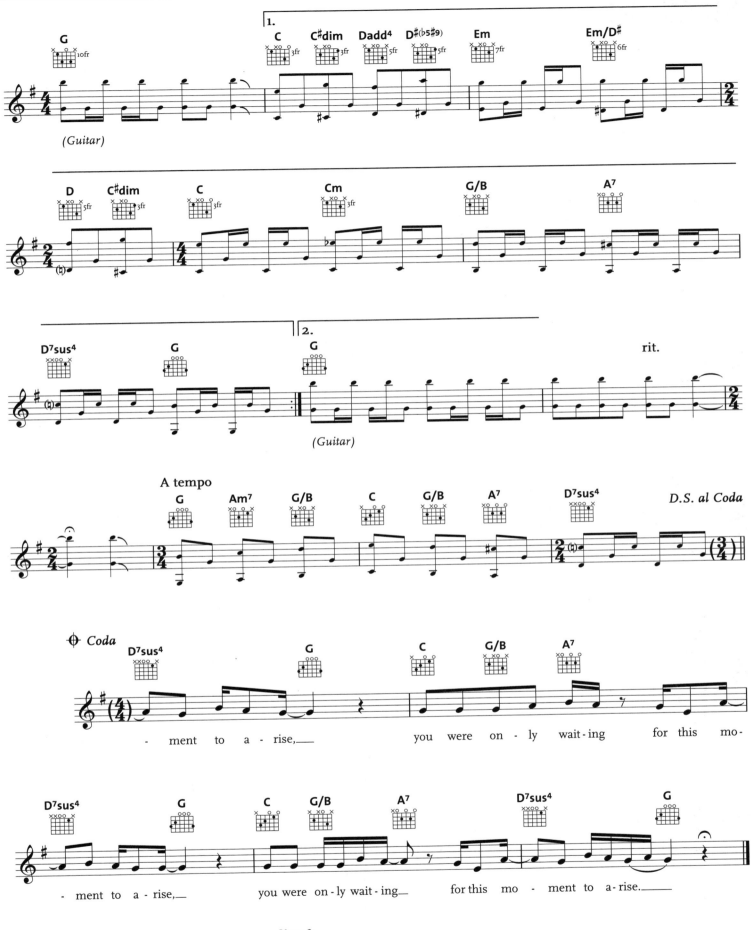

Verse 2:
Blackbird singing in the dead of night,
Take these sunken eyes and learn to see.
All your life, you were only waiting
For this moment to be free.

I Will

Words & Music by John Lennon
& Paul McCartney

you,___ your song___ will fill___ the air.___ Sing it loud___

___ so I___ can hear___ you, make it ea - sy to___ be near_

___ you, for the things___ you do___ en - dear___ you to___ me; ah,___

___ you know_ I will.___

(Guitar)

I will.___

Mm,_____ mm.___

Da da da da da da da.___ (Temple Blocks)

Verse 2:
For if I ever saw you,
I didn't catch your name.
But it never really mattered,
I will always feel the same.

Julia

Words & Music by John Lennon
& Paul McCartney
© Copyright 1968 Northern Songs.
All Rights Reserved.
International Copyright Secured.

♩ = 68

CAPO on 2nd fret

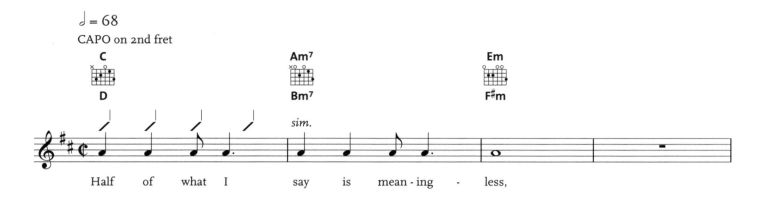

Half of what I say is mean-ing - less,

but I say it just to reach___ you, Ju - - - li -

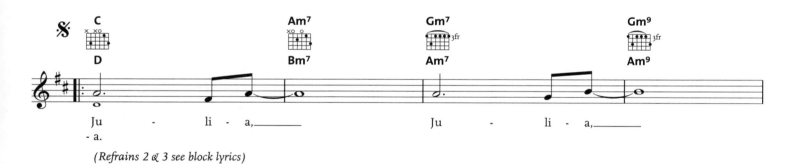

Ju - li - a,_____ Ju - li - a,_____
- a.

(Refrains 2 & 3 see block lyrics)

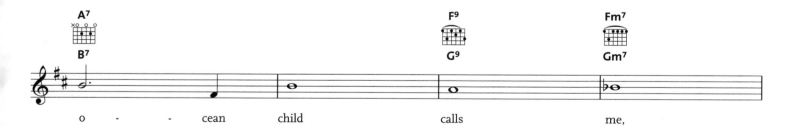

o - - cean child calls me,

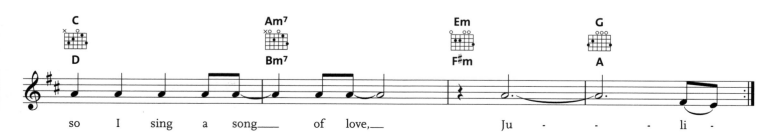

so I sing a song___ of love,___ Ju - - - li -

Refrain 2:
Julia, seashell eyes,
Windy smile calls me,
So I sing a song of love, Julia.

Refrain 3:
Julia, Julia,
Morning moon touch me,
So I sing a song of love, Julia.

Sexy Sadie

Words & Music by John Lennon
& Paul McCartney

427

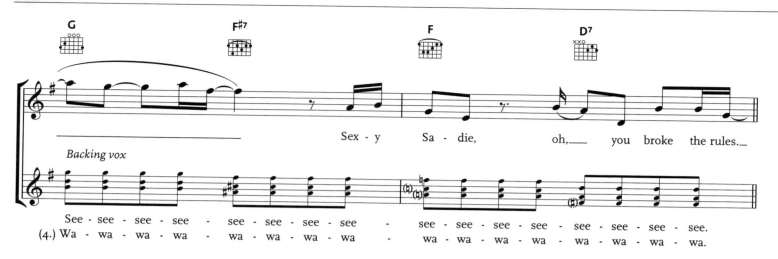

Sex - y Sa - die, oh,___ you broke the rules.___

Backing vox

See - see - see - see - see - see - see - see - see - see - see - see - see - see - see - see.
(4.) Wa - wa - wa - wa - wa - wa - wa - wa - wa - wa - wa - wa - wa - wa - wa - wa.

___ One sun - ny day, the world was wait - ing for a lov - er.
(Bridge 2 see block lyrics)

Sex - - - y Sa - - die.

She came a - long to turn___ on ev'ry - one._____ Sex - y Sa - die, the great - est of them all.___

Sex - y Sa - die, she's the great - est.

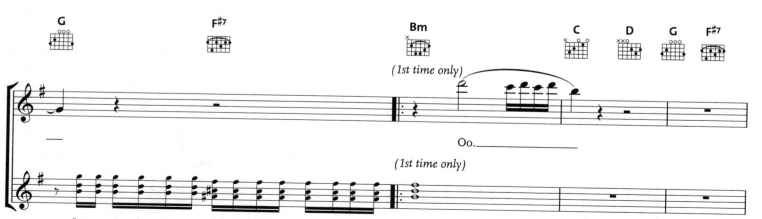

(1st time only)

Oo._____

(1st time only)

Sex - y Sa - die, she's the la - test and the great - est of them all.

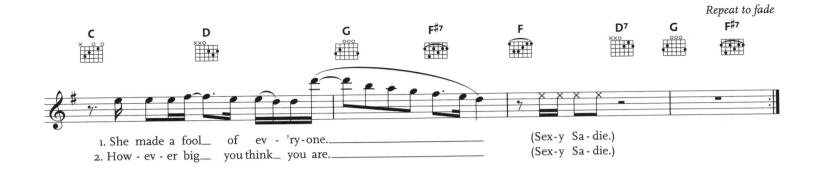

C   D   G   F#7   F   D7   G   F#7

Repeat to fade

1. She made a fool of ev-'ry-one. (Sex-y Sa-die.)
2. How-ev-er big you think you are. (Sex-y Sa-die.)

Verse 3:
Sexy Sadie, how did you know,
The world was waiting just for you,
The world was waiting just for you?
Sexy Sadie, oh, how did you know?

Verse 4:
Sexy Sadie, you'll get yours yet;
However big you think you are,
However big you think you are,
Sexy Sadie, oh, you'll get yours yet.

Bridge 2:
We gave her everything we owned
Just to sit at her table;
Just a smile would lighten everything.
Sexy Sadie, she's the latest and the greatest of them all.

1969

January

→ The FBI opened a file on John, alerted by the furore surrounding the nude sleeve for *Two Virgins*.

→ During an interview with the magazine *Nova*, Yoko coined the memorable phrase,

"Woman is the nigger of the world",

subsequently turned into a song by John.

2 January

→ *Get Back* filming started at Twickenham Studios.

→ Under pressure from Paul to return to live performance, the other Beatles had reluctantly agreed to make an appearance before a live audience, which would be filmed and released as a one-hour television show. However, it proved impossible to agree upon a venue: The Roundhouse in Chalk Farm was booked and cancelled, the idea of a Roman amphitheatre in Tunisia, filmed at dawn, empty of people, and slowly filling up with all races and creeds for the concert, was given serious consideration before Ringo vetoed it on the grounds that he wouldn't like the food.

→ Since they all agreed on the idea of the television film, Apple Films producer Denis O'Dell proposed that they begin rehearsing and suggested that they film the rehearsals for inclusion in the proposed film. He had Twickenham Film Studios booked from 3 February for use on *The Magic Christian* (starring Ringo with Peter Sellers) and he proposed they use the time until then to film on the sound stage in full 16-mm. It was a disaster. Each was still exhausted from the marathon sessions for *The Beatles*. Paul bossed George around; George was moody and resentful. John would not even go to the bathroom without Yoko at his side and for her part Yoko made sure she was in every shot. The tension was palpable, and it was all being caught on film.

→ The Beatles were scheduled to arrive every morning at 10am, a target they achieved only on the first day of shooting. Thereafter, the individuals arrived for work at Twickenham at varying times.

→ On the first day of filming, the group swapped fragments of their new songs. John unveiled 'Don't Let Me Down' and 'Dig A Pony'; George introduced 'All Things Must Pass' and 'Let It Down'. Eventually they worked on two Lennon songs, 'Don't Let Me Down' and 'Everybody Had A Hard Year', which Paul swiftly incorporated into his own song, 'I've Got A Feeling'.

3 January

→ Filming *Get Back* at Twickenham Studios. Paul played the others 'Let It Be' for the first time and they worked on George's 'All Things Must Pass' and their own oldie 'One After 909'.

→ Police in New Jersey impounded 30,000 copies of John and Yoko's *Two Virgins* album on the grounds that the cover was pornographic.

6 January

→ Filming *Get Back* at Twickenham Studios. They worked on 'Don't Let Me Down' and 'Two Of Us'. John, strung out on heroin, was mostly silent and withdrawn, leaving Yoko to do most of the talking on his behalf. As the session declined, Paul and George bickered over minor details in the songs.

George snapped: "You know, I'll play whatever you want me to play. I won't play at all if you don't want me to. Whatever it is that will please you, I'll do it."

January

→ Filming *Get Back* at Twickenham

"It's like hard work to do it," George complained during an early Twickenham session. "I don't want to work, really. It's a drag to get your guitar at eight in the morning, when you're not ready for it."

Opposite: The Beatles last informal concert: on the roof of their Apple office building at 3 Savile Row, 30 January.

Studios. Poor rehearsals of 'Maxwell's Silver Hammer' and John's 'Across The Universe', during which John forgot his own words. In an argument between George and Paul, George suggested that The Beatles should break up. That evening, George wrote 'I Me Mine', inspired by the pettiness and selfishness that he felt was afflicting The Beatles.

8 January

→ Filming *Get Back* at Twickenham Studios. Before John and Paul arrived for the day's shoot, George ran through 'I Me Mine' for the first time. 'I don't care if you don't want it on your show,' he half-joked to Ringo and the film crew. It was an ominous remark for the main feature of this day was an argument between John and George, with John putting down George's songwriting.

9 January

→ Filming *Get Back* at Twickenham Studios. Jam session on 'Suzy's Parlour' after Paul had introduced 'Her Majesty' and 'Another Day' to the sessions.

10 January

→ Filming *Get Back* at Twickenham Studios. After a fierce argument with John, George walked off the set from the studio canteen telling the others he'd 'see them round the clubs', and drove up to Liverpool to see his parents. George thus became the second Beatle to leave the group.

"If George leaves," John asked, "do we want to carry on The Beatles? I do. We should just get other members and carry on."

Ringo: "George had to leave because he thought Paul was dominating him. Well, he was."

→ The three remaining Beatles rehearsed and jammed fitfully throughout the afternoon with Yoko joining in with her trademark screeching.

12 January

→ The *Wonderwall* film opened at the Cinecenta cinema. George was the only

Beatle in attendance.

→ The Beatles met at Ringo's house to try and iron out their difficulties but the feud between John and George remained intractable.

13 January
→ Filming *Get Back* at Twickenham Studios. Ringo and Paul (with Linda) were the only Beatles to attend and spent the session discussing what to do about John's decision to let Yoko do all his talking for him. John and Yoko, both heavily medicated, made a brief appearance in the late afternoon, but no work was done.

→ The *Yellow Submarine* album was released in the US as Apple (Capitol) SW 385 (stereo only). Side A: 'Yellow Submarine', 'Only A Northern Song', 'All Together Now', 'Hey Bulldog', 'It's All Too Much', 'All You Need Is Love'; Side B: Seven soundtrack instrumental cuts by The George Martin Orchestra.

14 January
→ Filming *Get Back* at Twickenham Studios. The three mainly jammed, playing new improvised tracks of John's such as 'Madman' and 'Watching Rainbows'.

15 January
→ Filming *Get Back* at Twickenham Studios. George returned from Liverpool, and during a five-hour meeting, made up his difficulties with John. He said he would leave the group unless the idea of a live performance was dropped. He was prepared, however, to be filmed making an album, but wanted to use The Beatles' own state-of-the-art 72-track recording studio that 'Magic' Alex was supposed to be building for them at Savile Row.

17 January
→ *Yellow Submarine* was released in the UK as Apple (Parlophone) PMC 7070 (mono) and PCS 7070 (stereo) with the same tracks as the US release.

18 January
→ In an off-the-record remark on the stairs at Apple, John told the editor of *Disc And Music Echo*, Ray Coleman,

20 January
→ The *Get Back* film project was

> ## "Apple is losing money every week... if it carries on like this, all of us will be broke in the next six months."

switched to Apple's new basement recording studios at 3 Savile Row where John's guru, 'Magic' Alex, had supposedly built them a 72-track recording facility. Unfortunately, Alex did not have the slightest idea how a recording studio actually worked and had not even connected the studio with the control room. Confronted with an unusable studio, The Beatles called on George Martin to rescue them. He borrowed a pair of four-track machines from EMI, the leads were trailed in through the control room door, and two days later The Beatles began work.

21 January
→ Ringo was interviewed by David Wigg for the BBC Radio 1 programme *Scene And Heard*. In 1976 Wigg released all of his BBC interviews with The Beatles on a double album, *The Beatles Tapes*. Legal moves by George and Ringo failed to prevent its release.

22 January
→ *Get Back* sessions. With cameras and tapes rolling, The Beatles recommenced work on the album and film which would have broken up any normal group. On the first day they ran through 'All I Want Is You' (later called 'Dig A Pony'), 'I've Got A Feeling', 'Don't Let Me Down', 'She Came In Through The Bathroom Window' and a few cover versions including The Drifters' 'Save The Last Dance For Me' and Canned Heat's 'Going Up The Country'.

→ Billy Preston, a friend of The Beatles since Hamburg days, was visiting Apple and was recruited by George to play on The Beatles' sessions and in the film in order to help ease the tension between the four of them. By the end of the session, John was asking Preston:

> ## "Why don't you be on the album?"

23 January
→ *Get Back* sessions, including work on Paul's 'Get Back'.

24 January
→ *Get Back* sessions. Work on Paul's 'On Our Way Home' (later called 'Two Of Us'), 'Teddy Boy', 'Maggie Mae',

John's 'Dig It', 'Dig A Pony' and 'I've Got A Feeling'. The session began with a group discussion about how great a role Billy Preston should play in the sessions. John and George pushed for him to be included as a full member of The Beatles;

> ## "I'd like a fifth Beatle", John said. "It's bad enough with four!" Paul replied.

25 January
→ *Get Back* sessions. After jamming on the Everly Brothers' 'Bye Bye Love' they worked on Paul's 'Let It Be' and a new song of George's 'For You Blue' (originally titled on the tape box as 'George's Blues').

26 January
→ *Get Back* sessions. Work on 'Dig It' was followed by a long rock'n'roll jam to loosen themselves up: 'Shake Rattle And Roll', 'Kansas City', 'Miss Ann', 'Lawdy Miss Clawdy', 'Blue Suede Shoes', 'You Really Got A Hold On Me' and 'Tracks Of My Tears'. Then they were ready to work on Paul's 'The Long And Winding Road' and a song of George's which eventually appeared as 'Isn't It A Pity' on his *All Things Must Pass* triple album.

→ With the filmed live concert cancelled, the director of the film side of the project, Michael Lindsay-Hogg, realised that he might have months of filming ahead of him, judging by how long it took The Beatles to record an album. He proposed that they give a live concert, but all they would have to do was walk up one flight of stairs to the roof of their own building. Even this met with resistance, with George reluctant and Ringo determined not to do it. This time John and Paul combined persuaded the others, albeit only the day before the actual event.

27 January
→ *Get Back* sessions. Work on 'Get Back', 'Oh! Darling', 'I've Got A Feeling' and a jam on Jimmy McCracklin's 'The Walk'. John's 'Sweet Loretta Fart she thought she was a cleaner...' parody remark heard at the start of the *Let It Be* album version of 'Get Back' emanates from this session.

28 January

→ *Get Back* sessions. The Beatles recorded both sides of their next single, 'Get Back' and 'Don't Let Me Down', as well as shuffling through an improvised remake of 'Love Me Do', 'The One After 909', 'Dig A Pony', 'I've Got A Feeling' and 'Teddy Boy'.

→ Derek Taylor gave Allen Klein John's telephone number and John and Yoko met with Klein in the Harlequin suite of the Dorchester Hotel, London. They were very impressed with him, and John decided on the spot to make him his personal adviser. There and then he wrote to Sir Joseph Lockwood, the chairman of EMI:

"Dear Sir Joe: From now on Allen Klein handles all my stuff."

29 January

→ *Get Back* sessions. Work on versions of 'Teddy Boy', 'The One After 909', 'I Want You', Buddy Holly's 'Not Fade Away', 'Mailman, Bring Me No More Blues' as well as the old Hamburg and Cavern days standard, 'Besame Mucho'.

30 January

→ Mal set up the instruments, as of old, and The Beatles, with Billy Preston, took up position on the flat roof of their Savile Row headquarters. Traffic was brought to a halt as the lunchtime crowds gathered on the pavement below and all the windows and roofs nearby quickly filled with West End office workers, getting a privileged view of the last ever Beatles

Above: Allen Klein talks business with Neil Aspinall. After a meeting with John and Yoko on 28 January, Klein ended up representing Lennon, Harrison and Starr's business affairs.

live concert. The police tried to put a stop to it, but the combined Apple door security, and reluctance on the part of the police to actually pull the plug on such an extraordinary scene, meant that they played on for 42 minutes.

→ They began with a rehearsal of 'Get Back', 'Don't Let Me Down', 'I've Got A Feeling', 'The One After 909', 'Dig A Pony' (for this, an assistant had to kneel in front of John holding the words on a clipboard), 'God Save The Queen', 'I've Got A Feeling' (again), 'Don't Let Me Down' (again) and 'Get Back' (again). This final version of 'Get Back' was interrupted by the police and Paul ad-libbed,

"You've been playing on the roofs again and you know your momma doesn't like it, she's gonna have you arrested!"

At the end of the song, Maureen Starkey burst into loud applause and cheers, causing Paul to return to the microphone and acknowledge her,

"Thanks, Mo!"

→ John ended the set, and The Beatles' live career, with the memorable words

"I'd like to say thank you on behalf of the group and ourselves and I hope we passed the audition."

31 January

→ The last day of filming the *Get Back* sessions. Three of Paul's songs ('The Long And Winding Road', 'Let It Be' and 'Two Of Us') were unsuitable for the rooftop concert because they featured a piano or acoustic guitar. These were filmed at this session. A version of 'Lady Madonna' was also recorded. With the project in the can, The Beatles now put it on the shelf, where it would stay for more than a year.

→ Workmen moved in to tear out 'Magic' Alex's non-functioning studio.

2 February

→ The divorce of Yoko and her husband Anthony Cox in the Virgin Islands was ratified and Yoko was granted custody

Enter Allen Klein: 29 January

In the afternoon Allen Klein had a meeting with all four Beatles. Acting on the advice of John Eastman, Linda's brother, they had been about to buy NEMS for £1m, which EMI was prepared to lend them as an advance against royalties. (NEMS was entitled to take 25% of their record royalties for a further nine years even though Brian Epstein's management contract had expired, something that Epstein slipped into his renewal contract with EMI that The Beatles had not read or noticed.) Klein pointed out that royalties were subject to a high rate of tax, and they would have to earn £2 million to repay the debt. He said that until he had a chance to examine John's financial situation he wouldn't recommend buying NEMS. George and Ringo asked him to examine theirs too. Paul left the meeting.

433

of their child Kyoko, even though Cox had brought her up. Cox objected to these terms which were obtained by John's powerful lawyers and continued to look after Kyoko.

3 February

→ Ringo began an intense filming schedule at Twickenham Film Studios, playing support to Peter Sellers in Joe McGrath's *The Magic Christian*, based on the book by Terry Southern (who also wrote *Candy*). Filming went on from Monday to Friday for 13 weeks and Ringo was at the studio most days.

→ The Beatles, Allen Klein and John Eastman held a meeting. Klein was appointed as The Beatles' business manager, charged with examining their finances and finding a way to stop NEMS from bleeding them of a quarter of their income.

4 February

→ As a compromise to Paul, Eastman and Eastman, Linda's father and brother, were appointed as Apple's General Council, to keep an eye on Allen Klein's activities.

11 February

→ Abbey Road. John and Yoko did a mixing session of some of their experimental tapes.

12 February

→ Paul was made sole director of a new off-the-shelf company, Adagrose Limited, which was later renamed McCartney Productions Limited (MPL).

17 February

→ Leonard Richenberg of Triumph Investment Trust, a city merchant bank, acquired a 70 per cent stake in NEMS and Nemperor Holdings. The Beatles were horrified and wrote a letter to EMI, signed by all four Beatles, saying:

"We hereby irrevocably instruct you to pay Henry Ansbacher & Co. all royalties payable by you directly or indirectly to Beatles and Co. or Apple Corps."

EMI didn't know what to do so they froze the money – £1.3m in royalties – and put it into the nearest branch of

Opposite: Paul and Linda Eastman outside the Apple office. Above: Life inside the Apple building. John and Yoko kick back while George holds up an in-house paper.

Lloyds Bank. The album *James Taylor* (produced by Peter Asher and featuring Paul McCartney's bass playing on 'Carolina In My Mind') was released in the US as Apple SKAO 3352.

20 February

→ Ringo attended the UK premiere of *Candy* at the Odeon Cinema, Kensington, London.

22 February

→ Trident Studios, Soho. Work started on John's 'I Want You' (with Billy Preston on organ).

23 February

→ Trident Studios, Soho. John mixed 'I Want You.'

24 February

→ It was announced that the Triumph Investment group of companies had gained control of NEMS Enterprises.

25 February

→ Abbey Road. George, working by himself on his 26th birthday, cut three demo tapes of his latest songs: 'Old

Brown Shoe', 'Something' and 'All Things Must Pass'.

28 February

→ The album *Goodbye* by Cream (featuring George Harrison on 'Badge') was released in the UK as Polydor 583053.

→ The eviction action against Ringo by Bryman Estates for allowing John and Yoko to use drugs at 34 Montagu Square was settled out of court, allowing Ringo to sell his leasehold.

March

→ Dick James and Charles Silver sold their shares in Northern Songs to Lew Grade's ATV, who then announced that they wanted to buy a controlling interest.

1 March

→ Ringo continued work on The *Magic Christian* at Twickenham Film Studios.

2 March

→ John and Yoko appeared at an evening of avant-garde jazz and experimental music at Lady Mitchell

Hall, Cambridge University, joined by John Tchikai and John Stevens.

4 March

→ George was interviewed by David Wigg for the BBC Radio 1 programme *Scene And Heard*.

10 March

→ Engineer Glyn Johns began a four-day series of mixing sessions, attempting to salvage The Beatles' *Get Back* album.

12 March

→ Paul and Linda were married at Marylebone Register Office, with his brother Michael and roadie Mal Evans as witnesses. Afterwards they went to St John's Wood Church where their marriage was blessed by the Rev. Noel Perry-Gore. There was a luncheon reception afterwards at the Ritz Hotel given by Rory McKeown. Princess Margaret and Lord Snowdon were there and Patti's sister Paula tried to hand Margaret a joint in full view of everyone.

→ None of the other Beatles attended the wedding, though George and Patti went to the reception. They arrived very late because the notorious Sergeant Pilcher chose Paul's wedding day to raid George's house for drugs, bringing a large piece of hashish with them (in case they didn't find anything) which they 'found' on the floor. George commented, They were taken to Esher Police Station and formally charged with possession of cannabis resin. Pilcher was later found guilty in the police corruption trials of the early Seventies.

→ After the reception Paul returned to the studio to continue work on 'Thumbin' A Ride'.

→ Abbey Road. John and Yoko recorded 'Peace Song.'

13 March

→ Ringo shot a grouse-hunting scene on Chobham Common, Surrey, for *The Magic Christian*.

18 March

→ Ringo and Spike Milligan shot the traffic warden scene outside the Star and Garter pub in Putney, for *The Magic Christian*.

> **"I'm a tidy person. I keep my socks in the sock drawer and my hash in the hash box. It's not mine."**

→ George and Patti made an initial court appearance on their charges of cannabis possession, and were remanded on bail.

20 March

→ John and Yoko tried to get married on the cross-channel ferry but were refused permission to board *The Dragon* at Southampton because of 'inconsistencies in their passports'. Peter Brown at Apple found that they *could* get married on the British-governed island of Gibraltar. John, Yoko, Peter Brown and official photographer David Nutter flew to Gibraltar by private jet. They arrived at 8:30 am and were at the British Consulate when it opened at 9 am. There, registrar Cecil Wheeler married them with Peter Brown and David Nutter as their witnesses. They

remained in Gibraltar for just 70 minutes before flying straight to Paris.

21 March

→ Allen Klein was appointed business manager of Apple. His first task was to sort out the mess caused by Dick James selling his Northern Songs shares without first offering them to The Beatles. Klein told the *Daily Telegraph* that under a three year contract he would receive 20 per cent of all the money collected by Apple but no money from existing recording contracts. He would, however, receive 20 per cent of any increase he negotiated on those contracts.

→ As part of Klein's draconian restructuring of Apple, he sacked Alistair Taylor, the general manager of Apple who had previously been Brian Epstein's personal assistant and who witnessed The Beatles first contract with Epstein. Klein also tried to fire Neil Aspinall, although the latter decision was overruled at the Beatles' insistence.

23 March

→ Ringo flew to New York for a few days' location shooting on *The Magic Christian*.

25 March

→ John and Yoko flew to Amsterdam to begin a seven-day peace Bed-In in room 902 of the Hilton Hotel.

31 March

→ The last day of John and Yoko's seven-day bed-in. John and Yoko then flew to Vienna where they held a press conference from inside a white bag at the Hotel Sacher. It received worldwide coverage which a normal press conference would not, despite the fact that no-one was sure it really *was* them. They were in Vienna for the world television premiere of the film *Rape*, which they produced.

→ George and Patti were found guilty of possession of cannabis at Esher and Walton Magistrates' Court and were fined £250 each with ten guineas' costs each.

1 April

→ The *Hamlet* striptease scene was filmed at the Theatre Royal, in Stratford,

John: "We're staying in bed for a week, to register our protest against all the suffering and violence in the world. Can you think of a better way to spend seven days? It's the best idea we've had."

Beatles controlling about the same number of shares: ATV had acquired 1,604,750 shares from Silver and James, and already held 137,000, giving them nearly 35 per cent of the company. The Beatles between them controlled 29.7 per cent: Paul had the most at 751,000, John had 644,000 and held another 50,000 on trust and Ringo had 40,000. George had sold his but Patti had 1,000. Apple controlled another 30,000 through Subafilms.

"Monopoly with real money", John called it. "Businessmen play the game the way we play music and it's something to see."

The Northern Songs saga prompted Paul to write 'You Never Give Me Your Money'.

3 April

→ John and Yoko appeared on *The Eamonn Andrews Show* live from the Café Royal in Regent Street, where they tried to get Andrews to climb into a white bag with them. Fellow guests Jack Benny and Yehudi Menuhin were not amused.

→ George was interviewed by Sue McGregor for the lunchtime BBC Radio One programme *World At One* in which he discussed Ravi Shankar.

→ The single 'Badge' by Cream, written by George Harrison and Eric Clapton, was released in the UK as Polydor 2058 285

7 April

→ Disappointed by the way that 'Get Back' had sounded on the radio the previous day, Paul oversaw a remix session of the song at Olympic Studios.

9 April

→ The boat race scene at Barclays Bank Rowing Club on the Thames Embankment was filmed for *The Magic Christian*.

10 April

→ The Beatles rejected ATV's offer of £9 million for their shares in Northern Songs and announced that they were considering a counter bid (though where they would have obtained the £9.5 million required in real cash is hard to imagine). Lew Grade told the

East London, for *The Magic Christian*.

→ John and Yoko returned to London and gave a press conference at Heathrow. Later they appeared live on Thames Television's *Today* programme where they attempted to explain 'Bagism' to Eamonn Andrews.

2 April

→ John, Yoko and Paul, together with Allen Klein, visited The Beatles' merchant bankers, Henry Ansbacher and Company, to plot a strategy to try and get back Northern Songs for themselves. Their adviser was Mr Bruce Ormrod. It looked an evenly matched fight with ATV and The

Opposite: John listens to a playback at Apple Studios while Yoko sleeps. The couple made several experimental recordings together during 1968-69.

Daily Telegraph: 'We have 35 per cent of the shares and will not let go of that for anything.' The publicity caused market speculators to get in on the act and soon a powerful syndicate of holders of Northern Songs shares was formed known as The Consortium. Between them they had 14 per cent of the shares, enough to swing the outcome, and they met in secret to discuss their strategy.

11 April
→ 'Get Back'/'Don't Let Me Down', credited to The Beatles with Billy Preston, was released in the UK as Apple (Parlophone) R 5777.

12 April
→ John and Yoko had a meeting at Ansbachers in the City to work out the complicated financing necessary for The Beatles' counter bid for Northern Songs.

14 April
→ John and Yoko arrived at Paul's house in Cavendish Avenue so that Paul could go over 'The Ballad Of John And Yoko' with John. Despite their business problems, the Lennon and McCartney songwriting partnership was always held in very high regard by both partners, and was a major source of income for both of them. Once the song was complete, they went over to nearby Abbey Road and recorded it, without the aid of the other Beatles (George was abroad and Ringo was filming). Paul played drums, bass, piano and percussion. John did lead vocals and lead guitar.

15 April
→ More meetings at Ansbachers who, at one point had persuaded a number of City institutions who owned Northern Songs shares to go in with The Beatles in a deal that would have given The Beatles control but, with the papers all drawn up and waiting for John, Paul, George and Ringo's signature, John announced, The City businessmen decided that they would be better off siding with ATV.

16 April
→ Abbey Road. The group recorded George's 'Old Brown Shoe' and began work on his 'Something'.

> ## "I'm not going to be fucked around by men in suits sitting on their fat arses in the City."

18 April
→ Abbey Road. George's 'Old Brown Shoe' was completed and further work done on 'I Want You'.

20 April
→ There was a massive row at Ansbacher's because Paul, on Eastman's advice, refused to commit his shares in Northern Songs as part of the collateral required for the loan from Ansbacher's to finance The Beatles' bid. Their offer amounted to £2.1 million of which Ansbacher was lending them about £1.2 million against collateral. John and Paul together could just about manage it, but Paul refused to put up his shares. John's shares in Northern Songs were worth about £1.1 million, Maclen Music was worth just over half a million and Subafilms – which owned rights to *A Hard Day's Night, Help! and Yellow Submarine* – was worth about £350,000. Allen Klein had to put in all his shares in MGM: 45,000 shares worth about £650,000. The Beatles were now in a position to finance their bid.
→ Abbey Road. Work done on 'I Want You' and 'Oh! Darling!'

21 April
→ John and Yoko formed Bag Productions Limited.
→ In the City, the Consortium declared its hand and staged a blocking operation.

22 April
→ In a short formal ceremony on the roof of the Apple building at 3 Savile Row, John changed his middle name from Winston to Ono by deed poll before Commissioner of Oaths, Bueno de Mesquita.

John: "Yoko changed her name for me, I've changed mine for her. One for both, both for each other. She has a ring, I have a ring. It gives us nine 'O's between us, which is good luck. Ten would not be good luck."

Unfortunately for John, he technically became John Winston Ono Lennon (ten 'O's) as one can never fully revoke a name given at birth.

→ Abbey Road. John and Yoko taped the heartbeats used on *The Wedding Album*.

24 April
→ In a deal hammered out between Klein and Richenberg, NEMS surrendered its claim to 25 per cent of The Beatles royalties for the next nine years. Instead Triumph received £750,000 cash, 25 per cent of the royalties already frozen by EMI (over £300,000). Triumph received £50,000 for the 23 per cent that NEMS held in The Beatles' film company Subafilms and received 5 per cent of the gross record royalties from 1972 until 1976. This had been a sticking point but in the end Richenberg was satisfied because he knew that Klein would next turn his attention on EMI and obtain a substantial royalty rate increase. The Beatles also received an option on the 4.5 per cent of Northern Songs shares owned by NEMS, useful in the forthcoming battle for Northern Songs, and received 266,000 shares in Triumph (valued at £420,00) in exchange for The Beatles' 10 per cent share in NEMS.
→ On this same day, The Beatles offered 42s 6d per share for the 20 per cent of Northern Songs shares they needed to gain control. This would have cost them £2,100,000. They also said they would extend their contracts with Northern Songs for a further two years and would add other valuable assets to the company if they gained control. They added that they 'would not be happy to continue, let alone renew, their existing contracts with Northern under the aegis of ATV'.

25 April
→ John and Yoko attended a showing of their film *Rape* at the Montreux Television Festival in Switzerland.

26 April
→ Abbey Road. Paul added a lead vocal to 'Oh! Darling!' and work began on Ringo's 'Octopus's Garden'.

27 April
→ Abbey Road. John and Yoko made another recording of their heartbeats for use on *The Wedding Album*.

29 April
→ Abbey Road. Ringo added his lead vocal to 'Octopus's Garden'.

April 30
→ Abbey Road. New guitar added to 'Let It Be' and the rest of the session spent adding vocals and overdubs to 'You Know My Name (Look Up The Number)'.

1 May
→ Abbey Road. A mixing session for 'Oh! Darling!' and John and Yoko's heartbeat track 'John And Yoko'.

2 May
→ Abbey Road. The Beatles worked on George's 'Something'.
→ John and Yoko were interviewed for the BBC 1 television arts programme *How Late It Is*, discussing their film *Rape*.
→ ATV claimed that they had support from shareholders holding 45 per cent of the Northern Songs shares and extended their offer until 15 May.

4 May
→ John and Yoko bought a new home,

a Georgian mansion in 72 acres of land called 'Tittenhurst Park' in Sunninghill, Berkshire, once owned by the tycoon Peter Cadbury. It cost £145,000.

5 May
→ Olympic Sound Studios, Barnes. New bass and guitar added to 'Something.'
→ 'Get Back'/'Don't Let Me Down', credited to The Beatles with Billy Preston, was released in the US as Apple (Capitol) 2490.

6 May
→ Olympic Sound Studios, Barnes. Work began on 'You Never Give Me Your Money', Paul's response to the financial problems at Apple.

7 May
→ Olympic Studios: The session was spent mixing and listening to playbacks. Earlier, the group had a meeting with EMI chief Sir Joseph Lockwood.

8 May
→ John and Yoko were interviewed by

David Wigg for the BBC Radio One programme *Scene And Heard*.
→ John, George and Ringo signed a management contract with Allen Klein, in effect making him their manager. Paul held out.

9 May
→ Olympic Sound Studios, Barnes. The Beatles had a very stormy meeting in which Paul continued to hold out against the other three who wanted Allen Klein to manage them for a 20 per cent cut of their earnings. Paul thought 15 per cent would be sufficient. When Paul refused to sign the relevant documents until he had consulted his lawyer, the others stormed out of the studio, cancelling the planned recording session.
→ Allen Klein's ABKCO Industries (Allen and Betty Klein Corporation) was duly appointed business manager of The Beatles' companies but Paul all along refused to sign the contract and remained opposed to Klein's involvement with Apple or The Beatles, preferring his own in-laws, the Eastmans.
→ Paul stayed behind in the studio and after a long talk with American musician Steve Miller, he guested on 'My Dark Hour', on which Paul played drums, bass and did backing vocals. The track was included on Miller's album *Brave New World* and McCartney was credited as 'Paul Ramon'.
→ Zapple, Apple Records' new experimental and avant-garde label,

was launched with the release of two experimental Beatles solo albums.
→ The album *Unfinished Music No.2: Life With The Lions* by John Lennon and Yoko Ono, written and produced by John and Yoko, was released in the UK as Zapple 01. Side One: 'Cambridge 1969'; Side Two: 'No Bed For Beatle John', 'Baby's Heartbeat', 'Two Minutes Silence', 'Radio Play'.
→ The album *Electronic Sound*, performed and produced by George Harrison was released in the UK as Zapple 02. Side One: 'Under The Mersey Wall'; Side Two: 'No Time Or Space'.

15 May
→ Paul was interviewed by Roy Corlett for BBC Radio Merseyside's *Light And Local*

22 May
→ *Hey Jude* won the 1968 Ivor Novello award for top selling British song'.

24 May
→ John's drug bust meant that he was unable to enter the USA so John and Yoko planned another bed-in for peace in the Bahamas, thinking it was just off the coast of the US and therefore the American press would be able to cover the event.

25 May
→ John and Yoko found that the Bahamas were further from the US than they thought, so they flew on to Toronto where they were held at the

Losing Northern Songs: 19 May

Lew Grade's ATV gained control of Northern Songs Limited after a long and bitter battle. John had become disillusioned by the terms of the deal worked out by Ormrod and the Consortium in which the new board would have three representatives from each side with David Platz as the MD. John said he didn't see why The Beatles should bother to take over a company and then be told that they couldn't do what they liked with it. He said that he would rather let Grade have it than be dictated to like this. The company would not have been theirs to play with, of course, since all they were buying was control, and other shareholders were nervous that Klein might finish up running it. The Consortium sided with ATV who got the majority they needed a mere 15 minutes before The Beatles' offer expired. ATV now controlled virtually all of John and Paul's songs, and all future songs until 1973. The Beatles finished up owing Ansbacher's £5,000 for their services.

airport for two and a half hours before being allowed to enter the country.

26 May
→ The album *Unfinished Music No.2: Life With The Lions* by John Lennon and Yoko Ono, was released in the US as Zapple ST 3357.
→ The album *Electronic Sound* by George Harrison was released in the US as Zapple ST 3358.
→ John and Yoko began an eight-day Bed-In for peace in room 1742 of the Queen Elizabeth Hotel, Montreal, handily located for the New York press corps.

28 May
→ Glyn Johns assembled a working version of the *Get Back* LP for the approval of The Beatles.

29 May
→ John and Yoko were interviewed by phone over the air by radio station KSAN in San Francisco.

30 May
→ 'The Ballad Of John And Yoko'/ 'Old Brown Shoe' was released in the UK as Apple (Parlophone) R 5786.

1 June
→ John, Yoko and a roomful of visitors, including members of the Radha Krishna Temple, MOR singer Petula Clark, rock writer Paul Williams, comedian Tommy Smothers and Timothy Leary, recorded the peace anthem 'Give Peace A Chance'.

2 June
→ The last day of John and Yoko's Bed-In ended in the afternoon when John and Yoko went to Ottawa for a university conference on peace.

4 June
→ 'The Ballad Of John And Yoko'/'Old Brown Shoe' was released in the US as Apple (Capitol) 2531. Many radio stations refused to air the A-side, complaining that its lyrics were 'blasphemous'.

14 June
→ John and Yoko pre-recorded an appearance for the US edition of *The David Frost Show* recorded with a studio audience at InterTel Studios, Wembley.

Opposite: Paul at the Apple office. His attendances stopped after Allen Klein took control.
Below: John and Yoko hold another 'Bed-In' at the Queen Elizabeth Hotel, Montreal, 26 May. Their universal anthem, 'Give Peace A Chance' was recorded in the couple's suite with an array of visitors singing on the back-up chorus.

17 June
→ Kenneth Tynan's musical play *Oh! Calcutta!* opened at the Eden Theater in New York. One of its scenes, a masturbation fantasy entitled 'Four In Hand', was written by John.

22 June
→ John and Yoko were interviewed about their peace campaign on Radio Luxembourg.

23 June
→ Ringo and Peter Sellers shot the climactic scene of *The Magic Christian* near the National Film Theatre on the South Bank in which paper money was thrown into a huge tank full of slaughterhouse offal and manure.

1 July
→ Abbey Road. *Abbey Road* sessions. Paul added a new lead vocal to 'You Never Give Me Your Money'.

→ John and Yoko were involved in a car crash in Golspie, in the north of Scotland, when John let the car go out of control. They were taken to the Lawson Memorial Hospital where John had 17 stitches in a facial wound, Yoko 14 stitches and Kyoko four. John's son Julian was suffering from shock and they were all detained in hospital.

2 July
→ Abbey Road. *Abbey Road* sessions. Paul recorded the 'Her Majesty' fragment which was originally scheduled for the middle of the *Abbey Road* medley. When George and Ringo arrived they started work on 'Golden Slumbers'/ 'Carry That Weight'.

3 July
→ Abbey Road. *Abbey Road* sessions. More work done on 'Golden Slumbers'/ 'Carry That Weight.'

4 July

→ Abbey Road. *Abbey Road* sessions. More work on 'Golden Slumbers'/'Carry That Weight.'

→ The single 'Give Peace A Chance' (Lennon & McCartney)/'Remember Love' (Yoko Ono) by The Plastic Ono Band and produced by John and Yoko was released in the UK as Apple 13.

→ John sent Apple's Derek Taylor a mock begging letter from his hospital bed, signed 'Jack McCripple (ex-seamen)'.

6 July

→ John and Yoko chartered a helicopter to transfer them to a private jet for the flight back to London. The helicopter left from the lawn of the Lawson Memorial Hospital with the staff waving goodbye. The smashed car was crushed into a cube and exhibited on the lawn of Tittenhurst Park.

7 July

→ Abbey Road. *Abbey Road* sessions. The three Beatles, John at home recovering from his car crash, worked on George's 'Here Comes The Sun'.

→ The Plastic Ono Band single 'Give Peace A Chance'/'Remember Love' was released in the US as Apple 1809

8 July

→ Abbey Road. *Abbey Road* sessions. More work on 'Here Comes The Sun'.

9 July

→ Abbey Road. *Abbey Road* sessions. John arrived back in the studio and worked on Paul's 'Maxwell's Silver Hammer'. Yoko, more seriously injured than John, accompanied him as usual. A double bed was delivered to the studio by Harrods and Yoko lay in it, a microphone suspended above her mouth in case she wanted to add her thoughts.

10 July

→ Abbey Road. *Abbey Road* sessions. Overdubs added to 'Maxwell's Silver Hammer'.

11 July

→ Abbey Road. *Abbey Road* sessions. More overdubs added to 'Maxwell's Silver Hammer' (Ringo played anvil), and work done on 'Something' and

Opposite: Preparing to shoot the front sleeve for *Abbey Road*, the last Beatles album to be recorded and named after the location where the group had made virtually all of their classic recordings.

'You Never Give Me Your Money'.

15 July

→ Abbey Road. *Abbey Road* sessions. The vocals and chimes were overdubbed and added to 'You Never Give Me Your Money'.

16 July

→ Abbey Road. *Abbey Road* sessions. More work on 'Here Comes The Sun' and 'Something'.

17 July

→ Abbey Road. *Abbey Road* sessions. Paul added his lead vocal to 'Oh! Darling!' followed by all The Beatles working on Ringo's 'Octopus's Garden.'

18 July

→ Abbey Road. *Abbey Road* sessions. Paul had another try at the lead vocal to 'Oh! Darling!' followed by Ringo's vocal on 'Octopus's Garden.'

21 July

→ Abbey Road. *Abbey Road* sessions, Work began on 'Come Together'.

22 July

→ Abbey Road. *Abbey Road* sessions. Paul had another try at the vocal on 'Oh! Darling!' then the group worked on 'Come Together'.

23 July

→ Abbey Road. *Abbey Road* sessions. Rehearsals and recording of 'The End'.

24 July

→ Abbey Road. *Abbey Road* sessions. First Paul cut a demo of 'Come And Get It' for Apple band, The Iveys, soon to change their name to Badfinger. Then The Beatles recorded the 'Sun King'/'Mean Mister Mustard' medley.

25 July

→ Abbey Road. *Abbey Road* sessions. More work on 'Sun King'/'Mean Mister Mustard' and 'Sun King'. Work then began on John's 'Polythene Pam' and Paul's 'She Came In Through The Bathroom Window', recorded as one continuous number.

26 July

→ George gave a short radio interview to Kenny Everett to promote a forthcoming peace march in Hyde Park.

28 July

→ Abbey Road. *Abbey Road* sessions. More work on 'Polythene Pam'/'She Came In Through The Bathroom Window'.

29 July

→ Abbey Road. *Abbey Road* sessions. Guitar was added to 'Come Together' and work done on 'Sun King'/'Mean Mister Mustard'.

30 July

→ Abbey Road. *Abbey Road* sessions. A day of overdubs working on 'Come Together', 'Polythene Pam'/'She Came In Through The Bathroom Window', 'You Never Give Me Your Money' and 'Golden Slumbers'/'Carry That Weight'. After this they worked on a trial order for the medley, and Paul rejected 'Her Majesty' from the set, asking tape operator John Kurlander to edit it out and throw it away. EMI threw away nothing so Kurlander attached it to the end of the master tape on a long piece of leader tape. When an acetate was cut, the long gap, followed by 'Her Majesty' remained. Paul liked it that way, so it stayed.

31 July

→ Abbey Road. *Abbey Road* sessions. 'You Never Give Me Your Money' was completed and overdubs added to 'Golden Slumbers'/'Carry That Weight'.

1 August

→ Abbey Road. *Abbey Road* sessions. Work began on 'Because'.

4 August

→ Abbey Road. *Abbey Road* sessions. The gorgeous three part harmonies on 'Because' were recorded.

5 August

→ Abbey Road. *Abbey Road* sessions. 'Because' was completed by George playing the Moog synthesiser and vocals were added to 'The End'.

6 August

→ Abbey Road. *Abbey Road* sessions. George added guitar to 'Here Comes The Sun' and Paul added synthesiser to 'Maxwell's Silver Hammer'.

7 August

→ Abbey Road. *Abbey Road* sessions. Work on 'The End'. First vocals were added then a guitar track with Paul, George and John trading solos.

8 August

→ *Abbey Road* sessions: After lunch, in the studio, new bass and drum tracks were added to 'The End', work was done on 'I Want You' and Paul added lead guitar to 'Oh! Darling!'

The Abbey Road Sleeve: 8 August

At 11:35 am, with a policeman holding up the traffic, photographer Iain Macmillan climbed up a stepladder in the middle of Abbey Road and shot the now famous photograph of The Beatles walking across the zebra crossing near the recording studio. It was a hot day so Paul was not wearing shoes. The cover had been Paul's idea – he drew a sketch of how he wanted the photograph to look – and when the transparencies were developed, he was the one who chose which shot to use.

11 August

→ Abbey Road. *Abbey Road* sessions. Further work on 'I Want You', to which 'She's So Heavy' was added. More work was done on 'Oh! Darling!' and 'Here Comes The Sun'.

→ John and Yoko moved into their new mansion at Tittenhurst Park, Ascot.

12 August

→ Abbey Road. *Abbey Road* mixing session.

13 August

→ Abbey Road. *Abbey Road* mixing session.

14 August

→ Abbey Road. *Abbey Road* sessions. Editing work was done on the medley.

John was interviewed at the studio by Kenny Everett for his BBC Radio 1 show *Everett Is Here*.

15 August

→ Abbey Road. *Abbey Road* sessions. Orchestral overdubs were added to 'Golden Slumbers'/ 'Carry That Weight', 'The End', 'Something' and 'Here Comes The Sun'.

18 August

→ Abbey Road. *Abbey Road* sessions. Paul added piano to 'The End.'

19 August

→ Abbey Road. *Abbey Road* sessions. 'Here Comes The Sun' and 'Something' were completed.

20 August

→ Abbey Road. *Abbey Road* sessions. John's 'I Want You (She's So Heavy)' was completed, with its abrupt ending, made by literally cutting the tape. After this, The Beatles listened to the tracks in the proposed running order for the album. This was the last time that all four Beatles were together in Abbey Road.

22 August

→ The Beatles posed together for a photo session in the grounds of Tittenhurst Park. It was the last ever Beatles photo shoot and their last appearance together at any Beatles event.

27 August

→ As part of the deal struck on 24 April, The Beatles sold Triumph their shares in NEMS Enterprises Limited.

28 August

→ Paul and Linda's daughter Mary was born at Avenue Clinic, London.

8 September

→ Ringo was taken to the Middlesex Hospital, central London, suffering from an intestinal complaint and kept in for observation.

10 September

→ The Institute of Contemporary Arts held an evening of John and Yoko's avant-garde films, including the premiere of *Self Portrait* (an

entertaining study of John's penis in the process of becoming erect). Also screened were *Rape, Honeymoon, Two Virgins, Smile* and *Folding*. John and Yoko sent a couple to sit in a white bag on stage beneath the screen throughout the screening, thought by many people to be the Lennons themselves. The event was billed thus:

"John and Yoko's evening of film events will end towards midnight. It will happen once. It will be what they want it to be."

12 September

→ Rock promoter John Brower telephoned John and Yoko to invite them to attend the Toronto Rock'n'Roll Revival concert the next day to hear Little Richard, Chuck Berry and Jerry Lee Lewis, offering eight first-class tickets for them and six friends. John immediately agreed provided he and his band could play live. The astonished promoter accepted at once and, since John had no band – The Beatles had not played live in three years – he had to form one quickly. He summoned together Eric Clapton, Klaus Voormann and session drummer Alan White. Mal Evans was informed that he was handling the gear. Brower dealt with visas and immigration, still unable to believe that he had attracted a Beatle to his festival.

13 September

→ John and Yoko just made the plane and during the flight the Plastic Ono Band made a half-hearted attempt to rehearse a few songs. Meanwhile, Canadian radio stations were going wild and there were several hundred fans waiting at the airport, reminiscent of the old Beatlemania days.

→ They hastily rehearsed a few songs and before going on stage at the Varsity Stadium of Toronto University. John was so nervous he threw up. The Plastic Ono Band stuck to classics: 'Blue Suede Shoes', 'Money', 'Dizzy Miss Lizzy', 'Yer Blues', 'Cold Turkey' and 'Give Peace A Chance'. Yoko then took over for the avant-garde section of their set with 'Don't Worry Kyoko (Mummy's Only Looking For Her Hand In The

John quits: 20 September

At the meeting John and Yoko made Klein the business manager of their company, Bag Productions. John also used the occasion to finally tell the other Beatles that he was leaving the group:

John: 'I said to Paul, 'I'm leaving.' ... Paul said, 'What do you mean?'

'I said, 'I mean the group is over, I'm leaving.' Allen was saying don't tell. He didn't want me to tell Paul even. So I said 'It's out.' I couldn't stop it, it came out. Paul and Allen both said that they were glad that I wasn't going to announce it, that I wasn't going to make an event out of it. I don't know whether Paul said don't tell anybody, but he was darned pleased that I wasn't going to. He said, 'Oh that means nothing's really happened if you're not going to say anything.'

445

Above: Paul, Linda, Heather and baby Mary. In late 1969, Paul retreated out of the public eye into family life to the extent that a bizarre 'Paul Is Dead' rumour started to circulate in America. Opposite: Ringo and Peter Sellers at the premiere of *The Magic Christian*, Kensington Odeon, 11 December.

Snow)' and 'John, John (Let's Hope For Peace)'.

16 September
→ Maclen (Music) Limited instigated legal proceedings against Northern Songs Limited requesting a re-audit of royalty statements from February 11, 1965 onwards. This was an area that Klein specialised in and nearly always came up trumps.

19 September
→ Paul was interviewed by David Wigg for the BBC Radio 1 *Scene And Heard* programme.
→ BBC2's *Late Night Line-Up* previewed the entire *Abbey Road* album.

20 September
→ Allen Klein negotiated a tough new contract for The Beatles with EMI/Capitol giving them an increased royalty rate. Though their contract was

not due to expire until 1976, the group had virtually fulfilled the minimum provision of five long-playing records and five singles and so Klein was in a strong bargaining position.
→ Their previous deal with Capitol was already very good: 17.5 per cent of wholesale in the US, but Klein managed to get them 25 per cent. Paul gave credit where it was due and signed.

25 September
→ Abbey Road. John and Yoko supervised stereo mixes of their Toronto concert for release: 'Blue Suede Shoes', 'Money (That's What I Want)', 'Dizzy Miss Lizzy', 'Yer Blues', 'Cold Turkey', 'Give Peace A Chance', 'Don't Worry Kyoko (Mummy's Only Looking For Her Hand In The Snow)' and 'John, John (Let's Hope For Peace)'.
→ Afterwards John and Yoko, with The Plastic Ono Band (John on guitar and vocals, Eric Clapton on guitar,

Klaus Voormann on bass and Ringo on drums) returned to Abbey Road where they recorded 'Cold Turkey'. John had originally offered the song to The Beatles, but unsurprisingly Paul had turned it down.

26 September
→ *Abbey Road* was released in the UK as Apple (Parlophone) PCS 7088 (stereo only). Side A: 'Come Together', 'Something', 'Maxwell's Silver Hammer', 'Oh! Darling', 'Octopus's Garden', 'I Want You (She's So Heavy)'; Side B: 'Here Comes The Sun', 'Because', 'You Never Give Me Your Money', 'Sun King'/'Mean Mr. Mustard', 'Polythene Pam'/'She Came In Through The Bathroom Window', 'Golden Slumbers'/'Carry That Weight', 'The End', 'Her Majesty'.
→ Radio Luxembourg broadcast an interview with Ringo by David 'Kid' Jensen, talking about *Abbey Road*.

28 September
→ Trident Studios, Soho. The Plastic Ono Band, with the same line-up as on September 25, re-cut 'Cold Turkey'.

29 September
→ Abbey Road. John supervised the mixing of 'Cold Turkey'.

1 October
→ *Abbey Road* was released in the US as Apple (Capitol) SO 383 (stereo only).
→ The release of the album coincided with a US media frenzy inspired by the rumour started by an American DJ that Paul had died in 1966, ensuring that *Abbey Road* sold more quickly than any album since the height of Beatlemania in 1964. Paul denied the reports:
"I'm as fit as a fiddle,"
he told *Life* reporters.

3 October
→ Lansdowne Studios, London. A studio version of Yoko's 'Don't Worry Kyoko (Mummy's Only Looking For Her Hand In The Snow)' was recorded by The Plastic Ono Band as the B-side of 'Cold Turkey'.

5 October
→ Abbey Road. Overdubs on 'Cold Turkey'.

6 October

→ The single 'Something'/'Come Together' was released in the US as Apple (Capitol) 2654 – George Harrison's first (and only) Beatles A-side.

8 October

→ George recorded an interview with David Wigg at Apple for the BBC Radio 1 programme *Scene And Heard*.

9 October

→ On John's 29th birthday, Yoko was taken to King's College Hospital, London, for emergency blood transfusions when it seemed she might lose another baby. She and John had not long gone through cold turkey withdrawal from heroin addiction.

12 October

→ After four days in hospital, with John at her side throughout, Yoko miscarried her expected baby.

20 October

→ Abbey Road. John and Yoko did a new mix of the tapes of the Toronto Plastic Ono Band concert.

→ The single 'Cold Turkey'(Lennon)/ 'Don't Worry Kyoko (Mummy's Only Looking For Her Hand In The Snow') (Ono) by The Plastic Ono Band, produced by John and Yoko, was released in the US as Apple 1813.

→ The album *Wedding Album* by John Ono Lennon and Yoko Ono Lennon, was released in the US as Apple SMAX 3361. Side One: 'John And Yoko'; Side Two: 'Amsterdam'.

21 October

→ John was interviewed by David Wigg for the BBC Radio 1 programme *Scene And Heard*.

24 October

→ Paul, who was determined to put an end to the absurd 'Paul is dead' rumours coming from the States, was interviewed at his Scottish farm by Chris Drake for BBC Radio 4's *The World This Weekend*.

→ 'Cold Turkey'/ 'Don't Worry Kyoko' (Mummy's Only Looking For Her Hand In The Snow') by The Plastic Ono Band was released in the UK as Apple 1001.

26 October

→ John's interview with David Wigg for the BBC Radio 1 programme *Scene And Heard* was broadcast.

27 October

→ Abbey Road. Ringo began work on his first solo album *Sentimental Journey*, an album of standards. Ringo and a 17-piece orchestra recorded Cole Porter's 'Night And Day'.

31 October

→ 'Something'/'Come Together' was released in the UK as Apple (Parlophone) R 5814.

6 November

→ Abbey Road. *Sentimental Journey* sessions. Ringo recorded Lena Horne's 'Stormy Weather' with an 18-piece orchestra.

7 November

→ Abbey Road. *Sentimental Journey* sessions. Orchestral tracks were recorded for 'Stardust'. (Paul was credited on the sleeve for the arrangement.)

→ The album *Wedding Album* by John Ono Lennon and Yoko Ono Lennon, was released in the UK as Apple SAPCOR 11.

14 November

→ Abbey Road. *Sentimental Journey* sessions. Ringo added his vocal to 'Stardust' and began work on 'Dream'.

25 November

→ John returned his MBE to the Queen. It was delivered by his chauffeur in the morning. He attached the following note:

→ John was interviewed by David Bellan from BBC Radio 4. As with the original award of The Beatles' MBE's in 1965, his decision to send back his medal evoked a storm of protest from fellow award-holders.

26 November

→ Abbey Road. John and Yoko supervised remixes of 'What's The New Mary Jane' and 'You Know My Name (Look Up The Number)' for release as a Plastic Ono Band single because it seemed that The Beatles were not going to release them.

"Your Majesty, I am returning my MBE as a protest against Britain's involvement in the Nigeria – Biafra thing, against our support of America in Vietnam and against 'Cold Turkey' slipping down the charts. Love, John Lennon."

28 November

→ Abbey Road. *Sentimental Journey* sessions. Ringo recorded 'Blue Turning Grey Over You'.

1 December

→ Ringo was filmed at various London locations talking with Tony Bilbow for a full-length BBC2 documentary for an edition of *Late Night Line-Up* to be broadcast on the day of the world premiere of *The Magic Christian*.

→ George and Patti, Ringo and Maureen went to the first night of the Delaney & Bonnie & Friends tour which opened at the Royal Albert Hall, London. George enjoyed the show so much that he decided to join the tour and played two sets each night with them, standing unobtrusively at the back of the stage.

2 December

→ John was interviewed by anthropologist Desmond Morris, for a programme called *Man Of The Decade*. ATV had asked Alistair Cooke, Mary McCarthy and Morris to choose their own Man of the Decade. Cooke chose JFK, McCarthy chose Ho Chi Minh and Morris went for Lennon. The 20-minute section devoted to John also used archive footage as chosen by John.

→ The same day, the BBC began filming John and Yoko – including them being filmed by ATV – for their own 'The World of John and Yoko' documentary for the *24 Hours* series, presented by David Dimbleby.

→ George joined Delaney & Bonnie & Friends on stage at the Colston Hall, Bristol.

3 December

→ BBC1 filmed John and Yoko for *The World of John and Yoko*.

→ John was interviewed at Apple by American journalist Gloria Emerson. They argued furiously when she questioned his credibility.

→ George joined Delaney & Bonnie & Friends on stage at the Town Hall, Birmingham.

4 December

→ Abbey Road. *Sentimental Journey* sessions. Ringo and a 17-piece orchestra completed 'Blue Turning Grey Over You'.

→ Abbey Road. John and Yoko, Mal Evans, Eddie Klein, Anthony Fawcett,

Geoff Emerick and many others recorded two experimental tapes. The first was a track on which everyone laughed uproariously and shouted out things which was later given a percussion and chanting backing track. In the second all the participants approached the microphone and whispered a message. John and Yoko announced that this would be the fourth in the series following *Two Virgins*, *Life With The Lions* and *The Wedding Album* but it was never released. BBC1 filmed the entire thing for 'The World of John and Yoko'.

→ George joined Delaney & Bonnie & Friends on stage at City Hall, Sheffield.

5 December

→ The BBC filmed John and Yoko in the snow-covered Suffolk countryside, where they filmed *Apotheosis*,

Below: George onstage with Delaney & Bonnie & Friends.
Opposite: John and Yoko at a press conference in Montreal to launch their 'War Is Over (If You Want It)' poster campaign, 22 December.

capturing the ascent of a helium-filled balloon. John, Yoko and the BBC *24 Hours* film crew spent the night at The Bull in Long Melford, Suffolk.

→ George joined Delaney & Bonnie & Friends on the stage at the City Hall, Newcastle-upon-Tyne.

6 December

→ Three of the stars in *The Magic Christian* – Ringo, Peter Sellers and Spike Milligan – appeared together on *Frost On Saturday* to plug the film. The BBC crew finished their filming for 'The World of John and Yoko' with some footage of John and Yoko in their hotel room at The Bull in Long Melford.

→ George joined Delaney & Bonnie & Friends on stage at the Empire Theatre, Liverpool.

7 December

John and Yoko appeared on BBC1's religious programme *The Question Why*, in a debate chaired by Malcolm Muggeridge broadcast live from the BBC's Lime Grove Studios.

→ George joined Delaney & Bonnie & Friends on the stage at the Fairfield Hall, Croydon, for the final night of their tour. Both sets were recorded and released in May 1970 as the live album *Delaney & Bonnie On Tour With Eric Clapton*.

8 December

→ Abbey Road. A new vocal track for Ringo's 'Octopus's Garden' was recorded so that he could mime to it on George Martin's *With A Little Help From My Friends* television show without the Musicians' Union knowing.

10-12 December

→ George appeared with Delaney & Bonnie & Friends for all three nights of their residence at the Falkoner Theatre, Copenhagen, Denmark.

12 December

→ *The Plastic Ono Band – Live Peace In Toronto* by The Plastic Ono Band, produced by John and Yoko, was released in the UK as Apple CORE 2001. Side One: 'Introduction Of The Band', 'Blue Suede Shoes', 'Money (That's What I Want)', 'Dizzy Miss Lizzy', 'Yer Blues', 'Cold Turkey', 'Give Peace A Chance'; Side Two: Don't Worry Kyoko

(Mummy's Only Looking For Her Hand In The Snow)', 'John, John (Let's Hope For Peace)'. The album was released in the US as Apple SW 3362.
→ The various artists album *No One's Gonna Change Our World*, featuring the rejected 1968 recording of 'Across The Universe' by The Beatles, was released in the UK as EMI Regal Star Line SRS 5013.

14 December
→ Ringo taped his contribution to George Martin's *With A Little Help From My Friends* spectacular at the Talk Of The Town.

15 December
→ Ringo taped a two-minute appeal on behalf of the British Wireless for the Blind Fund, to be broadcast by BBC radio on Christmas Day.
John and Yoko's Plastic Ono Supergroup played at the 'Peace For Christmas' concert at the Lyceum Ballroom, Covent Garden, London, in aid of UNICEF. The musicians only had time for one brief rehearsal, in the afternoon before the show. George Harrison was among the musicians in the hastily assembled group: the first time he and John had appeared together on stage since August 1966. The other members of the line-up were Eric Clapton, Delaney and Bonnie, Alan White, Bobby Keyes, Keith Moon, Klaus Voormann, Jim Gordon and Billy Preston. They performed extended versions of 'Cold Turkey' and 'Don't Worry Kyoko (Mummy's Only Looking For Her Hand In The Snow)'. The entire show was recorded and later released on John and Yoko's 1972 double album *Sometime In New York City*.

16 December
→ Huge posters and billboards were erected in 11 cities across the world proclaiming 'War Is Over! If You Want It. Happy Christmas from John and Yoko.' In some countries the message was translated into the native language.
→ John and Yoko flew to Toronto, Canada, for their third visit that year. They stayed on Ronnie Hawkins' ranch, where they telephoned radio stations all over the world, giving

them a peace message to broadcast. Hawkins got left with the phone bill.

17 December
→ John also began the onerous task of signing all 3,000 copies of *Bag One*, his set of erotic lithographs.

19 December
→ The fan club flexi, *The Beatles Seventh Christmas Record* was sent out to members.

20 December
→ CBS TV (Columbia Broadcasting Corporation) filmed a conversation between John and Marshall McLuhan, author of *The Medium Is The Message*, at his office in the University of Toronto.
→ John was interviewed live on the CBC (Canadian Broadcasting Corporation) programme *Weekend*.

22 December
→ John and Yoko gave a press conference at the Château Champlain Hotel in Montreal.

23 December
→ John and Yoko had a 51-minute meeting with the Canadian Prime Minister, Pierre Trudeau, in Ottawa.

25 December
→ Ringo appeared in a BBC Radio 1 charity appeal on behalf of the British Wireless for the Blind Fund.

29 December
→ At a press conference in Ålborg in Denmark John and Yoko performed a Danish folk song called 'Kristelighed' and pledged to donate all their further record royalties to the peace movement.

John: "If all politicians were like Trudeau there would be world peace."

Get Back

Words & Music by John Lennon
& Paul McCartney

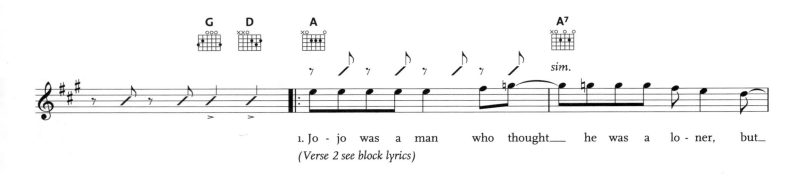

1. Jo - jo was a man who thought__ he was a lo - ner, but__
(Verse 2 see block lyrics)

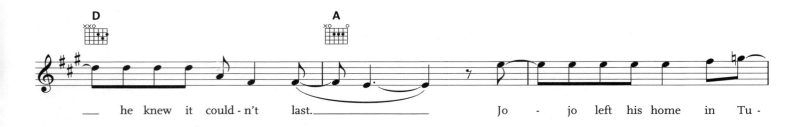

__ he knew it could-n't last._____ Jo - jo left his home in Tu -

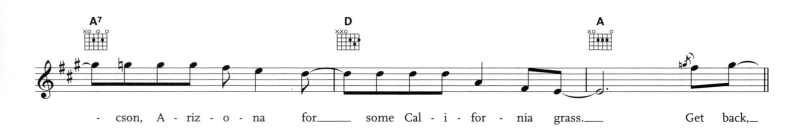

- cson, A - riz - o - na for__ some Cal - i - for - nia grass.__ Get back,__

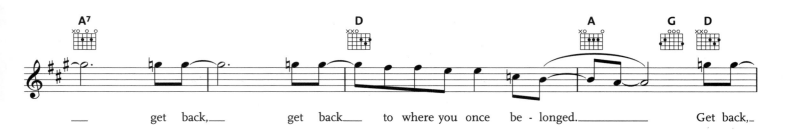

__ get back,__ get back__ to where you once be - longed._____ Get back,__

get back,___   get back___ to where you once   be-longed.

___ Get back, Jo - jo.   *(Guitar)*

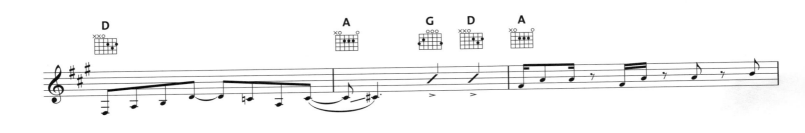

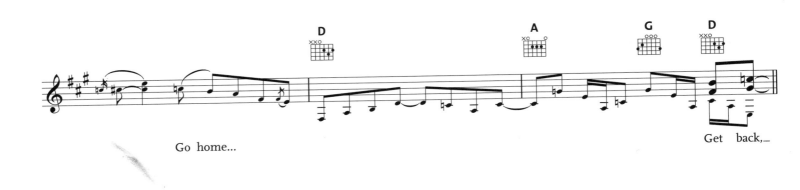

Go home...

Get back,___

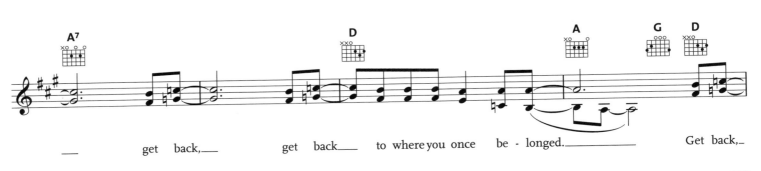

get back,___   get back___ to where you once   be - longed.___   Get back,___

get back,___ get back___ to where you once be - longed._____

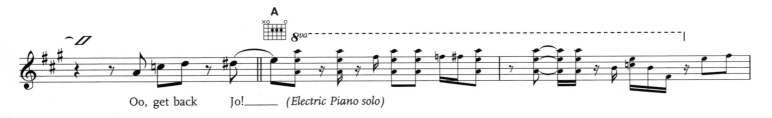

Oo, get back Jo!___ (Electric Piano solo)

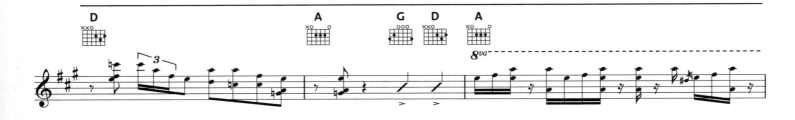

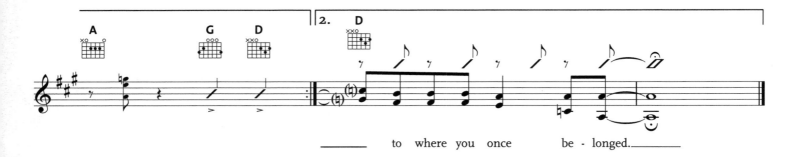

___ to where you once be - longed._____

Verse 2:
Sweet Loretta Martin thought she was a woman,
But she was another man.
All the girls around her say she's got it coming,
But she gets it while she can.

Get back...

Don't Let Me Down

Words & Music by John Lennon
& Paul McCartney
© Copyright 1969 Northern Songs.
All Rights Reserved.
International Copyright Secured.

Verse 2:
And from the first time that she really done me,
Oo she done me, she done me good.
I guess nobody ever really done me,
Oo she done me, she done me good.

Don't let me down, don't let me down.
Ee-ee wow, don't let me down.
Ee wow, girl, don't let me down.
Oh, don't let me down, don't let me down.

The Ballad Of John And Yoko

Words & Music by John Lennon
& Paul McCartney
© Copyright 1969 Northern Songs.

1. Stand-ing in the dock at South-amp-
(Bass riff)
(Verses 2, 3, 4 & 5 see block lyrics)

-ton,_____ trying to get to Hol-land or France.____ The

man in the mac___ said, "You've got to go back",_ you know they did-n't e-ven give us a chance.__

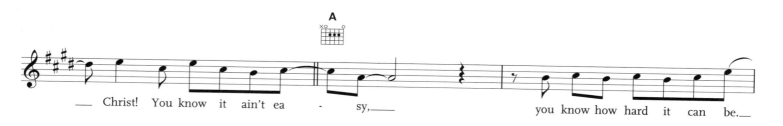

___ Christ! You know it ain't ea - sy,___ you know how hard it can be.__

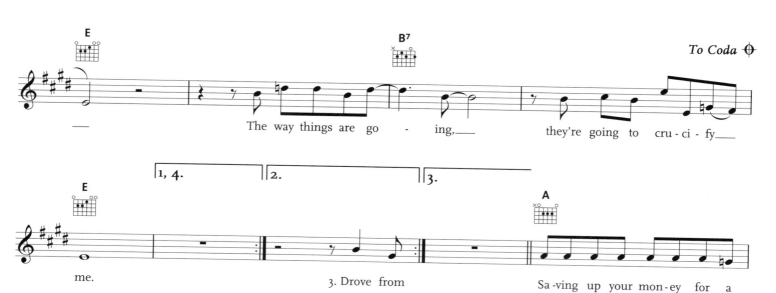

The way things are go - ing,___ they're going to cru-ci-fy___

me. 3. Drove from Sa-ving up your mon-ey for a

rain - y day,___ giv-ing all___ your clothes to char - i - ty. Last night the wife said,

"Oh boy, when you're dead, you don't take noth-ing with you but your soul".___ Think!

D.S. al Coda ⊕ *Coda*

(Drums) me. The way things are go - ing,___

they're going to cru - ci - fy___ me. *(Guitar)*

Verse 2:
Finally made the plane into Paris,
Honeymooning down by the Seine.
Peter Brown called to say, "You can make it O.K.,
You can get married in Gibraltar, near Spain."
Christ! You know it ain't easy,
You know how hard it can be.
The way things are going,
They're going to crucify me.

Verse 3:
Drove from Paris to the Amsterdam Hilton,
Talking in our beds for a week.
The newspeople said, "Say, what're you doing in bed?"
I said, "We're only trying to get us some peace."
Christ! You know it ain't easy,
You know how hard it can be.
The way things are going,
They're going to crucify me.

Verse 4:
Made a lightning trip to Vienna,
Eating chocolate cake in a bag.
The newspapers said, "She's gone to his head,
They look just like two gurus in drag."
Christ! You know it ain't easy,
You know how hard it can be.
The way things are going,
They're going to crucify me.

Verse 5:
Caught the early plane back to London,
Fifty acorns tied in a sack.
The men from the press said, "We wish you success,
It's good to have the both of you back."
Christ! You know it ain't easy,
You know how hard it can be.
The way things are going,
They're going to crucify me.

Come Together

Words & Music by John Lennon
& Paul McCartney

(Guitar)

Shoot me, shoot me, shoot me, shoot me.

1. Here come old flat top, he come groov-ing up slow-ly, he got joo - joo eye - ball, he one
(Verses 2, 3 & 4 see block lyrics)

hol - y rol - ler, he got hair down to his knee,

To Coda ⊕

got to be a jok - er, he just do what he please.___ got to be free.___ Come to - geth -

- er,___ right now,___ o - ver me. feel his dis - ease.___ Come to - geth -

- er,___ right now,___ o - ver me. Shoo, shoo.

(Guitar)

Verse 2:
He wear no shoe shine,
He got toe-jam football,
He got monkey finger,
He shoot Coca-Cola,
He say, "I know you and you know me,"
One thing I can tell you is you got to be free.
Come together, right now, over me.

Verse 3:
He Bag production,
He got walrus gumboot,
He got Ono sideboard,
He one spinal cracker,
He got feet down below his knee,
Hold you in his armchair, you can feel his disease.
Come together, right now, over me.

Verse 4:
He roller coaster,
He got early warning,
He got muddy water,
He one Mojo filter,
He say, "One and one and one is three,"
Got to be good looking 'cause he's so hard to see.
Come together, right now, over me.

Something

Words & Music by George Harrison
© Copyright 1969 Harrisongs Limited.
All Rights Reserved.
International Copyright Secured.

(Guitar)

1. Some - thing in the way____ she moves,____
(Verse 2 see block lyrics)

at - tracts me like no oth - er lov - er.

Some - thing in the way she woos____ me. I don't want to leave____ her now, you

know I be - lieve____ and how.____

(Guitar and Organ)

Double tempo feel

You're ask - ing me____ will my____ love grow, I don't know,_____ I____ don't

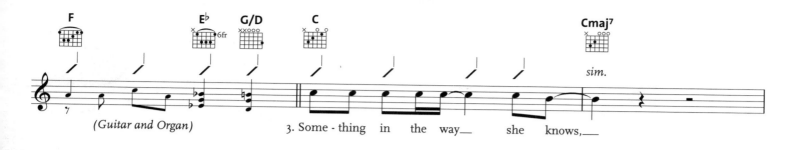

Verse 2:
Somewhere in her smile she knows,
That I don't need no other lover.
Something in her style that shows me.
I don't want to leave her now,
You know I believe and how.

Oh! Darling

Words & Music by John Lennon
& Paul McCartney

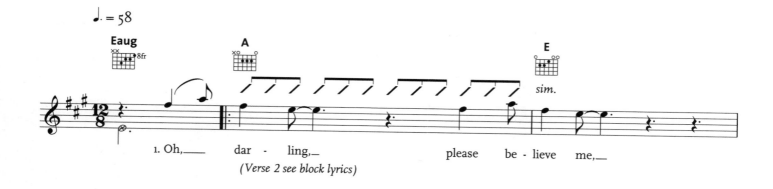

1. Oh,___ dar - ling,___ please be - lieve me,___

(Verse 2 see block lyrics)

I'll nev - er do you no harm.___ Be - lieve me when I tell___ you,___

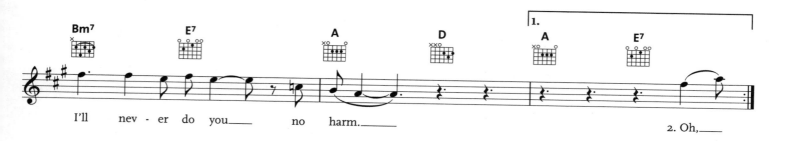

I'll nev - er do you___ no harm.___ 2. Oh,___

When you told___ me___ you did - n't need me an - y- more, well, you

know I near - ly broke down and___ cried.___ When you

told me___ you did-n't need me an-y-more,___ oh, well, you

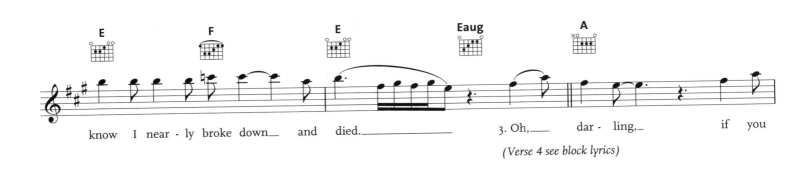

know I near-ly broke down___ and died._____ 3. Oh,___ dar-ling,___ if you

(Verse 4 see block lyrics)

leave me,___ I'll nev-er make it a-lone.___ Be-

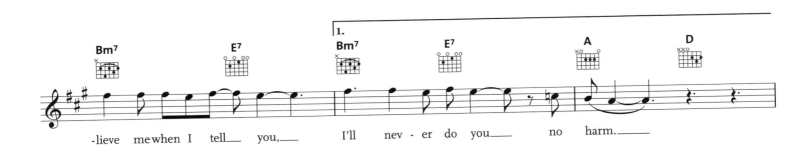

-lieve me when I tell__ you,___ I'll nev-er do you__ no harm.___

(Believe me, darling) When you I'll nev-er do you__ no harm.

Verse 2:
Oh, darling, if you leave me,
I'll never make it alone.
Believe me when I beg you,
Don't ever leave me alone.

Verse 4:
Oh, darling, please believe me,
I'll never let you down, (oh, believe me darling).
Believe me when I tell you,
I'll never do you no harm.

Here Comes The Sun

♩ = 126

Capo on 7th fret

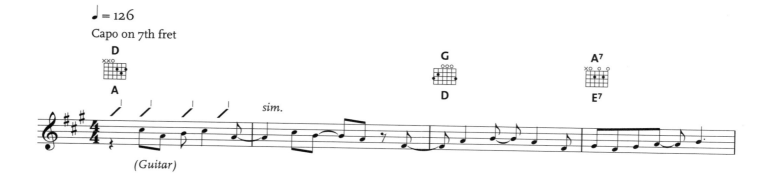

(Guitar)

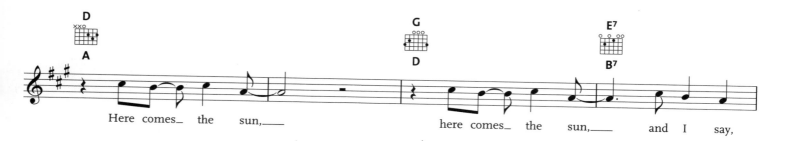

Here comes the sun, here comes the sun, and I say,

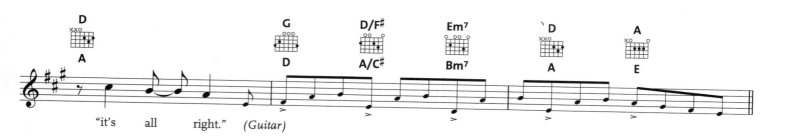

"it's all right." (Guitar)

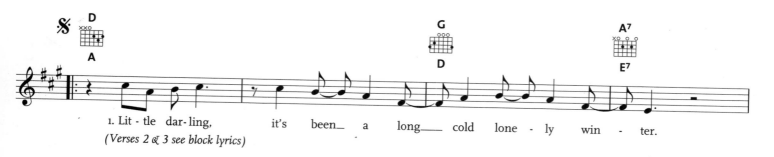

1. Lit-tle dar-ling, it's been a long cold lone-ly win-ter.

(Verses 2 & 3 see block lyrics)

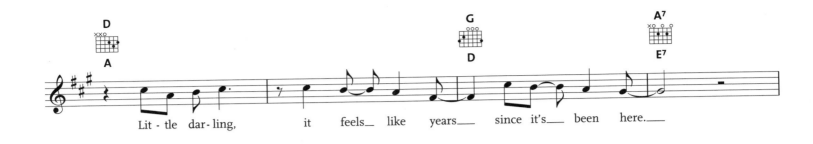

Lit - tle dar - ling, it feels__ like years__ since it's__ been here.__

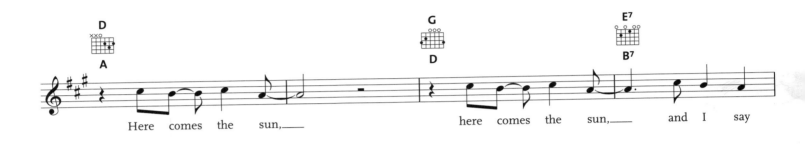

Here comes the sun,__ here comes the sun,__ and I say

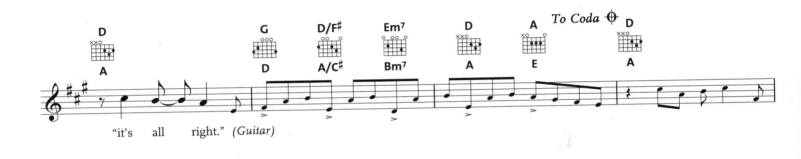

"it's all right." *(Guitar)*

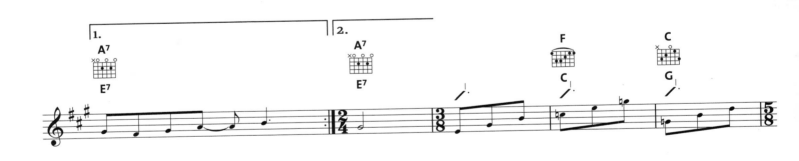

Sun,   sun,   sun,   here it   comes.

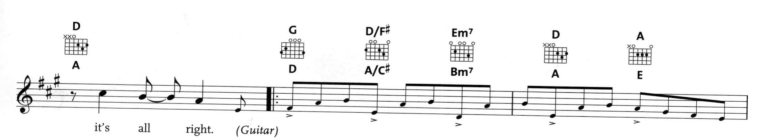

comes.   *(Guitar)*

Here comes the   sun,____   here comes the   sun,____

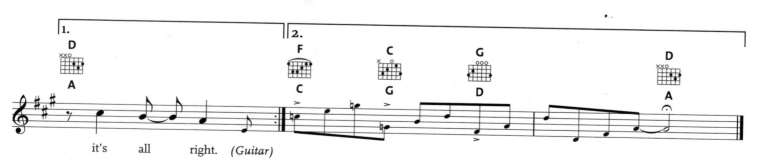

it's   all   right.   *(Guitar)*

it's   all   right.   *(Guitar)*

Verse 2:
Little darling, the smiles returning to their faces.
Little darling, it seems like years since it's been here.

Here comes the sun...

Verse 3:
Little darling, I feel the ice is slowly melting.
Little darling, it seems like years since it's been clear.

Here comes the sun...

Because

Words & Music by John Lennon
& Paul McCartney
© Copyright 1969 Northern Songs.
All Rights Reserved.
International Copyright Secured.

(Guitar/Harpsichord)

1. Ah,_____ be -

(Verses 2 & 3 see block lyrics)

- cause the world is round it turns me on._____ Be -

- cause_____ the world is round._____

Ah,_____ love is old, love is new. Love is all, love is

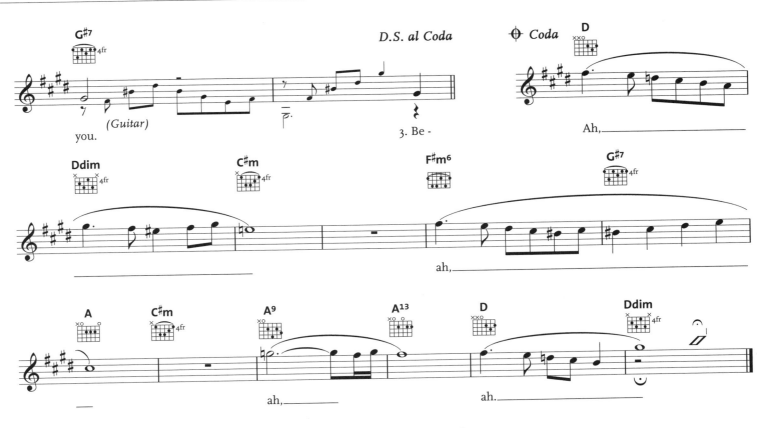

you. (Guitar) 3. Be-

Ah,_____

ah,_____

ah,_____ ah._____

Verse 2:
Ah, because the wind is high, it blows my mind.
Because the wind is high.

Verse 3:
Because the sky is blue, it makes me cry.
Because the sky is blue.

Golden Slumbers/Carry That Weight/The End

Words & Music by John Lennon & Paul McCartney
© Copyright 1969 Northern Songs.
All Rights Reserved.
International Copyright Secured.

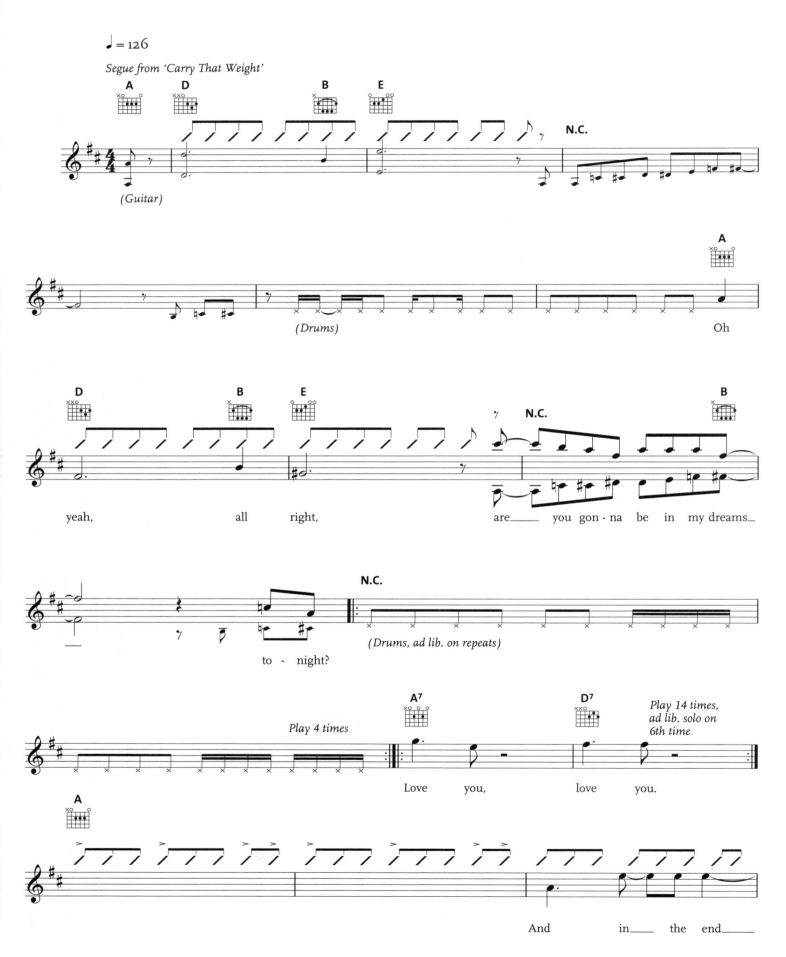

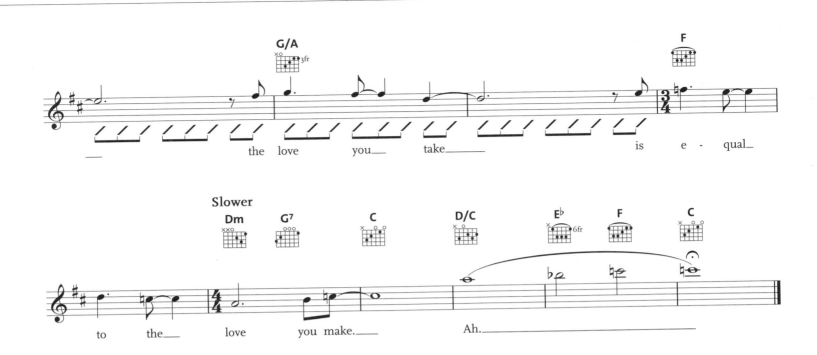

the love you___ take_____ is e - qual___

Slower

to the___ love you make.___ Ah._____

1970

3 January
→ Abbey Road. Paul, George and Ringo (John was still in Denmark) worked on overdubs to George's 'I Me Mine' for use on the *Let It Be* soundtrack album (as the *Get Back* film and soundtrack were now called).

4 January
→ Abbey Road. Further overdubs to 'Let It Be'.

8 January
→ Olympic Sound Studios, Barnes. George added a vocal overdub to the Glyn Johns production of 'For You Blue'.

12 January
→ The single 'Come And Get It' by Badfinger, produced by Paul McCartney, was released in the US as Apple 1815.

14 January
→ Olympic Sound Studios, Barnes. *Sentimental Journey* sessions. Ringo added his vocals to 'Love Is A Many Splendoured Thing' and 'Sentimental Journey'.

15 January
→ A two-week exhibition of John Lennon's 'Bag One' lithographs opened at the London Arts Gallery in New Bond Street.

16 January
→ Police detectives raided the London Arts Gallery and confiscated eight erotic lithographs. The exhibition continued with just six exhibits. On April 27, the gallery got the prints back, having argued in court that Picasso's erotic lithographs had been shown in Britain and not deemed obscene.

22 January
→ John's 'Bag One' lithographs were exhibited at the London Gallery in Detroit, Michigan without incident.

27 January
→ Abbey Road. John and The Plastic Ono Band cut a new single: 'Instant Karma!', which had been written that morning. The song was produced by Phil Spector, working with John for the first time. John took the vocals and played acoustic guitar, with Alan White on drums, Klaus Voormann on bass, Billy Preston on electric piano and George playing lead guitar. By 4 am it was finished and mixed.
→ The session was effectively an audition for Spector, who had requested the opportunity to produce The Beatles from their joint manager, Allen Klein. Delighted with the finished version of 'Instant Karma!', John quickly gave his approval for Spector to be allowed access to the tapes of their January 1969 sessions, in a last ditch effort to complete the *Get Back* project. But Spector had to wait for approval from all four Beatles, which delayed his involvement until late March.
→ In Los Angeles, Ringo taped an appearance before a live audience for the NBC-TV show, *Rowan and Martin's Laugh In*.

29 January
→ Ringo and Maureen attended the American premiere of *The Magic Christian* in Los Angeles.
→ Allen Klein was convicted of 10 tax offences in the New York Federal District Court.

30 January
→ The single 'All That I've Got (I'm Gonna Give It To You)' by Billy Preston, produced by George Harrison, was released in the UK as Apple 21.

3 February
→ Abbey Road. *Sentimental Journey* sessions. A 16-piece orchestra recorded the backing track for a remake of 'Love Is A Many Spendoured Thing' and Ringo added his vocal track.

4 February
→ In a rooftop ceremony with London Black Power leader Michael X (Michael Abdul Malik), John and Yoko swapped their shorn hair for a pair of Muhammad Ali's blood stained boxing shorts at the Black House in north London. John and Yoko intended to auction the boxing trunks to raise money for peace. The proceeds from their hair were to go to 'the Black community'.

5 February
→ Abbey Road. *Sentimental Journey*

sessions. Ringo recorded a new vocal for 'Love Is A Many Splendoured Thing'.

6 February
→ John and Yoko were interviewed at Apple by John Bellan for BBC Radio 1's *Scene And Heard*.
→ 'Instant Karma! (We All Shine On)' by The Plastic Ono Band/ 'Who Has Seen The Wind?' by Yoko Ono Lennon (side B produced by John Lennon) was released in the UK as Apple 1003.

7 February
→ Short-haired John and Yoko were interviewed for London Weekend Television's *The Simon Dee Show*. They brought with them Michael Abdul Malik – Michael X, the Black community leader to whom they had given their hair the previous week.

9 February
→ Abbey Road. *Sentimental Journey* sessions. Ringo added vocals to 'Have I Told You Lately That I Love You?'

11 February
→ John and The Plastic Ono Band taped two different live appearances before an audience for BBC 1's *Top Of The Pops* to promote 'Instant Karma!'. The line-up consisted of John on vocals and electric piano, Klaus Voormann on bass, Alan White on drums, Mal Evans on tambourine, and Yoko either holding cards or

knitting while blindfolded. In fact John's vocal was the only thing performed live, as the entire backing track was the one from the actual single, which had been specially mixed at Abbey Road the day before for the occasion. This was John's second time on TOTP – The Beatles had only appeared live in the studio once back in June 1966.

→ John paid outstanding fines amounting to £1,344 imposed on 96 anti-Apartheid protesters demonstrating against a South African rugby team which played a match in Scotland in December 1969.

→ Abbey Road. *Sentimental Journey* sessions. Klaus Voormann conducted a 15-piece orchestra in his own arrangement of 'I'm A Fool To Care' then Ringo added his vocal track.

→ *The Magic Christian (Original Soundtrack Album)* by Ken Thorne & Orchestra (additional tracks by Badfinger), produced by Paul McCartney, Ringo Starr and Peter Sellers, was released in the US as Commonwealth United CU 6004.

12 February
→ Abbey Road. *Sentimental Journey* sessions. A 31-piece orchestra plus nine singers recorded an arrangement of 'Let The Rest Of The World Go By', then Ringo added his vocal track.

16 February
→ John and Yoko began editing a film of their Montreal bed-in for peace.

18 February
→ Abbey Road. *Sentimental Journey* sessions. Ringo recorded new vocals for 'Have I Told You Lately That I Love You' and 'Let The Rest Of The World Go By'. This was followed by a midnight recording session for Ringo's composition 'It Don't Come Easy'.

George Martin produced the track, George Harrison conducted the musicians: George on acoustic guitar, Klaus Voormann on bass, Ringo on drums and Stephen Stills on piano. Ringo added his vocals to the best take and by 4:40 am it was mixed.

19 February
→ Abbey Road. Ringo recorded another vocal track for 'It Don't Come Easy'.

20 February
→ The Plastic Ono Band single 'Instant Karma! (We All Shine On)' /'Who Has Seen The Wind?' was released in the US as Apple 1818. The version of 'Instant Karma!' was suitably different to the one on the UK release, having been subtly remixed by Phil Spector without John's knowledge.

21 February
→ Abbey Road. *McCartney* solo sessions. Booked in as Billy Martin, Paul began mixing his eight-track masters.

22 February
→ Abbey Road. *McCartney* sessions. More mixing, then Paul recorded 'Every Night' and 'Maybe I'm Amazed'.

24 February
→ Abbey Road. *McCartney* sessions. Paul had a mixing session in Studio Two.
→ Abbey Road. *Sentimental Journey* sessions. In Studio One, Ringo added a new vocal to 'Blue Turning Grey Over You'.

25 February
→ Abbey Road. *McCartney* sessions. Paul recorded 'Man We Was Lonely', completing it and mixing it into stereo. As with each track on the album, Paul played all the instruments.
→ Ringo switched his sessions to De Lane Lea's new studio in Soho, where Johnny Dankworth conducted a 20-piece orchestra playing 'You Always Hurt The One You Love' to which Ringo added his vocals.

26 February
→ The album *Hey Jude* was released in

11 March

→ 'Let It Be'/'You Know My Name (Look Up The Number)' was released in the US as Apple (Capitol) 2764.

12 March

→ George and Patti moved out of 'Kinfauns', their bungalow in Esher, Surrey, and moved to Friar Park, a huge Victorian mansion in Henley-on-Thames, Oxfordshire.

14 March

→ John's 'Bag One' lithographs opened at the Denise René Hans Mayer Gallery in Düsseldorf. The show also opened without problems at the Lee Nordness Gallery in New York.

15 March

→ At Talk of The Town, Ringo shot a promotional film of himself (and backing singers) singing the title song from *Sentimental Journey* to promote the album. The shoot was directed by Neil Aspinall before an invited audience and featured the Talk Of The Town Orchestra, conducted by George Martin.

Above: George on the roof of the Apple building with members of the London chapter of the Radha Krishna Temple to promote the Harrison-produced RKT single 'Govinda', 5 March.

the US as Apple (Capitol) SW 385 (stereo only). Side A: 'Can't Buy Me Love', 'I Should Have Known Better', 'Paperback Writer', 'Rain', 'Lady Madonna', 'Revolution'; Side B: 'Hey Jude', 'Old Brown Shoe', 'Don't Let Me Down', 'The Ballad Of John And Yoko'. The record was the handiwork of Allen Klein, who had convinced John, George and Ringo that repackaging The Beatles' back catalogue in the US would bring them additional income without any effort on their part.

5 March

→ Yoko once more entered the London Clinic for observation, after discovering that once again she was pregnant. John stayed at her bedside throughout.

→ On Paul's recommendation, Ringo tried out Morgan Sound Studios, where he completed *Sentimental Journey*. On this day he recorded 'Whispering Grass' and 'Bye Bye Blackbird' with a 36-piece orchestra.

6 March

→ Ringo completed his *Sentimental Journey* album at Morgan: drums, piano and sax, played by Johnny Dankworth were added to 'You Always Hurt The One You Love' and four other tracks were mixed. The album was now ready for release.

→ The single 'Let It Be'/'You Know My Name (Look Up The Number)' was released in the UK as Apple (Parlophone) R 5833.

8 March

→ Trident Studios, Soho. Ringo did another remake of 'It Don't Come Easy' with George helping in the studio.

9 March

→ George was interviewed by Johnny Moran for a BBC Radio 1 Easter Monday special called *The Beatles Today*, recorded at the BBC's Aeolian Hall in New Bond Street.

→ That evening, George assisted Ringo in the studio for more work on 'It Don't Come Easy' which for some reason was not released as a single until April 1971.

→ Yoko was discharged from the London Clinic.

16 March

→ Abbey Road. *McCartney* sessions. Paul attended a playback session of his tapes.

23 March

→ Abbey Road. *McCartney* sessions. Paul finished the master tapes of *McCartney* to his satisfaction and took them away.

→ In Room Four at Abbey Road, at John and Allen Klein's request and without Paul's knowledge, Phil Spector was just beginning his remixing of the *Let It Be* tapes.

25 March

→ Abbey Road. Phil Spector remixed 'Two Of Us' and Paul's 'Teddy Boy'.

→ Ringo was interviewed at Apple by David Wigg for BBC Radio 1's *Scene And Heard*.

→ Around this date, psychologist Dr. Arthur Janov, the advocate of Primal Scream Therapy, arrived at Tittenhurst Park at John's invitation to treat the Lennons for their neuroses.

26 March

→ Abbey Road. Phil Spector continued his remix of *Let It Be*.

27 March

→ Abbey Road. Phil Spector continued his remix of *Let It Be*.

→ *Sentimental Journey* by Ringo Starr was released in the UK as Apple PCS 7101. Side One: 'Sentimental Journey', 'Night And Day', 'Whispering Grass (Don't Tell The Trees)', 'Bye Bye Blackbird', 'I'm A Fool To Care', 'Star Dust'; Side Two: 'Blue Turning Grey Over You', 'Love Is A Many Splendoured Thing', 'Dream', 'You Always Hurt The One You Love', 'Have I Told You Lately That I Love You', 'Let The Rest Of The World Go By'.

28 March

→ Five of John's 'Bag One' lithographs were confiscated by police from the Merrill Chase Gallery in Oak Brook, near Chicago, Illinois.

29 March

→ Ringo appeared live on David Frost's London Weekend Television show *Frost On Sunday* to promote his new album. John telephoned a message of support to a CND gathering in east London. In it he revealed that Yoko was pregnant again, but in mid-August she miscarried for the third time.

30 March

→ Abbey Road. Phil Spector continued his remix of *Let It Be*, adding fragments of dialogue from the film footage, none of which made it onto the finished album.

31 March

→ Ringo appeared live on the BBC Radio Two programme *Open House* where he was interviewed by Pete Murray.

1 April

→ Abbey Road. Ringo became the last Beatle to play at a Beatles recording session when, working with Phil Spector in Studio One, he overdubbed new drum parts on the tracks 'Across The Universe', 'The Long And Winding Road' and 'I Me Mine'.

→ Spector recorded a 50-piece orchestra and chorus to create a 'wall of sound' backing track for 'Across The Universe', 'The Long And Winding Road' and 'I Me Mine'. Spector was his usual temperamental self, and managed to anger and upset everyone involved with the session: the musicians downed instruments – but eventually picked them up again – the conductors and technical staff were all annoyed and Pete Brown, the balance engineer, stormed out of the building and went home. Spector had to call him and apologise before he would return. Ringo – the only Beatle there – had to order Spector to calm down and eventually the session was completed.

2 April

→ Abbey Road. Spector mixed the three orchestral tracks from the previous day and the *Let It Be* album was finished – at least as far as he was concerned. Acetates were submitted to all four Beatles for their approval. Initially, they all gave the OK for the album to be released.

10 April

→ Paul had his solo album, *McCartney*, ready for release on 17 April, but did not want to do any interviews for it.

→ Paul asked Peter Brown at Apple to write a questionnaire with the usual sort of things that journalists would want to know and he would answer it. Naturally Peter Brown slipped in the question that journalists had been clamouring to ask for six months: Brown opened up with fairly standard press questions but at question 8 he asked: Is this album a rest away from The Beatles or the start of solo career?
Paul: Time will tell. Being a solo album means 'the start of a solo career'... and not being done with The Beatles means it's a rest. So it's both.
Peter Brown: Have you any plans for live appearances?
Paul: No
Peter Brown: Is your break with The Beatles temporary or permanent, due to personal differences or musical ones?
Paul: Personal differences, business differences, but most of all because I have a better time with my family.

Ringo: "I spoke to Paul on the phone and said, 'Did you like it?', and he said, 'Yeah, it's OK'. He didn't put it down. And then suddenly he didn't want it to go out. Two weeks after that, he wanted to cancel it."

Temporary or permanent? I don't know.
Peter Brown: Do you foresee a time when Lennon-McCartney becomes an active songwriting partnership again?
Paul: No.
The press release was printed and enclosed with advance promotional copies of the album. The media went wild: 'The Beatles Break Up!' was headline news around the world.
The final press release for The Beatles, written by Derek Taylor, typed by Mavis Smith on the day that the news broke, read as follows: April 10, 1970 Spring is here and Leeds play Chelsea tomorrow and Ringo and John and George and Paul are alive and well and full of hope. The world is still spinning and so are we and so are you. When the spinning stops – that'll be the time to worry. Not before. Until then, The Beatles are alive and well and the Beat goes on, the Beat goes on.

8 May

→ *Let It Be* was released in the U.K. as Apple (Parlophone) PCS 7096 (stereo only). Side A: 'Two Of Us', 'Dig A Pony', 'Across The Universe', 'I Me Mine', 'Dig It', 'Let It Be', 'Maggie May'; Side B: 'I've Got A Feeling', 'The One After 909', 'The Long And Winding Road', 'For You Blue', 'Get Back'.

George Martin: "It was always understood that the album would be like nothing the Beatles had done before. It would be honest, no overdubbing, no editing, truly

Opposite: Paul, Linda, and sheepdog Martha on the McCartneys' Scottish farm. On 31 December, Paul began High Court proceedings for the dissolution of The Beatles.

live... almost amateurish. When John brought in Phil Spector he contradicted everything he had said before. When I heard the final sounds I was shaken. They were so uncharacteristic of the clean sounds The Beatles had always used. At the time Spector was John's buddy, mate and pal... still is, I don't know. I was astonished because I knew Paul would never have agreed to it. In fact I contacted him and he said nobody was more surprised than he was."

→ Glyn Johns had edited and mixed a completed album on January 5 but none of The Beatles were entirely happy with it, nor could John understand why Glyn Johns wanted credit as producer, even though he produced most of it.

11 May
→ The single 'The Long And Winding Road'/'For You Blue' was released in the USA as Apple (Capitol) 2832.

13 May
→ The film *Let It Be* premiered in New York.

18 May
→ *Let It Be* was released in the USA as Apple (Capitol) AR 34001.

20 May
→ *Let It Be* was premiered in Liverpool and London, but none of the Beatles turned up to see it.
→ The press release that Paul issued in April attracted headlines around the world. The greatest group in history was no more. Even Derek Taylor's whimsical optimism failed to disguise the awful truth: The Beatles had split into two camps with John, George and Ringo on one side and Paul on the other. The rift was irreversible and The Beatles would not work together again.
→ On 31 December, Paul began proceedings in the High Court of Justice in London to wind up The Beatles.

Paul: "I for one am very proud of the Beatle thing. It was great and I can go along with all the people you meet on the street who say you gave so much happiness to many people. I don't think that's corny... I believe that we did bring a real lot of happiness to the times."

Let It Be

Words & Music by John Lennon
& Paul McCartney

♩ = 76

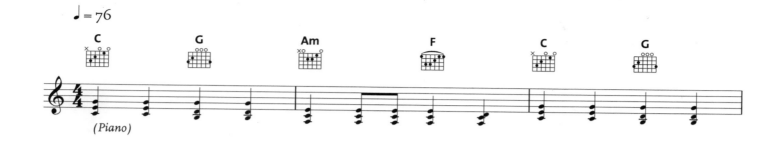

(Piano)

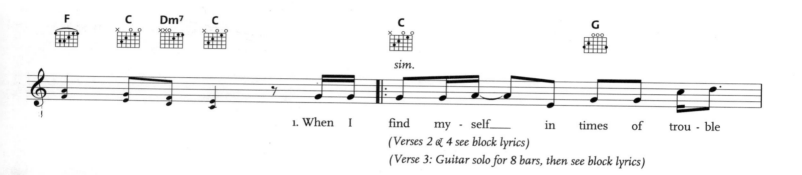

sim.

1. When I find my-self___ in times of trou-ble

(Verses 2 & 4 see block lyrics)

(Verse 3: Guitar solo for 8 bars, then see block lyrics)

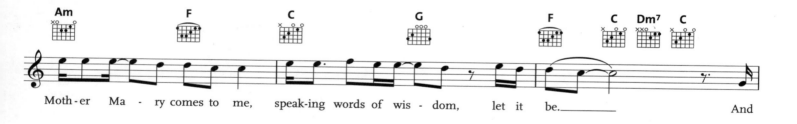

Moth-er Ma - ry comes to me, speak-ing words of wis - dom, let it be.___ And

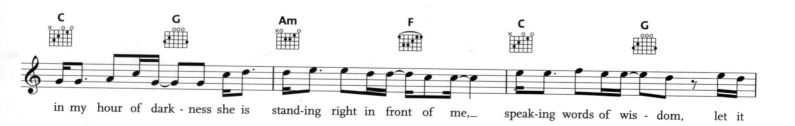

in my hour of dark - ness she is stand-ing right in front of me,___ speak-ing words of wis - dom, let it

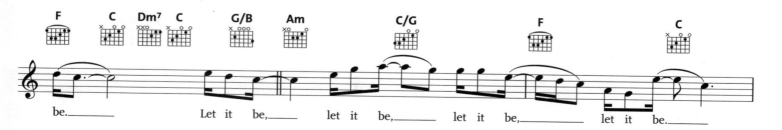

be.___ Let it be,___ let it be,___ let it be,___ let it be.___

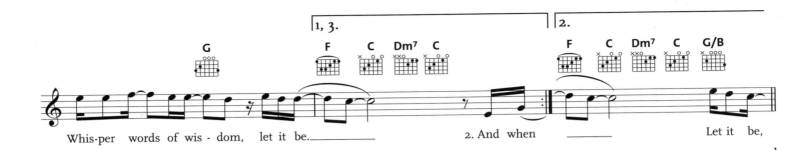

Whis-per words of wis - dom, let it be._____ 2. And when _____ Let it be,

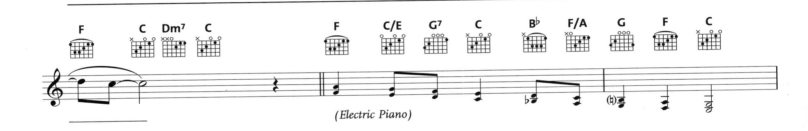

__ let it be,_____ let it be,_____ let it be.__ Whis-per words of wis - dom, let it be.__

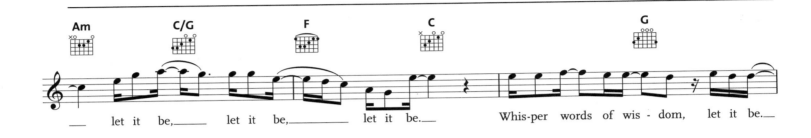

_____ *(Electric Piano)*

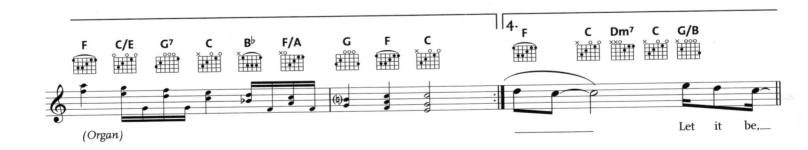

(Organ) Let it be,__

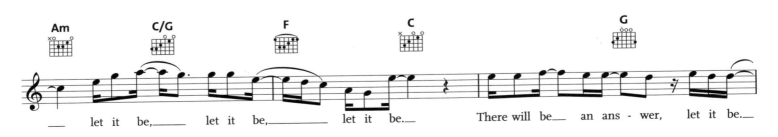

__ let it be,_____ let it be,_____ let it be.__ There will be_ an ans - wer, let it be.__

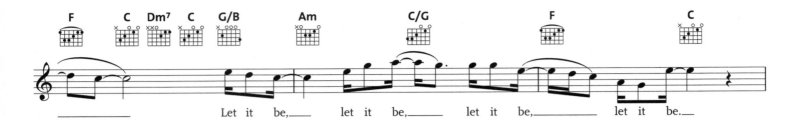

Whis-per words___ of wis - dom, let it be._____

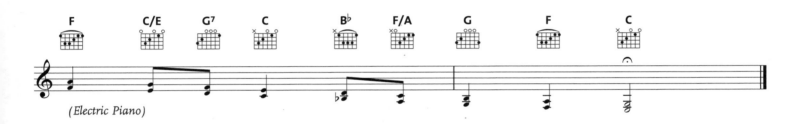

(Electric Piano)

Verse 2:
And when the broken hearted people
Living in the world agree,
There will be an answer, let it be.
For though they may be parted,
There is still a chance that they will see,
There will be an answer, let it be.

Let it be, let it be, let it be, let it be.
Yeah, there will be an answer, let it be.

Verse 3:
Instrumental: Guitar solo (for 8 bars)

Let it be, let it be, let it be, let it be
Whisper words of wisdom, let it be.

Verse 4:
And when the night is cloudy,
There is still a light that shines on me,
Shine until tomorrow, let it be.
I wake up to the sound of music,
Mother Mary comes to me,
Speaking words of wisdom, let it be.

Let it be, let it be, let it be, let it be.
There will be an answer, let it be.
Let it be, let it be, let it be, let it be.
There will be an answer, let it be.
Let it be, let it be, let it be, let it be.
Whisper words of wisdom, let it be.

Across The Universe

Words & Music by John Lennon
& Paul McCartney
© Copyright 1968 Northern Songs.
All Rights Reserved.
International Copyright Secured.

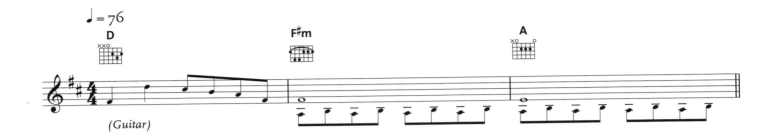

(Guitar)

1. Words are flow-ing out__ like end-less rain,__ in-to a pa-per cup.__ They

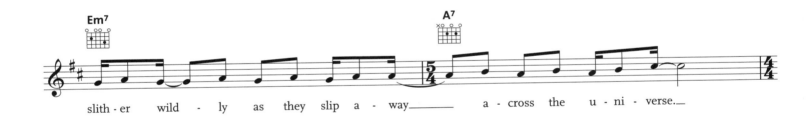

slith-er wild-ly as they slip a-way__ a-cross the u-ni-verse.__

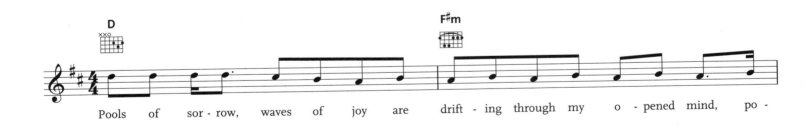

Pools of sor-row, waves of joy are drift-ing through my o-pened mind, po-

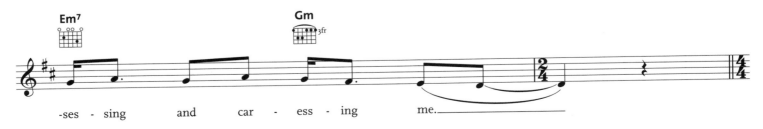

-ses-sing and car-ess-ing me.__

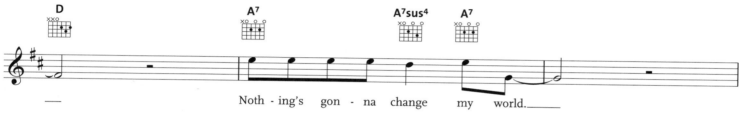

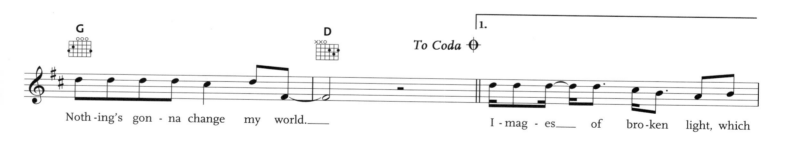

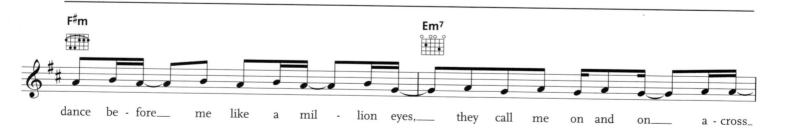

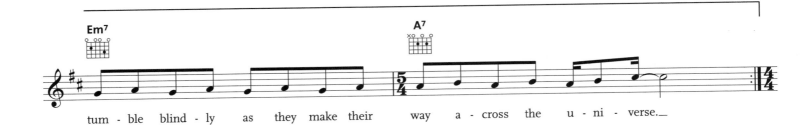

tum - ble blind - ly as they make their way a - cross the u - ni - verse.___

2.

Sounds of laugh - ter, shades of earth,___ are ring - ing through my o - pened ears,___ in -

-ci - ting and in - vi - ting me.___ Lim - it - less,___ un - dy - ing love,___ which

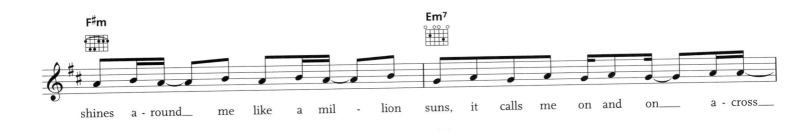

shines a - round___ me like a mil - lion suns, it calls me on and on___ a - cross___

D.S. al Coda   *Coda*   *Repeat to fade*

___ the u - ni - verse.___   Jai___ Gu - ru___ De - va.___

The Long And Winding Road

Words & Music by John Lennon
& Paul McCartney

Verse 2:
The wild and windy night
That the rain washed away,
Has left a pool of tears,
Crying for the day.
Why leave me standing here?
Let me know the way.

Verse 3:
But still they lead me back
To the long, winding road.
You left me standing here,
A long, long time ago.
Don't leave me waiting here,
Lead me to your door.

And... In the End

Regardless of how many rock and pop musicians stand up each year to receive their Grammys, Brits and platinum albums, The Beatles remain the benchmark by which their success is measured. Thanks to the ever increasing size of the global music industry they did so much to establish in the first place, many of the statistics that The Beatles once held have now been eclipsed, but no-one has ever really become "bigger than The Beatles" or even the "new Beatles", nor are they ever likely to because becoming "bigger than The Beatles" is simply unattainable today. Their achievements will forever remain unique because of the context in which they were accomplished.

"Bigger than The Beatles", of course, is the kind of emotive phrase that helps sell newspapers, and its perpetual use as a yardstick only adds to The Beatles' impregnable status. Nowadays, most acts compared briefly to The Beatles come pre-packaged by corporate interests and are referred to as "boy [or girl] bands", but many of them don't even play musical instruments, let alone write their own material, and their stage shows are often limited to displays of athletic formation dancing while they sing or mime to pre-recorded backing tapes. After a few years, when their audiences have matured and recognised their limitations, their careers are over and their back catalogues stagnate, only to be reactivated briefly as a 'Greatest Hits' collections a few more years down the line when the band reforms for commercial motives.

It is equally inconclusive to compare the success of The Beatles with serious stadium filler artists of the calibre of R.E.M., U2 or even Bruce Springsteen, none of whom were actually compared to The Beatles because their careers developed slowly and big success arrived only after several years of hard graft. Although all three have now produced more albums than The Beatles and their record sales (and concert ticket sales) certainly measure up, it took them at least three times as long to achieve this. Also, regardless of their integrity in an increasingly profit motivated industry, R.E.M., U2 and Springsteen never really changed society, and their names are known only to their fans, very few of whom are likely to mob them at Heathrow. John, Paul, George and Ringo, of course, were known to everyone, everywhere.

The Beatles, or at least three of them, played together for almost four years before they saw the inside of a real recording studio. In the meantime, somehow, they scratched a living by performing live. In the modern era it's unlikely that any group would stick it out together for four years from formation to recording. Among The Beatles' near contemporaries only The Who, again originally just three of them, made a living playing live for any appreciable time before recording. But The Who made only four albums in the Sixties, against The Beatles' 12. By comparison, less than six months elapsed between the formation of The Beatles' nearest rivals, The Rolling Stones, and the recording session that produced their first single.

Of course, the unremitting conditions under which The Beatles produced their work are unlikely ever to be repeated. It seems extraordinary to say it, but for all their modern-day sophistication, today's multi-national record companies are simply not equipped to handle two albums a year from the same artist, nor are they likely to welcome on average three non-album singles which would not act as promotional tools for the triennial album. Perhaps there's a lesson to be learned here: today's Top Five singles often sell less than 30,000; in their heyday The Beatles' singles sold over a million on advance orders alone and that's just in the UK!

Groups like Radiohead, Coldplay and Muse have enjoyed great success in the past decade, but it is unlikely that more than 2,000 other artists will record a cover version of any of their songs. Nor do more recent bands have the widespread appeal of The Beatles. Again, looking at the cover versions of their songs, they have been recorded by everyone from Ella Fitzgerald, Frank Sinatra, Ray Charles, Fats Domino and Peggy Lee at one end of the scale, to Laibach's industrial metal version of the entire *Let It Be* album on the other, to say nothing of Cathy Berberian's *Beatles' Arias*, an entire album of Beatles songs given operatic treatment, or the many brass band, string quartet and even steam organ versions of their songs.

The Beatles cast a giant shadow, a shadow so huge that many bands don't even realise they sit within its umbra. At the height of their fame, in the mid-Sixties, they influenced a huge number of their contemporaries: from Brian Jones period Rolling Stones (particularly his use of sitar, and the whole of *Their Satanic Majesties Request* which was derided as a *Sgt. Pepper* imitation), through Donovan, The Kinks to all the other pop acts who went on to produce more complex, lasting work, spurred on by the advances and experiments of The Beatles. Before the end of the Sixties their vocal harmonies were influencing everyone from The Hollies to The Bee Gees and by the end of the decade their impact was spreading out through ELO who took mid-period psychedelic Beatles songs as a blueprint for almost everything they did.

Another strand of their work, notably the guitar heavy 'White Album', was developed by Led Zeppelin, much more of a Beatles band than most people think; and Syd Barrett took much from The Beatles for the whimsical early Pink Floyd. Their influence was all encompassing. In the USA, one only has to look at the work of The Byrds, The Beach Boys and Buffalo Springfield – to name just those groups whose name also begins with 'B' – to see how the Americans coped with the British Invasion.

Interest in The Beatles' work remains far higher than any of their contemporaries, so much so that their complete repertoire remains in print at little short of full price, and fans still clamour for more. They have become the most collected group of all time and among the most bootlegged. In the years since The Beatles disbanded, lawyers and managers representing their interests have increased their tight stranglehold on the group's product. Although John and Paul lost control of their song publishing, the group and their advisors long ago turned around the slave and master situation that existed with EMI in the Sixties. The Beatles are now very much the masters.

The three volume *Anthology* series of rarities and outtakes, released in 1995 and 1996, together with the accompanying eight volume video collection, raised a sum adjacent to $400 million for the then three surviving Beatles and Yoko Ono Lennon. When it was released in November 2000, *1*, which contained 27 of The Beatles' greatest hits on one CD, became an instant best-seller and will probably ultimately become the best selling CD ever. George Harrison's sad passing a year later made headline news around the world. The *Love* album, an assortment of Beatles music mixed together by George Martin's son Giles to accompany the 2006 Cirque de Soleil show in Las Vegas, was among the most eagerly anticipated CDs of that year.

Evidently there can be no question that in the 21st Century, over 50 years after John first encountered Paul at the Woolton village fete, The Beatles remain the standard by which all others are and always will be measured.

Photography Credits

BBC Photo Library/Redferns: 66, 69
Bettmann/Corbis: 110, 111, 119, 120, 191, 194, 259, 315, 321
Jane Bown/Camera Press: 295, 297, 379
Tony Bramwell/LFI: 63, 386, 387, 391, 401, 407, 429
Beryl Bryden/Redferns: 209
Kevin Cole/Rex Features: 135, 256
Kay Cooper/Rex Features: 108
Cummings Archive/Redferns: 302, 312, 365, 376
Everett Collection/Rex Features: 116, 118
David Farrell/Redferns: 80
Fremantle Media: 186, 199
Gems/Redferns: 15
Harry Goodwin: 62, 144/145, 185, 277, 442, 469, 480
Jim Gray/Hulton Archive/Getty Images: 340
Tom Hanley/Redferns: 432, 435, 439, 440, 453, 471
M Haywood Archives/Redferns: 23, 48
Frank Hermann/Globe Photos/Camera Press: 298
Hulton Archive/Getty Images: 44, 109, 114/115, 121, 217, 230, 238, 279, 358, 370/371, 372, 374/375, 380, 382, 383, 390, 405, 436, 445, 448, 477, 478, 481
Hulton-Deutsch Collection/Corbis: 303
ITV/Rex Features: 103, 109
Keystone/Getty Images: 14, 52 (below)
Keystone USA/Rex Features: 45
K&K Ulf Kruger/OHG/Redferns: 10, 21, 24/25, 27, 28, 30, 33, 35, 38, 46, 49, 50, 55
Elliott Landy/Redferns: 378, 411
LFI: 6/7, 17, 61, 64/65, 67, 68, 72/73, 74, 76, 78, 79, 81, 89, 91, 106/107, 111, 113 (below), 117, 128, 129, 130/131, 132, 133, 134, 136, 137, 138/139, 142, 143, 149, 161, 169, 175, 177, 181, 182/183, 184, 188, 189, 190, 192/193, 195, 196, 207, 215, 231, 239, 244, 246, 250, 251, 252, 254, 258, 261, 267, 300, 306, 310/311, 318, 320, 322/323, 377, 383, 389, 392, 437, 441, 443, 444, 449, 476
Marvin Lichtner/Contributor/Getty Images: 326, 349
David Magnus/Rex Features: 47, 126, 245, 294, 308, 309, 333, 341, 353, 367
Bruce McBroom/Camera Press: 490/491
Bruce McBroom/LFI: 12, 475
Doug McKenzie/Hulton Archive/Getty Images: 248
Arthur Miller: 51
Tom Murray: 384/385
Harry Myers/Rex Features: 124, 125, 447
Michael Ochs Archives/Getty Images: 16, 19, 37, 52 (top), 53, 431, 434

Jan Olofsson/Redferns: 304/305
Terry O'Neill/Rex Features: 75
Photo News/Camera Press London: 123
Redferns/Redferns: 43, 393
David Redfern/Redferns: 140, 316, 317, 319
Rex Features: 77, 313, 463
John Rodgers/Redferns: 42
Cheniston Roland: 22
Richard Rosser/Rex Features: 127
Max Scheler/Redferns: 113 (top)
Scoopt/Contributor/Getty Images: 446
Sipa Press/Rex Features: 71
Various/New Orient/Rex Features: 271
Jurgen Vollmer/Redferns: 31, 36, 39, 49
Michael Ward/Rex Features: 54, 56/57, 60
Robert Whitaker: 247
Robert Whitaker/Contributor/Getty Images: 225, 270
Val Wilmer/Redferns: 70, 87, 95

Every effort has been made to trace the copyright holders of the photographs in this book but one or two were unreachable. We would be grateful if the photographers concerned would contact us.